TERRORISM AND COUNTERTERRORISM IN CANADA

Through close analysis of the Canadian context, *Terrorism and Counterterrorism in Canada* provides an advanced introduction to the challenges and social consequences presented by terrorism today. Featuring contributions from both established and emerging scholars, it tackles key issues within this fraught area and does so from multiple disciplinary perspectives, using historical, quantitative, and qualitative lenses of analyses to reach novel and much-needed insights.

Throughout the volume, the editors and contributors cover such topics as the foreign fighter problem, far-right extremism, the role of the internet in fostering global violence, and the media's role in framing the discourse on terrorism in Canada. Also included are essays that look at the struggles to develop specific counterterrorism policies and practices in the face of these threats.

In addition to offering a detailed primer for scholars, policymakers, and concerned citizens, *Terrorism and Counterterrorism in Canada* confronts the social and legal consequences of mounting securitization for marginalized communities.

(Canada Among Nations)

JEZ LITTLEWOOD is an independent researcher and policy analyst in the Government of Alberta.

LORNE L. DAWSON is a professor in the Department of Sociology and Legal Studies at the University of Waterloo.

SARA K. THOMPSON is an associate professor in the Department of Criminology at Ryerson University.

CANADA AMONG NATIONS

Canada Among Nations is an established series produced by the Norman Paterson School of International Affairs (NPSIA), Canada's oldest, largest, and top-ranked interdisciplinary graduate school of international affairs and a full and founding member of the Association of Professional Schools of International Affairs (APSIA). Canada Among Nations provides thematic reviews of key international policy issues affecting Canada and its place in the world, and volumes published in the series have been used extensively in university courses at both the graduate and undergraduate levels.

Terrorism and Counterterrorism in Canada

Canada Among Nations, Volume 30

EDITED BY JEZ LITTLEWOOD,
LORNE L. DAWSON,
AND SARA K. THOMPSON

UNIVERSITY OF TORONTO PRESS
Toronto Buffalo London

© University of Toronto Press 2020
Toronto Buffalo London
utorontopress.com

ISBN 978-1-4875-0186-0 (cloth) ISBN 978-1-4875-1412-9 (EPUB)
ISBN 978-1-4875-2170-7 (paper) ISBN 978-1-4875-1411-2 (PDF)

Library and Archives Canada Cataloguing in Publication

Title: Terrorism and counterterrorism in Canada / edited by Jez Littlewood,
   Lorne L. Dawson, and Sara K. Thompson.
Names: Littlewood, Jez, editor. | Dawson, Lorne L., 1954– editor. |
   Thompson, Sara K., 1971– editor.
Description: Series statement: Canada among nations ; vol. 30 | Includes
   bibliographical references and index.
Identifiers: Canadiana 20190192712 | ISBN 9781487521707 (softcover) |
   ISBN 9781487501860 (hardcover)
Subjects: LCSH: Terrorism – Canada. | LCSH: Terrorism – Canada –
   Prevention. | LCSH: Terrorism – Government policy – Canada. |
   LCSH: Terrorism – Social aspects – Canada.
Classification: LCC HV6433.C2 T47 2020 | DDC 363.3250971—dc23

University of Toronto Press acknowledges the financial assistance to its
publishing program of the Canada Council for the Arts and the Ontario Arts
Council, an agency of the Government of Ontario.

Canada Council   Conseil des Arts
for the Arts   du Canada

ONTARIO ARTS COUNCIL
CONSEIL DES ARTS DE L'ONTARIO
an Ontario government agency
un organisme du gouvernement de l'Ontario

Funded by the   Financé par le
Government   gouvernement
of Canada   du Canada

Canada

Contents

Figures and Tables

Figures

Tables

Acknowledgments

An edited collection focused on terrorism and counterterrorism inevitably involves a number of individuals working together to deliver a finished book. The bulk of the work has been undertaken by our authors and first and foremost our acknowledgment must recognize their commitment and patience with bringing the text to publication. More than twenty-five individuals were involved in the authoring and contributing to the individual chapters through editorial and peer review cycles. This book would not be possible without their commitment, professionalism, and patience. We are also grateful to the editorial team at the University of Toronto Press, to the Canadian Network for Research on Terrorism, Security, and Society (TSAS) for facilitating the call for proposals and providing the hub for coordination of the contributions, and the Norman Paterson School of International Affairs (NPSIA) and Carleton University for their generous administrative and financial support.

TERRORISM AND COUNTERTERRORISM
IN CANADA

1 Introduction

JEZ LITTLEWOOD, SARA THOMPSON,
AND LORNE DAWSON

The carnage of 11 September 2001 altered the sense of security of many Canadians and highlighted the threat that global terrorism posed to this nation. Yet terrorism had been a "Canadian issue" long before 9/11. The deadliest act of terrorism perpetrated against Canadians happened on 23 June 1985, when a bomb exploded on board Air India Flight 182 en route from Montreal to London and then New Delhi. The plane went down 110 miles southwest of Cork, Ireland, killing 329 people, including 268 Canadians. At the time, Canadians did not think of this incident as an act of terrorism against Canada. Canada's prime minister even sent his condolences to the prime minister of India. More than twenty years later, another Canadian prime minister made a statement recognizing the mistake: "Canadians who sadly did not at first accept that this outrage was made in Canada accept it now. Let me just speak directly to this perception, for it is wrong, and it must be laid to rest. This was not an act of foreign violence. This atrocity was conceived in Canada, executed in Canada, by Canadian citizens, and its victims were themselves mostly citizens of Canada" (Canada 2010).

Canada's history of terrorism differs, however, from that of the United States and Western European nations. The incidents have been fewer and, with the exception of the Air India bombing, generally less lethal. These differences notwithstanding, there is a long history of terrorism in Canada, and hence also a related history of counterterrorism (Ross 1988; Leman-Langlois and Brodeur 2005; Crelinsten 2012; Whitaker, Kealey and Parnaby 2012). Understanding this history is an important aspect of understanding contemporary terrorism and counterterrorism in Canada. In his distillation of lessons about terrorism from the past, Richard English remarked: "terrorism is a very old phenomenon, and we should use this to our advantage in learning what we can from this grim aspect of history. But the issue is of greatest importance because of what we are likely to face ahead; and an understanding of terrorism is most urgent at those moments of unanticipated crisis that puncture human history" (English 2009, 119). These remarks are particularly apt in light of recent and unanticipated events that have spurred a change in the discourse on terrorism and counterterrorism in Canada. After the lethal attacks on members of the Canadian armed forces on 20 and 22 October 2014 in Saint-Jean-sur-Richelieu (Quebec) and Ottawa, the government embarked on a reorganization of Canadian national security legislation. The then Conservative government argued that legislative amendments were required in order to identify and respond to threats; the resultant Bill C-51 sparked vociferous debate in Parliament, in the media, and on the streets. Passed in the last months of then Prime Minister Stephen Harper's tenure, the new legislation was complex and sweeping. Among other things, for the first time it permitted the Canadian Security Intelligence Service (CSIS) to disrupt terrorist activities; it also created a new information-sharing regime within the machinery of government, one that raised concerns about privacy and surveillance. The legislation also provided powers to remove content from websites and seize terrorist propaganda, and it created new offences related to the mere encouragement of terrorism. Lastly, it lowered the threshold for the preventive arrest of individuals who might be involved in terrorism. In 2015, the controversy over the legislation led the new prime minister, Justin Trudeau, to commit his government to addressing the "problematic elements of C-51" (Canada 2015). It would be nearly eighteen months, however, before the proposed changes to the legislation were tabled in Parliament (Harris 2017).

The debate over Bill C-51 is not the subject of this book, but it lurks in the background of the issues discussed in this collection. While there is a strong foundation of published work on terrorism in Canada, few collections have brought together different aspects of the problem of terrorism and counterterrorism. Everything said in this book is conditioned, however, by the changing nature of the threat posed by terrorism over the last decade or so (Burke 2015). With the train bombings in Madrid in 2004, and the suicide attacks on London's transit system in 2005, attention turned to the rise and spread of "homegrown terrorism." In the case of so-called jihadist terrorism, concerns over the threat posed by groups from abroad were expanded to include individuals who are citizens of the countries being attacked and who have undergone a process of radicalization leading to violence. Who was being radicalized, how, and why? These became the burning questions of the day as governments struggled to find effective but legitimate means to identify and intervene with disaffected elements of their own societies, while continuing to protect against intrusions by foreign terrorists (Ranstorp 2010). In the ensuing years, hundreds of homegrown terrorist plots were disrupted in the United States, the United Kingdom, and Australia and throughout Western Europe (Burke 2011; Bergen, Hoffman, and Tiedemann 2011; Nesser 2014; 2015; Pantucci, 2015). Several plots were disrupted in Canada as well (Crelinsten 2012; Mullins 2013; McCoy and Knight 2015). For example, the Toronto 18 plot in 2006 prompted Canadians to realize they are not safe from homegrown terrorism (Shepherd 2011; Dawson 2014).

No sooner had scholarly attention settled on this issue, though, than a new worry arose for governments: "lone wolf" terrorism. Individuals were being inspired by terrorist narratives and ideologies and launching attacks, seemingly with little or no support from established terrorist organizations or even groups of like-minded individuals. US Army psychiatrist Nadal Hassan, for example, opened fire on his fellow soldiers at Fort Hood, Texas, killing thirteen and wounding more than thirty. These lone-actor terrorists are thought to be particularly difficult to detect and stop, and this has prompted calls for academic research that could help us understand and interrupt the processes of radicalization leading to violence (Spaaij 2012; Gill, Horgan, and Deckert 2014; Hafez and Mullins 2015).

The burgeoning literature has clearly and consistently demonstrated that on their own, traditional coercive counterterrorism measures are not enough to counter this multidimensional terrorist threat. As a consequence, considerable attention has been paid to prevention and intervention initiatives in the "pre-criminal space." Community outreach by security agencies and, more generally, programs for countering violent extremism (CVEs) have begun to receive priority. Canada, however, under Stephen Harper's Conservative government, was late in developing such initiatives.

The outbreak of Syria's civil war in 2011 changed the global terrorism/counterterrorism landscape even more. That war gave rise to a variety of new jihadist groups (O'Bagy 2012), revitalized a flagging al Qaeda, and gave birth to the Islamic State of Iraq and al-Sham (ISIS). The complexity of the Syrian conflict led to internecine conflict between groups, which caused a split between the al Qaeda affiliate in Syria, Jabhat al-Nusra, and its parent group in Iraq (BBC 2016; Lister 2016). That split led to the emergence of a new, more lethal and successful group, ISIS. By June 2014, ISIS had seized control of vast tracts of territory in Syria and Iraq and declared the resurrection of the Muslim Caliphate (McCants 2015; Gerges 2016). The group's success inspired tens of thousands of young Muslims from around the world to travel to Syria and Iraq to fight for ISIS and other jihadist groups. As four to five thousand left from Western nations – almost one hundred are reported to have left from Canada (The Soufan Group 2015) – and ISIS perpetrated countless atrocities against its enemies, governments turned their attention to defeating ISIS and stemming the tide of foreign terrorist fighters. Over the course of 2016 and 2017, ISIS suffered a sharp reversal of its fortunes, losing much of the territory it had seized under a concerted assault by a multitude of local military forces backed by the West. But the loss of territory has not completely defeated ISIS (Burke 2017; Joscelyn 2018; Dawson 2018), which remains a potent inspirational force. These events in Syria and Iraq, and elsewhere (e.g., Yemen, Libya, Somalia, Nigeria, Mali, and Afghanistan), dramatically underscored the need to better understand how to counter violent extremism abroad and at home.

These events did not play out solely on the ground in Syria. Intertwined with these developments was the newly prominent role played by the Internet and social media in the spread of terrorist propaganda, the recruitment and mobilization of terrorists, and the facilitation of terrorist plots and attacks (Carter, Maher, and Neumann 2014; Berger and Morgan 2015). Counterterrorism more broadly, and CVE specifically, would necessarily entail developing expert knowledge of cyberspace. And in the midst of these trends and changes, awareness within democratic states slowly grew that other forms of violent extremism still mattered. The most significant threat was posed by the far right (Perry and Scrivens 2015; Koehler 2016). The massacre carried out by Anders Breivik in Norway in 2011 reminded the world of the large and growing threat associated with this brand of terrorism, which had long been ignored or underestimated. In Europe and North America, far-right extremism is enjoying a resurgence, in part as a response to the jihadist threat and mounting xenophobia related to immigration and refugee flows from the Muslim world, as well as the growth of populist politics in the North America and parts of Europe.

Here we can do no more than touch on these complex developments to highlight their general relevance for the studies presented in this volume. Yet even this cursory overview highlights that the threat to Canada posed by terrorism and violent extremism is complex and diffuse; it consists of established groups, cells, and inspired actors with a variety of ideological, political, and religious influences that have both real-world and virtual roots and connections. Further complicating the environment is the emergence of violent extremists who are not easily categorized as terrorists but who conduct deliberate attacks against civilians, such as Alek Minassian, who carried out a deadly vehicle attack on Yonge Street in Toronto on 23 April 2018 (CBC 2018).

Introduction to the Chapters

This book examines terrorist threats to Canada, the response to terrorism by Canadian authorities, and the impact of terrorism and counterterrorism on Canadian society. It is interdisciplinary in scope, drawing from political science, criminology, sociology, and history, and the authors use a variety of research methods and sources, including archives, semi-structured interviews, quantitative approaches, and content analyses. No book can hope to capture all aspects of terrorism and counterterrorism, even within one state. In this volume we have therefore chosen to explore a number of the pressing issues facing Canada: foreign fighters and radicalization to violence; police–community relations and ways of countering violent extremism; intelligence accountability; the impact of the internet on terrorism; media and public discourse about terrorism attacks; right-wing extremism; terrorism financing; and whether (or not) counterterrorism methods abroad reduce terrorism in Canada.

The volume is divided into three parts. The first deals with terrorism and threats to the security of Canada from violent extremist organizations. The second addresses security and responses to terrorism within Canada and by Canadian authorities. The third explores the implications of terrorism and counterterrorism for communities, the public discourse and understanding of terrorism, and the execution of security policy.

Terrorism

Canada is often referred to as the "Peaceable Kingdom," and existing studies and data on terrorism in Canada echo this perception (Charters 2008; Gartenstein-Ross and Frum 2012). Yet terrorism in Canada, whether domestic, transnational, or international, is more common than widely perceived. Until recently, though, researchers have been hard pressed to secure structured and systematic public data on terrorism in Canada and with a Canadian connection. As data collection on terrorism worldwide increased and improved post-9/11, Canadian scholars and those with a specific interest in Canada began to realize that even the most widely cited and used source of terrorism data – the Global Terrorism Database (GTD) – had significant deficiencies vis-à-vis Canada. As Tishler, Ouellet, and Kilberg outline in chapter 2, incidents within or with a connection to Canada are underrepresented in the most widely used terrorist incident datasets.

As a corrective, in part, the Canadian Incident Database (CIDB) was developed in 2012–13 with funding from the Canadian government.

Drawing on this new dataset, chapter 2 provides a survey of terrorism in Canada between 1960 and 2015. This fifty-five-year period provides the necessary historical context for thinking about terrorism and counterterrorism in Canada and anchors the post-9/11 period with a baseline of data that permits comparison of national, international, and regional incidents of terrorism and terrorist attacks. As the authors note, the CIDB "encompasses not only events that occurred within Canada, but also events involving Canadian victims, targets, or perpetrators abroad." Public access to data on incidents that have a direct and iden-tifiable Canadian connection is essential to ensure that political author-ities neither exaggerate the threat of terrorism and its consequences nor underplay or ignore its effects. As Tishler, Ouellet and Kilberg conclude from the survey, "Canada's exposure to terrorism may be construed as relatively mild [but] it is not so sparse as is frequently imagined."

Chapter 3 shifts to one of the more recent problems confronted by Western democratic states: foreign fighters. The conflict in Syria attracted thousands of individuals from around the world, who trav-elled there to join a range of violent non-state groups (The Soufan Group 2015; Barrett 2017). These foreign fighters pose a number of challenges, in terms of states' capacity to prevent individuals or sets of friends from joining a terrorist group abroad, establishing contacts and forming networks that facilitate recruitment, providing financial or other material support to such entities, gaining experience and training that might result in more sophisticated and deadly terrorist incidents when they return home or relocate to other conflict zones, and acting as an inspiration for others to join other conflicts (Hegghammer 2010; 2013; Nesser, Stenersen, and Oftedal 2016). Dawson and Amarasingam provide the context for Canadians to understand the foreign fighter phenomenon. Drawing on interviews with foreign fighters, relatives and friends of foreign fighters, and online supporters of jihadism, they argue that push factors such as a lack of economic, social, or politi-cal opportunities are far from being the sole drivers of such activity. Evident from this research is the interplay of push and pull factors; this, the authors note, challenges the common assertion that radicalization to violence is rooted in lack of opportunity in a society. Indeed, Dawson and Amarasingam observe that their primary data reveal that religious discourse and solidarity with fellow Muslims is a prominent factor and works alongside a moral rather than an economic explanation for the turn to extremism. The journey of each foreign fighter is a highly indi-vidual "quest of self-discovery ... [rather] than an explicitly political process." The authors do not discount the socio-economic and other conditions that are often seen as "pushing" individuals into terrorism;

rather, they argue that scholars and practitioners studying terrorism and radicalization to violence need to consider the complex interaction of "push" and "pull" variables. As they note, "an abiding need for a greater meaning and purpose in life, and the appeal of an ideology that appears to meet that need," must be included in any list of factors used to explain how individuals radicalize to violence.

Evident from other literature is the threat posed by right-wing terrorists, right-wing extremists, and white supremacists (Taylor, Currie, and Holbrook 2013; Ravndal 2015). This threat tragically revealed itself in early 2017 with the deadliest terrorist attack in Canada in recent years: the murder of six Muslims at a mosque in Quebec City following evening prayers. The political response to the killing of these six Canadians unequivocally referred to that event as an act of terrorism: the prime minister called it a "terrorist attack on Muslims" and "a despicable act of terror" (MacCharles 2017). Perry and Scrivens define the right-wing extremist movement in Canada as "a loose movement, animated by a racially, ethnically, and sexually defined nationalism. This nationalism is typically framed in terms of White power and is grounded in xenophobic and exclusionary understandings of the perceived threats posed by such groups as non-Whites, Jews, immigrants, homosexuals, and feminists" (Perry and Scrivens 2016, 821). Just as in the United States (Perliger 2012), the right-wing movement in Canada is heterogeneous, and assessments of its organizational structure and of the links between right-wing extremists reveal that "adherents are, rather, decidedly unorganized and constituted by small loosely linked cells, lone wolves, or ... 'three-man wrecking crews'" (Perry and Scrivens 2016, 834). Nevertheless, while right-wing extremism in Canada may not manifest itself as a coherent movement, its presence is certainly greater than most people realize, its terrorism identifiable, and its connections to wider political and extremist discourse evident (McCoy and Jones 2017; Perry 2017). With the emergence of the "alt right" in Canada, the United States, and parts of Europe, a struggle against violent extremism and terrorism from the right appears as likely as the continued struggle against the violent extremism and terrorism from al Qaeda, ISIS, and others of their ilk.

An understudied aspect of right-wing extremism is the Freemen-on-the-Land movement. In chapter 4, Hofmann provides the first detailed social and historical analysis of the Canadian manifestation of that movement. As he notes, the "anti-government mentality, acrimonious attitude towards police, and disregard for criminal and civil law has caused CSIS and the RCMP to classify them as an emerging security threat." Hofmann's research indicates that since 2012 at least six police officers have been killed "by individuals associated with or inspired by the Canadian Freemen."

Hofmann's analysis of the movement reveals its idiosyncrasies and particular Canadian flavour, which together distinguish it from its American counterpart. Like others who have studied Canadian right-wing extremist movements, including Perry and Scrivens (2015; 2016), he concludes that the Canadian Freemen "lack the organization, popular support, leadership, and resources" of the US right-wing extremist movement, and as such "they do not pose a serious threat to national security" at this time. He goes on to note, however, that this is not a reason to be sanguine; while the movement itself may not pose an immediate threat, its ideas are "fertile soil for the emergence of an ultra-radical fringe of small groups or lone actors" and may provide a right-wing extremist equivalent to the pull factors that Dawson and Amarasingam identify as significant contributing factors in the radicalization to violence of Canadian foreign fighters.

The final chapter in Part One focuses on one of the more perplexing and endemic aspects of contemporary life, one that serves as a facilitator of terrorism in all its forms: the internet, social media, and the digital world. Much has already been written about terrorism and the internet (von Behr et al. 2013; Benson 2014; Weimann 2015; Conway 2017; Gill et al. 2017), as well as the role the internet and social media play in facilitating terrorism or functioning as accelerants for radicalization to violence. Public and political discourse about the internet and terrorism tends to be permeated with the too simple assumption that exposure to propaganda or networks causes young people to be drawn into terrorism or even "brainwashed." In chapter 5, Bérubé and Ducol examine the Canadian context and response to what they refer to as "Jihadism in the digital era." Their assessment examines how Canada and Canadians have been portrayed in online jihadi propaganda, how and why Canada is mentioned within this material, and how the digital personae of Canadians like John Maguire, Mohamed Farah Shirdon, and André Poulin were developed for recruitment and propaganda purposes. The authors also examine how Canadian authorities have responded, both through legal means and by developing counter-narratives, to the challenge posed by digital media in the context of terrorism.

Security

Terrorism manifests itself in many different ways; how states respond to it takes equally diverse forms. Counterterrorism efforts are necessary but pose very real risks to democratic societies (Crenshaw 2010, 2).

In the Part Two of this volume, four chapters explore different aspects of counterterrorism in Canada. In chapter 6, Clément provides the historical context for Canada's response to terrorism. Through archival research, he outlines three stages in the evolution of counterterrorism in Canada. The first two stages cover the period from Confederation to the mid-twentieth century, when terrorism was one of a range of security threats to Canada, albeit at a lower level than in the contemporary period. The salience of this period to our current era is, however, evident, because Canada's concerns were not solely domestic, but also linked to those of its allies. The targeting of "suspect" immigrant communities, extensive liaison between intelligence agencies in Canada and their counterparts in Britain and United States, and a heavy-handed response to extant but relatively small-scale terrorist threats are part of the lineage of Canadian counterterrorism. These enduring aspects of counterterrorism in Canada are also evident in the third evolutionary stage of Canadian counterterrorism, which Clément traces from the 1970s to the current period. In the aftermath of the terrorist attack at the Munich Olympics, the experience with the Front de libération du Québec (FLQ), and the rise of terrorism in the 1970s, the Montreal Olympics of 1976 were the first modern test of Canadian counterterrorism planning.

Clément's archival research confirms that "international terrorism was supplanting communism as the dominant threat to national security," and that public and parliamentary criticism of "extreme measures" was limited until a series of crises in the late 1970s resulted in a Royal Commission that led to the founding of the Canadian Security Intelligence Service (CSIS) in 1984. As he goes on to note, while the terrorist threat today differs from that of the 1970s and 1980s, current Canadian counterterrorism practices have historical parallels that should not be ignored.

Building from a historical base and linked to the challenge of assessing the impact of counterterrorism measures, chapter 7 examines the effectiveness of Canadian counterterrorism. As counterterrorism became more extensive and required more resources post-9/11, a central question – what works? – was asked by scholars, concerned individuals, and political authorities. As Chenoweth and Dugan note, Canada's involvement in the Afghanistan campaign, alongside the United States and other NATO allies and partners, was in part justified by the claim that fighting terrorists abroad would help keep Canadians safer at home. But did it? Given that similar claims were used in the coalition efforts against ISIS, it is important to know whether, and to what extent, such operations did (and do) make Canadians safer. Using an approach developed to study other countries (LaFree, Dugan, and Miller 2015), the authors created a unique dataset to capture how the Canadian government responded to terrorism between 1985 and 2013. This dataset – Government Actions in Terror Environments (GATE) – is the first of its kind in Canada, designed to be used in conjunction with the GTD and the CIDB incident databases. Through a spectrum of responses ranging from accommodation and concessions at one end to deadly force at the other, the authors assess the impact of repressive and conciliatory actions on attacks and incidents of terrorism.

Such analyses of counterterrorism activity have not previously been conducted using Canadian data, and the authors readily acknowledge that their study has limitations and "uses fairly blunt measures of Canadian government actions." This does not, however, mean that the study has limited value; on the contrary, no other publicly available assessment of Canadian counterterrorism actions over time approaches the depth and sophistication of Chenoweth and Dugan's GATE. Its value, among other things, is that it identifies a wider range of measures of counterterrorism and is able to test claims and theories about what works. Chenoweth and Dugan's work has thus expanded the knowledge base regarding both what and what not to do in response to terrorism.

Chapter 8 returns us to the digital domain and the social structure of extremist websites. Acts of terrorism are rarely perpetrated without some connection to a wider political objective. Those who use terrorism rarely do so in isolation or without recourse to other political and social activities (Crenshaw 2011, 4). The internet is now a core medium used by terrorist groups to achieve a variety of communicative and instrumental ends. As Weimann (2015, 23–4) notes: "[c]ommunicative uses include spreading propaganda, launching psychological warfare campaigns, securing internal communications, and radicalizing recruits ... Instrumental uses include online teaching and training of terrorists, and establishing 'virtual training camps' for future assailants." As Dawson and Amarasingam, Hofmann, and Bérube and Ducol all indicate in Part One, extremism and radicalization to violence do not occur in complete isolation. Rather, extremism and radicalization exist within a "radical milieu – which shares their perspective and objectives, approves of certain forms of violence, and (at least to some extent) supports the violent group morally and logistically" (Malthaner and Waldmann 2014, 979). Such communities exist in the real world *and* the digital one (Amarasingam and Davey 2018; Williams 2018), and "there is no easy offline versus online violent radicalization dichotomy to be drawn" (Gill et al. 2017, 114). Moreover, as Conway observes, "research on the role of the internet needs to be widened beyond the present narrow focus on violent *jihadi* online content and interactions ... [It] needs to extend to enquire into the whole range of contemporary violent extremists and terrorists and their online activities." (Conway 2017, 82). The authors of chapter 8 do just that, examining the networks around the websites of four listed terrorist entities in Canada.

Bouchard and colleagues note that "the official website still serves a purpose as the public 'face' of the group, its first opportunity to define its goals and its cause." Understanding how a website is embedded in a wider network and community, who its users are, and how its links and connections function, is therefore important to understanding how a group operates and whether and how its actions resonate with the community it claims to be acting on behalf of or is seeking to win over. Bouchard and colleagues studied the official websites of four groups: the Revolutionary Armed Forces of Colombia (FARC), the Popular Front for the Liberation of Palestine (PFLP), Earth First! (EF), and the Animal Liberation Front (ALF). Each is a listed terrorist entity in Canada (though FARC has recently concluded a peace agreement with the Columbian government). Among other things, the authors explore whether and how Canadian-related content "is represented or discussed on these websites." As they note, "these groups and their websites were not specialized on Canadian content, [but] all sites analysed (except FARC's) either reference Canadian events, make analogies to Canadian specific struggles, or encourage users to support Canadian groups associated with the cause." This study has methodological value as a building block for more detailed research on terrorist group websites; in addition, its results reveal the importance of the size and density of the varied communities that are linked to such sites, besides providing assessments of extremism and recruitment related to these websites and the networks surrounding them.

Chapter 9, the final chapter in the security section, examines terrorist financing. While specific acts of terrorism may not be expensive, all activity costs something, and individuals, cells, and groups must find ways to fund what they do. At a simple level, the effort to understand and track how terrorists secure funding might be understood as a "follow the money" strategy. Schmidt explains, however, that such a singular focus only captures part of how, and why, terrorist groups seek resources to perpetuate their existence and activities. Schmidt builds upon earlier work to develop a model for understanding terrorist resourcing and the importance of a variety of resources to groups. He develops a model of terrorist resourcing that identifies five stages: acquisition of materials, goods, or knowledge of value; aggregation of these resources; transmission to the terrorist organization; transmission from the organization to the cell; and conversion of the artefacts with value into goods or services that support the activities of the terrorist organization. This latter stage may involve such things as purchasing weapons, paying for stolen documents, or producing propaganda materials. For larger groups, particularly those with some control (and responsibility) over a population, providing services to that population also costs money (schools, health, administration, etc.). Preventing, disrupting, and identifying the acquisition, flow, and use of resources therefore has significant value as part of an overall strategy against terrorist campaigns and terrorist groups.

Society

How states respond to terrorism has significant effects on terrorist groups and campaigns, society at large, specific communities within a given society, and even democracy itself. The final section of this volume brings Canadian perspectives to bear on enduring challenges in counterterrorism within Western democracies. Each chapter offers original data, evidence, and insights collected by the authors between 2014 and 2016, into how these challenges are being met (or not) in contemporary Canada. Chapter 10 examines intelligence accountability issues. Debates about the control, oversight, and accountability of Canada's national security community have been a constant feature of national security scholarship and discourse in Canada for more than two decades (Whitaker and Farson 2009). In the mid-1980s, Canada was at the forefront of accountability and control of intelligence through the *CSIS Act* (1985), which established the Security Intelligence Review Committee (SIRC) to review the actions of CSIS and created an Inspector General function designed to be the "eyes and ears" of the Minister of Public Safety and to ensure CSIS remained compliant with the law.

As intelligence activity emerged from the shadows in the 1980s, a role for Parliament emerged in a number of states, including the United Kingdom (UK), Australia, and New Zealand, three countries that alongside the United States are Canada's closest allies in the intelligence world. Repeated attempts to provide Canada's parliamentarians with a role in the accountability of intelligence failed in the late 1990s and 2000s, but the outcry against the *Anti-Terrorism Act, 2015,* gave new impetus to proponents of a Parliamentary committee (for a detailed critique of this legislation, see Forcese and Roach 2015). Such a committee had been rejected by the Conservative government at the time; a newly elected Liberal government promised to enact legislation that would create one. That legislation, Bill C-22, is the subject of chapter 10.

Decker charts its evolution, assesses its advantages and disadvantages, and compares it to the Intelligence and Security Committee in the UK. Her analysis identifies failings in the British system during its formative years and assesses how Canada can learn from its allies to ensure that the new committee fulfils its mandate and meets the expectations of the public and of parliamentarians themselves. She concludes that expectations for the new committee are very high – even allowing for the robust critiques of its limitations in the parliamentary and societal debates of 2016 – and that the committee has a significant task ahead of it.

Perry and Scrivens in chapter 11 explore a fundamental question related to public understanding, discourse, and communication over "who the terrorists are." The role of the media has long been recognized as fundamental in framing terrorism and counterterrorism (Nacos 2002). Using three Canadian incidents in 2014 – the killing of three RCMP officers in Moncton (New Brunswick) by Justin Bourque, the killing of one soldier and injury to another in Saint-Jean-sur-Richelieu (Quebec) by Martin Couture Rouleau, and the killing of one soldier and the storming of Parliament in Ottawa by Michael Zehaf-Bibeau – the authors examine the initial media representations of these lone actors in Canada's English-language print media. Their findings pose uncomfortable, but necessary, questions about how "terrorism" is constructed and reinforced so as to associate it with racialized "otherness." Their findings fit with a recent observation that in the United States "the threat of violence from sources such as white supremacists, antifederalists, and the Christian Identify movement does not have the same resonance for the security agenda" (Crenshaw and LaFree 2017, 4) as that posed by al Qaeda and Islamic State jihadist terrorism. As Perry and Scrivens conclude, "Islamic religious and ethnic groups draw the attention of media outlets, much more so than another very real political threat from the far right." The attacks on civilians in Quebec in 2017 and in Toronto in 2018 have underscored this threat and given rise to a debate in Canada about terrorism and the use of the term more broadly.

The creation or identification of "suspect communities" post-9/11 is a cause for concern in all democratic states (Vermeulen 2014). The experiences of communities that are the primary targets of counterterrorism activities are often reported via anecdotes or small samples from a given city or location. In chapter 12, Lenard and Nagra report on research conducted in five large Canadian cities that examines Muslim Canadians' perceptions of and experiences with counterterrorism measures in this country. Drawing on interviews with nearly one hundred community leaders in these cities, they demonstrate that "Muslims in Canada believe that terrorism has been 'Muslimized,' that is, that Canadians are being led – by political actors and the media – to believe that being Muslim is synonymous with being a terrorist." The ensuing belief and perception that Muslims are "stigmatized, alienated, and marginalized" in Canada undermines trust within and between communities.

That lack of trust has a direct impact on counterterrorism efforts, as the authors of chapter 13 illustrate. Thompson and Bucerius report on research with Somali Canadian youth and young adults, age sixteen to thirty, in Toronto and Edmonton. Drawing on more than four hundred in-depth interviews, the authors give voice to community concerns over radicalization to violence and these youths' relationships with local police services. They then assess how those relationships affect the levels of cooperation between the police and the community in the national security realm. Thompson and Bucerius conclude with the development of "general recommendations on whether and how the stronger relationships between Somali Canadian communities and the police required to implement effective CVE measures in both cities may be established."

Scholars often cry out for more data, but only in recent years has Canada developed a cohort of researchers interested in and capable of examining various aspects of terrorism and counterterrorism in this country. The chapters in this volume reflect this emerging scholarship, which is generating the kinds of empirical data, research methodologies, and policy-orientated interpretations required to devise and implement a distinctively Canadian response to the problems posed by terrorism and the securitization of society. The research findings reported in this volume are by no means the last word on terrorism and counterterrorism in Canada. Rather, they are illustrative of what more can be done, and should be done, to develop the foundation of sound knowledge needed to protect all Canadians and our democratic institutions in the future.

REFERENCES

Amarasingam, Amarnath, and Jacob Davey. 2018. "Fringe internet culture can't stay in the fringes." CBC, 27 April, http://www.cbc.ca/news/opinion/fringe-internet-culture-1.4636614.

Anti-terrorism Act. 2015. Anti-terrorism Act (S.C. 2015, c. 20). https://laws-lois.justice.gc.ca/eng/annualstatutes/2015_20.

Barrett, Richard. 2017. "Beyond the Caliphate: Foreign Fighters and the Threat of Returnees." The Soufan Group, http://thesoufancenter.org/research/beyond-caliphate.

BBC. 2016. "Syrian Nusra Front announces split from al-Qaeda." 29 July 29, http://www.bbc.com/news/world-middle-east-36916606.

Benson, David C. 2014. "Why the Internet Is Not Increasing Terrorism." *Security Studies* 23(2): 293–328. https://doi.org/10.1080/09636412.2014.905353.

Berger, J.M., and Jonathon Morgan. 2015. "The ISIS Twitter Census: Defining and Describing the Population of ISIS Supporters on Twitter." The Brookings Project on US Relations with the Islamic World. Analysis Paper no. 20, March.

Bergen, Peter, Bruce Hoffman, and Katherine Tiedemann. 2011 "Assessing the Jihadist Terrorist Threat to America and American Interests." *Studies in Conflict and Terrorism* 34(2): 65–101. https://doi.org/10.1080/10576 10X.2011.538830.

Burke, Jason. 2011. *The 9/11 Wars*. London: Allen Lane.

– 2015. *The New Threat*. London: The Bodley Head.

– 2017. "Rise and Fall of Isis: Its Dream of a Caliphate Is Over, So What Now?" *The Guardian*, 21 October, https://www.theguardian.com/world/2017/oct/21/isis-caliphate-islamic-state-raqqa-iraq-islamist.

Canada. 2010. Statement by the Prime Minister of Canada at the Commemoration Ceremony for the 25th Anniversary of the Air India Flight 182 Atrocity. 23 June.

– 2015. Minister of Public Safety and Emergency Preparedness Mandate Letter, http://pm.gc.ca/eng/minister-public-safety-and-emergency-preparedness-mandate-letter.

Carter, Joseph, A., Shiraz Maher, and Peter R. Neumann. 2014. "#Greenbirds: Measuring Importance and Influence in Syrian Foreign Fighter Networks." International Centre for Studies in Radicalization and Political Violence Report.

CBC. 2018. "All 10 of those killed in Toronto van attack identified." 27 April, http://www.cbc.ca/news/canada/toronto/van-attack-victims-identified-1.4638102.

Charters, David. 2008. "The (Un)Peaceable Kingdom? Terrorism and Canada before 9/11." *IRPP Policy Matters* 9(4).

Conway, Maura. 2017. "Determining the Role of the Internet in Violent Extremism and Terrorism: Six Suggestions for Progressing Research." *Studies in Conflict and Terrorism* 40(1): 77–98. https://doi.org/10.1080/10576 10X.2016.1157408.

Crelinsten, Ronald. 2012. "Canada's Experience with Terrorism and Violent Extremism." In *Terror in the Peaceable Kingdom*, ed. Daveed Gartenstein-Ross and Senator Linda Frum, 9–27. Washington, D.C.: FDD Press.

Crenshaw, Martha, ed. 2010. *The Consequences of Counterterrorism*. New York: Russell Sage Foundation.

– 2011. *Explaining Terrorism*. London and New York: Routledge.

Crenshaw, Martha, and Gary LaFree. 2017 *Countering Terrorism*. Washington, D.C.: Brookings Institution Press.

CSIS Act. 1985. Canadian Security Intelligence Service Act R.S.C., 1985, c. C-23. https://laws-lois.justice.gc.ca/eng/acts/c-23/FullText.html.

Dawson, Lorne. 2014. "Trying to Make Sense of Home-Grown Terrorist Radicalization: The Case of the Toronto 18." In *Religious Radicalization and Securitization in Canada and Beyond*, ed. Paul Bramadat and Lorne Dawson, 64–91. Toronto: University of Toronto Press

– 2018. "The Demise of the Islamic State and the Fate of Its Western Foreign Fighters: Six Things to Consider." Policy brief no. 9, International Centre for Counter-Terrorism, The Hague.

English, Richard. 2009. *Terrorism: How to Respond*. Oxford: Oxford University Press.

Forcese, Craig, and Kent Roach. 2015. *False Security: The Radicalization of Canadian Anti-Terrorism*. Toronto: Irwin Law.

Gartenstein-Ross, Daveed, and Senator Linda Frum, eds. 2012. *Terror in the Peaceable Kingdom*. Washington, D.C.: FDD Press.

Gill, Paul, Emily Corner, Maura Conway, Amy Thornton, Mia Bloom, and John Horgan. 2017. "Terrorist Use of the Internet by the Numbers." *Criminology and Public Policy* 16(1): 99–117. https://doi.org/10.1111/1745-9133.12249.

Gill, Paul, John Horgan, and Paige Deckert. 2014. "Bombing Alone: Tracing the Motivations and Antecedent Behaviors of Lone-Actor Terrorists." *Journal of Forensic Sciences* 59(2): 425–35. https://doi.org/10.1111/1556-4029.12312.

Gerges, Fawaz A. 2016. *ISIS: A History*. Princeton: Princeton University Press.

Hafez, Mohammed, and Creighton Mullins. 2015. "The Radicalization Puzzle: A Theoretical Synthesis of Empirical Approaches to Homegrown Extremism." *Studies in Conflict and Terrorism* 38(11): 958–75. https://doi.org/10.1080/1057610X.2015.1051375.

Harris, Kathleen. 2017. "Liberals to create 'super' national security watchdog as part of anti-terror overhaul." 20 June, http://www.cbc.ca/news/politics/security-terrorism-legislation-1.4168780.

Hegghammer, Thomas. 2010. "The Rise of Muslim Foreign Fighters: Islam and the Globalization of Jihad." *International Security* 35(3): 53–94. https://doi.org/10.1162/ISEC_a_00023.

– 2013. "Should I Stay or Should I Go? Explaining Variation in Western Jihadists' Choice between Domestic and Foreign Fighting." *American Political Science Review* 107(1): 1–15. https://doi.org/10.1017/S0003055412000615.

Joscelyn, Thomas. 2018. "Analysis: ISIS Hasn't Been Defeated." 22 February, https://www.longwarjournal.org/archives/2018/02/analysis-isis-hasnt-been-defeated.php.

Koehler, Daniel. 2016. "Right-Wing Extremism and Terrorism in Europe: Current Developments and Issues for the Future." *PRISM* 6(2): 85–104. https://cco.ndu.edu/PRISM/PRISM-Volume-6-no-2/Article/839011/right-wing-extremism-and-terrorism-in-europe-current-developments-and-issues-fo.

LaFree, Gary, Laura Dugan, and Erin Miller, with Erica Chenoweth. 2015. "Government Responses to Terrorism." In LaFree, Dugan, and Miller, *Putting Terrorism in Context*, 205–25. London and New York. Routledge.

Leman-Langlois, Stéphane, and Jean-Paul Brodeur. 2005. "Terrorism Old and New: Counterterrorism in Canada." *Police Practice and Research: An International Journal* 6(2): 121–40. https://doi.org/10.1080/15614260500121096.

Lister, Charles. 2016. "Profiling Jabhat al-Nusra." Analysis paper no. 24, The Brookings Project on US Relations with the Islamic World. Washington, D.C.: The Brookings Institution.

MacCharles, Tonda. 2017. "Canadian leaders drop partisanship to denounce Quebec mosque attack." *Toronto Star*, 30 January, https://www.thestar.com/news/canada/2017/01/30/trudeau-faces-challenging-times-after-quebec-city-attack-and-chaos-in-us.html.

McCants, William. 2015. *The ISIS Apocalypse*. New York: St Martin's Press.

Malthaner, Stefan and Peter Waldmann. 2014. "The Radical Milieu: Conceptualizing the Supportive Social Environment of Terrorist Groups." *Studies in Conflict & Terrorism* 37 (12) 979–98. https://doi.org/10.1080/10576 10X.2014.962441.

McCoy, John, and David Jones. 2017. "Look beyond Trump to explain the rise of right wing extremism." *Globe and Mail*, 17 August, https://www.theglobeandmail.com/opinion/look-beyond-trump-to-explain-the-rise-of-right-wing-extremism/article36014162.

McCoy, John, and W. Andy Knight. 2015. "Homegrown Terrorism in Canada: Local Patterns, Global Trends." *Studies in Conflict and Terrorism* 38(4): 253–74. https://doi.org/10.1080/1057610X.2014.994349.

Mullins, Sam. 2013. "'Global Jihad': The Canadian Experience." *Terrorism and Political Violence* 25(5): 734–76. https://doi.org/10.1080/09546553.2012.693552

Nacos, Brigitte, L. 2002. *Mass-Mediated Terrorism*. Lanham: Rowman and Littlefield.

Nesser, Petter. 2014. "Toward an Increasingly Heterogeneous Threat: A Chronology of Jihadist Terrorism in Europe 2008–2013." *Studies in Conflict and Terrorism* 37(5): 440–56. https://doi.org/10.1080/1057610X.2014.893405.

– 2015. *Islamist Terrorism in Europe: A History*. Oxford: Oxford University Press.

Nesser, Petter, Anne Stenersen, and Emile Oftedal. 2016. "Jihadi Terrorism in Europe: The IS-Effect." *Perspectives on Terrorism* 10(6): 3–24. https://doi.org/10.1093/acprof:oso/9780190264024.001.0001.

O'Bagy, Elizabeth. 2012. "Jihad in Syria." Washington, D.C.: Institute for the Study of War.

Pantucci, Raffello. 2015. *We Love Death as You Love Life*. London: Hurst.

Perliger, Arie. 2012. "Challengers from the Sidelines: Understanding America's Violent Far-Right." The Combating Terrorism Center at West Point, www.ctc.usma.edu.

Perry, Barbara. 2017. "The Threat of Right Wing Extremism." *Policy Options*, 13 September, http://policyoptions.irpp.org/magazines/september-2017/the-threat-of-right-wing-extremism.

Perry, Barbara, and Ryan Scrivens. 2015. Right-Wing Extremism in Canada: An Environmental Scan. Ottawa: Public Safety Canada.

– 2016. "Uneasy Alliances: A Look at the Right Wing Extremist Movement in Canada." *Studies in Conflict and Terrorism* 39(9): 819–41. https://doi.org/10.1 080/1057610X.2016.1139375.

Ranstorp, Magnus, ed. 2010. *Understanding Violent Radicalisation*. London and New York: Routledge.

Ravndal, Jacob Aasland. 2015. "Thugs or Terrorists? A Typology of Right-Wing Terrorism and Violence in Western Europe." *Journal for Deradicalization* 15(3): 1–38. http://journals.sfu.ca/jd/index.php/jd/article/view/16/16.

Ross, Jeffrey, Ian. 1988. "Attributes of Domestic Political Terrorism in Canada, 1960–1985." *Terrorism* 11(3): 213–33. https://doi.org/10.1080/10576108808435712.

Shepherd, Michelle. 2011. *Decade of Fear*. Vancouver: Douglas and McIntyre.

Spaaij, Ramon. 2012. *Understanding Lone Wolf Terrorism*. New York: Springer.

Taylor, Max, P.M. Currie, and Donald Holbrook, eds. 2013. *Extreme Right-Wing Political Violence and Terrorism*. New York: Bloomsbury Academic.

The Soufan Group. 2015. *Foreign Fighters: An Updated Assessment of the Flow of Foreign Fighters into Syria and Iraq*. New York. http://soufangroup.com/wp-content/uploads/2015/12/TSG_ForeignFightersUpdate3.pdf.

Vermeulen, Floris. 2014. "Suspect Communities – Targeting Violent Extremism at the Local Level: Policies of Engagement in Amsterdam, Berlin, and London." *Terrorism and Political Violence* 26(2): 286–306. https://doi.org/10.1 080/09546553.2012.705254.

von Behr, Ines, Anaïs Reding, Charlie Edwards, Luke Gribbon. 2013. "Radicalisation in the Digital Era: The Use of the Internet in 15 Cases of Terrorism and Extremism. Cambridge and Brussels: RAND Europe. http://www.rand.org/content/dam/rand/pubs/research_reports/RR400/RR453/RAND_RR453.pdf.

Weimann, Gabriel. 2015. *Terrorism in Cyberspace*. New York: Columbia University Press.

Whitaker, Reg, and Stuart Farson. 2009. "Accountability in and for National Security." *IRPP Choices* 15(9). https://irpp.org/wp-content/uploads/assets/

research/security-and-democracy/accountability-in-and-for-national-security/vol15no9.pdf).

Whitaker, Reg, Gregory S. Kealey, and Andrew Parnaby. 2012. *Secret Service.* Toronto: University of Toronto Press.

Williams, Zoe. 2018. "'Raw hatred': Why the 'incel' movement targets and terrorises women." *The Guardian*, 25 April, https://www.theguardian.com/world/2018/apr/25/raw-hatred-why-incel-movement-targets-terrorises-women.

PART ONE

Terrorism

2 A Survey of Terrorism in Canada: 1960–2015

NICOLE TISHLER, MARIE OUELLET,
AND JOSHUA KILBERG

Accounts of Canada's experience with terrorism are often based on a small selection of foundational sources. These sources, restricted to specific time periods or definitions of terrorism, provide only a selective sampling of incidents.[1] In this chapter, we present comprehensive data derived from Canadian Incident Database (CIDB), an event-based database chronicling incidents of terrorism and violent extremism related to Canada between 1960 and 2015.[2] Consisting of 1,846 Canadian-affiliated incidents, the CIDB nearly doubles previous assessments of the scope of Canadian extremism. This chapter uses CIDB data to review, and where needed revise, the history of terrorism in Canada.

Although the CIDB encompasses a broad scope of violent extremist activity, this chapter focuses exclusively on events that meet Canada's *Criminal Code* definition of terrorism. After presenting an overview of earlier datasets and the major trends they document, the chapter provides a survey of both historical and contemporary Canadian terrorism incidents. Descriptive statistics and infographics derived from the CIDB provide a snapshot of the evolution of terrorism in Canada from 1960 to 2015, emphasizing trends over time, by geographic distribution, perpetrator motivations, tactics and targets, and incident fatalities. To contextualize these data, the chapter then presents a detailed tracing of the predominant organizations and ideologies that have shaped terrorism in Canada. While this terrorism narrative extends to Canada's early campaigns of the 1960s, '70s, and '80s, the emphasis is on post-9/11 trends – namely, jihadi-inspired plots and eco-terrorist incidents. This detailed narrative and overview of key trends together provide a much-needed context for understanding Canada's experience with terrorism as well as a necessary foundation for designing policy responses. Peaceful though it may be, Canada – both at home and abroad – has faced more than 1,800 incidents of terrorism and violent extremism since 1960.

Sources of Events Data

While much of the literature on terrorism in Canada consists of anecdotal case studies, some rigorous empirical analyses have been conducted. The majority of these centre on key incidents[3] and/or groups,[4] or they consist of Canada-centric thematic appraisals of terrorism types[5] and problem areas.[6] These accounts range widely, but they are also fragmentary and fail to offer a complete picture of the terrorist threat to Canada. To provide a more representative view of trends in Canadian terrorism, statistical analyses based on events data (where the unit of analysis is the terrorist event itself) are useful.

While Canadian incidents are included in well-known cross-national terrorism databases such as the Global Terrorism Database (GTD) and International Terrorism: Attributes of Terrorism Events (ITERATE), they are frequently underrepresented.[7] As Table 2.1 shows, both ITERATE and the GTD include a scant number of events relating to Canada and Canadians, as compared with CIDB counts.

Prior Sources of Canadian Events Data

Prior to the CIDB, the most comprehensive and widely cited Canada-specific events data collection efforts were published in works by Anthony Kellett and colleagues (1991), Jeffrey Ian Ross (1988; 1992a; 1994), David Charters (2008), and Stéphane Leman-Langlois and Genviève Ouellet (2009).

The chronology presented by Kellett and colleagues (1991)[8] is often referred to as the National Security Coordination Centre (NSCC) database, in reference to the office of the Solicitor General of Canada in which it was developed. It has been recognized as the "monumental reference on terrorism and political violence [in Canada]" (Leman-Langlois and Brodeur 2005, 122) and is widely referenced in current reviews. In 1992, the NSCC database included 428 incidents of terrorism that had occurred on Canadian territory (366 purely domestic, and 62 with an international dimension)[9] between 1960 and 1989, as well as 511 "excluded" events[10] and 93 terrorist support activities over the same period (Kellett 1995, 286). Kellett's (1995) book chapter synthesizes key findings from the NSCC data and includes a short section on the approximately one dozen incidents occurring in Canada in the subsequent two years (1990–92). The NSCC data collection effort ceased in late 1992 after it was transferred to the Canadian Security Intelligence Service (CSIS).

Incorporated into the NSCC chronology is a revised version of the events data collected under Jeffrey Ian Ross's Attributes of Terrorism

Table 2.1. Coverage of Canadian incidents in terrorism databases

Dataset (year range)	Incidents in Canada	International incidents involving Canadians
ITERATE (1968–2013)	55	144
GTD (1970–2014)	69	74
CIDB (1960–2015)	871	262

in Canada (ATIC) project.[11] ATIC-I, presented in Ross's (1988) evaluation of Canadian domestic terrorism, covers the years 1960 to 1989 and includes almost 500 discrete events coded according to 40 variables. In ATIC-IV, Ross (1994) revises the entries and extends the period under study to 1990. ATIC-IV includes 469 events (411 domestic, 58 with an international dimension).[12]

More recently, Charters (2008) published a review of Canada's pre-9/11 experience with terrorism dating back to 1945, with an emphasis on the years 1960 to 2001. This report relies heavily on NSCC data, using some primary news sources and annual CSIS reports to extend the coverage to 2001. His review is noteworthy for its inclusion of attacks occurring outside Canada, where they involve Canadian perpetrators or interests. Because they adhered to strict geographical requirements, NSCC and ATIC data had excluded the bombing of Air India Flight 182,[13] which more contemporary reviews (Charters 2008; Ouellet 2009; Crelinsten 2012) rightly treat as the most lethal terrorist event in Canadian history.

The most current pre-CIDB database of Canada's experience with terrorism was the one maintained by the Équipe de recherche sur le terrorisme et l'antiterrorisme (ERTA), managed by Jean-Paul Brodeur. Like Charters's chronology, this database is built largely on NSCC data, with updates based on a systematic review of media.[14] Unlike the datasets described above, ERTA expands event coverage beyond actual terrorist attacks to include three other matters: peripheral (i.e., support) activities; details of foiled and abandoned plots; and the response (including previous surveillance) to these and to the terrorist acts themselves.

ERTA, however, begins only in 1973, with the end of the Front de Libération du Québec (FLQ) crisis. With this contemporary focus – and despite relying on a definition of terrorism so broad that even the authors recognize the database likely includes events not categorized as terrorism elsewhere (Leman-Langlois and Ouellet 2009, 62) – ERTA identifies only 326 terrorist events between 1973 and 2006. Of these, 232 are of such a low level that the authors categorize them as "bruit de fond," separate from their analysis of violent acts (Leman-Langlois and Ouellet 2009, 62). Although Crelinsten (2012) incorporates ERTA into his most recent review of terrorism in Canada, ERTA's data and its most detailed information are published only in French and are available neither for public consultation nor for purchase.

Introduction to the CIDB

The CIDB, as described above, is an event-based dataset chronicling incidents of terrorism and violent extremism related to Canada between 1960 and 2015. This database encompasses not only events that occurred within Canada but also events involving Canadian victims, targets, or perpetrators abroad.[15] Incidents for the database were compiled in two stages. First, coders imported all Canadian-related incidents from extant databases, chronologies, and reports.[16] Second, coders conducted open source searches of media, legal, and government reports to validate and update existing event profiles and introduce new incidents.

Consistent with Canada's *Criminal Code* definition of terrorism,[17] as well as the GTD's guidelines for event inclusion, the CIDB records events as acts of terrorism if they meet three criteria:

1 The incident must be intentional – the result of a conscious calculation on the part of a perpetrator;
2 The incident must entail some level of violence or threat of violence – including property violence, as well as violence against people; and
3 The perpetrators of the incident must be subnational actors (i.e., not state actors).

The CIDB also includes extremist activity that does not satisfy all three of these criteria. Thus, it defines non-terrorist violent extremism as serious threats, harm, murder, mayhem, and damage to property motivated and justified by extremist beliefs (such as hate crimes where no violence is perpetrated, and low-level incidents resulting in little damage, such as vandalism). The CIDB does not include (as does ERTA) details of peripheral or support activities, nor does it incorporate elements of counterterrorism surveillance and response, except when these details are relevant to descriptions of actual terrorist incidents. It does, however, incorporate incidents of varying degrees of success (i.e., including foiled and abandoned plots), by means of an indicator variable for incident success.

Comprising 1,846 incidents between 1960 and 2015, the CIDB is the largest open-source database of Canadian violent extremism events.[18] This count includes Canadian-affiliated incidents perpetrated abroad (21% of the total sample), and incidents that failed to meet one of the three criteria for terrorism defined above (39%), as well as other extremist incidents (14%). In the sections that follow, the analyses emphasize the CIDB's 871 (47%) events that occurred within Canada and that meet the three definitional requirements for terrorism described above.

Terrorism in Canada

This section presents descriptive statistics and infographics to highlight trends in the evolution of terrorism in Canada since 1960, including the temporal and geographic distribution of incidents, perpetrator motivations, tactics and targets employed, and resulting fatalities.

Geographic and Temporal Trends

While the CIDB includes incidents occurring in every Canadian province and territory except Nunavut and Yukon (see Figure 2.1), the bulk of these incidents are concentrated in particular geographic regions and time periods. Figure 2.2 presents the temporal distribution of CIDB's terrorism incidents (n = 1,133),[19] demonstrating a broad shift from within-country incidents (n = 871) to Canadian-affiliated incidents (i.e., with Canadian victims, targets, or perpetrators) abroad (n = 262). By the mid-2000s, the frequency of Canadian-affiliated terrorist incidents perpetrated abroad (23% of the total sample) had surpassed that of terrorist incidents within Canada (77%).

For incidents within Canada, two peaks in the 1960s and 1970s correspond to surges in the terrorist activities of the Sons of Freedom (SOF) in British Columbia (BC) and the FLQ in Quebec (described in greater detail in the following section). The decrease in incidents by the mid-1970s reflects the subsequent demise of both campaigns. The less pronounced peaks of activity in the 1980s capture a resurgence of terrorist incidents associated with émigré groups – that is, perpetrators using Canada as a base for addressing foreign grievances. While émigré incidents occurred persistently across the 1960s and 1970s (largely reflecting the activities of anti-Castro Cubans, and activities related to Yugoslavia prior to its break-up in the 1990s), the apparent burst of terrorist acts in the 1980s predominantly reflects the activities of the Armenian Secret Army for the Liberation of Armenia (ASALA).[20] The small increase in incidents in the 2000s reflects a wave of threats and incidents associated with environmental and jihadi-inspired terrorism.

Perpetrators' Motivations and Attack Frequency

The incidents for which perpetrators have been identified encompass a wide range of motivations and involve separatist, religious,

Figure 2.1. Distribution of terrorist events by province/territory, 1960–2015

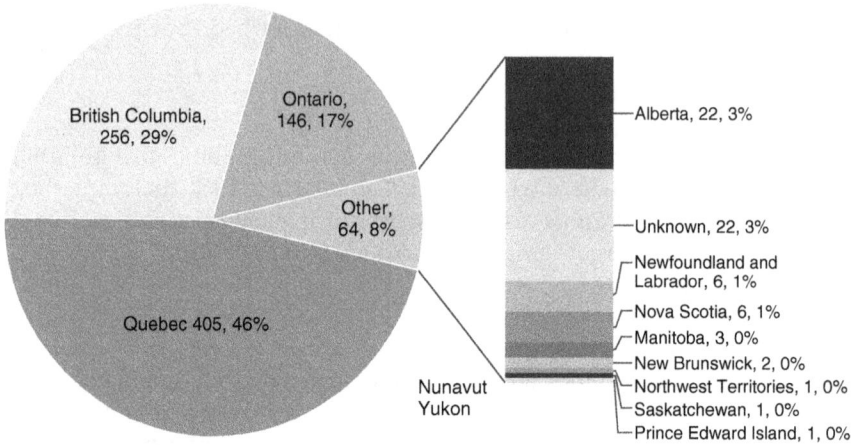

Figure 2.2. Temporal trends in Canadian terrorism incidents, 1960–2015

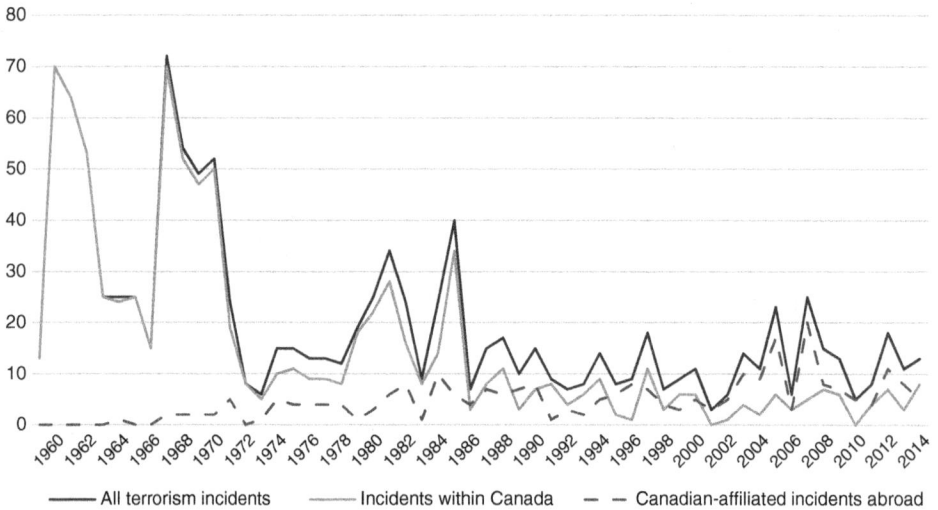

leftist, rightist, environmentalist, supremacist, and ethnic-based forms of extremism.[21] Despite this heterogeneity, as Figure 2.3 shows, patterns in terrorist motivation are evident.

Most incidents are motivated by separatist (31%) or religious (26%) ideologies, reflecting the high number of incidents perpetrated by the

Figure 2.3. Motivational orientation of terrorist attack perpetrators in Canada, 1960–2015

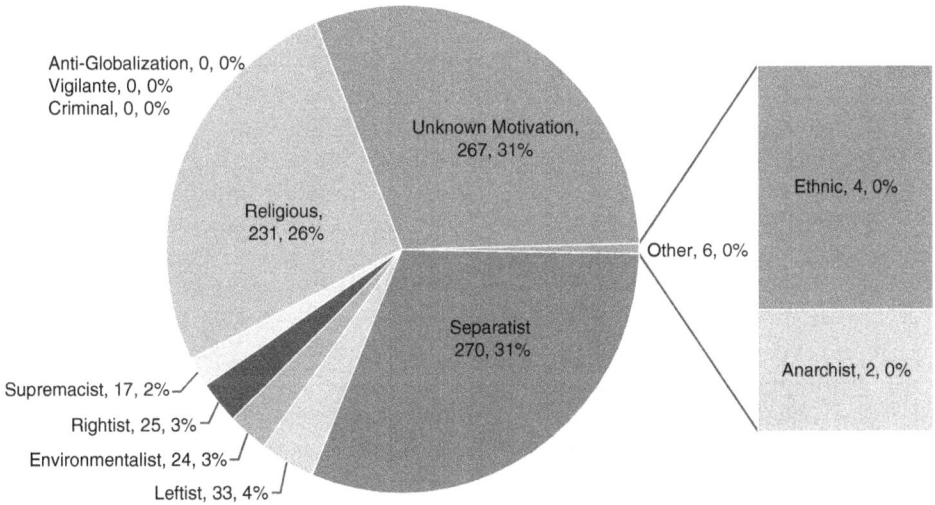

FLQ and SOF, respectively. Combined, supremacist and rightist organizations account for a mere 5 per cent of incidents.[22] While other data sources frequently conflate these two categories under the "right-wing" moniker,[23] the CIDB maintains a sharp distinction: supremacist organizations are those that pursue a racial agenda, advocating for the inherent supremacy of a specific race over others; rightist organizations are those that pursue economically right-wing policies, such as extreme laissez-faire, small government, or the preservation of status quo economic elites. While supremacist attacks are spread relatively evenly across the decades, nearly half of the CIDB's rightist incidents occurred in the 1970s, capturing the anti-Castro Cuban émigré incidents (among others) of the same period. At the opposite end of the spectrum, almost half of Canada's leftist attacks occurred in the 1980s, reflecting the campaigns of BC-based Direct Action (DA) and the related (although unaffiliated) Groupe action directe, active primarily in Montreal. Environmentally motivated incidents emerged in the 1980s and have since increased in frequency: 32 per cent of environmentalist incidents occurred in the 1990s, and 54 per cent in the 2000s.

This diversity of motivations is reflected in the number of terrorist perpetrators active in Canada since 1960. The CIDB identifies ninety-seven distinct perpetrators, including both established groups and lone actors. Of these perpetrators, 75 per cent conducted only a single attack. Just three identified perpetrators – the FLQ, SOF, and ASALA—carried out campaigns involving ten or more incidents.

Tactics and Targets

Figures 2.4 and 2.5 highlight overarching trends in the tactics used by terrorists in Canada between 1960 and 2015. As illustrated in Figure 2.5, 65 per cent of all terrorism incidents involved the use or threatened use of explosives, bombs, or dynamite. The frequency of explosives use is reflected in the broader categorization of event type (see Figure 2.4), whereby bombings and explosions constitute 52 per cent of all incidents. Given their pervasiveness, it is no surprise that 74 per cent of threat events involved the threatened use of explosives.

Throughout the 1960 to 2015 period, the second-most-popular event type was attacks on facilities or infrastructure. These attacks have the primary objective of causing damage to a non-human target (such as buildings, monuments, pipelines, or transport infrastructure), without the use of explosives. The vast majority (97%) of these attacks were conducted using incendiary weapons, which burn but do not explode (such as Molotov cocktails), although they may also involve non-incendiary forms of sabotage (such as cutting guy wires or smashing glass).

The CIDB also incorporates a dummy indicator for hoaxes ($n = 153$), that is, those incidents in which perpetrators use benign materials to give the impression that a terrorist act is, or has been, underway; threaten a future terrorist attack with no intention of actually carrying it out; or claim responsibility for incidents they did not cause. As indicated in Figure 2.6, the vast majority of these hoax incidents involved hoaxed explosives, bombs, or dynamite – consistent with the trend of actual weapons' uses.

While tactical and weapon choices were concentrated in a few select categories, Figure 2.7 shows that perpetrators' target selections were far more diverse. Approximately one fifth of attacks targeted private citizens and property, a category that includes not only attacks on individuals and their private residences, but also attacks on public areas such as markets, commercial streets, busy intersections, and pedestrian malls. Governments (their buildings, representatives, convoys, and/ or events) were targeted 16 per cent of the time, followed closely by commercial businesses (13% of attacks).

Terrorist tactics are generally evenly distributed across target types, as per the proportions presented for the overall sample of events in Figure 2.4. However, a subset of targets are far more prone to experiencing certain tactics over others. For instance, in the case of bombing events (which themselves account for 52% of the full sample), attacks on utilities almost

Figure 2.4. Types of terrorist events in Canada, 1960–2015

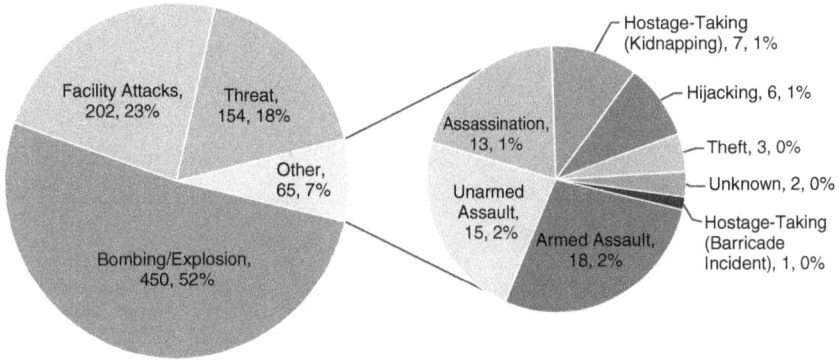

Figure 2.5. Primary weapon type used in terrorist events in Canada, 1960–2015

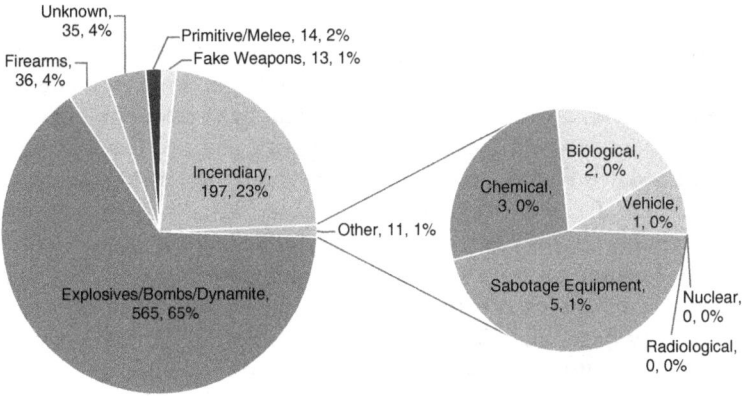

Figure 2.6. Weapons implied in terrorist hoaxes in Canada, 1960–2015

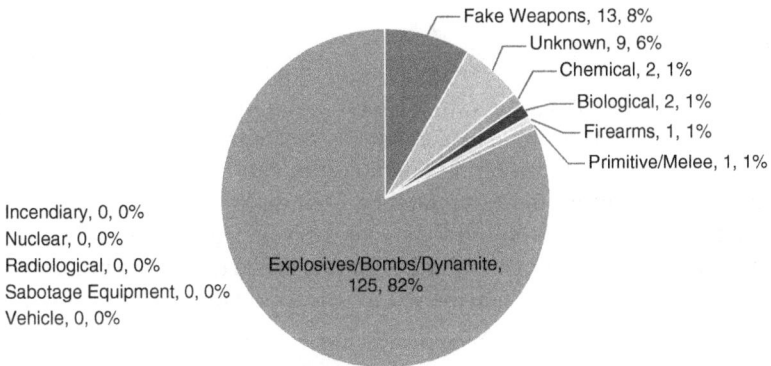

Figure 2.7. Primary targets of terrorism incidents in Canada, 1960–2015

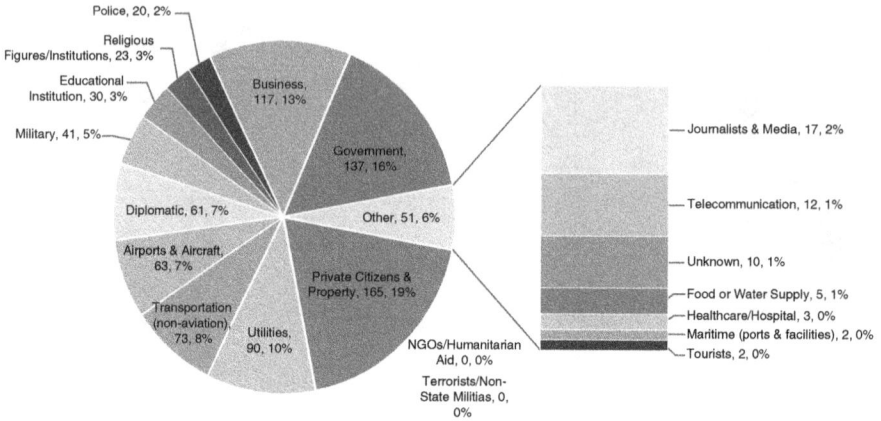

Police, 20, 2%

Religious Figures/Institutions, 23, 3%

Educational Institution, 30, 3%

Military, 41, 5%

Business, 117, 13%

Government, 137, 16%

Diplomatic, 61, 7%

Other, 51, 6%

Airports & Aircraft, 63, 7%

Transportation (non-aviation), 73, 8%

Utilities, 90, 10%

Private Citizens & Property, 165, 19%

NGOs/Humanitarian Aid, 0, 0%

Terrorists/Non-State Militias, 0, 0%

Journalists & Media, 17, 2%

Telecommunication, 12, 1%

Unknown, 10, 1%

Food or Water Supply, 5, 1%

Healthcare/Hospital, 3, 0%

Maritime (ports & facilities), 2, 0%

Tourists, 2, 0%

exclusively (97% of the time) involve bombs or explosions, as compared with only 11 per cent of attacks on airports and aircraft. Conversely, although threats occur across the general sample 18 per cent of the time, such threats almost never target utilities (1%) and far more frequently (33%) target airports and aircraft. These relationships suggest that terrorists are far more inclined to only threaten attacks against hardened targets (such as airports and aircraft), and to actually carry out serious attacks against softer, more accessible targets (such as utilities), which are often unguarded.

Finally, hostage-taking incidents are highly concentrated against certain target types: in Canada the CIDB's only barricade scenario occurred on a military base, and 71 per cent of kidnapping scenarios involved diplomats (the other two kidnapping incidents involved government and police). Private citizens were never targeted for hostage scenarios outside of transportation (predominantly aviation) hijackings, and none were injured or killed in such hostage-taking events.

Fatalities

Very few terrorist attacks in Canada have resulted in death. That is not to say, however, that there have been few deaths. Since 1960, only 3 per cent of all incidents have resulted in any fatalities and, of these, only six incidents involved more than one fatality. Despite this infrequency of fatal incidents, however, 374 individuals have been killed as a result of terrorism in Canada between 1960 and 2015. Prior to 9/11, the 1985 bombing of Air India Flight 182 had been the world's deadliest terrorist attack against a Western state (Charters 2008, 20; Ouellet 2009, 74). All 329 people aboard the aircraft perished in the incident, accounting for 88 per cent of Canada's terrorism-related deaths since 1960. The bombing's alleged perpetrators were Canada-based Sikhs, seeking to avenge Indian governmental policies (Air India Flight 182, 2010; discussed in greater detail below).

Of the remaining forty-five fatalities, the bulk resulted from incidents with no identified perpetrator motivation. Where motivations were identified, the most lethal motivational orientations were religious and separatist, each responsible for seven fatality-generating incidents and resulting in ten and nine deaths, respectively.[24] With the Air India bombing excluded, the most lethal terrorist weapon type in Canada is firearms, which were responsible for thirty-four fatalities across fifteen incidents. Setting aside the Air India explosives, firearms are the only weapon type to have resulted in more than one fatality per attack.

Terrorism in Canada: A Narrative Lens

To contextualize the statistical overview of terrorism trends presented above, this chapter now takes a more narrative orientation, presenting a detailed tracing of the predominant organizations and ideologies that have shaped terrorism in Canada from 1960 to present. This section has two parts. First, it examines Canada's early terrorism campaigns of the 1960s, '70s, and '80s: namely the SOF, FLQ, and various factions of imported (or émigré) terrorism. Second, it presents a comprehensive overview of terrorist incidents between 2001 and 2015, emphasizing a spate of eco-terrorism incidents and a series of well-known jihadi-inspired plots and events.

Drivers of Terrorism in Canada: The Early Decades

Given the CIDB's reliance on the NSCC (and its component ATIC) data for the first decades under examination, its data tell a story similar to those presented in other contemporary reviews of terrorism in Canada, namely Charters (2008) and Crelinsten (2012).[25] This section illuminates central parallels with existing narratives and highlights instances where a CIDB-based narrative diverges from previous understandings.

Both Charters and Crelinsten divide their reviews into domestic incidents and what NSCC calls "international" terrorism, better understood as imported homeland conflicts. The CIDB mirrors their portrayal of the country's two major domestic campaigns, as identified above and described in greater detail below: the SOF, peaking in 1961–62, and Quebec separatists (mainly the FLQ and its related cells), with events clustered in two peaks at the beginning and end of the 1963–72 period.

While existing reviews describe DA – known locally as the Squamish Five – as Canada's third most high-profile domestic campaign, the CIDB does not reflect this prominence in terms of attack frequency ($n = 5$) or lethality (no associated deaths). The dataset does, however, include DA's two most infamous attacks, responsible for a collective $8–9 million in property damage: the May 1982 bombing of a BC Hydro substation on Vancouver Island, and the October 1982 bombing of Litton Industries' Toronto plant. The CIDB better captures DA activities in the context of a broader trend toward a concentration of leftist activities in the 1980s (almost half of all leftist incidents occurred in that decade). The vast majority of leftist events perpetrated in that decade were attributed to groups closely linked with the DA and its motivating ideology, which blended anti-capitalist, anti-nuclear, environmental, and feminist ideals (Charters 2008, 17; Crelinsten 2012, 14).[26]

Sons of Freedom (SOF) Doukhobors

The SOF were a militant wing of the otherwise pacifist Doukhobor Christian sect, responsible for perpetrating more than half of all Canada's religious terrorism in the 1960–2015 period.[27] Although the SOF's violent activities date back to 1923 – arising from conflict with government authorities sparked by the community's denial of secular authority and corresponding refusal to register their homesteads and land – the CIDB captures the resurgence and pinnacle of SOF violence that occurred following the Doukhobor church's 1960 decision to buy back land previously confiscated by the BC government (Charters 2008, 15). Between 1960 and 1986, the SOF conducted 133 terrorist attacks, more than 63 per cent of which occurred in 1961 and 1962.

Most of these attacks were committed in the Kootenay region of rural British Columbia and targeted the property of private citizens as well as energy transmission networks and transportation infrastructure. The SOF frequently used arson and blunt objects to attack the homes and local community halls of Doukhobors who supported the church's land negotiations with the government. Attacks on utilities and transportation infrastructure were more frequent and consisted predominantly of explosives used to sabotage hydro poles and railway tracks. Despite the frequency of attacks, however, the SOF intentionally avoided causalities; the one exception was a perpetrator death and four perpetrator injuries resulting from a premature bomb detonation while five SOF members were en route to bombing a post office. SOF activity eventually declined – their final incident occurred in 1986 – after a series of confessions by SOF community members (Charters 2008, 15).

The Front de Libération du Québec (FLQ)

The FLQ and its affiliated cells were the most prolific terrorist perpe-trators within a broader separatist campaign for Quebec independ-ence. Between 1963 and 1972, the FLQ carried out 176 terrorist attacks (accounting for the majority of non-émigré separatist terrorism in the country). These attacks were perpetrated mainly against targets on the island of Montreal and other areas of Quebec; there were also a hand-ful of attacks in the country's capital, Ottawa. The FLQ's first action was an attempt to bomb a Canadian Broadcasting Corporation (CBC) radio tower in February 1963 – consistent with its general strategy of targeting symbols of the federal government and anglophone presence in Quebec (Charters 2008, 16). This attempt failed, but the group was not deterred. The following seven months – the most active period in the group's nine-year campaign – saw eighteen successful bombings and explosive or incendiary attacks on facilities and infrastructure, and a nearly equal number of unsuccessful attacks, threats, and hoaxes. The group's activity surged again in 1968 and to a lesser degree in 1970.

In 1970, the FLQ abducted British attaché James Cross as well as Quebec's deputy premier and labour minister Pierre Laporte – whom they would eventually murder. This precipitated the October Crisis, "one of the most significant political crises in Canadian history" (Crelinsten 2012, 11). In response to these kidnappings, which have similarly been described as "the most serious security emergency in [Canadian] history" (Whitaker, Kealey, and Parnaby 2012, 271–2), the federal government invoked the *War Measures Act*, thus granting itself sweeping emer-gency powers of arrest and detention. The FLQ's prominent position in Canadian historical memory is thus a result not of its organizational or tactical prowess – it was, in fact, rather amateurish – but of its ability to "str[ike] at the heart of the Canadian political culture" (Charters 1997, 133). The group's sharp decline is attributed to police informant infiltra-tion of active FLQ cells by 1971, to the extent that by 1972 the group "was in essence a pawn of the security service" (Crelinsten 2012, 14).

Imported Terrorism

The CIDB uses the "émigré" indicator to capture what is referred to in ATIC and NSCC data as "international" terrorism, or "imported homeland conflicts." Canada experienced variously oriented waves of émigré terrorism in the 1960–2000 period (outlined above). The most significant incident of this kind was the June 1985 bombing of Air India Flight 182. As noted above, this bombing was allegedly perpetrated by a network of Sikh extremists who were seeking to avenge the Indian government's assault on the Sikh Golden Temple shrine in Amristar (Charters 2008, 20; Air India Flight 182, 2010, 21–31; Crelinsten 2012, 18). The bombing resulted in the death of all on board. The plot had been conceived and implemented in Canada, and the flight was en route to Delhi from Montreal when the bomb exploded over the Atlantic Ocean in Irish airspace. Of the 329 people killed, 280 were Canadian citizens.[28]

Drivers of Terrorism in Canada from 2001 to 2015

Between 2001 and 2015, Canada experienced sixty-two terrorism incidents, nearly half of which (44%) involved threats or unsuccessful attempts to carry out an attack. Only three terrorism events – an anti-separatist incident in 2012, in which a stagehand was shot at a political rally in Montreal, and two jihadist-inspired incidents against members of the Canadian Forces in 2014 – resulted in any fatalities. Other contemporary reviews have recognized the low attack frequency in this period (Leman-Langlois and Ouellet 2009; Crelinsten 2012, 22) but have presented only sparse descriptions of the events themselves. The sections that follow examine the two most prominent motivational trends for terrorist attacks between 2001 and 2015: environmental and jihadi-inspired. Again, incidents of violent extremism not meeting the *Criminal Code* definition for terrorism are excluded from the analysis.

Environmental Extremism

Between 2001 and 2015, Canada experienced eleven incidents motivated by environmental concerns, all of which occurred within a five-year span: 2005 to 2009. The Earth Liberation Front (ELF) in Ontario perpetrated three of these incidents. Adopting arson as their main tactic, ELF targeted businesses and construction sites, burning down a pro shop on a golf course in 2005 and two under-construction houses in 2006, cumulatively causing more than $600,000 in damage.

The remaining eight incidents occurred in 2008 and 2009 in western Canada, along the BC–Alberta border. In these attacks, unidentified eco-terrorists targeted the oil-and-gas industry, usually employing explosive devices to damage pipelines and wellheads. A still-at-large individual, who came to be known as the "Tomslake/EnCana Bomber," in reference to the campaign's location and corporate target, perpetrated the most notorious of these attacks (Joosse 2017). In several threat letters to local media, the perpetrator had expressed concerns regarding the "crazy expansion of deadly gas wells" (MacDonald 2009).

In their failed effort to identify and prosecute the culprit, the RCMP had deployed more than 250 investigators, including members of the Integrated National Security Enforcement Team (INSET); and EnCana had offered a $1 million reward for information.

Jihadi-Inspired Incidents

Notwithstanding the post-9/11 attention accorded to jihadist terrorism in Western countries, Canada has escaped relatively unscathed. Between 2001 and 2015, the country experienced only nine jihadist incidents, seven of which were foiled by law enforcement before the attackers' plans could come to fruition.[29] Differing from earlier religious terrorism in Canada, which primarily aimed to destroy facilities and infrastructure, Canada's two successful jihadist incidents targeted members of the armed forces, and the foiled plots each aimed to target civilians. Since each of the incidents was perpetrated by a distinct set of actors and did not form part of a single coordinated campaign, they are detailed independently below. A common thread is law enforcement's capacity to foil plots and neutralize attackers: every one of these incidents resulted in the perpetrators' arrest or death. In post-9/11 Canada, increased vigilance, the deployment of counterterrorism teams (such as INSETs), and legislative reforms have led to the successful detection and prevention of several potentially large-scale attacks.

Momin Khawaja (2004). Canadian citizen Momin Khawaja was arrested in his Orleans, Ontario, home for helping a British jihadi group plot a series of fertilizer bomb attacks in England. Khawaja was involved in facilitating financing for the group, training its members, and assisting with the development of explosive devices (*R. v. Khawaja* 2006). Evidence presented at trial indicated that the likely targets were a nightclub and a shopping mall in London. In 2010, Khawaja received a life sentence.

The "Toronto 18" (2006). In this notable plot, eighteen individuals (four of them youths) planned to conduct bombings against public targets, including various Ontario power plants, the Toronto Stock Exchange, and the Toronto offices of CSIS. The group was seeking to persuade Canada to withdraw its military support for the war in Afghanistan (*R v. Ahmad* 2010). The group came under intense RCMP surveillance from early on, but by then it had already organized two training camps and amassed bomb-making materials. The successful infiltration of two informants led to the arrest of all members in 2006. Ten adults and one minor were eventually convicted, with sentences ranging from two and a half years to life.

The "Maskinongé Terrorist" (2007). Canadian citizen Said Namouh was arrested in Maskinongé, Quebec, for plotting to detonate a car bomb in Austria with a team of at least three other al Qaeda sympathizers. Online communications with his European co-conspirators identified Namouh as the attack's designated suicide bomber (*R. v. Namouh* 2010). Namouh had also been an active member of the Global Islamic Media Front (GIMF) and had published much of the group's online propaganda. In 2010, he received a life sentence.

Ottawa Plot (2010). This incident was initially reported as involving three Canadian men who were plotting to bomb targets in Ottawa. One of the three had attended an al Qaeda–affiliated terrorist training camp in Afghanistan (*R. v. Ahmed* 2014). He allegedly recruited the two others upon his return to Canada and supplied the necessary components and instructions for constructing improvised explosive devices. Only two of the men were convicted for their involvement in the plot, receiving sentences of twelve and twenty-four years; the third was acquitted in 2014, marking Canada's first acquittal of an individual charged under the *Anti-Terrorism Act.*

Via Rail Plot (2013). Two men were convicted for plotting to derail a train with the intent of killing all its passengers (*R v. Esseghaier and Jaser* 2015). The train in question was a VIA Rail passenger train running between the Greater Toronto Area and New York City. Detecting this cross-border incident thus relied on collaboration (including surveillance) between the RCMP and the Federal Bureau of Investigation (FBI), with an FBI agent playing a key role in infiltrating the small group and securing evidence necessary for convictions. Both men were sentenced to life in prison.

Victoria Legislature Plot (2013). On 1 July 2013, a couple planted what they believed to be two explosive devices on the grounds of the BC Legislature in Victoria. The improvised bombs – pressure cookers filled with nails and bolts – were intended to detonate during the popular Canada Day celebrations at the site. Fortunately, the couple had been placed under RCMP surveillance earlier that year, after a neighbour reported that they had espoused extremist sentiments; they were arrested shortly after planting the devices. As part of an undercover sting operation, the RCMP had posed as Muslim extremists, befriending the couple for the purpose of gathering intelligence about a potential conspiracy. In June 2015, the couple were convicted by a jury for terrorism-related offences (*R. v. Nuttall* 2014); approximately one year later, however, a BC Supreme Court judge entered a stay of proceedings, stating that the plot had been instigated by the RCMP and that the couple lacked the mental capacity and motivation to conduct the planned bombing on their own (CBC 2016). This was the first case in Canadian history where entrapment was successfully used as a defence against terrorism charges. As of January 2018, the Crown is appealing the ruling.

Saint-Jean-sur-Richelieu Attack (2014). On 20 October 2014, Martin Couture-Rouleau drove his vehicle into two Canadian Forces members in the parking lot of a strip mall in Saint-Jean-sur-Richelieu, Quebec. He killed Warrant Officer Patrice Vincent and injured the other soldier. A police chase ensued, during which the perpetrator phoned 9-1-1 to tell police he had been "acting in the name of Allah." The chase ended abruptly when Couture-Rouleau was fatally shot by a responding police officer.

Ottawa Parliament Shooting (2014). Less than two days later, on 22 October 2014, another individual, Michael Zehaf-Bibeau, travelled to Ottawa, where he fatally shot Corporal Nathan Cirillo, a sentry at the National War Memorial, before entering Parliament Hill, where he in turn was fatally shot in an exchange of gunfire with House of Commons Security and RCMP officers. In this case and in the attack in Saint-Jean-sur-Richelieu, questions about the lone attackers' mental stability led to a national debate surrounding whether such incidents should be labelled as terrorism (see Bouchard and Thomas 2015).

Toronto Plot (2015). A thirty-three-year-old Pakistani man based in Canada, Jahanzeb Malik, was accused of plotting remote-controlled bomb attacks against the US Consulate and financial district in Toronto. A six-month undercover operation provided evidence that he had received military and weapons training in a Libyan camp and that he sympathized with al Qaeda and ISIS (Perkel 2015). He was arrested in March 2015 and ordered to be deported to Pakistan by the Immigration and Refugee Board.

Conclusion

Although Canada's exposure to terrorism may be construed as relatively mild (see, for example, MacLeod 2011), it is not so sparse as is frequently imagined. Canada's early experience with terrorism is punctuated by three surges reflecting the activities of the SOF and FLQ in the early 1960s and 1970s, and a later small wave of leftist incidents in the 1980s. Compared to these early decades, contemporary terrorism in Canada has been relatively infrequent. Among the only sixty-two incidents occurring within Canada between 2001 and 2015, two clusters can be discerned: a series of eco-terrorism incidents, mostly comprised of arson attacks against oil industry targets; and a collection of jihadi-inspired foiled plots and serious incidents, notably the October 2014 attacks that led to the deaths of two Canadian Forces members. In the same post-2000 period, the CIDB documents a shift towards Canadian-affiliated incidents (i.e., with Canadian victims, targets, or perpetrators) abroad. It also notes an increase in right-wing extremist activity. A thorough treatment of these developments is beyond the scope of this chapter, but they are covered elsewhere in this volume (Dawson and Amarasingam; Hofmann; Perry and Scrivens) and in other literature cited in this chapter.

In his 2008 review of terrorism in Canada, Charters aptly recognized that "[f]or a country once referred to as "the peaceable kingdom" ... Canada has a remarkably rich history of political violence" (8). The data contained within the CIDB and presented in this chapter paint a comprehensive picture of this history.

NOTES

1 With the exception of Charters (2008), these efforts predated the creation of a national legal definition of terrorism.
2 The CIDB was funded by Public Safety Canada and Defence Research and Development Canada (DRDC), under the National Security Data Initiative (NSDI) of the Canadian Safety and Security Program (CSSP). It was compiled by a team of research affiliates of the Canadian Network for Research on Terrorism, Security, and Society (TSAS), including this chapter's three authors.
3 Namely the 1985 bombing of Air India Flight 182 and the 1970 October Crisis.
4 Namely the Front de libération du Québec (FLQ; Crelinsten 1987; Charters 1997); Sons of Freedom Doukhobors (Woodcock and Avakumovik 1968; Yerbury 1984; Ouellet 2009); Direct Action (Ouellet 2009, 80–5); Sikh Militant Movements (Razavy 2006); and the Toronto 18 (Dawson 2014).
5 For example, separatist/nationalist (Ross 1995); religious (Wilner 2009; McCoy and Knight 2015); and right-wing (Ross 1992b; Bérubé and Campana 2015; Perry and Scrivens 2016).
6 For example, foreign fighters (Mullins 2013; Amarasingam 2015; Anzalone 2015); radicalization (Parent and Ellis 2011; Ilardi 2013; Jakobsh 2014); terrorism financing (Passas 2010; Financial Transactions and Reports Analysis Centre of Canada (FINTRAC) 2012); and public response (Bourne 1978; Lee, Dallaire, and Lemyre 2009; McCauley et al. 2011; Bramadat 2014; Jamil 2014).
7 Ross (1992b) attributes this underrepresentation of Canadian (and other countries') incidents in cross-national datasets to the globally oriented publications used as sources for chronology construction and coding.

Accordingly, he concludes that such datasets are useful for cross-national statistical tests but not for individual country analyses (72).

8 The full data are presented in Kellett and colleagues' 1991 report. Kellett's (1995) book chapter presents a more detailed – and widely referenced – interpretation of the data.

9 The NSCC defines domestic terrorism as "terrorist events or activities aimed ultimately at altering the Canadian social or political system, and in which Canadians, their personal or business property, or the property of some level of government, are targeted" (Kellett et al. 1991, 29). International incidents are those "directed toward the prosecution of conflicts outside Canada" (ibid.) and can include foreign victims or targets located within Canada. Accordingly, the NSCC database excludes acts perpetrated by Canadians abroad or attacks against Canadian interests abroad.

10 The "excluded events" category encompasses incidents for which there is insufficient information; incidents that occurred outside of Canada; and those that lack a clearly identified political motivation or that were politically oriented (but not terroristic) protests.

11 Ross (1988) chronicles the development of this new dataset, including the processes of constructing a chronology, selecting variables, and coding.

12 While ATIC is limited to incidences of terrorism, Ross (1992a) expands upon this coding to create a new dataset examining right-wing violence in Canada: RWVIC.

13 ATIC-IV's coverage of international terrorism is limited to "acts of terrorism carried out by Canadians against foreign targets in Canada; foreigners against Canadian targets in Canada, and foreigners against foreign targets in Canada" (Ross 1994, 39; emphasis added), and the NSCC includes events occurring outside of Canada only in its "excluded event" appendix (Kellett et al. 1991, 437).

14 ERTA's methodology for data collection is most effectively summarized in Leman-Langlois and Ouellet (2009) and in Brodeur's Social Sciences and Humanities Research Council (SSHRC) funding application (available at http://erta-tcrg.org/textes/CRSH-bdd.pdf). Although dated, the most comprehensive English-language summary of this work is presented in Leman-Langlois and Brodeur (2005).

15 Incidents with a Canadian connection that occur abroad are important for any comprehensive evaluation of Canada's experience with terrorism. The human and financial costs of terrorism to Canada include Canadian victims and targets, whether at home or abroad, and irrespective of whether Canadian entities were deliberately targeted. Similarly, Canadian perpetrators of terrorist activity abroad impose reputational costs, and elicit international legal obligations, for the country (such as UN Security Council Resolution 2178 [S/RES/2178(2014)], which requires member-states to prevent travel through their territory for terrorist purposes.

16 Cross-national terrorism datasets consulted in the first stage of CIDB event coding include: Energy Infrastructure Attack Database (EIAD); Energy Incident Database (EIDB); Global Terrorism Database (GTD); International Terrorism: Attributes of Terrorist Events (ITERATE); Jane's Database; Mickolus et al. (1989) Terrorism Chronologies; Monterey WMD Terrorism Database; RAND Database of Worldwide Terrorism Incidents (RDWTI); and Worldwide Incidents Tracking System (WITS). Canada-specific reports/chronologies consulted include: Attributes of International Terrorism in Canada (ATIC) (Kellett et al. 1991); Ross, 1992a; Burak, 2014); Integrated Terrorism Assessment Centre, Notable Incidents (2014); Perry and Scrivens (2015); Chronology of Criminal Extremist Incidents in Canada from 1970 (2002); and Right-Wing Violence in Canada (RWVIC) (Ross, 1992b).
17 *Criminal Code*, R.S.C. (1985), c. C-46, s.83.01
18 The CIDB is available at no cost at www.extremism.ca.
19 This figure captures incidents that meet all three criteria for terrorism defined above, both within Canada and abroad.
20 Émigré terrorism occurred in Canada across the 1960s ($n = 12$), 1970s ($n = 22$), 1980s ($n = 25$), and 1990s ($n = 5$). In the earlier two decades, however, émigré incidents were dwarfed by the more significant campaigns of the SOF and FLQ. Accordingly, it is misleading to interpret the seeming surge of émigré terrorism in the 1980s as an increase in this type of activity; it is merely more visible following the demise of the SOF and FLQ.
21 Perpetrator motivation is unknown for 31 per cent of Canadian terrorist events. Only two incidents were identified as having multiple ideological motivations, including the 1985 Air India Bombing (classified as both separatist and religious).
22 The chapter's focus on events that satisfy the Criminal Code's three conditions for terrorism accounts for the lack of detail on supremacist and right-wing extremist events that have been documented in other work (Ross 1992b; Parent and Ellis 2011; Bérubé and Campana 2015; Perry and Scrivens 2015; 2016; Hofmann, this volume).
23 For instance, Ross's (1992b) study uses the right-wing label to encompass activities by "radical-right, fringe right, fundamentalist right-wing, lunatic right, racist, anti-Semitic, fascist, neo-fascist, Nazi and neo-Nazi" groups, although he acknowledges that racist violence is not always of a right-wing orientation, and vice versa (74).
24 Perpetrators adhering to other terrorist motivations carried out fatal incidents at a rate of one death per fatal attack: supremacist ($n = 3$); ethnic ($n = 2$); and rightist ($n = 1$). No leftist, environmentalist, anarchist, or anti-globalization attacks resulted in death.
25 For the 1960–89 period, both Charters (2008) and Crelinsten (2012) rely explicitly on NSCC data, which documents 366 incidents of domestic

terrorism; CIDB documents 749 incidents for the same period (689 if émigré incidents – the CIDB's equivalent indicator for NSCC's "international" or "imported" terrorism classification – are filtered out). Consistent with the NSCC, which identifies 62 such "international" incidents, the CIDB codes 64 émigré events, 60 of which occurred prior to 1989.

26 These include activities by the Wimmins Fire Brigade, which included two of DA's five members; as well as activities by Groupe action directe and Friction directe, which share a common titular inspiration: the French revolutionary group, Action directe.

27 CIDB codes 133 SOF terrorism incidents. An additional ten (occurring mostly in 1962) are coded as "doubt terrorism" incidents, for their probable lack of intentionality, and an additional single incident is coded as non-terrorist violent extremism.

28 The bombing's Canada-based perpetrators were also allegedly responsible for a concurrent explosion at Narita International Airport, in which two baggage handlers died.

29 This overview does not address the wave of foreign fighter incidents that has emerged since 2013. While some foreign fighter incidents are included in the CIDB as Canadian-affiliated incidents abroad, incidents such as peace bonds intended to prevent Canadians from going abroad, or suspicions of individuals potentially becoming involved in terrorist activity, are not included in the CIDB.

REFERENCES

Air India Flight 182: A Canadian Tragedy. Final report of the Commission of Inquiry into the Investigation of the Bombing of Air India Flight 182. Ottawa.

Amarasingam, Amarnath. 2015. "The Clear Banner: Canadian Foreign Fighters in Syria: An Overview." *Jihadology*, 4 March. https://jihadology.net/2015/03/04/the-clear-banner-canadian-foreign-fighters-in-syria-an-overview.

Anzalone, Christopher. 2015. "Canadian Foreign Fighters in Iraq and Syria." *CTC Sentinel* 8(4): 14–19.

Bérubé, Maxime, and Aurélie Campana. 2015. "Les violences motivées par la haine. Idéologies et modes d'action des extrémistes de droite au Canada." *Criminologie* 48(1): 215–34. https://doi.org/10.7202/1029355ar.

Bouchard, Martin, and Evan Thomas. 2015. "Radical and Connected." In *Social Networks, Terrorism, and Counter-Terrorism: Radical and Connected*, ed. Bouchard, 218–30. New York: Routledge.

Bourne, Robin. 1978. "Terrorist Incident Management and Jurisdictional Issues: A Canadian Perspective." *Terrorism and Political Violence* 1(3–4): 307–13. https://doi.org/10.1080/10576107808435416.

Bramadat, Paul. 2014. "The Public, the Political, and the Possible: Religion and Radicalization in Canada and Beyond." In *Religious Radicalization and Securitization in Canada and Beyond*, ed. Paul Bramadat and Lorne Dawson, 3–33. Toronto: University of Toronto Press.

Burak, Kyle. 2014. "Asymmetric Warfare in an Asymmetric World: A Theoretical Analysis of Canadian Antiterrorism Policy and Spending." MA thesis, University of Victoria.

CBC. 2016. Nuttall and Korody free after B.C. judge overturns terror convictions," 29 July, http://www.cbc.ca/news/canada/british-columbia/nuttall-and-korody-free-after-b-c-judge-overturns-terror-convictions-1.3700599.

Charters, David A. 1997. "The Amateur Revolutionaries: A Reassessment of the FLQ." *Terrorism and Political Violence* 9(1): 133–69. https://doi.org/10.1080/09546559708427393.

– 2008. "The (Un)Peaceable Kingdom? Terrorism and Canada before 9/11." *IRPP Policy Matters* 9(4): 1–43.

Crelinsten, Ronald. 1987. "The Internal Dynamics of the FLQ during the October Crisis of 1970." *Journal of Strategic Studies* 10(4): 59–89. https://doi.org/10.1080/01402398708437315.

– 2012. "Canada's Experience with Terrorism and Violent Extremism." In *Terror in the Peaceable Kingdom: Understanding and Addressing Violent Extremism*, ed. Daveed Gartenstein-Ross and Senator Linda Frum, 9–27. Washington, D.C.: Foundation for the Defense of Democracies.

Criminal Code, R.S.C. (1985), c. C-46, s.83.01.

Dawson, Lorne. 2014. "Trying to Make Sense of Home-Grown Terrorist Radicalization: The Case of the Toronto 18." In *Religious Radicalization and Securitization in Canada and Beyond*, ed. Paul Bramadat and Lorne Dawson, 64–91. Toronto: University of Toronto Press.

FINTRAC (Financial Transactions and Reports Analysis Centre of Canada). 2012. "Money Laundering and Terrorist Financing Trends in FINTRAC Cases Disclosed between 2007 and 2011." Ottawa.

Ilardi, Gaetano Joe. 2013. "Interviews with Canadian Radicals." *Studies in Conflict and Terrorism* 36(9): 713–38. https://doi.org/10.1080/10576 10X.2013.813248.

Jakobsh, Doris R. 2014. "The Sikhs in Canada: Culture, Religion, and Radicalization." In *Religious Radicalization and Securitization in Canada and Beyond*, ed. Paul Bramadat and Lorne Dawson, 164–200: Toronto: University of Toronto Press.

Joosse, Paul. 2017. "Leaderless Resistance and the Loneliness of Lone Wolves: Exploring the Rhetorical Dynamics of Lone Actor Violence." *Terrorism and Political Violence* 29(1): 52–78. https://doi.org/10.1080/09546553.2014.987866.

Kellett, Anthony. 1995. "Terrorism in Canada, 1960–1992." In *Violence in Canada: Sociopolitical Perspectives*, ed. Jeffrey Ian Ross, 284–312. Toronto: Oxford University Press.

Kellett, Anthony, Bruce Beanlands, and James Deacon, with Heather Jeffrey and Chantal Lapalme. 1991. *Terrorism in Canada, 1960–1989*. Ottawa: Solicitor General.

Lee, Jennier E.C., Christine Dallaire, and Louise Lemyre. 2009. '"Qualitative Analysis of Cognitive and Contextual Determinants of Canadians' Individual Response to Terrorism." *Health, Risk, and Society* 11(5): 431–50. https://doi.org/10.1080/13698570903184564.

Leman-Langlois, Stéphane, and Jean-Paul Brodeur. 2005. "Terrorism Old and New: Counterterrorism in Canada." *Police Practice and Research* 6(2): 121–40. https://doi.org/10.1080/15614260500121096.

Leman-Langlois, Stéphane, and Geneviève Ouellet. 2009. "L'évolution du Terrorisme au Canada, 1973–2006." In *Terrorisme et antiterrorisme au Canada*, ed. Stéphane Leman-Langlois and Jean-Paul Brodeur, 58–72. Montréal: Les Presses de l'Université de Montréal.

MacDonald, Jake. 2009. "EnCana's ticking timebomb." *Globe and Mail,* 24 September.

MacLeod, Ian. 2011. "Terror risk in Canada lowest among major Western economies: Study." *Ottawa Citizen,* 7 July 2016. Web.

McCauley, Clark, Christian Leuprecht, Todd Hataley, Conrad Winn, and Bidisha Biswas. 2011. "Tracking the War of Ideas: A Poll of Ottawa Muslims." *Terrorism and Political Violence* 23(5): 804–19. https://doi.org/10.1080/09546553.2011.596774.

McCoy, John, and Andy Knight. 2015. "Homegrown Terrorism in Canada: Local Patterns, Global Trends." *Studies in Conflict and Terrorism* 38(4): 253–74. https://doi.org/10.1080/1057610X.2014.994349.

Mickolus, Edward, Todd Sandler, and Jean M. Murdock. 1989. *International Terrorism in the 1980s: A Chronology of Events*, vol. 2: *1984–97*. Ames: Iowa State University Press.

Mullins, Sam. 2013. "'Global Jihad': The Canadian Experience." *Terrorism and Political Violence* 25(5): 734–76. https://doi.org/10.1080/09546553.2012.693552.

Ouellet, Geneviève. 2009. "Les causes célebres." In *Terrorisme et antiterrorisme au Canada*, ed. Stéphane Leman-Langlois and Jean-Paul Brodeur, 72–102. Montréal: Les Presses de l'Université de Montréal.

Parent, Richard B., and James O. Ellis III. 2011. "Countering Radicalization of Diaspora Communities in Canada." Working Paper no. 11–12, September. Vancouver: Metropolis British Columbia. http://mbc.metropolis.net/assets/uploads/files/wp/2011/WP11-12.pdf.

Passas, Nikos. 2010. "Understanding Terrorism Financing." In *Commission of Inquiry into the Investigation of the Bombing of Air India Flight 182*, vol. 2: *Terrorism Financing, Charities, and Aviation Security*, 15–117.

Perkel, Colin. 2015. "Jahanzeb Malik ordered out of Canada." *CBC News,* 7 July 2016. Web.

Perry, Barbara, and Ryan Scrivens. 2015. "Right Wing Extremism in Canada: An Environmental Scan." Ottawa: Public Safety Canada.
– 2016. "Uneasy Alliances: A Look at the Right-Wing Extremist Movement in Canada." *Studies in Conflict and Terrorism* 39(9): 819–41. https://doi.org/10.1080/1057610X.2016.1139375.
R. v. Ahmad. 5874. Ontario Superior Court of Justice (ONSC). 2010. CanLii.
R. v. Ahmed. 6153. Ontario Superior Court of Justice (ONSC). 2014. CanLii.
R. v. Esseghaier and Jaser. 5855. Ontario Superior Court of Justice (ONSC). 2015. CanLii.
R. v. Khawaja. 63685. Ontario Superior Court of Justice (ONSC). 2006. CanLii.
R. v. Namouh. 943. Court of Quebec (QCCQ). 2010. CanLii.
R. v. Nuttall. 2355. Supreme Court of British Columbia (BCSC). 2014. CanLii.
Razavy, Maryam. 2006. "Sikh Militant Movements in Canada." *Terrorism and Political Violence* 18(1): 79–93. https://doi.org/10.1080/09546550500174913.
Ross, Jeffrey Ian. 1988. "Attributes of Domestic Political Terrorism in Canada, 1960–1985." *Terrorism* 11(3): 213–33. https://doi.org/10.1080/10576108808435712.
– 1992a. *Attributes of Terrorism in Canada (ATIC)*, vol. 4: *Chronology of Domestic and International Terrorist Events in Canada, 1960–1990*. Montreal: International Centre for Comparative Criminology.
– 1992b. "Contemporary Radical Right-Wing Violence in Canada: A Quantitative Analysis." *Terrorism and Political Violence* 4(3): 72–101. https://doi.org/10.1080/09546559208427161.
– 1994. "Low Intensity Conflict in the Peaceable Kingdom: The Attributes of International Terrorism in Canada, 1968–1990." *Conflict Quarterly* (Summer): 36–62.
– 1995. "The Rise and Fall of Quebecois Separatist Terrorism: A Qualitative Application of Factors from Two Models." *Studies in Conflict and Terrorism* 18(4): 285–97. https://doi.org/10.1080/10576109508435986.
Whitaker, Reg, Gregory S. Kealey, and Andrew Parnaby. 2012. *Secret Service: Political Policing in Canada from the Fenians to Fortress America*. Toronto: University of Toronto Press.
Wilner, Alex. 2009. *Canada's Role in Combating al Qaeda: International, Regional, and Homegrown Dimensions*. Toronto: Canadian International Council.
Woodcock, George, and Ivan Avakumovik. *The Doukhobors*. Toronto: Oxford University Press, 1968.
Yerbury, Colin J. 1984. "The 'Sons of Freedom' Doukhobors and the Canadian State." *Canadian Ethnic Studies* 16(2): 47–70.

3 Canadian Foreign Fighters in Syria and Iraq, 2012–16

LORNE DAWSON AND AMARNATH AMARASINGAM

The conflict in Syria and Iraq has attracted jihadist "foreign fighters" (Malet 2013) from around the globe in unprecedented numbers. Most of these 25,000 to 30,000 fighters have come from countries in the Middle East, but probably 4,000 to 5,000 have come from Europe, the United Kingdom, the United States, Canada, and Australia (Soufan Group 2015; Neumann 2015a). Most of them, largely young men but also some young women, are joining the Islamic State (aka the Islamic State of Iraq and Sham, or Iraq and Syria, or Iraq and Levant, or ISIS or ISIL), perhaps the most radical and dangerous of all jihadi groups.[1] The foreign fighter problem is not as serious in Canada as elsewhere; even so, in a statement before the Public Safety Committee of the Canadian House of Commons on 23 February 2016, Michel Coulombe, director of the Canadian Security Intelligence Service (CSIS), said that "the total number of people overseas involved in threat-related activities – and I'm not just talking about Iraq and Syria – is probably around 180." "In Iraq and Syria," he said, "we are probably talking close to 100" (Fife 2016).

The Canadian government worries about what these citizens are doing, what the implications are for international relations, and what might happen when any return. Precedent suggests that 20 to 30 per cent of these foreign fighters may return (Hegghammer 2011); however, British officials estimate that as many as 425 of their 850 foreign fighters have returned (Barrett 2017). Although the director of CSIS noted that around sixty individuals had returned to Canada, there are no accurate figures for the number of returnees to Canada from Syria and Iraq (Public Safety Canada 2017). Relying on news accounts and on our network of contacts in Muslim communities, as of February 2018 we could identify only seventeen individuals who had returned to Canada from the conflict in Syria and Iraq, and eight of these people had merely tried to travel there and had been turned back by authorities in Turkey or

Egypt. But whether the returnees are disillusioned and disengaged, or still operational and dangerous, they pose security challenges. It now appears, for example, that as many as seven of the perpetrators of the tragic attacks in Paris that killed 130 people on 13 November 2015 were either returnees or agents sent by ISIS (Callimachi 2016a). This also appears to have been the case with several of the perpetrators of the bombings in Brussels on 22 March 2016. Indeed, the *New York Times* reported that these attacks were part of a larger campaign of attacks in Europe (some successful, some not) led by ISIS operatives trained in Syria (Callimachi 2016b).

In this chapter we set the context of the foreign fighter issue for Canadians and reflect on the policy implications of this new kind of terrorist threat. Setting the context entails describing the ways Canadians are involved in the conflict in Syria and Iraq and discussing the new and rather popular theory that Western foreign fighters are part of a new "youth subculture of 'no future'" (Roy 2015; Coolsaet 2016). These young people are motivated to become jihadists primarily by socio-economic push factors, and as Olivier Roy (2015) states aptly, we may be witnessing more the "Islamization of radicalization" than the "radicalization of Islam." On the basis of twenty-two interviews with foreign fighters, we propose an alternative view, one that assigns more significance to existential and ideological pull factors. It is not lack of social and economic opportunity that drives Western foreign fighters, but the lure of participating in a deeply fulfilling new life opportunity, sanctioned by the call to defend all Muslims from their "Zionist and Crusader" oppressors.

We frame the implications of the jihadi foreign fighter phenomenon in terms of who cares about it and why. This phenomenon has repercussions for the communities the fighters come from, the Canadian government, and the countries to which the fighters travel. In the end, we argue, this new type of terrorist activity provides a strong impetus for the further expansion of Canada's capacity to detect, detain, and intervene with potential terrorists, as well as for stronger efforts to develop specialized rehabilitative programs for "wannabe," returned, and convicted jihadi foreign fighters.[2]

The Canadian Foreign Fighter Phenomenon

While the number of Canadians travelling to Syria is relatively low, some of those fighters have figured prominently in the Islamic State's English-language videos. The worldwide publicity generated by these videos increased the attention paid by Canadians to the new threat.

Andre Poulin, from Timmins, Ontario, was the first Canadian to appear in Islamic State propaganda (CBC 2014a). In that video, Poulin – known as Abu Muslim – explains how he was an average Canadian, with a good life, yet felt compelled to come to the defence of his fellow Muslims in Syria. The video ends with footage of his martyrdom during battle. Two more videos soon followed. In one, Farah Shirdon, from Calgary – known as Abu Usamah al-Somalee – burns his Canadian passport and threatens Western powers (CBC 2014b). Shirdon achieved further notoriety when he appeared in an interview with Vice News (Vice News 2014). Another video features John Maguire from Ottawa. Like Poulin, he implores his fellow Muslims in the West to make *hijrah* (emigrate) to the Islamic State (Bell 2014a). He goes on to praise the ISIS-inspired lone-actor attacks in October 2014 in Saint-Jean-sur-Richelieu and Ottawa. These attacks were in retaliation, he says, for Canada joining the bombing campaign against ISIS:

> Your people will be indiscriminately targeted as you indiscriminately target our people. I warn you of punishment in this worldly life at the hands of mujahedeen, and I also like to warn you of a greater punishment and that is the eternal punishment of hell-fire promised to those who died not having submitted as Muslims to the one true God of all that exists ... So, the mujahideen continue to call you to one of two options: hijrah or jihad. You either pack your bags or you prepare your explosive devices. You either purchase your airline ticket or sharpen your knife.

In the face of this threat it is imperative that we develop a better grasp of how these young Canadians were radicalized. However, research on this process is hampered by a lack of primary data derived from talking to terrorists, particularly those from Canada (e.g., Bartlett and Miller 2012; Ilardi 2013). In his authoritative survey of the literature, Andrew Silke laments that systematic interviews have been used in "only 1 per cent of research reports" (Silke 2008, 101). This chapter offers some findings from our interactions with twenty-two foreign fighters, five of whom were Canadians.

Studying Western Foreign Fighters

In early 2013 it became apparent that many foreign fighters were using Twitter and other social media platforms to talk about their experiences (Prucha and Fischer 2013; Carter, Maher, and Neumann 2014; Klausen 2015). This kind of mass, real-time communication by individuals engaged in terrorism had never happened before. Terrorist organizations were early adopters of online propaganda, but the independent spread of the jihadist message through social media was not foreseen. Many of the young people travelling to Syria and Iraq simply kept their accounts active. ISIS became aware of this and decided to capitalize on it. They allowed much of the communication to continue, though often with some guidelines in place (e.g., see SecDev 2015).[3] Reporters and researchers adapted to the new reality so quickly that we tend to forget how novel this situation was, as was the originality of exploiting these channels of communication to secure information about how and why people become foreign fighters.

Between May 2014 and July 2017, we conducted interviews with thirty-six fighters (men and women) in Syria and Iraq, and fifty-three relatives and friends of foreign fighters, and a further ten with online supporters of jihadism.[4] The "interviews" with the foreign fighters took the form of extended social media dialogues stretching over days, weeks, or months. This was the case as well with many of the "interviews" with online supporters. The interviews with relatives and friends were conducted face-to-face and audio-recorded. While we originally intended to interview only Canadians, in the end we interviewed whoever was willing. Thus, five of the interviews were with Canadian fighters, and the rest were with fighters from the United Kingdom, the United States, Europe, Australia, India, and Africa. Thirty-seven of the relatives and friends interviewed were Canadian, and most of the rest were American, British, or European. Most of the fighters interviewed were affiliated with either ISIS or Jabhat al-Nusra (the name of the al Qaeda group in Syria at the time), and many had been with both groups at different times. A few were from other, smaller, largely jihadist rebel groups.

Our semi-structured, open-ended, and informant-oriented interviews with the fighters focused on the following: (1) their personal and family background; (2) their social networks and sense of identity; and (3) the process of becoming foreign fighters. We were after their "definition of the situation," and to minimize ethical and legal risks we did not gather operational data (e.g., about travel arrangements, contacts, collaborators, specific violent actions, or plots). The research was labour-intensive, and exceptional measures were taken to ensure the confidentiality of the information (see Dawson and Amarasingam 2016).

We also sought to acquire more general information about Canadians engaged in jihadism. In February 2016 the official number of Canadians fighting in Syria and Iraq was "close to 100." We confirmed the identity of sixty-two (see Table 3.1) but have heard rumours of many more. Of course, like the government, we are using the term "fighter" rather broadly, to refer to those who left for Syria and Iraq, whether or not they actually engaged in combat. To the best of our knowledge, though, as

Table 3.1. Canadian foreign fighters we have identified (2011–16)

Gender	Provinces	Ethnic Background
Male 52	Ontario 22	Unknown 11
Female 10	Alberta 17	Somali 11
	Quebec 16	Algerian 8
	Unknown 4	Lebanese 5
	British Columbia 3	Bangladeshi 4
		Pakistani 4
		Syrian 4
		White 4
		Afghan 3
		Jamaican 2
		Moroccan 2
		Bosnian 1
		Indian 1
		Libyan 1
		Sudanese 1

of March 2016 at least nineteen Canadian fighters had died in Syria and Iraq: eight from Ontario, eight from Alberta, and three from Quebec. All of these were men, and five of them were converts to Islam. We have good reason to believe that most of the Canadians in Syria and Iraq are fighting with ISIS. This holds true for our sample of fighters as well, and we can identify twelve or more Canadians fighting with Jabhat al-Nusra, Ahrar as-Sham, or other jihadi and rebel groups. Twenty or more Canadians appear to have fought with Kurdish or Christian militias; these are round figures based on what people have reported to us. As of this writing, ten to fifteen women have left Canada to live under the so-called caliphate in Syria and Iraq. We know that three have given birth after marrying ISIS fighters, most whom were foreign-born. At least two other Canadian women were pregnant at the time this chapter was being written.

The Canadian Clusters

Canadians leaving to fight in Syria and Iraq add support to two of the more robust findings from studies of homegrown terrorism: pre-existing social networks, of kinship and friendship, play a central role in the radicalization of extremists; and so do the social-psychological dynamics of small groups (Sageman 2004; 2008; McCauley and Moskalenko 2011; Hafez and Mullins 2015). Over the course of this study it became increasingly apparent that most Canadian foreign fighters had left to join the fight in "clusters," so presumably they radicalized together as well.

One of the first clusters formed in Calgary, Alberta. This one consisted of Damian Clairmont, Salman Ashrafi, and Gregory and Collin Gordon, along with a few other individuals we have tentatively identified but still need to fully confirm (Stark 2014; Bell 2014b). They left for Syria sometime in November or December 2012. They were friends, yet their biographical details are quite varied. Ashrafi was born Muslim, educated at the University of Lethbridge, held a prestigious job with Talisman Energy, and was married with a child. In November 2013, he died in a suicide attack in Iraq that killed forty others (Bell 2014c). Clairmont, by contrast, was a white convert, suffered from bipolar disorder, was a high school dropout, and was homeless for a time in Calgary. Clairmont and Ashrafi were close friends and part of an Islamic study circle with the Gordon brothers and several others. Interviews with their friends in Calgary indicate that Clairmont was the dominant personality and influenced many of the other young men in this cluster. He left Calgary in late 2012 and fought with the al Qaeda–affiliated Jabhat al-Nusra and later ISIS. He was captured and killed by the Free Syrian Army in January 2014 (Bell 2014d). Not much is known about the Gordon brothers, except that they converted to Islam in their early twenties and left for Syria soon after, in August 2014. Gregory Gordon is reported to have been "quiet and courteous" and to have suffered from sickle-cell anemia, while Collin was a very outgoing volleyball player at the Alberta Institute of Technology and then Thompson Rivers University in Kamloops, British Columbia, where he studied business. By December both brothers had died fighting for ISIS near Dabiq, in Syria (Stark 2014; Roberts 2014; Molnar 2015). When their deaths were reported, no family members and friends would speak with us, and we chose not to press the issue since there had been several other recent deaths in the family as well.

Another fighter with some connection to the Calgary study circle was Ahmed Waseem, from Windsor, Ontario. Waseem's story is particularly interesting because he returned to Canada after an injury sometime in 2013 (Kwong 2014; Logan 2014). After experiencing increased surveillance, he secured a fraudulent passport and left again for Syria. According to his Twitter feed, he was then regularly involved in fierce battles in Syria. Around January 2015 he joined ISIS; in March 2015, he was killed in battle at Tal Hamis.

Farah Shirdon, discussed above, also left from Calgary for Syria and ISIS. He had some contact with the others who departed from there and is often associated with them in media reports, but he was not part of this cluster. To the best of our knowledge, he is still active as a fighter.

While it was the Calgary cluster that initially made the news in Canada, more foreign fighters came from Ontario. Of the sixty-plus Canadian foreign fighters in Syria and Iraq we have tried to investigate, close to half are from Ontario. Perhaps the most intriguing case is the story of Andre Poulin (aka Abu Muslim) from Timmins, discussed above. Born in 1989, Poulin converted to Islam from Roman Catholicism in 2009 and travelled to Syria in November or December 2012. Initially he did not seem to be part of a "cluster" – indeed, the media attention he received stressed how outlandish and threatening it was that someone from Timmins, an isolated northern town with few Muslims and no mosque, could become the star of an ISIS propaganda video. But our research, and the investigations of reporters, showed the truth to be otherwise.

Around 2011, Poulin told family and friends that he was moving to Toronto to be closer to other Muslims. In Toronto, he met with Muhammad Ali from Mississauga (Bell 2014e). They had become friends in an online forum long before this first meeting, and in Toronto they would see each other regularly. Ali was born in 1990 and went to Ryerson University to study aerospace engineering. He did not do well, and failed out after a year. At that point he started asking questions about life and the afterlife, and found many of the answers in Islam, the religion of his upbringing. He joined online forums and began interacting with fellow Muslims, one of whom was Poulin. Ali would leave for Syria in April 2014, almost a year after Poulin's death. Of course, Poulin made other friends while he was in Toronto, some of whom he seems to have influenced significantly. At least four young men in Toronto (three Bangladeshi Canadians and one Indian Canadian) became his friends and left for Syria around the same time he did. At this time very little is known about these men, except that some or all of them may have returned to Toronto in late 2013, only to leave again in July 2014. Interestingly, on 13 July 2014, Muhammad Ali posted a screenshot of a text-message conversation he was having on his phone. That message read: "This is the friends of Abu Muslim [i.e., Poulin] from Canada. We are in Turkey now and we want to know which way to get into Syria and join Islamic State." From this message we can deduce that while Ali and Poulin were friends in Toronto, Ali likely did not know Poulin's other Toronto friends until later.

Early in 2015, news broke about another cluster of young men from Ottawa. In January, charges of participation in a terrorist activity were brought against Suliman Mohamed and the twin brothers Ashton and Carlos Larmond for seeking to fly to Turkey and then travel on to join ISIS in Syria. In February, more charges were laid against three others: Awso Peshdary, John Maguire, and Khadar Khalib. All of these men knew one another, and Peshdary is thought to have played a key role in radicalizing them. Maguire (discussed above) and Khalib made it to Syria, where Maguire died. It is thought that they had been reaching out from Syria to other members of their network of friends to encourage them to come to Syria as well (Baksh and Arsenault 2015; Helmer and Dimmock 2016).

Almost simultaneously, another group of young people – at least two women and four men – left Montreal together for Turkey and then Syria (January 2015). Four had been students together at the Collège de Maisonneuve in Montreal, and one was an older man of twenty-nine. As one news report states: "Their online profiles, families, friends and former classmates paint a picture of people who are a far cry from basement-dwelling conspiracists divorced from reality and social engagement" (Perreaux and Stevenson 2015). In May 2015, ten more young people were detained at the Montreal airport on their way to join the militants in Syria. Because most of them were underage, they were returned to their parents, and we do not know much about them. But it is thought they had ties with the same college and with the six who had left earlier (CBC News 2015a; 2015b).

Community sources have told us about other possible clusters, but it is often hard to confirm the details of what we have been hearing from confidential sources. We were told some time ago about four Somali Canadians from Edmonton who had died fighting in Syria – Omar Abdirahman, brothers Hamza and Hersi Kariye, and their cousin Mahad Hersi. Eventually we interviewed some family members and friends of three of these men, and ISIS application documents leaked to the media in March 2016 confirm that all four entered ISIS territory in Syria on 12 November 2013 (Arsenault and Baksh 2016; Shepard and Bailey 2016). We heard that as many as ten others may have departed Edmonton in 2013 and 2014.

Since then a number of other individuals, singly or in pairs, either have been arrested for attempting to travel to Syria to join terrorist groups, or have had their activities restricted by the government via the application of peace bonds. Four of the most recent and well-publicized examples are Aaron Driver from Winnipeg (Barghout 2015), Kevin Omar Mohamed from Waterloo (Bell 2016a), Kadir Abdul and Samuel Augustine Aviles from Toronto (Bell 2016b), and Seyed Amir Hossein Raisolsadat from Prince Edward Island (CBC 2015c). Overall, we estimate that eighteen individuals were either arrested or placed on peace bonds in Canada in 2015.

The Comparative Context: Socio-Economic Versus Existential-Ideological Factors

The radicalization process is too complex to discuss in this context (Dalgaard-Nielsen 2010; Hafez and Mullins 2015). We can, however, frame the foreign fighter issue in terms of some key interpretive options by contrasting some findings from twenty-two of the foreign fighter interviews conducted by the second author of this chapter with the conclusions reached by three recent studies of European foreign fighters.[5]

The scholarly literature on the Syrian conflict, ISIS, and the foreign fighter phenomenon is growing rapidly (see e.g., Batrawi 2013; Gudmundson 2013; Pantucci 2013; Zammit 2013; Zelin 2013; Hegghammer 2013; Reinares and Garcia-Calvo 2014; Saarinen 2014; McCants 2015; Stern and Berger 2015). Two brief publications focus on Canadian foreign fighters (Anzalone 2015; Amarasingam 2015). With a few exceptions, however, these studies are largely descriptive and rely on publicly available information. Two of the three studies we wish to highlight stand out because they introduce new primary data. Weggemans, Bakker, and Grol (2014) interviewed eighteen people who knew five Dutch individuals who became foreign fighters. Bakker and Grol (2015) did interviews with people who knew six Dutch men who wanted to be foreign fighters. They also interviewed four of the six men. The third study, by Rik Coolsaet (2016), does not use new primary data, but it provides the most current and comprehensive assessment of Belgian foreign fighters and their motivations. The language of this study creates the impression that Coolsaet's insights are based on some kind of direct knowledge of the thoughts and motivations of the foreign fighters. The references supplied, however, are from a variety of secondary sources. Taken together, the three studies provide the most immediate and empirically rich context for comparing the insights we have gleaned from our new primary data.

Two Studies of Dutch Foreign Fighters

Regrettably, the results of the two Dutch studies are not presented in a uniform manner and there is some ambiguity, as we discuss below. A critical synthesis of the conclusions, however, creates a somewhat common impression about the motivations for joining the jihad: most foreign fighters and wannabe fighters are young people with limited prospects in life, who are relatively unhappy with what is happening in their lives, are looking for some greater meaning and sense of belonging, and are heavily influenced by the small groups they come into contact with as they seek some relief from their condition. More specifically, the fighters and wannabe fighters were in their twenties, predominantly from immigrant Muslim families, and had lower- or lower-middle-class backgrounds and modest levels of education. Prior to leaving for Syria, or planning to do so, most of the individuals became increasingly isolated from their social networks, developed bonds with new networks that reinforced their radical views, and fell under the influence of "charismatic persons" or "inspiring figures" (Weggemans, Bakker, and Grol 2014, 108; Bakker and Grol 2015, 13). The foreign fighters had "feelings of apathy and lack of meaningfulness in their lives in the period before they left for Syria" (Weggemans, Bakker, and Grol 2014, 108); most of the non-leavers had "limited chances on the labour market and of a social career" (Bakker and Grol 2015, 13). The study of leavers further notes that some had experienced personal losses and significant disappointments prior to radicalizing, "such as loss of a loved one or experiencing difficulties at school or work and trouble with authorities" (Weggemans, Bakker, and Grol 2014, 108). No similar finding is reported in the case of the non-leavers. In the end, both reports surmise that they sought to participate in the Syrian conflict because it "seemed to provide them with a sense of purpose and fulfil their need to belong" (Weggemans, Bakker, and Grol 2014, 108), though the discussion of this point is muted and indirect.

The descriptive result of the two studies is helpful, but very limited. In terms of the balance of push and pull factors accounting for recruitment to social movements, the emphasis falls on the push factors.

A Study of Belgian Foreign Fighters

In the study of Belgian foreign fighters, this emphasis is even more explicit. Coolsaet chastises radicalization studies for being too preoccupied with tracing how individuals became terrorists at the expense of grasping the "wider circumstances and context" in which terrorism arises (Coolsaet 2016, 12–13). Insufficient attention, he argues, has been given to the role of "a conducive or instigating environment" (Coolsaet 2016, 13). He also stresses: "Radicalisation is first and foremost a socialization process in which group dynamics (kinship and friendship) are more important than ideology ... for most of the individuals involved, it is not the narrative (i.e., the ideology) that eventually lures them into terrorism" (Coolsaet 2016, 12). As Coolsaet further notes, the radicalization of anyone is a messy and complex process and merely holding radical beliefs is a poor indicator of the potential to be violent (see Bartlett and Miller 2012; Khalil 2014; McCauley and Moskalenko 2014). We agree, but we also think Coolsaet establishes too strong a dichotomy between social processes and ideology. Social contexts and small-group dynamics are crucial to the process. Nothing would happen, however, without the framing work done by ideology, and consequently the religiosity of these foreign fighters is paramount in interpreting their actions. The religious ideology plays a constitutive role in their new identity and their sense of purpose in life. Terrorism is not the result of bad ideas; rather, deep identification with ideas is instrumental to the radicalization of jihadists.

Coolsaet subscribes to Olivier Roy's (2015) notion that contemporary jihadism is rooted in a "'no future' youth subculture" and not religion per se. Roy, an influential French sociologist and scholar of contemporary Islam, argues we are not witnessing "the radicalization of Islam" so much as "the Islamization of radicalism." Today's "terrorists are not the expression of a radicalization of the Muslim population, but rather reflect a generational revolt that affects a very precise category of youth" (Roy 2015, cited in Coolsaet 2016, 26). Describing the most recent wave of Belgian foreign fighters, Coolsaet comments (Coolsaet 2016, 24):

> They often mention earlier personal difficulties [of various kinds], that left them feeling stifled and discontented. Frequently, they express feelings of exclusion and absence of belonging, as if they didn't have a stake in society. One gets the impression of solitary, isolated adolescents, frequently at odds with family ... and friends, in search of belonging. The succession of such estrangements result at a certain age in anger.

In the end, he concludes: "Going to Syria is an escape from a life seemingly without prospects" (Coolsaet 2016, 27).

The argument is similar to the one made by the Dutch studies.[6] It is also broadly in line with discussions of marginalized immigrant youth in much of the literature on radicalization in Europe (e.g., Spalek, 2007; Cesari 2008; 2011; Githens-Mazer 2010). The problem is that Coolsaet provides little in the way of direct or primary evidence for his view, beyond references to a few brief comments attributed to individuals in the media and some academic articles. Even more fundamentally, the specificity problem looms large. The description applies to many more youth in Europe than the tiny handful who even think about becoming foreign fighters, let alone acting on the idea. Something else, then, must be at play.

Our Sample of Foreign Fighters

The basic characteristics of our sample of twenty-two foreign fighters are not too dissimilar to those in the other studies. Individuals varied, however, in the information they were willing to provide. They all claimed, with some credibility, to have been engaged in combat. They were all male, and with one exception they were all in their twenties (22 to 28). Most were single, but two were married and at least one had children. Five of the twenty-two were Canadians; four were American; six were from the UK; four were European; one was Australian; and one was from India. Several had a mixed ethnic background and had lived for a time in the home country of one of their parents, so they did not identify exclusively, it seems, with any one country. They were mainly from Muslim families, but four were converts and one was the child of a convert in a mixed marriage.

More thematically, the converts and the Muslim youth in this sample said they either experienced conversion or became much more religious in their teen years (14–18). Only one person said he became much more religious at a somewhat later age, after graduating from university. In one way or another, almost all of them dwelled on the significance of this youthful turn to religion in explaining why they became foreign fighters. In a few instances, the full turn to religion seems to have been preceded by a partial process of radicalization stemming from anger over the Israeli treatment of Palestinians, or the atrocities committed by the Syrian regime of Bashar al-Assad against Sunni Muslims. In our small sample no other conflicts were specifically named. Several were the only child in their family, and no one mentioned a sibling radicalizing. Several mentioned that their brothers and sisters were actively opposed to their decision to make *hijrah*, and most of their parents were pained by the decision as well. The families were largely unsympathetic to jihadism. Nevertheless, most of the young men still respected and cared about their parents, while also disparaging some of them as "coconuts" (i.e., brown on the outside and white on the inside). Reports of the religiousness of the parents varied widely, but about half of the group received some formal religious education as children (i.e., Quranic studies and Islamic schooling). For a few the religious education in childhood was intensive and prolonged, and this was true for fighters whether they grew up in Africa, the Middle East, or the West.

About half of our sample reported at least going to university, and one third mentioned graduating with a degree. Many of these individuals only fully radicalized after graduating. Several indicated that they had enjoyed their studies, but most said they had been discontented while in school because they felt the need for something more in their lives. No one in our sample reported having come from a familial situation of poverty or marginality. On the contrary, most indicated they had a fairly happy and privileged – or at least comfortable – childhood. Several participants made a point of stating that they had abandoned lives of relative "luxury" or "comfort" to become *mujahidin*. No one specifically mentioned any personal crises that prompted their radicalization or departure for Syria. One individual radicalized after failing out of his first year at university, but added that he had lost interest and never really tried to succeed at school.

Overall, our findings conform with many of the conclusions reached in the research literature on the process of radicalization to violence. The process started in early adolescence, it involved a small group of friends, and the internet and social media played a fairly prominent role. The decision to "go forth" to jihad was kept secret from most people, especially parents. Our sample commonly received assistance in preparing and actually travelling to Syria from people in Syria or "brothers" in their communities. This information reinforces our understanding of the key role played by "social networks" and, even more, "facilitators" or "brokers" in the mobilization of foreign fighters (Sageman 2004; Hegghammer 2011; Holman 2016). Several were inspired by the fact that others from their community had left already and sometimes become martyrs. Surprisingly, all of our small sample were the first individuals in their immediate group to make *hijrah*. In some cases others followed, but in several cases they ended up being the only one to make the journey.

All calmly reiterated their desire to achieve martyrdom and celebrated the martyrdom of others. When asked why they had undertaken jihad, many gave answers that prioritized their fear of being blocked from entering *Jannah* (paradise) because they led comfortable lives when their fellow Muslims were suffering. Several participants declared forcefully that when young they worried that they would burn in hell if they did not change their ways, and this worry prompted their increased religiosity and interest in radical ideas. Their justifications for becoming foreign fighters were largely moral and religious rather than explicitly political, although the blend of religious and political views they espoused suggested that in their own minds, there was little real separation between the two. Over and over again, they expressed the need to reject the moral corruption of life in the West, and this emerged as the principal justification for leaving to live in the ISIS caliphate. In general, our interactions with them were laced with comments about the need to strictly observe the differences between true Muslims and others and to achieve the unity of belief and action they associated with true practice.

There was certainly a rhetorical aspect to the statements they made to us. But we have no reason to question the basic sincerity of their claims, and the sheer repetition of themes across the sample, and in diverse contexts, causes us to ascribe some significance to what they were asserting. In doing so we are paying attention to the overall nuance of the dialogues as much as to their specific statements.

Three interrelated features stand out in the accounts we have analysed so far: (1) the prominence of religious discourse and considerations, and solidarity with their fellow Muslims; (2) the focus on moral rather than economic challenges when they condemned their past lives and explained their turn to extremism; and (3) the personal nature of their journeys, which they tended to understand more as a process of self-discovery rather than as explicitly political. None of those interviewed indicated, let alone explicitly stated, that their decision had been influenced by their "limited chances on the labour market and of a social career" (Bakker and Grol 2015, 13). "Lack of prospects," or some equivalent notion, never emerged as a relevant factor.

Our sample is small and non-random, so it difficult to generalize. That said, we interviewed more active fighters than anyone else has to date. Perhaps the Dutch and Belgian cases reflect the real deprivation of Muslims in those countries, who are experiencing less socio-economic success and integration than are Muslims in Canada, the United States, and Australia. But our sample includes a diversity of individuals from Europe, North America, Australia, Africa, and elsewhere, and the data point to the greater importance of existential and ideological pull factors – to the promise of something more in life than material prosperity and ordinary domesticity – in the decision to become a foreign fighter. In terms of what they told us and the tone of the conversations, the interviewees emphasized their positive reasons for becoming *mujahid* rather than the material and social drawbacks of their prior lives.

So in seeking to discern why a tiny handful of disgruntled youth actually become jihadists, we are inclined to follow the lead of our data and balance an interest in the socio-economic push factors for radicalization with a fuller inquiry into the role of pull factors, such as an abiding need for greater meaning and purpose in life, and the appeal of an ideology that appears to meet that need (Crenshaw 1988; Orsini 2009; Ginges, Atran, Sachdeva and Medin 2011; Cottee and Hayward 2011; McBride 2011; Maynard 2014). This is a modest point, but an important one, given the marked bias in much of the research literature against taking religion seriously as a motivator for terrorism (see Dawson 2017).

Policy Implications: Foreign Conflicts, Local Consequences

Understandably, discussions about foreign fighters tend to dwell on the threat posed by returnees. To fully grasp the policy implications of the foreign fighter problem, however, we need to ask who cares about the problem and why. Who is impacted and in what ways, and hence what should be our response? Three groups have reason to be concerned: the communities from which the radicalized Canadians are coming, the Canadian government, and the countries where Canadians are fighting.

The communities care because the families of the fighters are suffering from the loss of a child, and because other families wonder, quite justifiably, whether their children also are susceptible. The loss in question may be because the son or daughter is killed, or because he or she cannot return home for fear of being prosecuted and imprisoned. This aspect of terrorism's impact is rarely given much consideration. But the parents and siblings of foreign fighters are not only emotionally stricken by the loss; in many cases they are also shunned or stigmatized by their ethnic communities, the members of their mosques, and their neighbourhoods (see Thompson and Bucerius in this volume). Some of the parents we interviewed expresssed concern that other children in the household might find it difficult to attend school or obtain employment once the name of their foreign-fighter sibling appeared in the media. More generally, of course, the media attention the issue draws exacerbates the distrust and discrimination experienced by their ethnic and religious community as a whole. These implications need to be understood better and factored into how law enforcement, security services, social agencies, and even the media respond to these situations if the government wishes to recruit these communities as active partners in countering extremism (Koehler 2015).

The federal government should care because the foreign fighters are Canadian citizens and as such the government remains legally responsible for their welfare. But even more, Canada can be held responsible, to some degree, for their actions. Canada is a signatory to many international conventions condemning terrorism, and the government has an obligation to prevent its citizens from going abroad and harming others. If the Canadian government expects other states to take seriously their obligations to help protect us from terrorism, then Canada must reciprocate, or even display leadership, in preventing its citizens from becoming terrorists.

Most importantly, however, the government must seek to protect its own citizens from harm by addressing more constructively the threats posed by returnees from foreign conflicts. Based on the study of jihadists fighting in past conflicts in Afghanistan, Bosnia, Chechnya, Iraq, and elsewhere, it is estimated 20 to 30 per cent of the foreign fighters will return and that one in nine of these returnees may be dangerous (Hegghammer 2011, 2013). Yet we still lack a clear picture of the actual threat posed by returnees, since the evidence in hand is incomplete and often anecdotal (de Roy van Zuijdewijn and Bakker 2014). J.M. Berger (2011), for example, followed the fate of thirty of the larger set of Americans who went to Afghanistan or Bosnia to fight. He found that at least four who returned were convicted later of serious terrorism offences. The contingent of foreign fighters in Syria and Iraq is much larger, and they have participated in a more prolonged and destructive war. Consequently, the threat they pose is more ominous. Many have argued that these fighters are more likely to return as battle-hardened veterans, with a more advanced understanding of urban tactics, weapons, and explosives than earlier waves of foreign fighters. They will return, moreover, with established ties to larger networks of jihadists around the world, facilitating their access to training and weapons (Watts 2009, 4; Byman 2015, 582; Barrett 2017). The specific threat they pose is heightened by the blowback to the overt military actions taken against ISIS and by that group's explicit calls for Muslims to strike out against the Western countries involved.

Overall, the probability of an attack in Canada remains low, but less so than before the mass migration of fighters to Syria and Iraq. The political fallout from any kind of returnee attack could be significant. Extraordinary efforts should be taken, then, to detect and track the movements of those suspected of going (or wanting to go) and those who have returned. This is expensive, and it is difficult to determine what resources are needed, when, and where. But the attacks in Paris (2015) and Brussels (2016) have shown what can happen when security officials are not vigilant enough. In addition, veterans of foreign conflicts often are the most effective recruiters of new volunteers, in terms of both ideology and instrumentality (Sageman 2004, Watts 2008, Berger 2011, Byman 2015, Nesser 2015, Holman 2016). As our interviews indicate, the example set by those who left to fight can be potent for those contemplating doing the same.

Yet historical precedent (Hegghammer 2011; de Roy van Zuijdewijn 2014) suggests that not all returnees will be dangerous, and care must be taken to develop the means to differentiate the operational from the disengaged or disillusioned. Some of the returnees undoubtedly will have been disillusioned by their experiences (Smith 2014; de Freytas-Tamura 2015; Neumann 2015b). Do we want to dedicate scarce resources to investigating and prosecuting them? Will that deter others from going or encourage families and communities to cooperate with the government in detecting and stopping others? Many think that more thought should be given to how we might best assess these returnees, seek to reintegrate the disillusioned ones, and even elicit their help in educating and dissuading others from going to fight. A program aimed at treating and reintegrating foreign fighters has been operating in Aarhus, Denmark's second-largest city, for some time. It is attracting attention from around the world (e.g., Henley 2014; Braw 2014; Agerschou 2014). Similar efforts are under way in Germany (Hayat-Germany 2016; Koehler 2015) and elsewhere in Europe (Vidino and Brandon 2012). This rehabilitative approach is controversial, and its success depends on a complex array of factors, ranging from the careful conceptualization of the task, through resourcing such programs adequately and training appropriate personnel, to developing the political commitment to undertake such measures (see, e.g., Harris-Horgan, Barrelle, and Zammit 2015; Khalil and Zeuthen 2016; Berger 2016). In Canada, until recently, the government has shown little sustained interest in developing such an option. In particular, the status of Canadians who have returned from abroad or have been prevented from going is unclear. Many have been placed under some sort of legal restraint (e.g., a peace bond), but are they receiving any kind of treatment or other forms of assistance to diminish the threat they pose to themselves and others? Moreover, returnees suffering from post-traumatic stress disorder will need to be treated, if only to minimize the harm they might do to themselves and others. This is equally true if they have been convicted and imprisoned. But in Canada, unlike in some countries (e.g., Vidino and Brandon 2012; Schuurman and Bakker 2016), there are few specific programs for dealing with these individuals either before, during, or after incarceration.

The countries where Canadian jihadists go to fight obviously bear the brunt of the problem. Our citizens kill theirs and often carry out indiscriminate violence or even atrocities. Yet there is little research on the impact of foreign fighters on the nations that become their hosts. In the existing research there is also some divergence of views (e.g., Vidino 2006; Moore and Tumelty 2008). On the whole, however, it is recognized that foreign-born jihadists tend to have a detrimental impact on the course of the wars they join. They tend be more destructive and lethal because they are more ideologically committed and lack any natural ties to the communities in which they are fighting. They are less restrained by the immediate or long-term consequences of their actions for the people, economies, or heritages of the places where they are fighting. For similar reasons, they are more likely to oppose and disrupt efforts to establish peace between warring parties and to fanatically sustain conflicts at all costs. For many, the only acceptable end is either complete victory or annihilation, and along the way they frequently perpetrate horrendous atrocities (Kohlmann 2004). But analyses suggest that the most significant consequence of the intrusion of foreign fighters may be more indirect: their disruptive effect on the organizational cohesion of insurgencies often prolongs conflicts and escalates violence (Bakke 2014; Rich and Conduit 2015). The foreigners often bring new resources that are welcomed by the insurgents, but they also bring "new ideas about what the struggle is about and how it should be fought" (Bakke 2014, 153). More often than not, some local factions come to resent and resist the intrusion of foreign fighters and ideas. In Chechnya and Syria the result has been twofold: internecine struggles that have fragmented and weakened the insurgent forces; and cycles of out-bidding among insurgent groups, where groups compete for attention and influence, have escalated the violence and aggravated tensions. Invariably, the presence of jihadist foreign fighters, and the drift toward more radical positions and acts of indiscriminate violence, undermine the international support that insurgent groups can garner for their cause. The same factors play into the hands of their government opponents, who use the presence of such outsiders to deflect attention from their own culpability for the conflict and to justify taking ever more extreme measures against the insurgents. If the faction with which the foreign fighters are aligned overcomes these drawbacks and succeeds, there is usually a higher social and political price to be paid. The more radical the victors, the more likely they are to engage in severe persecution of those who opposed them, including other insurgents, and this perpetuates the cycle of violence and inflates the flow of refugees. In some measure, all of these things have come to pass in Syria and Iraq. The tide of foreign fighters has been crucial to the escalation of hostilities. Stemming the tide is imperative if there is to be any hope of resolving the refugee crisis that is straining the resources of Syria, Iraq, Turkey, Jordan, Lebanon, much of Europe, and even Canada.

For all these fairly obvious yet rarely itemized reasons, we do not think Canadians can simply let these discontented young people leave the country and die – as some might be inclined to suggest. Rather, our long-term best interests, both domestic and international, are served by making the necessary investments in the personnel and systems required to detect these individuals, prevent them from leaving, and if necessary detain, convict, and rehabilitate them, either before they leave or when they return. This must be done, moreover, in a sustained way, as stressed in Resolution 2178 (2014) of the United Nations Security Council. In this regard, some leading scholars have largely dismissed the role of ideology, and especially religion, in both the radicalization and the deradicalization or disengagement of foreign fighters (e.g., Sageman 2004; McCauley and Moskalenko 2011; Schuurman and Horgan 2016). Like Coolsaet (2016), they contend that the relevant issues are socio-economic, personal, and political – in various combinations – and that religious ideologies merely provide a convenient post hoc justification for the choices made. But other leading researchers staunchly disagree (e.g., Orsini 2012; Neumann 2016; Koehler 2017), arguing like us that religio-ideological commitments are at the core of the insurgent identity of foreign fighters. Consequently, any effort to disengage and reintegrate returned foreign fighters must tackle the thorny challenge of confronting the ideology. How is another matter, and one that far exceeds what can be said here.

The current flow of fighters to Syria and Iraq may be episodic, and ISIS is being defeated on the battlefield. But the continued instability of much of the Middle East, and the relative popularity of jihadist ideas, means it is unlikely that the threat of jihadist terrorism will disappear. Jihadism has become a global social movement with an appeal that transcends what is happening in Syria and Iraq. Other conflicts will give rise to new cohorts of jihadist foreign fighters.

NOTES

1 For definitions of the terms jihadist and jihadism, see Neumann (2014).
2 Of course it is the Canadian government, lockstep with many other states, that has labelled these travellers terrorists. In their own view, and that of many others, they are, like the *mujahidin* who fought before them in Afghanistan against the Soviets, just "freedom fighters" or "defenders of the faith" and not terrorists.
3 In the first half of 2016, however, the social media activity of ISIS members fell off sharply. No one knows exactly why, but it coincides with the new military campaigns to defeat ISIS in Iraq and Syria.
4 The research is ongoing.
5 When this chapter was submitted we had only analysed twenty-two interviews with foreign fighters, and new interviews were being done. As often happens, this chapter was submitted a year before an article that offers a more detailed analysis of a sample of twenty interviews with foreign fighters was pubished (Dawson and Amarasingam 2017). The samples are largely similar, but there are some differences.
6 Coolsaet specifically draws a connection to information on the Dutch foreign fighter contingent, noting the similarities, on page 36 of his report.

REFERENCES

Agerschou, T. 2014. "Preventing Radicalization and Discrimination in Aarhus." *Journal for Deradicalization* (Winter): 5–22.

Amarasingam, Amarnath. 2015. "Canadian Foreign Fighters in Syria: An Overview." *Jihadology – The Clear Banner*. https://jihadology.net/2015/03/04/the-clear-banner-canadian-foreign-fighters-in-syria-an-overview.

Anzalone, Christopher. 2015. "Canadian Foreign Fighters in Iraq and Syria." *CTC Sentinel* (Combating Terrorism Center at West Point). https://www.ctc.usma.edu/posts/canadian-foreign-fighters-in-iraq-and-syria.

Arsenault, Adrienne, and Nazim Baksh. 2016. "ISIS paperwork reveals names of 6 Canadians." 11 March. http://www.cbc.ca/news/canada/isis-documents-canadians-1.3486552.

Bakke, Kristin M. 2014. "Help Wanted? The Mixed Record of Foreign Fighters in Domestic Insurgencies." *International Security* 38(4): 150–87. https://doi.org/10.1162/ISEC_a_00156.

Bakker, Edwin, and Peter Grol. 2015. "Motives and Considerations of Potential Foreign Fighters from the Netherlands." International Centre for Counter Terrorism (ICCT) Policy Brief (July).

Baksh, Nazim, and Adrienne Arsenault. 2015. "Terrorism-related charges laid against Ottawa men with alleged ISIS ties." *CBC News*. http://www.cbc.ca/news/canada/terrorism-related-charges-laid-against-ottawa-men-with-alleged-isis-ties-1.2943313.

Barghout, Caroline. 2015. "Aaron Driver defends ISIS, attack on Parliament, but denies he's a threat." *CBC News*. http://www.cbc.ca/news/canada/manitoba/aaron-driver-defends-issis-attack-onparliament-but-denies-he's-a-threat.

Barrett, Richard. 2017. "Beyond the Caliphate: Foreign Fighters and the Threat of Returnees." The Soufan Center. https://thesoufancenter.org/wp-content/uploads/2017/11/Beyond-the-Caliphate-Foreign-Fighters-and-the-Threat-of-Returnees-TSC-Report-October-2017-v3.pdf.

Bartlett, Jamie, and Carl Miller. 2012. "The Edge of Violence: Towards Telling the Difference between Violent and Non-Violent Radicalization." *Terrorism and Political Violence* 24(1): 1–21. https://doi.org/10.1080/09546553.2011.594923.

Batrawi, Samar. 2013. "The Dutch Foreign Fighter Contingent in Syria." *CTC Sentinel* (Combating Terrorism Center at West Point). http:www.ctc.usma.edu/posts/the-dutch-foreign-fighter-contingent-in-syria.

Bell, Stewart. 2014a. "ISIS Fighter from Ottawa appears in video threatening Canada with attacks 'where it hurts you the most.'" *National Post*, 7 December 2014. http://news.nationalpost.com/2014/12/07/john-maguire-an-isis-fighter-from-ottawa-appears-on-video-warning-canada-of-attacks-where-it-hurts-you-the-most/.

– 2014b. "The path to extremism: The story of how one young man from Calgary ended up dead in Syria." *National Post*, 25 April. http://news.nationalpost.com/2014/04/25/the-path-to-extremism-the-story-of-how-one-young-man-from-calgary-ended-up-dead-in-syria/.

– 2014c "It's a mystery how middle-class Calgary man turned suicide bomber was recruited into ISIS terror group: Family." *National Post*, 12 June. http://news.nationalpost.com/2014/06/12/its-a-mystery-how-middle-class-calgary-man-turned-suicide-bomber-was-recruited-into-isis-terror-group-family/.

– 2014d. "Canadian killed in Syria: Calgary man, 22, joined fight after converting to Islam." *National Post*, 15 January. http://news.nationalpost.com/2014/01/15/canadian-killed-fighting-in-syria-calgary-man-22-joined-fight-after-converting-to-islam.

– 2014e. "Canadian Jihadist unmasked." *National Post*, 16 September. http://news.nationalpost.com/canadian-isis-fighter-abu-turaab-identified-as-mohammed-ali.

– 2016a. "RCMP arrest 23-year-old Ontario man suspected of plotting to leave Canada to engage in terrorism." *National Post*, 26 March. http://news.nationalpost.com/news/canada/rcmp-arrest-23-year-old-man-suspected-of-plotting-to-leave-canada-to-engage-in-terrorism.

– 2016b. "Toronto-area men may commit terrorism unless peace bond imposed: RCMP." *National Post*, 21 April. http://news.nationalpost.com/news/canada/toronto-area-men-may-commit-terrorism-unless-peace-bond-imposed-rcmp.

Berger, J.M. 2011. *Jihad Joe: Americans Who Go to War in the Name of Islam.* Washington, D.C.: Potomac Books.

– 2016. "Making CVE Work: A Focused Approach Based on Process Disruption." *ICCT Research Paper*. https://doi.org/10.19165/2016.1.05.

Braw, Elisabeth. 2014. "Inside Denmark's Radical Jihadist Rehabilitation Program." *Newsweek*, 17 October. http://www.newsweek.com/2014/10/24/denmark-offers-returning-jihadis-chance-repent-277622.html.

Byman, Daniel. 2015. "The Homecomings: What Happens When Arab Foreign Fighters in Iraq and Syria Return?" *Studies in Conflict and Terrorism* 38(8): 581–602. https://doi.org/10.1080/1057610X.2015.1031556.

Callimachi, Rukmini. 2016a. "ISIS video appears to show Paris assailants earlier in Syria and Iraq." *New York Times*, 25 January. http://www.nytimes.com/2016/01/25/world/middleeast/isis-video-paris-attacks.html?emc=edit_th_20160125&nl=todaysheadlines&nlid=27320165.

– 2016b. "How ISIS Built the Machinery of Terror under Europe's Gaze." *New York Times*, 29 March. https://www.nytimes.com/2016/03/29/world/europe/isis-attacks-paris-brussels.html.

Carter, Joseph A., Shiraz Maher, and Peter R. Neumann. 2014. "#Greenbirds: Measuring Importance and Influence in Syrian Foreign Fighter Networks." The International Centre for the Study of Radicalisation and Political Violence. https://icsr.info/wp-content/uploads/2014/04/ICSR-Report-Greenbirds-Measuring-Importance-and-Infleunce-in-Syrian-Foreign-Fighter-Networks.pdf.

CBC. 2014a. "Andre Poulin: Dead Canadian jihadist used in ISIS recruitment video." 12 July. http://www.cbc.ca/news/world/andre-poulin-dead-canadian-jihadist-used-in-isis-recruitment-video-1.2705115.

– 2014b. "Farah Mohamed Shirdon of Calgary fighting for Islamic State of Iraq and Syria." 18 June. http://www.cbc.ca/news/canada/farah-mohamed-shirdon-of-calgary-fighting-for-islamic-state-of-iraq-and-syria-1.2680206.

CBC News. 2015a. "Syrian jihadists believed to have recruited 6 young Quebecers." 26 February. http://www.cbc.ca/news/canada/montreal/syrian-jihadists-believed-to-have-recruited-6-young-quebecers-1.2973089.

– 2015b. "10 Montreal young people arrested on suspicion of wanting to join jihad." 19 May. http://www.cbc.ca/news/canada/montreal/10-montreal-young-people-arrested-on-suspicion-of-wanting-to-join-jihad-1.3079873.

– 2015c. "Terrorism-related peace bond for Seyed Amir Hossein Raisolsadat extended." 22 May. http://www.cbc.ca/news/canada/prince-edward-island/terrorism-related-peace-bond-for-seyed-amir-hossein-raisolsadat-extended-1.3083226.

Cesari, Jocelyne. 2008. "Muslims in Europe and the Risk of Radicalism." In *Jihadi Terrorism and the Radicalisation Challenge in Europe*, ed. Rik Coolsaet, 97–107. Aldershot: Ashgate.

– 2011. "Muslims in Europe and the US: A Shared but Overrated Risk of Radicalism." In *Jihadi Terrorism and the Radicalisation Challenge*, ed. Rik Coolsaet, 101–16. Farnham: Ashgate.

Coolsaet, Rik. 2016. "Facing the Fourth Foreign Fighter Wave: What Drives Europeans to Syria, and to Islamic State? Insights from the Belgian Case." Egmont – Royal Institute for International Relations (March).

Cottee, Simon, and Keith Hayward. 2011. "Terrorist (E)motives: The Existential Attractions of Terrorism." *Studies in Conflict and Terrorism* 34(12): 963–86. https://doi.org/10.1080/1057610X.2011.621116.

Crenshaw, Martha. 1988. "The Subjective Reality of the Terrorists: Ideological and Psychological Factors in Terrorism." In *Current Perspectives on International Terrorism*, ed. Robert O. Slater and Michael Stohl, 12–46. London: Macmillan.

Dalgaard-Nielsen, Anja. 2010. "Violent Radicalization in Europe: What We Know and What We Do Not Know." *Studies in Conflict and Terrorism* 33(9): 797–814. https://doi.org/10.1080/1057610X.2010.501423.

– 2017. "Discounting Religion in the Explanation of Homegrown Terrorist Radicalization: A Critique." In *The Cambridge Companion to Religion and Terroris*, ed. James R. Lewis, 32–45. Cambridge: Cambridge University Press.

Dawson, Lorne L., and Amarnath Amarasingam. 2016. "Trying to Talk to the Terrorists: Ethical and Methodological Challenges in Canada," Canadian Network for Research on Terrorism, Security, and Society, working paper.

– 2017. "Talking to Foreign Fighters: Insights into the Motivations for *Hijrah* to Syria and Iraq," *Studies in Conflict and Terrorism* 40(3): 191–210. https://doi.org/10.1080/1057610X.2016.1274216.

De Freytas-Tamura, Kimiko. 2015. "ISIS Defectors Reveal Disillusionment." *New York Times*, 20 September. http://www.nytimes.com/2015/09/21/world/europe/isis-defectors-reveal-disillusionment.html?_r=0.

De Roy van Zuijdewijn, Jeanine. 2014. "Research Note: The Foreign Fighters' Threat: What History Can(not) Tell Us." *Perspectives on Terrorism* 8(5): 59–73. http://www.terrorismanalysts.com/pt/index.php/pot/article/view/378/753.

De Roy van Zuijdewijn, Jeanine, and Edwin Bakker. 2014. "Returning Western Foreign Fighters: The Case of Afghanistan, Bosnia, and Somalia." International Centre for Counter-Terrorism, Background Note (June). www.icct.nl.

Fife, Robert. 2016. "Sharp increase in number of Canadians involved in terrorist activities abroad." *Globe and Mail*, 24 Febrary, A1 and A4.

Ginges, Jeremy, Scott Atran, Sonya Sachdeva, and Douglas Medin. 2011. "Psychology Out of the Laboratory: The Challenge of Violent Extremism." *American Psychologist* 66(6): 507–19. https://doi.org/10.1037/a0024715.

Githens-Mazer, Jonathan. 2010. "Mobilization, Recruitment, Violence, and the Street: Radical Violent *takfiri* Islamism in Early Twenty-First-Century Britain." In *The New Extremism in 21st Century Britain*, ed. Roger Eatwell and Matthew J. Goodwin, 47–66. London: Routledge.

Gudmundson, Per. 2013. "The Swedish Foreign Fighter Contingent in Syria." *CTC Sentinel* 6(9) (Combating Terrorism Center at West Point). http:www.ctc.usma.edu/posts/the-swedish-foreign-fighter-contingent-in-syria.

Hafez, Mohammed, and Creighton Mullins. 2015. "The Radicalization Puzzle: A Theoretical Synthesis of Empirical Approaches to Homegrown Extremism." *Studies in Conflict and Terrorism* 38(11): 958–75. https://doi.org/10.1080/1057610X.2015.1051375.

Harris-Horgan, Shandon, Kate Barrelle, and Andrew Zammit. 2015. "What Is Countering Violent Extremism? Exploring CVE Policy and Practice in Australia." *Behavioral Sciences of Terrorism and Political Aggression* 8(1): 6–24. https://doi.org/10.1080/19434472.2015.1104710.

Hayat-Germany. 2016. http://hayat-deutschland.de/english.

Hegghammer, Thomas. 2011. "The Rise of Muslim Foreign Fighters: Islam and the Globalization of Jihad." *International Security* 35(3): 53–94. https://doi.org/10.1162/ISEC_a_00023.

– 2013. "Should I Stay or Should I Go? Explaining Variation in Western Jihadists' Choice between Domestic and Foreign Fighting." *American Political Science Review* (February). doi:10.1017/S0003055412000615.

Helmer, Aedan, and Gary Dimmock. 2016. "Who is Awso Peshdary: The case against an alleged Ottawa extremist." *Ottawa Citizen*, 4 April. http://ottawacitizen.com/news/local-news/who-is-awso-peshdary-the-case-against-an-alleged-ottawa-extremist.

Henley, Jon. 2014. "How do you deradicalize returning ISIS fighters?" *The Guardian*, 12 November. http://www.theguardian.com/world/2014/nov/12/deradicalise-isis-fighters-jihadists-denmark-syria.

Holman, Timothy. 2016. "'Gonna Get Myself Connected': The Role of Facilitation in Foreign Fighter Mobilizations." *Perspectives on Terrorism* 10(2). http://www.terrorismanalysts.com/pt/index.php/pot/article/view/497.

Ilardi, Gaetano Joe. 2013. "Interviews with Canadian Radicals." *Studies in Conflict and Terrorism* 36(9): 713–38. https://doi.org/10.1080/1057610X.2013.813248.

Khalil, James. 2014. "Radical Beliefs and Violent Actions Are Not Synonymous: How to Place the Key Disjuncture between Attitudes and Behaviors at the Heart of Our Research into Political Violence." *Studies in Conflict and Terrorism* 37(2): 198–211. https://doi.org/10.1080/1057610X.2014.862902.

Khalil, James, and Marine Zeuthen. 2016. "Countering Violent Extremism and Risk Reduction: A Guide to Programme Design and Evaluation." Royal United Services Institute for Defence and Security Studies.

Klausen, Jytte. 2015. "Twitting the *Jihad*: Social Media Networks of Western Foreign Fighters in Syria and Iraq." *Studies in Conflict and Terrorism* 38(1): 1–22. https://doi.org/10.1080/1057610X.2014.974948.

Koehler, Daniel. 2015. "Family Counselling, De-radicalization, and Counter-Terrorism: The Danish and German Programs in Context." In *Countering Violent Extremism: Developing an Evidence-base for Policy and Practice*, ed. Sara Zeiger and Anne Aly, 129–36. Perth, Australia: Hedayah Center and Curtin University. http://www.hedayahcenter.org/Admin/Content/File-23201691817.pdf.

– 2017. *Understanding Deradicalization: Methods, Tools and Programs for Countering Violent Extremism*. London: Routledge.

Kohlmann, Evan F. 2004. *Al-Qaida's Jihad in Europe: The Afghan–Bosnian Network*. London: Bloomsbury.

Kwong, Matt. 2014. "Ahmad Waseem case illustrates Canada's foreign fighter problem." *CBC News*, 5 August. http://www.cbc.ca/news/canada/ahmad-waseem-case-illustrates-canada-s-foreign-fighter-problem-1.2727328.

Logan, Nick. 2014. "The trouble with charging Canadian ISIS fighters."
   Global News, 12 December. http://globalnews.ca/news/1723036/
   the-trouble-with-charging-canadian-isis-fighters.
Malet, David. 2013. *Foreign Fighters: Transnational Identity in Civil Conflicts.*
   New York: Oxford University Press.
Maynard, Jonathan Leader. 2014. "Rethinking the Role of Ideology in Mass
   Atrocities." *Terrorism and Political Violence* 26(5): 821–41. https://doi.org/
   10.1080/09546553.2013.796934.
McBride, Megan K. 2011. "The Logic of Terrorism: Existential Anxiety, the
   Search for Meaning, and Terrorist Ideologies." *Terrorism and Political
   Violence.* 23(4): 560–81. https://doi.org/10.1080/09546553.2011.575486.
McCants, William. 2015. *ISIS Apocalypse: The History, Strategy, and Doomsday
   Vision of the Islamic State.* New York: St Martin's Press.
McCauley, Clark R., and Sophia Moskalenko. 2011. *Friction: How Radicalization
   Happens to Them and Us.* New York: Oxford University Press.
– 2014. "Toward a Profile of Lone Wolf Terrorists: What Moves an Individual
   from Radical Opinion to Radical Action." *Terrorism and Political Violence*
   26(1): 69–85. https://doi.org/10.1080/09546553.2014.849916.
Molnar, Coleman. 2015. "My Friend the Terrorist." *The Walrus*, 6 July. http://
   thewalrus.ca/my-friend-the-terrorist.
Moore, Cerwyn, and Paul Tumelty. 2008. "Foreign Fighters and the Case of
   Chechnya: A Critical Assessment." *Studies in Conflict and Terrorism* 31(5):
   412–33. https://doi.org/10.1080/10576100801993347.
Nesser, Petter. 2015. *Islamist Terrorism in Europe: A History.* Oxford: Oxford
   University Press.
– 2014. "The New Jihadism: A Global Snapshot." International Centre for
   the Study of Radicalization and Political Violence (ICSR), King's College
   London. http://icsr.info/wp-content/uploads/2014/12/ICSR-REPORT-
   The-New-Jihadism-A-Global-Snapshot.pdf.
– 2015a. "Foreign Fighters Total in Syria /Iraq Now Exceeds 20,000; Surpasses
   Afghanistan Conflict in the 1980s." International Centre for the Study of
   Radicalization and Political Violence (ICSR), King's College London, 26
   January. www.icsr.info.
– 2015b. "Victims, Perpetrators, Assets: The Narratives of Islamic State
   Defectors." International Centre for the Study of Radicalization and Political
   Violence (ICSR), King's College London. www.icsr.info.
– 2016. *Radicalized: New Jihadists and the Threat to the West.* London: I.B. Tauris.
Orsini, Alessandro. 2009. *Anatomy of the Red Brigades: The Religious Mindset of
   Modern Terrorists*, trans. Sarah J. Nodes. Ithaca: Cornell University Press.
– 2012. "Poverty, Ideology, and Terrorism: The STAM Bond." *Studies in
   Conflict and Terrorism* 35(10): 665–92. https://doi.org/10.1080/10576
   10X.2012.712030.

Pantucci, Rafaello. 2013. "British Fighters Joining the War in Syria." *CTC Sentinel* 6(2) (Combating Terrorism Center at West Point). https://ctc.usma.edu/british-fighters-joining-the-war-in-syria.

Perreaux, Les, and Verity Stevenson. 2015. "Quebeckers who left to join IS defy easy stereotypes." *Globe and Mail*, 28 February, A6.

Prucha, Nico, and Ali Fischer. 2013. "Tweeting for the Caliphate: Twitter as the New Frontier for Jihadist Propaganda." *CTC Sentinel* 6(6) (Combating Terrorism Center at West Point). https://ctc.usma.edu/tweeting-for-the-caliphate-twitter-as-the-new-frontier-for-jihadist-propaganda.

Public Safety Canada. 2017. *Public Report on the Terrorist Threat to Canada: Building a Safe and Resilient Canada.* https://www.publicsafety.gc.ca/cnt/rsrcs/pblctns/pblc-rprt-trrrst-thrt-cnd-2017/index-en.aspx.

Reinares, Fernando, and Carola Garcia-Calvo. 2014. "The Spanish Foreign Fighter Contingent in Syria." *CTC Sentinel* 7(1) (Combating Terrorism Center at West Point). https://ctc.usma.edu/the-spanish-foreign-fighter-contingent-in-syria.

Rich, Ben, and Dara Conduit. 2015. "The Impact of Jihadist Foreign Fighters on Indigenous Secular-Nationalist Causes: Contrasting Chechnya and Syria." *Studies in Conflict and Terrorism* 38(2): 113–31. https://doi.org/10.1080/1057610X.2014.979605.

Roberts, Nadim. 2014. "Gregory and Collin Gordon, Calgary brothers, join ranks of Canadians fighting for ISIS." *CBC News*, 28 August. http://www.cbc.ca/news/gregory-and-collin-gorfon-calgary-brothers-join-ranks-of-candians-fighting-for-ISIS.

Roy, Olivier. 2015. "What Is the Driving Force behind Jihadist Terrorism? A Scientific Perspective on the Causes/Circumstances of Joining the Scene." Speech delivered to BKA Autumn Conference (*Bundeskriminalamt* [German Federal Police]), 18–19 November, Fiesole, Italy. www.bka.de/nn_256982/.../herbsttagung2015RoyAbstract.pdf.

Saarinen, Juha. 2014. "The Finnish Foreign Fighter Contingent in Syria." *CTC Sentinel* 7(3) (Combating Terrorism Center at West Point). https://ctc.usma.edu/the-finnish-foreign-fighter-contingent-in-syria.

Sageman, Marc. 2004. *Understanding Terror Networks.* Philadelphia: University of Pennsylvania Press.

– 2008. *Leaderless Jihad.* Philadelphia: University of Pennsylvania Press.

Schuurman, Bart, and Edwin Bakker. 2016. "Reintegrating Jihadist Extremists: Evaluating a Dutch Initiative, 2013–2014." *Behavioral Sciences of Terrorism and Political Aggressiion* 8(1): 66–85. https://doi.org/10.1080/19434472.2015.1100648.

Schuurman, Bart, and John Horgan. 2017. "Rationales for Terrorist Violence in Homegrown Jihadist Groups: A Case Study from the Netherlands." *Aggression and Violent Behavior* 27(March–April): 55–63. https://doi.org/10.1016/j.avb.2016.02.005.

SecDev. 2015. "ISIS Steps Up Information Control in Raqqa and Dier Ez," SecDev Flash Notes, 5 August. https://secdev-foundation.org/isis-steps-up-information-control-in-raqqa-and-deir-ezzor.

Shephard, Michelle, and Andrew Bailey. 2016. "The Daesh files." *Toronto Star*, 30 May, A1.

Silke, Andrew. 2008. Research on Terrorism: A Review of the Impact of 9/11 and the Global War on Terrorism. In *Terrorism Informatics: Knowledge Management and Data Mining for Homeland Security*, ed. Hsinchun Chen, Edna Reid, Joshua Sinai, and Andrew Silke, 27–50. New York: Springer.

Smith, Lewis. 2014. "Syria crisis: British jihadists becoming disillusioned at fighting rival rebels and want to come home." *The Independent*, 5 September. http://www.independent.co.uk/news/world/middle-east/syria-crisis-british-jihadists-becoming-disillusioned-at-fighting-rival-rebels-and-not-assad-regime-9713279.html.

Soufan Group. 2015. "Foreign Fighters: An Updated Assessment of the Flow of Foreign Fighters into Syria and Iraq." New York. http://soufangroup.com/wp-content/uploads/2015/12/TSG_ForeignFightersUpdate3.pdf.

Spalek, Basia. 2007. "Disconnection and Exclusion: Pathways to Radicalisation?" In *Islamic Political Radicalism: A European Perspective*, ed. Tahir Abbas, 192–206. Edinburgh: University of Edinburgh Press.

Stark, Erika. 2014. "Calgary brothers the latest Canadians identified as fighting for ISIS" *National Post*, 28 August. http://news.nationalpost.com/2014/08/28/calgary-brothers-the-latest-canadians-identified-as-fighting-for-isis.

Stern, Jessica, and J.M. Berger. 2015. *ISIS: The State of Terror*. New York: Ecco.

Vidino, Lorenzo. 2006. "The Arab Foreign Fighters and the Sacralization of the Chechen Conflict." *Al Nakhlah* (Spring): 1–11.

Vidino, Lorenzo, and James Brandon. 2012. "Countering Radicalization in Europe." International Centre for the Study of Radicalisation and Political Violence. www.icsr.info.

Vice News. 2014. "Exclusive: Islamic State member warns of NYC attack." 25 September. https://www.youtube.com/watch?v=j8TLu514EgU.

Watts, Clint. 2008. "Foreign Fighters: How Are They Being Recruited? Two Imperfect Recruitment Models." *Small Wars Journal*. smallwarsjournal.com.

– 2009. "Countering Terrorism from the Second Foreign Fighter Glut." *Small Wars Journal*. smallwarsjournal.com.

Weggemans, Daan, Edwin Bakker, and Peter Grol. 2014. "Who Are They and Why Do They Go? The Radicalisation and Preparatory Processes of Dutch Jihadist Foreign Fighters." *Perspectives on Terrorism* 8(4): 100–10. http://www.terrorismanalysts.com/pt/index.php/pot/article/view/365.

Zammit, Andrew. 2013. "Tracking Australian Foreign Fighters in Syria." *CTC Sentinel* 6(11–12) (Combating Terrorism Center at West Point). https://ctc.usma.edu/tracking-australian-foreign-fighters-in-syria.

Zelin, Aaron Y. 2013. "Who Are the Foreign Fighters in Syria?" Washington Institute for Near East Policy. http:www.washingtoninstitute.org/policy-analysis/view/who-are-the-foreign-fighters-in-syria.

4 Breaking Free: A Socio-Historical Analysis of the Canadian Freemen-on-the-Land Movement

DAVID C. HOFMANN

In September 2013, a two-year legal battle between a Calgary landlady and her tenant caught the attention of the Canadian media. Normally, this type of commonplace disagreement is hardly newsworthy. However, this particular case drew interest due to the bizarre behaviours exhibited by Andreas Pirelli, the tenant involved in the dispute (Graveland 2013a). In November 2011, Pirelli moved from Montreal to Calgary and rented a duplex from Rebekah Caverhill. When Caverhill went to collect the rent, she discovered that he had changed the locks. Upon confronting Pirelli, he declared that the property was an embassy and now belonged to him. Caverhill then received a number of fictitious invoices and liens from Pirelli by mail, demanding payment in gold bullion for work he had supposedly done on the property. When Caverhill took her dispute to the media, reporters interested in interviewing Pirelli were greeted by signs affixed around the rental unit declaring himself a diplomat and threatening monetary fines for those who trespassed on his property. Due to the civil nature of the dispute, the police were unable to intervene until it was discovered that Pirelli was actually Mario Antonnaci, a man accused of pushing a Montreal landlady down the stairs in 2007 (Graveland 2013b). On 27 September, the Calgary police arrested Pirelli on several outstanding warrants issued in Quebec, ending the two-year ordeal.

At first glance, Pirelli's justification for reneging on his rental agreement with Caverhill seems outlandish. Yet in Pirelli's mind, he was exercising his personal rights and freedoms as a Freeman-on-the-Land.[1] The resultant media coverage of Pirelli and Caverhill's dispute, along with several other contemporaneous events involving other Freemen (Yogaretnam 2012; Carter 2013; CBC 2013; Wilhelm 2013), helped pique public interest in the movement (Graveland 2013c). Questions about the Freemen abounded in the media: Just who are these individuals operating in our midst (Bell 2010; Moore 2013)? What is the basis of their unusual ideology, which seems to haphazardly blend ideas involving individual rights, freedoms, and religion with pseudo-legalistic terminology (Vandenbrink 2011)? Are they a danger to public safety, or merely a benign social and political movement, as several of their leaders insist (Bell 2013; Bronskill 2013; Global Toronto 2013; Wilhem 2013)?

For governments and law enforcement, the emergence of the Freemen in Canada over the past fifteen years has raised a parallel set of concerns. With Islamist-inspired terrorism looming large in the collective consciousness of security scholars and governments, alternative threats to national security have received less attention and resources. However, recent empirical evidence has highlighted the potential of the Freemen and other ideologically similar anti-government movements to develop into serious security threats in the United States (Anti-Defamation League 2012; Rivinius 2014).[2] In the Canadian context, the Freemen's anti-government mentality, acrimonious attitude toward police, and disregard for criminal and civil law have caused CSIS and the RCMP to classify them as an emerging security threat (CSIS 2012; RCMP 2014). While they are not nearly as lethal as their American counterparts (Southern Poverty Law Center 2009; Anti-Defamation League 2012), over the past five years there have been several violent incidents between law enforcement and individuals associated with or inspired by the Canadian Freemen (see Table 4.1), such as the 2012 shooting of two RCMP officers in Killam, Alberta (Yogaretnam 2012), the 2014 shooting deaths of three RCMP officers in Moncton, New Brunswick, (Brean 2014), and the 2015 shooting death of a west Edmonton police constable (Pruden 2015).

These recent violent events, and the paucity of academic studies of Canadian far-right and anti-government movements (Tanner and Campana 2014; Bérubé and Campana 2015; Perry and Scrivens 2015; Perry, Hofmann, and Scrivens 2017), suggest there is a need for terrorism scholars in Canada to take a more proactive approach to emerging security threats posed by anti-government movements. A holistic overview of the landscape of terrorism and counterterrorism in Canada requires a better understanding of the motivations and methods of active Canadian anti-government movements. In this chapter, I contribute to the nascent body of knowledge on potentially violent Canadian anti-government movements by providing academics, police, and security practitioners with a primer on the beliefs, practices, and history of the Canadian Freemen-on-the-Land. Given the nature of this volume, I also briefly explore whether and to what degree the Canadian Freemen pose a threat to national security. I start with a descriptive overview of

Table 4.1. Known acts of Freeman-on-the-Land-inspired violence in Canada (2012–15)

Actor(s)	Date	Location	Result
Brad Clarke and Sawyer Robinson	February 2012	Killam, AB	Two RCMP officers shot and injured.
Justin Bourque	June 2014	Moncton, NB	Shooting deaths of three RCMP officers.
Norman Walter Raddatz	June 2015	Edmonton, AB	Shooting death of police constable. One other police constable injured.

the beliefs and methods of the Canadian Freemen-on-the-Land. This is followed by a socio-historical analysis that links the ideological roots of the Canadian Freemen to the legacy of far-right anti-government thought in the United States over the past forty years. Finally, based on key concepts taken from the literature on the root causes of terrorism (Crenshaw 1981; Bjorgo 2004; Newman 2006; Noricks 2009) and what we have gleaned from previous cases of North American far-right anti-government violence (Sargent 1995; Wessinger 1999; Wright 1995; 2007; Levitas 2002; Noble 2010; Perliger 2012), I conclude this chapter with a discussion of two conditions that may cause the Freemen to develop into a serious threat to Canadian national security.[3]

Who Are the Canadian Freemen-on-the-Land?

The Canadian Freemen are a loosely knit, highly fractionalized, and decentralized anti-government movement with pseudo-religious and libertarian overtones. While commonly and correctly associated with far-right forms of extremism in the United States, the Canadian movement actually first emerged in the early 2000s from the extremes of Canada's political left (Netolitzky 2016a, 624–7, discussed further below). The Canadian Freemen hold a number of society-rejecting and conspiratorial beliefs couched in pseudo-legal language and semiotics, whereby they claim the right to be exempt from paying taxes, debts, mortgages, and other monetary, civil, and legal obligations. The movement's refusal to recognize the legitimacy of provincial and federal governmental authority means that members often do not carry any government-issued documentation (e.g., SIN cards, driver licences, passports). Furthermore, certain Canadian Freemen espouse the libertarian ideal of unfettered access to firearms and/or narcotics (Vandenbrink 2011; Quan 2012; Graveland 2013d). While some individual members and supporters of the Canadian Freemen hold racist and antisemitic world views (Topham 2012), the organization itself is not overtly associated with organized Canadian hate movements (Tanner and Campana 2014; Bérubé and Campana 2015). The Freemen's anti-government ideology means they are often vexatious and confrontational when they come into contact with law enforcement (CBC 2013; Graveland 2013c; Humphreys 2013; Wilhelm 2013) and the legal system (*Meads v. Meads* 2012; Netolitzky 2016b), whose representatives they view as illegitimate agents of the state trying to impose unjust legal obligations upon them.

Canadian Freemen ideology is spread mainly by individual leaders, referred to as "gurus," each of whom peddles his particular brand of Freemen thought. Canadian gurus engage heavily in cyberspace, where they teach and proselytize, sharing their concepts and methods through personal websites, open and closed online forums, and social networking platforms,[4] as well as posting ideological and instructional videos on sites like YouTube (e.g., World Freeman Society 2015). Once exposed to the Freemen world view, prospective members may choose to attend public seminars hosted by Canadian or international gurus purporting to teach them the secrets of Freemen Common Law necessary to liberate themselves from governmental control and obligations (Menard 2012; Carter 2013).[5] In his analysis of the pseudo-legal practices of the Canadian Freemen, Justice Rooke emphasizes the role of small face-to-face gatherings in the spread of anti-government ideology: "[Freemen] ideas appear to be developed in social groups ... [and] litigants frequently say they work or study in groups" (*Meads v. Meads* 2012, 17, 59–60). These small work or study groups are important for the development of new concepts and pseudo-legal tactics, which are later shared with the broader Freemen community via the internet (Menard and Denis 2011).

Due to the loose-knit nature of the Canadian Freemen, their ideas and methods are not monolithic. Most individual Freemen are ideological bricoleurs who pick and choose elements, tactics, and theories from the teachings of several gurus and a variety of conspiracy, antisemitic, religious, racist, and fringe political thinkers, bloggers, and journalists (Johanson 2009; Netolitzky 2016a, 625–6). There are, however, common elements across the various interpretations of Freemen Common Law. A prominent theme in Freemen rhetoric is that at some point the Government of Canada was co-opted by a shadowy cabal of social elites. There are numerous theories as to who these individuals actually are: some Freemen subscribe to the "one world government"[6] theory popular among the American anti-government far right, while others turn to antisemitic, conspiratorial, and/or fantastical explanations (i.e., David

Icke's "lizard people" theory).[7] Building upon the notion of the illegitimacy of the Canadian government, the defining feature of Freemen ideology is the belief that individuals are only obligated to follow laws to which they consent. According to Freemen Common Law, when a baby is born the government creates a fictitious legal persona (a "straw man") attached to their birth certificate that is distinct from the physical individual (a "living person of flesh and blood"). Since this legal persona is a creation of the state, it is the only aspect of the individual over which they can claim legitimate authority. The Freemen argue that by tacitly consenting to be associated with their legal personae, the vast majority of Canadians are acquiescing to governmental control over their lives. Therefore, Freemen believe that by severing their connection with their fictitious legal personae, they can withdraw their consent to be governed and thereby "break free" from any governmental or legal obligations (Chapman 2010). The methods used to become a Freeman vary widely depending on the teachings of individual gurus. They include techniques such as the completion of pseudo-legal documentation declaring emancipation from their associated "straw man" identity, issuing a written or verbal denunciation of governmental authority prior to the destruction of related documents (SIN numbers, passports, etc.), pledging allegiance to the Freemen movement, and similar symbolic, pseudo-religious, and pseudo-legal acts. Freemen believe that after one or more of these rituals have been completed, the connection to the "straw man" is severed; from that point on, efforts by the state to control Freemen (i.e., government documentation, levying taxes, issuing tickets) are seen as an illegitimate and unilateral imposition of obligations from which they believe they are exempt as physically and legally distinct "living persons of flesh and blood."

The typical response of Canadian Freemen to what they perceive as illegitimate government action is to employ a number of ritualistic, semi-religious, and/or pseudo-legal tactics based on their personal interpretation of Freemen Common Law. These include practices such as the adoption of certain naming conventions (e.g., John-George: Smith or John George of the Family/Clan/House of Smith), odd spelling and formatting choices in written documents (e.g., Freemen-on-the-Land), the invocation of certain religious terms and terminology (e.g., John-George: Smith who is the creation of the Lord God Almighty Jehovah), the uttering of formulaic statements laced with pseudo-legal jargon when confronted by agents of the state, and the use of pseudo-legal paper warfare tactics based upon antiquated, religious, or misunderstood legal/political concepts and documents.[8] These ritualistic behaviours can be linked to a Common Law concept called "joinder," whereby Freemen believe that *any* verbal or written acknowledgment of a link between oneself and their straw man identity legally fuses the two identities together, providing the legal justification for the state to exercise coercive control over previously emancipated individuals.[9] Another common motif in Canadian Freemen Common Law is the existence of esoteric knowledge that can negate or alleviate financial and legal burdens. For example, websites of Canadian Freemen gurus often offer advice on how to avoid financial obligations such as parking tickets and student loans by using pseudo-legal fill-in-the-blank documentation (e.g., Think Free Be Free 2015). Scholars of Freemen ideology have likened the use of these tactics to a form of magic, whereby practitioners believe they can employ secret knowledge to subvert and control others for their own well-being (Wessinger 2000, 160; *Meads v. Meads* 2012, 15–16, 68).

Perhaps one of the most puzzling aspects of the Canadian Freemen is their lack of a distinct political orientation. Reflecting the bricoleur nature of Canadian Freemanism, individual adherents and small clusters of Freemen identify with and espouse far-left, far-right, and even centrist political ideologies, sometimes even shifting between the categories when convenient (Perry, Hofmann, and Scrivens 2017). Early incarnations of the Canadian Freemen were clearly inspired by far-left anti-globalization and social activist movements (Netolitzky 2016a, 624–5). However, as the movement attracted increased attention during the early 2000s, anti-government ideas and world views developed by American far-right actors in the United States between the late 1970s to mid-1990s began to seep into the Canadian Freemen ideology, spearheaded by competing ideologues engaged in efforts to attract and retain followers. The amorphous political orientation of the Canadian Freemen is likely due to concerted efforts by the early Freemen leadership to "Canadianize" ideological and pseudo-legal concepts taken from the American Sovereign Citizens and several other similar anti-government and far-right movements (Perry, Hofmann, and Scrivens 2017, 14–15). The end result was the creation of a product and belief system couched in leftist liberal ideology meant to better resonate with Canadian values, while still espousing the core components of American anti-government and far-right world views.

Despite the far-left origins of the Canadian Freemen, right-wing rhetoric and world views have increasingly taken root among some of the more devoted adherents. For example, when asked his opinion of the government during an interview with a journalist, Canadian Freeman Mika Rasila replied: "It is basically us against the government now. If we don't rein them in then they are just going to take over every possible freedom that we have ... I mean if it comes down to defence, we are willing to defend ourselves. [I would go] as far as I'd have to go [in order to defend myself]" (Bell 2010). This type of rhetoric is emblematic of the influence that core tenets of American far-right and anti-government conspiratorial world views have upon Canadian Freemen ideology. Regardless of individual political affiliation, central themes that espouse certain inalienable rights, the use of pseudo-legal harassment tactics, the rejection of certain or all forms of authority, and the legitimization of violent self-defence against outside hostile forces remain cornerstones of Canadian Freemen ideology (see, Netolitzky 2016b; Perry, Hofmann and Scrivens 2017, 56–7).

Therefore, situating the origin of the Canadian Freemen's beliefs and practices in the larger context of American anti-government thought is an important component to understanding their particular world view, and provides unique insight into the conditions that may precipitate violent political action among Canadian Freemen and their supporters. In the following section, I discuss the growth, development, and spread of the far-right American anti-governmental ideology, paying particular attention to the impact it has had on the Canadian Freemen world view.

The Ideological Roots of the Canadian Freemen-on-the-Land

The collective research on the emergence of American far-right and anti-government ideology is varied and vast and cannot be surveyed in its entirety here (Bjorgo 1995; Coates 1995; Diamond 1995; Sargent 1995; Barkun 1996; 1997; Hamm 1997; 2002; Levitas 2002; Wright 2007; Noble 2010; Perliger 2012). However, scholars recognize that the emergence of a new wave of far-right movements in the United States coincided with a series of economic, political, and social crises in the late 1970s and early 1980s. During this tumultuous period, the leadership of the American far-right capitalized on the social, economic, and political turmoil caused by events such as the Farm Crisis (Diamond 1995, 259–65; Wessinger 2000, 161–3; Levitas 2002, 168–76), the increased militarization of American police forces (Miller 1996; Balko 2013), and the introduction of stricter gun control legislation (Durham 2000, 63–83; Wright 2007, 114–48). These and other events allowed far-right leaders to construct a credible narrative of imminent threat that was central to the development of an anti-government ideology that appealed to angry and disenfranchised segments of the American population. The concept of a hostile government controlled by Jews and banking elites (i.e., the "New World Order") resonated with anti-tax protesters and with a subset of American farmers facing foreclosure on their farms and the erasure of their livelihoods. By packaging patriotic narratives with religious, racist, and anti-government themes, leaders of the far right also found adherents among Christian Patriots and Identity Christians (Barkun 1997; Noble 2010). At the national level, the adoption of a military model of crime control by American police (e.g., President Reagan's "War on Drugs") fed into the fears of gun rights advocates, who saw this as evidence that the government was bent on stripping its citizens of their individual rights (Gibson 1994). Furthermore, the escalating tension between far-right actors and agents of the state, what Stuart Wright (2007, 26–43) calls the opportunity/threat spiral, was exacerbated by several violent confrontations between police and members of far-right movements (Noble 2010, 151–6).

Anti-government sentiment among far-right movements hit a fever pitch in the early 1990s after the sieges at Ruby Ridge (Hamm 1997; Levitas 2002, 301–4) and the Branch Davidian compound in Waco, Texas (Tabor and Gallagher 1995; Wright 1995; Doherty 2001). These deadly stand-offs, caused by police intervention over weapons violations, entrenched the idea among far-right actors that the government was actively attempting to disarm gun owners as a prelude to a mass takeover. The legacy of these events and the fears they instilled among the far right led to the growth of American militia movements during the 1990s (Crothers 2004, 75–122). Despite a decline in popularity in the aftermath of the 1995 Oklahoma City bombing (Crothers 2004, 145–72; Wright 2007, 194–5) the core anti-government ideology established by the far right during this period endures among the larger sympathetic support base of far-right conservatives in the American population, as well as Canadians involved in fringe social activism on both ends of the political spectrum.[10]

The ideological lineage of the Canadian Freemen-on-the-Land can be traced directly to one particular militia movement: the Montana Freemen. They are best known for their eighty-one day stand-off with the FBI in 1996, which ended with their peaceful surrender (Rosenfeld 1997; Wessinger 1999; 2000, 158–217). Established during the early 1990s, the Montana Freemen were a revolutionary movement of Christian Patriots focused on overthrowing what they perceived to be a hostile federal government under the control of Jews and the World Bank. Much like other American militia movements at the time, the Montana Freemen believed that the powers exercised by the US federal government were unconstitutional and anti-Christian and that they were engaged in a deliberate plot to strip its citizens of their personal rights and freedoms as a prelude to a mass takeover. In safeguarding themselves from this perceived imminent threat, their primary goal was to establish of a utopic sovereign republic governed by a mixture of Old Testament law and the pre–Civil War constitution (Wessinger 1999, 37–8).

Like similar American far-right militias, the Montana Freemen were heavily armed and prepared to fight to protect themselves from the perceived hostile agents of the federal government. However, they differentiated themselves from their contemporaries by attempting to subvert or control the established legal system by engaging in pseudo-legal paper warfare tactics against the government. The Montana Freemen's use of paper warfare was pivotal in the creation of an alternative legal framework for anti-government actors who refuse to recognize the legitimacy of state and federal authority. The documents and tactics used by the Montana Freemen harkened back to an idealized time-period that resonated with the patriotic, religious, and personal world views of their sympathetic support base. It served to reinforce core beliefs in the illegitimacy of government, the supremacy of God's law over man's law, and the inalienable rights of the individual. To the Montana Freemen and their supporters, this was a way to beat the government at its own game, using what they viewed as divinely inspired (i.e., the US Constitution and the Declaration of Independence) and legally superior (i.e., the Magna Carta) documents as legal precedent and justification. Perhaps most importantly, the Montana Freemen actively disseminated the ideas and the methods involved in their use of paper warfare. In September 1995, they established "Justus Township" on a farm near Jordan, Montana, and proceeded to teach an estimated 700 to 800 people their interpretation of Common Law (Wessinger 2000, 163–167). In addition to these seminars, they produced videotapes of lectures explaining the principles of Freeman Common Law, some of which were handed out to reporters covering the stand-off between the Montana Freemen and the FBI (Wessinger 2000, 167). The Montana Freemen dissolved after their peaceful surrender to law enforcement in 1996, but their pseudo-legal tactics and ideological concepts continue to be used by a multitude of far-right and sovereigntist movements (Fleishman 2004; Bilinsky 2012; *Meads v. Meads* 2012).

A close reading of the ideological and pseudo-legal material produced by the Canadian Freemen reveals that, despite their origins as part of the extreme political left in Canada, the influence and legacy of American far-right anti-government thought permeates almost all facets of their beliefs and practices. The themes of inalienable personal liberty, resistance to an illegitimate government, and defence of fundamental rights advanced by the Montana Freemen all endure in contemporary Canadian Freemen rhetoric (Menard 2012). Furthermore, Canadian Freemen's ideology is founded on arguments that have been transplanted from a distinctly American context that explicitly uses American historical events and case law as justification for their actions (Wise 2013a; 2013b). In writings and videos posted online, Canadian Freemen gurus like Robert Menard and Dean Clifford make efforts to "Canadianize" these justifications and strip them of overt Christian, racist, and right-wing ideals (Menard and Denis 2011; Clifford 2013); even so, they often present whitewashed and rehashed arguments taken from the original strategies used by the Montana Freemen and their ideological successors in the United States.[11] Other Freemen gurus like dual American/Canadian citizen Glenn Winningham (2011b) outright cite the authority of the US constitution when discussing the application of Freeman Common Law in Canada. Freemen gurus often explain away cross-border institutional and legal differences by evoking conspiratorial "one world" government theories that point to the machinations of a single clandestine international organization of ruling elites (i.e., Jews, the IMF, the United Nations, the Vatican) or by stressing the expansive nature of Common Law jurisdiction by virtue of the authority of the Magna Carta (Chapman 2010; Winningham 2011a).

The clear link between the ideologies of American far-right anti-government movements and Canadian Freemen-on-the-Land provides a useful starting point for exploring their respective threats to national security. Needless to say, there are distinct cultural and political differences between Canada and the United States that need to be taken into account during any sort of cross-national comparison. In terms of frequency and character, far-right and anti-government violence in the United States (Southern Poverty Law Center 2009; Perliger 2012) differs vastly from what is encountered in Canada (Perry and Scrivens 2015, 34–5). There are also larger socio-cultural issues to consider and contrast, such as differences in gun control laws and the amorphous political make-up of the Canadian Freemen. American anti-government and militia movements are steeped in a broader, older, pro-gun, Second Amendment culture spurred by lobbying groups such as the National Rifle Association. As a result, it is easier for them to gain access to automatic firearms compared to their Canadian contemporaries, who are constrained by more restrictive gun laws (see *Criminal Code* 1985). Notwithstanding a certain amount of pro-gun advocacy among some Canadian Freemen, legislative barriers preventing the ownership and acquisition of automatic firearms mean that the security threat posed by the Canadian Freemen is not completely analogous with similar American movements. Furthermore, the political leanings of Canadian Freemen are more varied than those of their largely far-right counterparts in the United States; north of the border, some adherents subscribe to leftist social-activist and anti-globalization ideals (Kivanc 2016), and others embrace an ideology more in line with that of American Sovereign Citizens (Brean 2014; Pruden 2015). The following section explores these and other cross-cultural differences in order to discern useful insights into what propels members of the Canadian Freemen to embrace terrorist violence.

Are the Canadian Freemen-on-the-Land a Threat to National Security?

The Canadian Freemen present particular challenges for front-line police officers and the legal system; however, in their current incarnation they likely do not pose a serious threat to national security. This is largely because they lack the organization, popular support, leadership, and resources that violent American anti-government far-right movements possessed in the 1980s and 1990s (Levitas 2002; Wright 2007). This does not mean, though, that the Canadian Freemen are a completely benign socio-political movement. The threat posed by the Canadian Freemen lies not in the movement itself but rather in their paranoid, conspiratorial, anti-government world view. In other words, the Freemen ideology is fertile soil for an ultra-radical fringe – that is, for small groups or lone actors who adopt a strategy of organized political violence against the state.[12]

A full exploration of the social dynamics involved in radicalization toward violence within Canadian anti-government movements like the Freemen is much needed, but impossible to address in the limited space available here. However, I hope to begin closing this lacuna in knowledge by identifying at least two conditions that may motivate fringe elements of the Canadian Freemen to escalate toward organized acts of terrorist violence: (1) the emergence of one or more charismatic leaders capable of credibly blending themes of violent resistance with the Freemen world view, and (2) one or more precipitating events (Crenshaw 1981) that galvanize collective sentiments of anger and outrage among the Canadian anti-government community. Below, I briefly outline how and why these conditions matter.

Charismatic Leadership

As I have pointed out elsewhere (Hofmann and Dawson 2014; Hofmann 2015; 2016), scholars have paid scant attention to how charismatic leaders influence radicalization toward violence within extremist political and terrorist organizations. The social-scientific concept of charisma and charismatic authority has been largely misapplied or misunderstood when the dynamics of terrorist radicalization are explored (Hofmann and Dawson 2014, 355–60). Yet many security studies scholars implicitly or explicitly recognize that charismatic leaders play an important role in determining whether or not certain groups ultimately adopt violence (Hofmann 2015, 711). In the context of North American anti-government extremism, it is evident that the violent world view adopted by certain members of far-right movements can be attributed, at least in part, to the narrative of armed resistance woven by a series of highly influential leaders and ideologues. By the 1960s, the core ideology of the American far right was being shaped by charismatic individuals such as William Potter Gale, Robert DePugh, James Ellison, David Duke, Louis Beam, Robert Miles, Robert Millar, and many others (Levitas 2002; Wright 2007, 44–69; Noble 2010). Over time, these leaders constructed a cohesive world view that blended elements of conspiracy theories, Christian identity, patriotism, antisemitism, and racism within an anti-government framework. But perhaps most importantly, the vast majority of these American leaders actively preached armed and in some cases violent resistance. By casting far-right actors as the final line of defence against the machinations of satanic enemies, they set the stage for acts of political violence inspired by far-right ideology (Juergensmeyer 2003). Indeed, violent far-right and anti-government actors almost universally justify their actions as a pre-emptive defence against the hostile intentions of their perceived enemies. Considering that similar themes of armed resistance and self-defence against a hostile government manifest themselves in Canadian Freemen rhetoric (Bell 2010; Hitchen 2014), a call to arms from a credible charismatic guru will likely find a certain number of followers among the movement's radical fringe.

At the time of writing, the Canadian Freemen do not possess a charismatic leader akin to those in the United States during the 1980s and early 1990s. It is evident on Web forum posts, online blogs, videos of seminars, and the comment sections of ideological videos that the most prominent Canadian Freemen guru, Robert Menard, has certain charismatic qualities that are legitimated and recognized by at least some of his followers; however, evidence suggests that repeated failures have diminished or weakened his credibility among his followers (Netolitzky 2016a, 626). Even so, unlike the leaders of American far-right anti-government movements that stimulated politically inspired violence in the 1980s and 1990s, Menard does not preach violent or armed resistance against the state. He plainly contends that the movement is not about violence, and he is quick to distance the Canadian Freemen from their counterparts in the United States (Global Toronto 2013; Kivanc 2016), although he previously stated that he has not completely discounted the need for armed resistance (CBC 2012). As a result, Menard likely has a moderating effect on attitudes toward organized political violence among his followers.

However, the potential remains for fringe members of the Canadian Freemen to adopt dangerous interpretations of his teachings. This danger is heightened for two reasons: first, Menard's weakened charismatic authority opens the door for other charismatic leaders with more violent agendas to arise (Dawson 2002); and second, the decentralized, cell-like nature of the Canadian Freemen is conducive to the emergence of "larger than life" charismatic leaders to arise in small, socially encapsulated groups of Freemen (Hofmann 2015). Both factors have been identified in the wider scholarly literature as precipitants to violence in socially isolated new religious movements (Bird 1993; Hall 2000; Robbins 2002; Lewis 2011) and in the radicalization toward violence in terrorist groups (Hofmann and Dawson 2014; Hofmann 2015).

Precipitant Events

The importance of precursor or precipitant events in the genesis of various types of social movements and collective action has been widely observed (Lieberson and Silverman 1965; Olzak 1989; Wiktorowicz 2002, 193; Snow et al. 2005). A near-universal component in the creation of any social movement of note has been some form of watershed moment that galvanized collective feelings of anger, discontent, fear, and other powerful emotions.[13] Like other social and political movements, precipitant events play an important role in motivating fringe members of these groups to embrace terrorist violence as a means of achieving their long-term organizational goals (Crenshaw 1981; Noricks 2009).[14]

In the context of North American anti-government movements over the last forty years, precipitant events have played an extremely important role in the radicalization toward violence among far-right actors and groups, such as Timothy McVeigh (Hamm 1997; Wright 2007), the Covenant, the Sword, and the Arm of the Lord (Noble 2010; Hofmann 2015), the Aryan Republican Army (Hamm 2002), and others (Levitas 2002). Highly publicized confrontations involving shootouts with law enforcement that resulted in the deaths of Christian Patriot martyrs Gordon Kahl and Robert Mathews in the 1980s (Wright 2007, 84–90), and the violent outcomes of the sieges at Ruby Ridge and Waco in the early 1990s (Doherty 2001; Levitas 2002; Tabor and Gallagher 1995; Wright 1995), helped unify a largely divided American far right. By no means were these precipitant events the sole causal factor; even so, they served as the metaphorical "last straw" that helped propel a number of far-right actors to embrace terrorism as a tactic. Perhaps most importantly, the defining feature of these precipitant events was some form of violent confrontation with agents of the state. These conflicts were held up by the leaders of far-right movements as definitive proof of the hostile intentions of the federal government and helped legitimate the collective fears of anti-government movements. This fact was not lost on American law enforcement. Guided by the efforts of religious studies scholars (Tabor and Gallagher 1995; Wright 1995; Wessinger 1999), American law enforcement agencies learned from their mistakes at Ruby Ridge and Waco and adopted a less belligerent and more conciliatory approach to dealing with contentious religious and anti-government movements. This, for the most part, has been an effective strategy. Subsequent standoffs with anti-government movements that ended relatively peacefully, such as the episode with the Montana Freemen (Rosenfeld 1997; Wessinger 1999; 2000), failed to spark the same sort of sentiment among the far right as the outcomes at Ruby Ridge and Waco.

While the values, world view, and mindset of 1980s and 1990s America are not completely analogous with contemporary Canadian society, there is an important lesson to be learned from the mistakes of American law enforcement. Canada's government and police must make a conscious effort to avoid initiating violence when confronted by individual or small groups of Freemen. The symbiotic relationship between perceived or actual persecution and the escalation toward violence in socially encapsulated movements has been noted by scholars of new religions (Hall and Schuyler 1998; Wessinger 2000; Robbins 2002, 63–5), particularly in cases where the "oppressed" group holds a paranoid, apocalyptical, and/or catastrophic world view.

Since casting the state as an active enemy engaged in overt or covert warfare against law-abiding citizens is at the core of Freeman thought, perceived or actual persecution is likely to reinforce their world view and catalyse hostile action. Gurus can use even justified acts of self-defence or pro-active policing to fuel the flames of discontent among the Freemen's sympathetic support base. This point is doubly important in the event of a prolonged armed stand-off between Canadian Freemen and law enforcement akin to Ruby Ridge and Waco. If such an event does occur, it is important that Canadian law enforcement confer with academics and experts versed in the ideology, rhetoric, and world view of the Freemen in order to avoid bloodshed (Rosenfeld 1997; Wessinger 1999). The hard lessons that US law enforcement learned from past confrontations helped them avoid violence during later events, such as the recent stand-off with an armed militia at the Oregon Malheur National Wildlife Refuge in 2016 (see Simon 2017). Any violent outcome, regardless of who initiated it, may serve as a tipping point for a radical fringe of Canadian Freemen to embrace terrorist violence in perceived defence of their rights. Knowledge of the beliefs, motives, and end goals of the Freemen, and of other anti-government movements, may be pivotal in negotiating a peaceful outcome to stand-offs with law enforcement and help prevent future acts of violence by anti-government movements.

Conclusion

Compared to the Islamist-inspired terrorist plots and attacks on Canadian soil over the last fifteen years, the security threat posed by Canadian anti-government movements like the Freemen-on-the-Land seems relatively small. Yet there is legitimate concern over the Freemen's potential for violence among Canadian security practitioners and law enforcement agencies (CSIS 2012; RCMP 2014), as well as a growing concern over right-wing extremist violence in general (Public Safety Canada 2017). Issues related to Canadian national security are dynamic and ever-changing, and like their partners in government and law enforcement, security scholars need to be prepared to adapt to emergent threats posed by anti-government movements. This chapter is a first attempt at understanding the beliefs, practices, and methods of the Canadian Freemen-on-the-Land and the conditions in which they could develop into a serious threat to national security.

Much more research is required before we can begin to develop a holistic understanding of the methods and motives of Canadian anti-government movements. There are several fruitful avenues that warrant scholarly attention. If, as I argue in this chapter, it is the Freemen's world view that poses the greatest threat to Canadian national security, then the extent to which ideology plays a role in the escalation toward terrorist violence among anti-government movements needs to be explored in more depth (Maynard 2014). It may be useful to explore the many interesting parallels in the use of social media and the internet by jihadists recruiting foreign fighters for Syria and Iraq and Canadian Freemen gurus reaching out to potential recruits. The comparison may prove to be important in helping construct credible counter-narratives (Klausen 2015; Gendron 2016). Finally, to better understand how and why only a small number of the radical fringe of larger anti-government movements radicalize toward terrorist violence (Della Porta 1988; Horgan 2005, 83–4; Dawson 2014, 66–7), efforts need to be made to identify and flesh out additional conditions that may propel anti-government actors toward violent political action. The logical next step is to begin gathering robust primary statistical and interview data from law enforcement, government agencies, and members of anti-government movements. The production of additional research on the Canadian Freemen and other anti-government movements, informed by quality primary data, is essential if we are to truly understand their place in the Canadian terrorism and counter-terrorism landscape.

NOTES

1 While grammatically incorrect, the use of dashes and the capitalization of "Land" is a convention used by Freemen.
2 The Freemen-on-the-Land movement is not unique to Canada. Members of the Freemen and their sympathizers are found in the United States (see Berger 2016), the United Kingdom (see Chapman 2010), Australia (see Thomas 2015), and other English-speaking countries. Various incarnations of the movement may refer to themselves as Freemen, Sovereign (or Sovran/Sovren) Citizens, Livings Souls, and/or Natural Persons, with naming choices based on nuances related to geographic, nationalistic, and doctrinal differences.
3 By necessity, these discussions are relatively brief and are not meant to be an exhaustive analysis. To my knowledge, this chapter is the first attempt to understand and analyse the Canadian Freemen as a socio-political movement. The existing legal and academic scholarship on the Canadian Freemen has focused largely on the methods and implications of their use of pseudo-legal paper warfare strategies, which involve filing or threatening to levy fictitious debts, liens, and legal obligations to privately prosecute detractors (see, *Meads v. Meads* 2012; Kent and Willey 2013, 324–9; Perry and Scrivens 2015, 21–30; Netolitzky 2016a, 2016b).
4 See, for example, http://worldfreemansociety.org/forum/index and http://wfs.me and https://www.facebook.com/TheFreemanMovement for open, closed, and social networking examples respectively.
5 Harkening back to the authoritative legal roots of the Magna Carta, "Common Law" is the alternative pseudo-legal system to which the Freemen-on-the-Land subscribe.
6 The "one world government" or "New World Order" conspiracy theory posits the existence of a shadowy cabal of social and economic elites who have a globalist agenda of uniting the world under a single, totalitarian regime. Adherents of this theory argue that the establishment of a one-world government will lead to the dissolution of sovereign nation-states, the stripping of inalienable rights (e.g., to gun ownership), and the

centralization of political power among a small number of elites, as well as, possibly, serve as the precursor to some form of apocalyptical event (i.e., the time of tribulations prior to the second coming of Christ).

7 David Icke's lizard people theory contends that giant shapeshifting reptilian humanoids have infiltrated the highest echelons of government, media, and popular culture around the globe and are secretly controlling and manipulating world events. For more information on the lizard people and similar conspiratorial theories, see Barkun (2013).

8 A comprehensive overview of the pseudo-legal paper warfare techniques used by the Canadian Freemen and other Organized Pseudolegal Commercial Arguments (OPCA) movements is beyond the scope of this chapter. It has been covered in detail elsewhere (see *Meads v. Meads* 2012; Netolitzsky 2016b).

9 For example, if a police officer or judge asks a Freeman, "Are you John Smith?" (their "straw man" identity), and the Freeman confirms this rather than using his "living person" identity (i.e., John of the Family/Clan/House of Smith), they believe this establishes "joinder," which legally fuses the two identities together. In short, Freeman believe that if they are not careful in their verbal and written interactions with agents of the government, they can accidentally enter into a legally binding contract with the state.

10 For example, the election of President Barack Obama in 2008 led to fears of a hostile military takeover and a resurgence of militia and Patriot movements in the United States (Southern Poverty Law Center 2009). Another more recent example is the paranoia surrounding a large-scale US military training exercise during the summer of 2015, dubbed operation "Jade Helm." Far-right conspiracy theorists and their adherents saw that exercise as a prelude to the establishment of martial law by President Obama, and encouraged citizens to stockpile weapons and ammunition in order to protect themselves (see Fernandez 2015). In Canada, there is growing concern that Freemen ideology has found traction among certain segments of angry and disenfranchised First Nations communities (see Bronskill 2013; Moore 2013).

11 Most of the efforts of prominent Canadian gurus to hybridize Freemen thought with Canadian values involve distancing themselves from the actions and ideology (i.e., gun rights, Christian overtones, racism/anti-semitism) espoused by certain of their American counterparts. An example of this can be found in a recent interview (see Kivanc 2016), in which Freemen guru Robert Menard acknowledges that Canada does not have "the gun mentality that [American sovereign citizens] have" and that he "could see [a Canadian] revolution, if it happened, to be far more peaceful [than a similar American revolution]." Despite these cosmetic rhetorical differences in the interviews he gives to the media, Menard's core message

in the ideological material he posts online is remarkably similar to the one embraced by American Freemen/Sovereign Citizens (see Berger 2016): belief in the widespread dissatisfaction of the common man with unjust government, conspiratorial overtones that cast the government as a hostile entity, and the ability/duty to free oneself from governmental control.

12 The inability of terrorism scholars to explain why only a select few individuals among a larger support base escalate toward the commission of terrorist violence is better known as the "explanatory gap" (see Della Porta 1988; Horgan 2005, 83–4; Dawson 2014, 66–7). The brief discussion that follows is not meant to drastically narrow the explanatory gap, but rather, is intended to be a first step in understanding some of the potential motivations that may cause a small subset of Canadian Freemen to engage in political violence.

13 A recent example of this is the emergence of the Black Lives Matter movement in the United States after the 2013 acquittal of George Zimmerman in the shooting death of Trayvon Martin.

14 There are numerous relevant examples of precipitant events contributing to the creation of terrorist movements, such as the 1969 shooting of Black Panther Fred Hampton (Weather Underground), Ariel Sharon's visit to the Temple Mount in 2000 (the second Palestinian intifada), and the 2011 failure of the Arab Spring in Syria (the rise of ISIS and other jihadist groups).

REFERENCES

Anti-Defamation League. 2012. *The Lawless Ones: The Resurgence of the Sovereign Citizen Movement.* http://www.adl.org/combating-hate/domestic-extremism-terrorism/c/the-lawless-ones-sovereign-citizen-movement.html.

Balko, R. 2013. *Rise of the Warrior Cop: The Militarization of America's Police Forces.* New York: PublicAffairs.

Barkun, M. 1996. Religion, Militias, and Oklahoma City: The Mind of Conspiratorialists. *Terrorism and Political Violence* 8(1): 50–64. https://doi.org/10.1080/09546559608427332.

– 1997. *Religion and the Racist Right: The Origins of the Christian Identity Movement.* Chapel Hill: University of North Carolina Press.

– 2013. *A Culture of Conspiracy: Apocalyptic Visions in Contemporary America.* Berkeley: University of California Press.

Bell, S. 2010. "Who are Canada's 'Freemen'?" *National Post*, 29 October.

– 2012. "Slapping down Freeman 'scams'; Judge's ruling denounces anti-government 'gurus.'" *National Post*, 29 September.

– 2013. Domestic extremists commit more terrorist acts in Canada than Islamists: report. *Postmedia News*, 3 January.

Berger, J.M. 2016. *Without Prejudice: What Sovereign Citizens Believe*. Occasional Paper, GW Program on Extremism. https://cchs.gwu.edu/sites/cchs.gwu. edu/files/downloads/Occasional%20Paper_Berger.pdf.

Bérubé, M., and A. Campana. 2015. "Les violences motives par la haine. Idéologies et modes d'action des extrémistes de droite au Canada." *Criminologie* 48(1): 215–34. https://doi.org/10.7202/1029355ar.

Bilinsky, D. 2012. "The Freeman-on-the-Land Movement." *Law Society of British Columbia Bencher's Bulletin* 4. https://www.lawsociety.bc.ca/page. cfm?cid=2627.

Bird, F.B. 1993. "Charisma and Leadership in New Religious Movements." In *Handbook of Cults and Sects in America*, vol. B, ed. D.G. Bromley and J.K. Hadden, 75–92. Greenwich: JAI Press.

Bjorgo, T. 1995. *Terror from the Extreme Right*. London: Frank Cass.

– 2004. *Root Causes of Terrorism: Myths, Reality, and Ways Forward*. London: Routledge.

Brean, J. 2014. "Moncton shooting accused may be a classic 'pseudo-commando' with anti-government Freeman ideology." *National Post*, 5 June.

Bronskill, Jim. 2013. "Freemen-on-the-Land movement a 'threat to officer and public safety': report." *Postmedia News*, 24 October.

Carter, Adam. 2013. "Dean Clifford, Freemen guru, arrested on Canada-wide warrant." *CBC News*, 26 November. http://www.cbc.ca/news/canada/ hamilton/news/dean-clifford-freemen-guru-arrested-on-canada-wide-warrant-1.2439237.

CBC. 2012. "The National: Interview with Robert Menard." https://www. youtube.com/watch?v=AH4E1gYjL2M.

– 2013. "'Freemen' take over Grande Prairie cabin, trappers say." *CBC News Edmonton*, 4 October. http://www.cbc.ca/news/canada/edmonton/ freemen-take-over-grande-prairie-cabin-trappers-say-1.1912428.

Chapman, Veronica. 2010. *Freedom ... is more than just ... a seven letter word*. [UK]: TamaRe House.

Clifford, D. 2013. "Making It Simple – Dean Clifford – Part 1/2." Video. https://www.youtube.com/watch?v=9xpisHFB0jw.

Coates, J. 1995. *Armed and Dangerous: The Rise of the Survivalist Right*. New York: Hill and Wang.

Crenshaw, M. 1981. "The Causes of Terrorism." *Comparative Politics* 13(4): 379–99. https://doi.org/10.2307/421717.

Criminal Code, R.S.C. 1985, c.46, s.84.

Crothers, L. 2004. *Rage on the Right: The American Militia Movements from Ruby Ridge to Homeland Security*. Lanham: Rowman and Littlefield.

CSIS (Canadian Security Intelligence Service). 2012. *Threat of Domestic Extremism – The Intelligence Assessment, Domestic Threat Environment in Canada: Left-Wing/Right-Wing Extremism*. Ottawa.

Dawson, L.L. 2002. "Crises of Charismatic Legitimacy and Violent Behaviour in New Religious Movements." In *Cults, Religion, and Violence*, ed. D.G. Bromley and J.G. Melton, 80–101. Cambridge: Cambridge University Press.

– 2014. "Trying to Make Sense of Home-Grown Terrorist Radicalization: The Case of the Toronto 18." In *Religious Radicalization and Securitization in Canada and Beyond*, ed. P. Bramadat and L.L. Dawson, 64–91. Toronto: University of Toronto Press.

Della Porta, D. 1988. "Recruitment Process in Clandestine Political Organizations: Italian Left-Wing Terrorism." In *International Social Movement Research*, ed. B. Klandermans, H. Kriesi, and S. Tarrow, 155–69. Greenwich: JAI Press.

Diamond, S. 1995. *Roads to Dominion: Right-Wing Movements and Political Power in the United States*. New York: Guilford Press.

Doherty, J.S. 2001. *Learning Lessons from Waco: When the Parties Bring Their Gods to the Negotiation Table*. Syracuse: Syracuse University Press.

Durham, M. 2000. *The Christian Right, the Far Right, and the Boundaries of American Conservatism*. Manchester: Manchester University Press.

Fernandez, M. 2015. "Jade Helm military exercise ends, with little fanfare and less paranoia." *New York Times*, 16 September. http://www.nytimes.com/2015/09/17/us/jade-helm-military-exercise-ends-with-little-fanfare-and-less-paranoia.html?_r=0.

Fleishman, D. 2004. "Paper Terrorism: The Impact of the 'Sovereign Citizen' on Local Government." *Public Law Journal* 7: 7–10.

FreeMan Society of Canada. 2012. Claim Your Rights As A Freeman on the Land [*sic*]. http://freemansocietyofcanada.webs.com/aboutus.htm.

Gendron, A. 2016. "The Call to Jihad: Charismatic Preachers and the Internet." *Studies in Conflict and Terrorism* [early access]. http://www.tandfonline.com/doi/abs/10.1080/1057610X.2016.1157406?src=recsys.

Gibson, J.W. 1994. *Warrior Dreams: Paramilitary Culture in Post-Vietnam America*. New York: Hill and Wang.

Global Toronto. 2013. "Interview with Robert Menard: Director of the World Freeman Society." 11 September. https://www.youtube.com/watch?v=4_xYH2GUyN8.

Graveland, B. 2013a. "Freemen-on-the-Land 'embassy' takes over Alberta pensioner's rental property." *National Post*, 23 September. http://news.nationalpost.com/news/canada/freemen-on-the-land-embassy-takes-over-alberta-pensioners-rental-property.

– 2013b. « La police de Calgary arête un militant antigouvernemental recherché au Québec. » *La Presse Canadienne*, 27 September. http://quebec.huffingtonpost.ca/2013/09/27/la-police-de-calgary-arr_n_4006042.html.

– 2013c. "Little-known 'sovereign citizen' movement emerged from shadows in 2013." *Canadian Press*, 18 December.

– 2013d. "'Sovereign citizen' movement in spotlight: Authorities in Canada more aware." *Saskatoon StarPhoenix*, 21 December.

Hall, J.R. 2000. *Apocalypse Observed: Religious Movements, Social Order, and Violence in North America, Europe, and Japan*. London: Routledge.

Hall, J.R., and P. Schuyler. 1998. "Apostasy, Apocalypse, and Religious Violence: An Exploratory Comparison of Peoples Temple, the Branch Davidians, and the Solar Temple." In *The Politics of Religious Apostasy: The Role of Apostates in the Transformation of Religious Movements*, ed. D.G. Bromley, 139–70. Westport: Prager.

Hamm, M.S. 1997. *Apocalypse in Oklahoma: Waco and Ruby Ridge Revenged*. Boston: Northeastern University Press.

– 2002. *In Bad Company: America's Terrorist Underground*. Boston: Northeastern University Press.

Hitchen, I. 2014. "Accused threatened police: Crown." *Brandon Sun*, 9 December.

Hofmann, D.C. 2015. "Quantifying and Qualifying Charisma: A Theoretical Framework for Measuring the Presence of Charismatic Authority in Terrorist Groups." *Studies in Conflict and Terrorism* 38(9): 710–33. https://doi.org/10.1080/1057610X.2015.1048100.

– 2016. "The Influence of Charismatic Authority on Operational Strategies and Attack Outcomes of Terrorist Groups." *Journal of Strategic Security* 9(2): 14–46. https://doi.org/10.5038/1944-0472.9.2.1486.

Hofmann, D.C., and L.L. Dawson. 2014. "The Neglected Role of Charismatic Authority in the Study of Terrorist Groups and Radicalization." *Studies in Conflict and Terrorism* 37(4): 348–68. https://doi.org/10.1080/10576 10X.2014.879436.

Horgan, J. 2005. *The Psychology of Terrorism*. London: Routledge.

Humphreys, A. 2013. "Judges losing patience as anti-government tax-deniers clogging courts with 'absurd' claims." *Postmedia News*, 7 August.

Juergensmeyer, M. 2003. *Terror in the Mind of God: The Global Rise in Religious Violence*. Berkeley: University of California Press.

Johanson, Jace. 2009. "Resources, Gurus, and Followers." Web forum post. http://worldfreemansociety.org/forum/43-general-discussion/14509-resources-gurus-and-followers.

Kent, Stephen A., and Robin Willey. 2013. "Sects, Cults, and the Attack on Jurisprudence." *Rutgers Journal of Law and Religion* 14: 306–60.

Kivanc, J. 2016. "We spoke to a leader in the Freemen on the land movement about the Oregon standoff." *Vice Canada*, 8 January. https://www.vice.com/en_ca/read/we-spoke-to-a-leader-in-the-freemen-on-the-land-movement-about-the-oregon-standoff.

Klausen, J. 2015. "Tweeting the *Jihad*: Social Media Networks of Western Foreign Fighters in Syria and Iraq." *Studies in Conflict and Terrorism*m 38(1): 1–22. https://doi.org/10.1080/1057610X.2014.974948.

Levitas, D. 2002. *The Terrorist Next Door: The Militia Movement and the Radical Right*. New York: Thomas Dunne Books.

Lewis, J.R. 2011. *Violence and New Religious Movements*. New York: Oxford University Press.

Lieberson, S., and A.R. Silverman. 1965. "The Precipitants and Underlying Conditions of Race Riots." *American Sociological Review* 26: 902–8. https://doi.org/10.2307/2090575.

Maynard, J.L. 2014. "Rethinking the Role of Ideology in Mass Atrocities." *Terrorism and Political Violence* 26(5): 821–41. https://doi.org/10.1080/09546553.2013.796934.

Meads v. Meads. 2012. ABQB 571. Court of Queen's Bench of Alberta.

Menard, R. 2012. "Freeman on the land: Robert Menard in Toronto – December 2010 – Part 2." Video. 31 May. https://www.youtube.com/watch?v=BbGU1Y91KwE.

Menard, R., and L. Denis. 2011. "Freeman Lectures – Robert Menard, Luke Denise – On Money." Video. 30 November. https://www.youtube.com/watch?v=3h6-_qhiTnc.

Miller, R.L. 1996. *Drug Warriors and Their Prey: From Police Power to Police State*. Westport: Praeger.

Moore, Dene. 2013. "'Sovereign citizen' movement worrying officials as 30,000 claim they 'freed' themselves from Canada's laws." *National Post*, 2 September. http://news.nationalpost.com/news/canada/sovereign-citizen-movement-worrying-officials-as-30000-claim-they-freed-themselves-from-canadas-laws.

Netolitzky, D. 2016a. "The History of the Organized Pseudolegal Commercial Argument Phenomenon in Canada." *Alberta Law Review* 53(3): 609–42. https://doi.org/10.29173/alr422.

– 2016b. "Organized Pseudolegal Commercial Arguments [OPCA] in Canada: An Attack on the Legal System." *Journal of Parliamentary and Political Law* 10: 1–44.

Newman, E. 2006. "Exploring the 'Root Causes' of Terrorism." *Studies in Conflict and Terrorism* 29(8): 749–72. https://doi.org/10.1080/10576100600704069.

Noble, K. 2010. *Tabernacle of Hate: Seduction into Right-Wing Extremism*. Syracuse: Syracuse University Press.

Noricks, D. 2009. "The Root Causes of Terrorism." In *Social Science for Counterterrorism: Putting the Pieces Together*, ed. P.K. Davis and K. Cragin, 11–70. Arlington: RAND Corporation.

Olzak, S. 1989. "Labor Unrest, Immigration, and Ethnic Conflict in Urban America, 1880–1914." *American Journal of Sociology* 94(6): 1303–33. https://doi.org/10.1086/229156.

Perliger, A. 2012. "Challengers from the Sidelines: Understanding America's Violent Far-Right." Combatting Terrorism Center at West Point. http://oai.dtic.mil/oai/oai?verb=getRecord&metadataPrefix=html&identifier=ADA576380.

Perry, Barbara, David Hofmann, and Ryan Scrivens. 2017. "Broadening Our Understanding of Anti-Authority Movements in Canada." Working paper no. 17–02. The Canadian Network for Research on Terrorism, Security and Society (TSAS). http://tsas.ca/wp-content/uploads/2017/08/2017-02-Perry.compressed-1.pdf.

Perry, Barbara, and Ryan Scrivens. 2015. "Right Wing Extremism in Canada: An Environmental Scan." Public Safety Canada (Kanishka Project Contribution Program). Ottawa.

Pruden, J.G. 2015. "Police shooter espoused extremist Freemen-on-the-Land ideology on Facebook page." *Edmonton Journal*, 10 June. http://www.edmontonjournal.com/Police+shooter+espoused+extremist+Freemen+Land+ideology+Facebook+page/11127580/story.html.

Public Safety Canada. 2017. "2017 Public Report on the Terrorist Threat to Canada." https://www.publicsafety.gc.ca/cnt/rsrcs/pblctns/pblc-rprt-trrrst-thrt-cnd-2017/index-en.aspx.

Quan, D. 2012. "'Freeman on the Land' movement worries CSIS." *Times Colonist* [Victoria], 30 December. http://www.timescolonist.com/news/national/freeman-on-the-land-movement-worries-csis-1.37071.

RCMP. 2014. "Armed with Awareness." *Gazette Magazine* 76. http://www.rcmp-grc.gc.ca/gazette/vol76no1/cover-dossier/freeman-eng.htm.

Rivinius, Jessica. 2014. "Sovereign citizen movement perceived as top terrorist threat." National Consortium for the Study of Terrorism and Responses to Terrorism (START). http://www.start.umd.edu/news/sovereign-citizen-movement-perceived-top-terrorist-threat.

Robbins, T. 2002. "Sources of Volatility in Religious Movements." In *Cults, Religion, and Violence*, ed. D.G. Bromley and J.G. Melton, 57–79. Cambridge: Cambridge University Press.

Rosenfeld, J. 1997. "The Importance of the Analysis of Religion in Avoiding Violent Outcomes." *Nova Religio* 1(1): 72–95. https://doi.org/10.1525/nr.1997.1.1.72.

Sargent, L.T. 1995. *Extremism in America: A Reader*. New York: NYU Press.

Simon, N. 2017. "Oregon Standoff: A timeline of how the confrontation unfolded." *The Oregonian*, 9 February. http://www.oregonlive.com/pacific-northwest-news/index.ssf/2016/01/oregon_standoff_a_timeline_of.html.

Snow, D.A., S.A. Soule, and D.M. Cress. 2005. "Identifying the Precipitants of Homeless Protest across 17 U.S. Cities, 1980 to 1990." *Social Forces* 83(3): 1183–210. https://doi.org/10.1353/sof.2005.0048.

Southern Poverty Law Center. 2009. "The second wave: The return of the militias." https://www.splcenter.org/20090801/second-wave-return-militias.

Tabor, J.D., and E.V. Gallagher. 1995. *Why Waco? Cults and the Battle for Religious Freedom in America*. Berkeley: University of California Press.

Tanner, S., and A. Campana. 2014. "The Process of Radicalization: Right-Wing Skinheads in Quebec." TSAS working paper no. 14–107.

Think Free Be Free. 2015. "Violation tickets and student loans." http://www.thinkfree.ca/violation-tickets and http://www.thinkfree.ca/student-loans.

Thomas, J. 2015. "Sovereign citizens: Terrorism assessment warns of rising threat from anti-government extremists." *ABC News*, 30 November. http://www.abc.net.au/news/2015-11-30/australias-sovereign-citizen-terrorism-threat/6981114.

Topham, A. 2012. "Zionist-Jew controlled CSIS spy agency joins ADL in smear campaign again [*sic*] the Freemen on the Land movement in Canada." 13 October. http://www.radicalpress.com/?p=1856.

Vandenbrink, D. 2011. "Man insists laws do not apply to him." *Cornwall Standard Freeholder*, 15 August.

Wessinger, C. 1999. "Religious Studies Scholars, FBI Agents, and the Montana Freemen Standoff." *Nova Religio* 3(1): 36–44. https://doi.org/10.1525/nr.1999.3.1.36.

– 2000. *How the Millennium Comes Violently: From Jonestown to Heaven's Gate.* New York: Seven Bridges Press.

Wiktorowicz, Q. 2002. "Islamic Activism and Social Movement Theory: A New Direction for Research." *Mediterranean Politics* 7(3): 187–211. https://doi.org/10.1080/13629390207030012.

Wilhelm, T. 2013. "Former funeral director charged with threatening justice officials." *Postmedia News*, 17 April.

Winningham, G. 2011a. "Sovereignty – do you know who you are?" Pt 1 of 7. Video. 21 April. https://www.youtube.com/watch?v=SAVIh7MipX8.

– 2011b. "Sovereignty – do you know who you are?" Pt 3 of 7. Video. 21 April. https://www.youtube.com/watch?v=AlxqDUdf5Io.

Wise. 2013a. "Do you consent?" *World Freeman Society News*, 11 September. http://worldfreemansociety.org/do-you-consent.

– 2013b. "The great birth certificate (Ttust) scam: This is how they are enslaving you." *World Freeman Society News*, 1 September. http://worldfreemansociety.org/the-great-birth-certificate-trust-scam-this-is-how-they-are-enslaving-you.

World Freeman Society. 2015. *YouTube Channel.* Video. https://www.youtube.com/channel/UCk9a3COa_JDkzsvwS1BPMfA.

Wright, S.A. 1995. *Armageddon in Waco: Critical Perspectives on the Branch Davidian Conflict.* Chicago: University of Chicago Press.

– 2007. *Patriots, Politics, and the Oklahoma City Bombing.* Cambridge: Cambridge University Press.

Yogaretnam, S. 2012. "Accused in RCMP shootings released from Remand Centre." *Edmonton Journal*, 29 June.

5 Jihadism in the Digital Era: The Canadian Context and Responses

MAXIME BÉRUBÉ AND BENJAMIN DUCOL

In recent years, jihadist[1] terrorism has become an issue of top concern, and public authorities both in Europe and in North America are grappling with the shift this violent extremism is making toward smaller-scale, locally conceived attacks and/or attacks on foreign countries by individuals who are "inspired," "directed," or "remote-controlled" by jihadist organizations and their propaganda (Hegghammer 2016; Neumann 2016; Callimachi 2017). Many have identified the internet as a crucial element when it comes to understanding the transnational diffusion of jihadi narratives over the past decade (Torres, Jordán, and Horsburgh 2006; Ducol, 2015). Indeed, digital environments provide new avenues for jihadi organizations and their followers to mobilize, disseminate, and frame their militancy across territorial borders (Zelin 2013; Lohlker 2013). They allow the jihadi movement to convey motivational frames that increase the likelihood that some individuals will sympathize with and join violent extremist groups and clandestine networks (Matusitz 2015; Veilleux-Lepage 2016).

In this chapter, we explore how Canada has been directly affected by this new digital era of jihadism. Our attention focuses foremost on the social and communication uses of the internet by jihadi militants and sympathizers in the Canadian context. We discuss the dissemination of jihadi narratives through the lens of cyberspace and online environments, as well as measures that have been taken in the Canadian context to undermine this phenomenon.

The first section of this chapter offers an overview of how Canada and Canadians have been portrayed in online jihadi propaganda. More specifically, we address why, how, and under what circumstances Canada has been mentioned in this material, as well as how Canadians – including Mohamed Farah Shirdon, André Poulin, and John Maguire, who joined jihadi groups abroad, and Martin Couture-Rouleau and

Michael Zehaf-Bibeau, who carried out attacks on Canada soil in the name of jihad – have been portrayed or "crafted" for recruitment purposes. In the second section, we examine recent counter-measures that have been developed in Canada in response to the proliferation of jihadi material on the internet. We locate these measures within a typology that classifies them along a continuum ranging from legislative initiatives – including provisions of the *Anti-Terrorism Act, 2015,* (also known as Bill C-51 or more simply C-51) – through "softer" activities involving online awareness campaigns and counter-narrative approaches. We conclude by assessing the potential these measures may hold for countering online jihadi propaganda and by discussing some of the challenges practitioners and policy-makers face in their efforts to accomplish this goal.

Canada and Canadians in Online Jihadi Propaganda: Towards an Increasing Trend?

Jihadi groups and their sympathizers, like almost everyone in our "digital society," have increased their presence on the internet over the past two decades. They use it mainly "for propaganda, psychological warfare, and weapons tutorials" (Weimann 2014, 1), but also to inform, communicate with, and mobilize followers through a variety of diffusion channels (Conway 2012; Winter 2015). A significant amount of jihadi material is available on almost all common social media platforms, including Facebook, Twitter, and YouTube (Weimann 2009; Prucha and Fisher 2013; Stern and Berger 2015, 147–75; Klausen 2015), as well as through instant messaging systems, such as KIK, WhatsApp, and Telegram (Bloom, Tiflati, and Horgan 2017). Nearly all major violent jihadi groups, be they global or local, have also developed a strong media production capacity that includes small media teams and official media production houses. These structures mainly produce videos and audio messages, though some also manufacture online propaganda magazines, such as (in English) *Inspire, Dabiq, Resurgence, al-Risalah,* and (in French) *Dar al-Islam.* This "high jihadisphere"[2] has emerged out of the main official media production houses of al Qaeda (AQ), such as as-Sahab Foundation for Media Production (al Qaeda Central), Al-Andalus Foundation (al Qaeda in the Islamic Maghreb), and Al-Malahem Media (al Qaeda in the Arabic Peninsula). Regarding Islamic State (IS), the al-Furqan Media Foundation is a leading media group; others include al-Hayat Media Center, al-I'tisaam Media Foundation, Ajnaad Media, al-Himma Foundation, and the A'maq News Agency. In recent years, this "high jihadisphere" has been complemented by the emergence of a "low jihadisphere" of unaffiliated sympathizers who have helped legitimize and publicize jihadi narratives, predominantly through social media and encrypted communication channels (Veilleux-Lepage 2016; Huey and Peladeau 2016).

Content, from both the "high" and "low" jihadispheres, has increased in recent years (Fisher 2015; Winter and Bach-Lombardo 2016), and as we illustrate below, Canada has become a target of that content. In addition, Canadians jihadi sympathizers have produced and disseminated their own propaganda and narratives. For example, Quebec resident Saïd Namouh was convicted in 2010 for his role in a bomb plot in Austria and Germany while serving as a key member of the Global Islamic Media Front (GIMF), an al Qaeda–affiliated online media infrastructure that disseminates jihadi propaganda internationally. Even before Namouh's arrest, ties between the online jihadi movement and Canada were observable; for example, the GIMF's initial website was referred to as the work of a mysterious "Abu Banan," based in Montreal (Torres Soriano 2012, 772–3).

The amount of online content designed to appeal to Canadian audiences has increased in the recent years. Given that jihadi online narratives and figures may play a role in the phenomenon of Canadians joining jihadi groups abroad (Carter, Maher, and Neumann 2014; Dawson and Amarasingam in this volume), or threatening or carrying out violent actions in Canada, it is essential to have a better understanding of how jihadi propaganda and this online counterculture (Ramsay 2013) is currently targeting Canadian audiences, through the increasing presence of (a) Canadian figures and (b) mentions of Canada in jihadi propaganda.

Prior to the Syrian conflict, Canada and Canadians were rarely mentioned explicitly in jihadi propaganda. The increasing attention paid to Canada and other Western nations in this material is likely related to the proliferation of English-language jihadi propaganda since 2009.[3] For example, in March 2013, al Qaeda in the Arabian Peninsula (AQAP), the Yemeni branch of AQ, launched its tenth issue of *Inspire* magazine (Lemieux, Brachman, Levitt, and Wood 2014), in which the prominent jihadi ideologue Abu Musab al-Suri identified Canada as one of the most important Western states to target for terrorism (*Inspire* 2013, 24). In fact, Canada was cited by al-Suri as a close ally of the United States and as a prospective target for jihadi violent actors because of its significant community of Muslim citizens. Abu Musab al-Suri has been advocating decentralized and individual jihad since the early 2000s (Lia 2009) and has repeatedly attempted to convince Muslims living in countries like Canada to practise a decentralized form of jihad by committing attacks in their own countries.

*Canadian Figures in Jihadi Propaganda: Personal Stories
as Mobilizing Examples*

It appears that in 2014, in the context of the Syrian conflict, the Canadian presence in jihadi propaganda intensified; a surge of Canadian nationals or residents joining jihadi groups on the ground could be linked to this. Farah Mohamed Shirdon (aka Abu Usamah Somali) was one of the first Canadians to appear in an IS propaganda video; he was quickly spotted by Canadian media after its online release (CBC News 2014; Vice News 2014). In April 2014, the young Calgarian appeared in an al-Furqan Media video, in which he gave a short speech that explained why he had "emigrated" from Canada to Syria: "This is a message for Canada ... we are coming, we will destroy you ... I made *hirjah* to this land for one reason alone, I left comfort for one reason alone, for Allah." The video concluded with Shirdon burning his Canadian passport on camera (Al-Furqan Media 2014a). In this video, Shirdon was portrayed not only as a charismatic leader with considerable influence (he is standing in front a group of other "fighters"), but also as a Western youth who had chosen the path of jihad. A few months later, Shirdon was contacted by a VICE reporter; live from Mosul, he granted a webcam interview that offered a highly positive picture of IS. He also tried to inspire fear among Western populations, especially among Americans, by claiming that IS was mobilizing in the United States and that sophisticated plots were under way (Vice News 2014). Another framing of Shirdon was his claim that he and his friends would prefer to be home but were fighting because they were "tired of oppression"; he emphasized that they *had* to fight. All of Shirdon's appearances helped IS present a personification of the jihadi ideal for Canadian audiences: the sincere commitment and true devotion of a young Canadian to the larger jihadi cause.

Another Canadian figure who has been widely shown in jihadi propaganda out of Syria is André Poulin (aka Abu Muslim), a young Ontarian who left Canada in 2012 soon after converting to Islam. He appeared in an eleven-minute video that was posted online in July 2014 (al-Hayat Media 2014a). The video, part of which was included in the documentary-style video *Flames of War* released in 2014 by al-Hayat Media (al-Hayat Media 2014b), provided detailed information on the history, background, and martyrdom of this Canadian foreign fighter. It included poignant sequences of Poulin alive, explaining who he was and why he went to Syria; other sequences showed him fighting for IS during the assault at Aleppo airport during which he lost his life; in final images, a narrator glorified him, presenting him as a heroic role model. In form and content, André Poulin's staged video amounted to a typical IS recruitment narrative whose purpose was to convince others to join the group. As Braddock and Horgan (2016) noted in their case study of Poulin, the use of biographical information and the example of a young Canadian who gave up everything to embrace the path to jihad resulted in a strong narrative crafted with different levels and themes and thereby speaking to a range of audiences (Braddock and Horgan 2016, 395–8).

John Maguire (aka Abu Anwar al-Canadi), also from Ontario, was another convert Canadian foreign fighter who joined jihadi groups in Syria in early 2013. He too participated in staged IS propaganda. In a video released by al-I'tisaam Media in December 2014, he urged Canadians to influence the government to cease military operations in Muslim countries (al-I'tisaam Media 2014; CBC 2014). In that same video, he referenced the October 2014 attacks in Canada in Saint-Jean-sur-Richelieu and Ottawa and encouraged Muslims in Canada to "follow the example of brother Ahmad Rouleau [Martin Couture-Rouleau]" by carrying out lone-wolf attacks on Canadian soil.

Print and online media have also featured Canadian-specific individual stories. In early 2016, two Canadian converts from Alberta were featured in *Dabiq* in an article titled "Among the Believers Are Men" (*Dabiq* 2016, 37). In addition to the symbolic dimension attached to their conversion from Christianity to Islam, the article emphasized the heroic journey of these two young men from Calgary to Egypt, and then to Syria. Stressing the exploits and pious values of these two Canadian figures, the same *Dabiq* edition praised another Canadian, Ali Mohamed Dirie, who was sentenced to seven years as a member of the Toronto 18 plot in 2006, released in 2012, and is believed to have been killed in Syria in 2013 (CBC News 2013).

Canadian Mentions in Jihadi Propaganda: Canada as a Target for Jihadists

Any discussion of recent jihadi propaganda related to Canada would be incomplete without mention of the deceased IS spokesperson Abu Muhammad al-Adnani and his call for terrorist attacks in Canada. In June 2014 a soundtrack was posted by al-Furqan Media in which al-Adnani urged the killings of American, European, Australian, or Canadian disbelievers (Al-Furqan Media 2014b). First delivered in Arabic, it was subsequently translated into English and published in the September 2014 issue of *Dabiq* (2014, 9), and inter alia included the infamous call: "If you can kill a disbelieving American or European – especially the spiteful and filthy French – or an Australian, or a Canadian, or any other disbeliever from the disbelievers waging war, including the citizens of the countries that entered into a coalition against the Islamic State, then rely upon Allah, and kill him in any manner or way however it may be" (Weiss 2014). The following month, two Canadians decided to conduct terror attacks on their own. First, Martin Couture Rouleau (aka Ahmad Rouleau) rammed two Canadian soldiers with his car in Saint-Jean-sur-Richelieu, killing Warrant officer Patrice Vincent. Then, two days later, Michael Zehaf-Bibeau shot and killed a Canadian soldier at the War Memorial in Ottawa before launching an armed assault on Parliament Hill. Those two incidents were subsequently highlighted and celebrated in jihadi propaganda material, particularly in IS's *Dabiq* magazine. John Cantlie, a British journalist kidnapped by IS in 2012, states that "these attacks were the direct result of the Shaykh's [Abu Muhammad al-Adnani] call to action" (*Dabiq* 2014, 37). IS was not the only jihadi group to have used the two Canadians for propaganda purposes. In May 2017, AQAP released a video message from its emir, Qasim al-Raymi, calling on Muslims to undertake lone-actor attacks against the West in retaliation for "a tragedy upon Muslims." In the video, Al-Raymi noted that attacks can be "easy and simple," and the opening sequence showed a number of successful solo jihadi attacks, pointing to the Canadian domestic terrorists Michael Zehaf-Bibeau and Martin Couture-Rouleau (al-Malahem Media 2017). In May 2017, an article published in the ninth issue of *Rumiyah* magazine titled "Just Terror Tactics: Hostage-Taking" identified Canada, among other Western countries, as a target for terrorist attacks, and named Michael Zehaf-Bibeau and Martin Couture-Rouleau as examples worthy of emulation (*Rumiyah* 2017, 46).

Until his death in 2016, Al-Adnani's repeated appearances in *Dabiq* magazine after the fifth edition were accompanied by specific mentions of Canada. For its part, AQ mentioned Canada specifically on several occasions in its propaganda materials, including the second issue of *Resurgence* magazine in June 2015 (*Resurgence* 2015, 68) and the fourteenth issue of *Inspire* magazine in September 2015 (*Inspire* 2015, 9). In December 2017, the release of the seventeenth issue of *Inspire* by AQAP included an article titled "Train Derail Operations," which encouraged jihadi sympathizers to sabotage passenger and freight trains in the United States and suggested how (*Inspire* 2017). The same edition contained visual and textual references to Canada, including photographs appearing to show the aftermath of the 2013 catastrophic train derailment in Lac-Mégantic, and an allusion to the 1979 freight train derailment in Mississauga, offering these as examples of potential action against trains for jihadi militants (*Inspire* 2017, 92).

All these examples demonstrate that Canada has been increasingly prominent in jihadi online content in recent years and that Canadian figures involved in the Syrian jihad have been more visible than any other Canadian jihadists before them. These trends may be explained by the greater linguistic diversification of jihadist propaganda in general (especially the growth of English-language material) over the past decade, as well as the presence of a number of Canadians among jihadi groups in Syria. Thus, there are increasing opportunities for jihadist organizations to use them for mobilization and propaganda purposes.

Countering Jihadism Online: A Typology of Measures

In the second part of this chapter, we look at the multiple strategies that have been developed in response to the increasingly important digital footprint of the global jihadi movement. Our discussion provides an overview of recent initiatives aimed at countering online jihadism in the Canadian context. Canadian measures and strategies that intend to counter or at least to address online jihadi discourses and contents can be categorized along a bidimensional typology (Figure 5.1). The first dimension (X) refers to the actors involved in countering jihadi materials and narratives online. This includes counter-measures led by Canadian government and other governmental agencies, as well as initiatives and programs advanced by civil society actors. The second dimension (Y) refers to the nature of the initiatives intended to counter jihadi narratives and content in cyberspace. This refers to the counter-measures themselves, whether hard or soft (Saltman and Russell 2014). Hard counter-measures or initiatives might be defined as measures that aim to target extremist messaging through negative, coercive, and punitive actions. Soft counter-measures or initiatives are oriented more toward addressing and challenging extremist propaganda by limiting its appeal and empowering alternative narratives online that might emerge from various community voices.

This spectrum of hard and soft measures deployed by multiple actors is in line with contemporary counterterrorism strategies – for example, with Canada's Building Resilience Against Terrorism (2012). Chenoweth and Dugan (in this volume) in their dataset note the range of actions undertaken by government to address terrorism. Similarly, Crenshaw and LaFree (2017, 28–31) note the expansive nature of contemporary counterterrorism, which encompasses measures at the subnational, national, international, and other levels. That multiple approaches to countering online jihadist (and other) terrorism exist and are contemplated is, therefore, no surprise.

Figure 5.1. Typology of Canadian counter-measures and initiatives against online jihadism

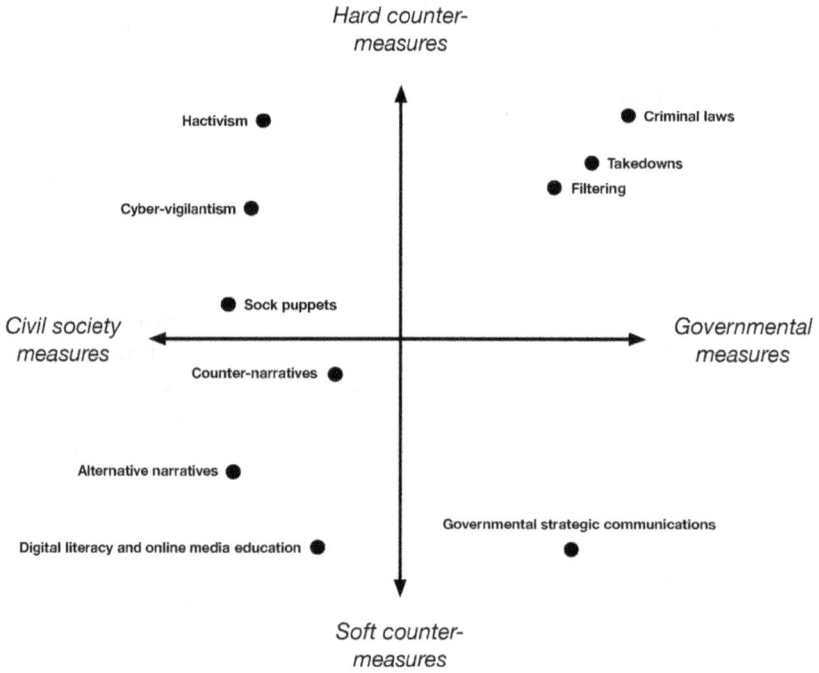

Governmental Hard Counter-Measures: The Criminalization of Online Jihadism?

In the Canadian context, hard counter-measures or initiatives are those initiated by the governmental apparatus. The first category of repressive counter-measures can be traced to the judicial domain (Forcese 2007). With the *Anti-Terrorism Act, 2015*, these include new criminal offences related to advocating or promoting "terrorism offences in general" and the introduction of a new concept of "terrorist propaganda" defined as "any writing, sign, visible representation or audio recording that advocates or promotes the commission of terrorism offences in general ... or counsels the commission of a terrorism offence" (Forcese and Roach 2015a, 323–4). These judicial measures in part target the advocacy or the promotion of terrorism offences online; they include the prohibition of communicating and spreading through cyberspace extremist content and jihadi propaganda. Since 2007, the Canadian government had repeatedly expressed its interest in complementing the existing antiterrorism legal framework (Forcese and Roach 2015a, 323–6) by taking punitive measures against the "glorification of terrorist activity" (Forcese and Roach 2015b).

In response to the two terror incidents that took place in October 2014 and the growing number of Canadian foreign fighters travelling to Syria/Iraq, the Conservative government adopted punitive measures to facilitate the prosecution of online extremist material. Bill C-51 distances itself from the United Kingdom's glorification offence – whereby under the UK *Terrorism Act* (2006) it is now an offence to express "any form of praise or celebration" for terrorist activity or entities (United Kingdom 2006); however, it does criminalize extremist speech, and in doing so appears to draw more directly from the Australian "advocacy of terrorism" offence framework (Forcese and Roach 2015a, 329). Under the Australian legislation, it is an offence to intentionally urge, counsel, promote, or encourage an act of terrorism (Australia 2015). As discussed by Forcese and Roach (2015b), the new Canadian offence introduced by Bill C-51 into the *Criminal Code* was framed as a "speech crime," but it raised several issues, including its practical application and its compatibility with the Canadian Charter of Rights and Freedoms. Following a report by the Standing Committee on Public Safety and National Security (2017), Bill C-59 was introduced in June 2017 by the new Liberal government with the intention of reforming the terrorist speech offences introduced in C-51. Ratified in June 2019, C-59 maintains the overall criminalization of extremist content and propaganda while proposing to change the *Criminal Code* wording from "knowingly advocates and promotes the commission of terrorism offences in general" to "counsels another person to commit a terrorism offence without identifying a specific terrorism offence." Similarly, the definition of "terrorist propaganda" has been modified by C-59 from "any writing, sign, visible representation or audio recording that advocates or promotes the commission of terrorism offences in general ... or counsels the commission of a terrorism offence" to "any writing, sign, visible representation or audio recording that counsels the commission of a terrorism offence," to overcome criticisms about the vagueness of C-51's formulations (Platt 2017).

In addition to the creation of new criminal offences in C-51, other "hard" counter-measures have been taken related to the filtering, blocking, and taking down of illegal content on the internet. Building on a provision introduced by the *Anti-Terrorism Act* of 2001 – that is, the omnibus legislation passed in the wake of 9/11, the *Anti-Terrorism Act of* 2015, allowed for court-ordered actions to remove terrorism material from the internet. Although a departure from previous Canadian counterterrorism, when compared to similar coercive measures in other states, Canada remained strictly bound by its normative and legal framework. For example, France has authorized the removal of online extremist materials and the takedown of entire websites simply through administrative decisions and without judicial oversight. Canadian law remains much more cautious when it comes to allowing public authorities to delete extremist materials online.

These new provisions are designed to reduce the volume of online propaganda, but their practical applications may be limited, for several key reasons. One such reason is the ease with which extremist organizations or sympathizers can simply upload new material, reopen new accounts, or repost content on any number of online spaces, including social media platforms. Indeed, as Fisher (2015) demonstrates, multiple postings by a range of actors on diverse platforms and applications is a purposeful strategy to ensure that material is available for sympathizers to access and disseminate. Thus, the takedown approach has led to a "whack-a-mole" situation, due in large part to the limited technical and human capacity of various actors, including law enforcement, to monitor the vast amount of data disseminated online on a daily basis (Arthur 2014). Nevertheless, some maintain that the suspension and suppression of online extremist content holds promise for curbing the spread of jihadi narratives through the internet (Berger and Perez 2016).

Positive perceptions of the whack-a-mole approach are premised on non-governmental actors identifying and reporting extremist content. An important aspect of this is the internet service providers (ISPs) themselves enforcing their terms of service as they relate to violent, criminal, terrorist, and other offences. Few envisage responsibility for policing the online world as being the sole responsibility of government security agencies. Indeed, several countries, including the UK (United Kingdom 2015) and Australia (2015), have asked the public to help authorities by reporting extremist materials distributed online. In a 2009 publication the RCMP noted that Canadians could respond in a variety of ways, including by reporting the material to ISPs or to the national ISP association, or by using the national security tip line to report extremist material encountered online (RCMP 2009). However, there is as yet no indication that the Canadian government intends to promote broader reporting practices as an national strategy for countering extremist material online. The RCMP has, however, made information more accessible to non-expert audiences with the online publication of the *Terrorism and Violent Extremism Awareness Guide* (RCMP 2016).

Non-Governmental Hard Counter-Measures: Hacktivism
and Cyber-Vigilantism

In the collective imagination, hard counter-measures are rarely associated with civil society actors. However, ISPs have considerable capacity and authority to take down offensive content or content that violates their terms of service. And ISPs are not the only civil society or non-governmental actors responding to online extremist material. The emergence of "cyber-vigilantes" (Huey, Nhan, and Broll 2012) suggests that a broader array of social actors are becoming more involved in the "policing" of online content. These are mainly anonymous Web users engaging in retributive actions (hacking, reporting, harassment, and so on) against online jihadi propaganda and armchair sympathizers, independent of any association with law enforcement. The rise of "cyber-vigilantes" battling the jihadi narrative in cyberspace is a relatively new phenomenon (Gladstone 2015). By exposing suspected social media accounts of jihadi sympathizers (on Twitter, Facebook, etc.) and encouraging users to report material that violates the law or an ISP's terms of service, "cyber-vigilantes" have introduced another means for the general public to initiate harder counter-measures (Huey, Nhan and Broll 2012).

The famous hacker group Anonymous has repeatedly declared war on the armed group IS; however, the vast majority of retributive actions appear to be carried out by individuals or small groups of loosely related cyber-activists. Gladstone (2015) highlights the "sock puppet accounts" (Huey and Kalyal, 2015) that are set up with the plain intention of deceiving others and overwhelming discussion forums, and Cottee (2015) observed that anonymous individuals respond online to mock pro-jihadi supporters on social media platforms. Indeed, the Canadian sock puppet activists on social media who have emerged over the past year have been engaged in a wide array of actions ranging from hacking and disruptive operations to more humorous ones such as the creation of parody social media accounts mocking IS itself as well as jihadi sympathizers (Leung 2015).

Governmental Soft Counter-Measures: Canada's Indirect
Counter-Narrative Strategy

By governmental soft counter-measures, we are referring mainly to counter-narrative initiatives as well as prevention and education programs whose aim is to strengthen individual resilience against the jihadi narrative and to empower communities to speak out against violent extremism. Counter-narrative strategies encompass a wide range of activities (Van Ginkel 2015), ranging from government strategic communications and targeted public information campaigns to online media initiatives promoting either "counter-" or "alternative" narratives.[4] In this domain, Canada has remained relatively cautious, and a broad Canadian public information campaign has yet to be unveiled (Bell 2015). Governmental counter-narrative efforts, especially on the internet and social media, are not risk-free and can lead to serious concerns about counter-productive messaging (Briggs and Feve 2013). Also, trust issues between governments and local communities and bureaucracy are among the reasons why governments may not be the best choice for taking the lead with digital counter-narrative initiatives. In this regard, foreign initiatives such as the French government's counter–violent extremism (CVE) campaign "Stop djihadisme"[5] and the US State Department's "Think Again, Turn Away" campaign launched in 2013[6] have been criticized for the strongly "moralistic" and "binary" tone they take. The Americans' "Welcome to the 'Islamic State' land" video became a viral success (Miller and Higham 2015) but was also criticized for its embrace of graphic violence and mocked for its lack of credibility (O'Grady and Groll 2015; Beauchamp 2015). It also offered an important platform for jihadi propagandists to respond directly to US officials. Those propagandists mocked the campaign and exploited the visibility of the program's Twitter account to justify and clarify certain aspects of their own discourse (Miller and Higham, 2015; Winter and Bach-Lombardo 2016).

Rather than engineering strategic/targeted CVE campaigns, many governments develop more indirect counter-narrative strategies by supporting civil society initiatives and local actors who are willing to engage in such activities. In Canada, funding provided by the government's Kanishka Project[7] and by the current Canada Centre for Community Engagement and Prevention of Violence (CCEPV)[8] through the Community Resilience Fund have supported this approach through several programs, including the Extreme Dialogue and SOMEONE projects.

Civil Society Soft Counter-Measures:
Raising Awareness and Building Resilience

The most visible initiative funded by the Government of Canada, albeit developed by civil society, has been the Extreme Dialogue project, launched in February 2015. Developed by the UK-based Institute for Strategic Dialogue (ISD), it aims to reduce the appeal of extremist narratives among young people and to offer positive alternative narratives to the extremist material available online. The website offers the personal life stories of those who have been deeply affected by violent extremism. Initially, the initiative produced two videos of different testimonies, one from a former member of the extreme far right, Daniel Gallant, the other detailing the experience of the mother of Damian Clairmont, a young man from Calgary who was killed fighting for IS in Syria. Extreme Dialogue's website now offers additional testimonies, including those of a former member of an extreme Islamist group, a man whose father was murdered by the IRA, a Somali refugee and community activist now living in Toronto, a Syrian refugee adapting to life in Germany, and a Roma family contending with right-wing extremism in Hungary. These videos offer inspirational testimonies with the goal of "reduc[ing] the appeal of extremism among young people" and building resilience among Canadian audiences.

In Canada, as in other countries, civil society's response to the growing digital footprint of jihadism has sometimes been much more rapid than the government's. More localized CVE initiatives have emerged without necessarily being widely publicized at the national level. Several such initiatives have been launched to counter the effects of jihadist discourse. For example, in Quebec the Observatoire sur la radicalisation et l'extrémisme violent (OSR) and the Groupe Philosophie, éducation et société (PES)[9] have developed educational support materials. These are intended to assist local actors and communities and have not yet been disseminated to a wider audience. Similarly, the Extreme Dialogue website offers additional resources and support materials to help groups explore and discuss the issues among youth and other sectors of society. Many civil society initiatives have carefully expanded beyond jihadist violent extremism to encompass all forms of extremist narratives online.

Civil society soft counter-measures also aim to foster critical thinking skills and cognitive awareness regarding the effects of extremist discourses and hate speech encountered online. Another initiative, SOMEONE (SOcial MEdia EducatiON Every day),[10] focuses on sensitizing the public about the detrimental effects of online hate speech. Built around the issues of digital literacy, the need to improve critical thinking in the consumption of digital content, and understanding one another online, the SOMEONE initiative emphasizes strengthening individuals' capacity to resist *all* forms of violent narratives, not only jihadi narratives.

Finally, youth-led CVE campaigns have emerged across Canada as a result of the Peer-to-Peer (P2P) Challenging Extremism initiative,[11] a US government effort supported in part by Facebook that uses the creativity of university students to develop campaigns and social media strategies to combat extremism. Canada-based P2P campaigns include, for example, Carleton University's "60 Days of PVE" (Wilner and Rigato 2017), Université Laval's "L'un, L'autre," and Concordia University's "The Rest of Us" campaigns.

Soft counter-measures aimed at countering online jihadism and other forms of violent extremism do not necessarily set out to address the components of the extremist narrative itself, but rather the social and individual conditions thought to affect individuals' receptivity to such narratives (poor critical thinking, lack of understanding of online media's impact, etc.). Educational programs that encourage broad critical thinking skills and digital literacy in Canada might represent a productive soft counter-measure to weaken the reception of jihadi narratives among Canadian audiences indirectly or within a much broader social goal or public good. The What If I Was Wrong?[12] (Et Si J'avais Tort? in French) awareness campaign launched in the fall of 2017 by the Montreal-based Centre for the Prevention of Radicalization Leading to Violence (CPRLV) is the most recent example of such an approach. With its focus on fostering cognitive complexity and developing critical thinking skills, the What If I Was Wrong? initiative has been deployed both online through a website and communication campaign and offline through art workshops across Quebec and an activity guide for teachers and youth workers.

Challenges of Counter-Messaging Campaigns

Counter- and alternative narrative campaigns find it a severe challenge to measure their actual impact on the jihadi phenomenon (Silverman, Stewart, Amamullah, and Birdwell 2016). However good the intentions of these initiatives, evaluating their impact remains problematic (Davies et al. 2016). Berger has suggested that a good way to assess the effectiveness of a counter-messaging campaign is to measure any decline in the resonance of the discourse it seeks to address: "The metric for success should be reducing the number of followers reached by content, engagement with the content, and the length of time that the content is widely available (trending)" (Berger 2016, 26). We would emphasize, however, that the audience for any speech can be highly diverse: it may include not only potential adherents or the target audience, but other communities (see Bouchard et al. this volume) as well as researchers, law enforcement, and journalists. So it is no easy task to collect data on engagement with any content. In addition, one of many criticisms often raised in research that aims to assess propaganda is that its impact is rarely due to a single factor, so it is difficult to identify the real influence of propaganda with respect to other factors occurring simultaneously in the same context (Bryant and Thompson 2002). Evaluating the effectiveness of counter-measures against online jihadism remains one of today's biggest challenges.

Conclusion

The internet's responsibility for, and contribution to, radicalization to violence remains a contentious issue. As Conway notes, there is to date no "proven connection between consumption of and networking around violent extremist online content and adoption of extremist ideology and/or engagement in violent extremism" (Conway 2017, 77). For instance, in the Canadian context, circumstantial evidence might suggest that Martin Couture-Rouleau and Michael Zehaf-Bibeau answered the call of IS and al-Adnani, yet the difficulty of proving such a connection remains. The issues are inevitably complex (Conway 2017, 77–80); that said, though scholars remain divided regarding the impact of the Internet overall, few doubt that along with social media and other communication technologies it likely has some effect. Exposure to propaganda, videos, and other materials as well as the internet itself rarely "causes" radicalization to violence, but according to more empirical studies (von Behr et al., 2013, Gill et al. 2017; Ducol et al. 2016), it can act as a catalyst and accelerant.

In this chapter we have outlined how the internet can be viewed as an important means by which jihadi narratives are disseminated to a broad international audience. In the case of Canada, our chapter demonstrates how this country became identified more prominently as a target and how Canadian jihadists then came to be used in online propaganda materials. The internet, however, can be and indeed has also been used in a counterterrorism context. As the literature shows, both state and non-state actors have countered jihadist content online. In this chapter we have developed a typology of measures taken by Canadian governments and civil society to counter online jihadism, categorizing these measures as soft or hard, depending on whether they aim to eradicate online propaganda material or to soften its impacts through counter-narratives or alternative narratives. Government initiatives fall mainly, but not exclusively, at the repressive end of the spectrum of counter-measures, whereas civil society has developed alternative discourse promotion campaigns. It is important to note, though, that many of these civil society initiatives receive financial support through various government programs. Overall, hard counter-measures to fight online jihadism have predominated in Western countries over the past years. In this regard, Canada is no exception, having introduced in 2015 several new legal provisions through Bill C-51. However, policing the internet is not without risks. Hard and overly simplistic counter-measures against violent extremism can have detrimental effects that should not be underestimated, especially regarding restriction of freedom of speech, the introduction of intrusive surveillance measures, and the use of administrative measures to police extremist material.

With regard to counter-narratives or alternative narratives, as with other types of measures, closer attention must be paid to which narrative is intended to be countered and the context in which it occurs (Briggs and Feve 2013; Braddock and Horgan 2016). The growing presence of Canadians in jihadi propaganda is a reality. When countering a particular discourse, any response must be attuned to Canada's political and social reality. Every society is different, and the context in which a Canadian may be lured into violent extremism differs significantly from, those for, say, French, Belgian, or other European nationals. Indeed, as Dawson and Amarasingam outline (in this volume), radicalization to violence can be a result of local friends and networks, but also subject to highly individualized "pull" factors revolving around identity and belief. The speeches of Shirdon, Maguire, and Poulin all refer to the quality of life they enjoyed in Canada, but they nonetheless decided to leave.

It therefore seems necessary to offer a counter-narrative or an alternative narrative, one that Canadians themselves recognize and that relates to the specific factors pushing and pulling Canadians into violent extremism. This can be achieved through a better understanding of the jihadi narratives and the development of other initiatives with respect to the cases we discussed in the first part of this chapter. A good understanding of this material can help us distinguish what is highlighted in the jihadi discourse related to Canada and Canadians, as well as what to emphasize in a discourse that deconstructs the way jihadism frames a different reality. Braddock and Horgan (2016) have used the case of André Poulin as an example of constructing counter-narratives to reduce support for terrorism. In addition to how counter-narratives should be constructed, these researchers have raised the question of how to distribute them. Indeed, this represents a major challenge, and it is essential for these narratives to reach and persuade the appropriate audience. To that end, there is a need to find the most appropriate dissemination strategies with respect to each particular measure. Relevant strategies differ because the target audience is not always the same. Some types of narratives can be designed for the general public with more generic preventive objectives, or even an educative role. The videos and support materials on the Extreme Dialogue website are one example of a general education and awareness-raising approach. Other efforts must seek to address specific audiences.

However, we do not know yet which strategies are most effective for each type of measure, and the challenge of evaluating effectiveness is much greater than the mere work of simply disseminating counter- or alternative narratives. One approach would be to assess the direct effects on jihadism mobilization capacity. Overall, it is still important to be able to ensure that these counter-measures contribute to a broader strategy. Despite the good intentions behind all these initiatives, their effectiveness and efficiency is difficult to assess. Indeed, evaluation approaches are a major challenge in themselves. Accordingly, if Canadians want to avoid financial investments in some very costly initiatives with poor returns, it is essential to ensure that effective evaluation programs are implemented for all the measures taken with regard to this particular issue.

NOTES

1 We define jihadism as an extremist form of Islamist activism. Contemporary jihadi militancy in its current and globalized form can be seen as a collective action frame structured around narratives that intend to mobilize a community of "true Muslim believers" against what is perceived as a diversity of threats weighing on Islam and the community of believers – the Ummah. Unlike other Islamist movements such as the Muslim Brotherhood and Salafists, jihadi militancy is characterized above all by its belief that armed violence represents a legitimate means of action. For a synthesizing work on jihadism and its intellectual foundations, see Maher (2016).
2 The term "high jihadisphere" is used here to designate all online activities of media production and content diffusion that are primarily related to official and well-recognized jihadi organizations. In opposition, the term "low jihadisphere" refers to all online activities of media production and content diffusion that are emanating from armchair jihadists and sympathizers.
3 In April 2009, Samir Khan, a young, Web-savvy American, launched the first issue of *Jihad Recollections*, an English-language jihadi magazine aimed at providing access to jihadi propaganda for non-Arabic audiences. After the publication of three issues of *Jihad Recollections*, Khan launched another infamous English-language jihadi magazine: *Inspire*.

4 Alternative narratives differ slightly from counter-narratives in that they are aimed not at deconstructing the extremist narrative per se, but rather at providing alternative narratives that offer a different picture of the social reality and ongoing political events and societal issues. Counter-narratives "directly deconstruct, discredit and demystify violent extremist messaging," whereas alternative narratives "undercut violent extremist narratives by focusing on what we are 'for' rather than 'against,'" as detailed in Briggs and Feve (2013, 6–7).
5 For more information about this initiative, visit Stop-Djihadisme's website: www.stop-djihadisme.gouv.fr.
6 The US Department of State used a Twitter account @ThinkAgain_DOS as a means to undertake global engagement. The effort was subsequently reorganized in March 2016 as the Global Engagement Center.
7 For more information about the Kanishka Project, visit http://www.publicsafety.gc.ca/cnt/ntnl-scrt/cntr-trrrsm/r-nd-flght-182/knshk/index-eng.aspx.
8 For more information about the Centre for Community Engagement and Prevention of Violence, visit https://www.publicsafety.gc.ca/cnt/bt/cc/index-en.aspx.
9 Visit Extreme Dialogue's website, http://extremedialogue.org, for more information about this initiative.
10 Visit https://radicalisationforum.org and https://observatoire-radicalisation.org and https://philosophie-education-societe.org.
11 Visit http://projectsomeone.ca and, for an overview of videos developed by SOMEONE's initiative, https://vimeo.com/someonecanada/videos.
12 For more information about the "What If I Was Wrong?" awareness campaign, visit http://etsijavaistort.org.

REFERENCES

al-Furqan Media. 2014a. "He named you Muslims." Al-Furqan Media, 13 April.
– 2014b. "This is the promise of Allah." Al-Furqan Media, 29 June.
al-Hayat Media. 2014a. "Al-Ghuraba – the chosen few of different lands Abu Muslim from Canada." 11 July.
– 2014b. "Flames of War." 19 September.
al-I'tisaam Media. 2014. "Canadian John Maguire appears in new ISIS video." 7 December.
al-Malahem Media. 2017. "An Inspire Address #1: A Lone Mujahid or An Army By Itself." 7 May.
Arthur, Charles. 2014. "Taking Down ISIS Material from Twitter or YouTube Not as Clear Cut as it Seems" The Guardian, 23 June.

Australia. 2015. "Report Online Extremist Material." https://www.
reportextremism.livingsafetogether.gov.au. *See also* Living Safely Together:
Building Community Resilience to Violent Extremism. https://www.
livingsafetogether.gov.au/pages/home.aspx.

Bell, Stewart. 2015. "RCMP set to tackle extremism at home with program to
curb radicalization of Canadian youth." *National Post*, 4 March.

Berger, J.M. 2016. *Making CVE Work: A Focused Approach Based on Process
Disruption.* The Hague: International Centre for Counter-Terrorism.

Berger, J.M. and Heather Perez. 2016. "The Islamic State's Diminishing
Returns on Twitter: How Suspensions Are Limiting the Social Networks of
English-Speaking ISIS Supporters." George Washington University Program
on Extremism, Washington, D.C.

Beauchamp, Zack. 2015. "Why the US is so bad at countering ISIS
propaganda." *Vox*, 5 October.

Bloom, Mia, Hicham Tiflati, and John Horgan. 2017. "Navigating ISIS's
Preferred Platform: Telegram." *Terrorism and Political Violence*, forthcoming,
1–13. https://doi.org/10.1080/09546553.2017.1339695.

Braddock, Kurt. and John Horgan. 2016. "Towards a Guide for Constructing
and Disseminating Counternarratives to Reduce Support for Terrorism."
Studies in Conflict and Terrorism 39(5): 381–404. https://doi.org/10.1080/105
7610X.2015.1116277.

Briggs, Rachel, and Sebastien Feve. 2013. "Review of Programs to Counter
Narratives of Violent Extremism. What Works and What Are the
Implications for Government?" London: Institute for Strategic Dialogue.

Bryant, Jennings, and Susan Thompson. 2002. *Fundamentals of Media Effects.*
Boston: McGraw-Hill.

Callimachi, Rukmini. 2017. "Not 'lone wolves' after all: How ISIS guides
world's terror plots from afar." *New York Times*, 5 February, A1.

Carter, Joseph A., Shiraz Maher, and Peter R. Neumann. 2014. "#Greenbirds:
Measuring Importance and Influence in Syrian Foreign Fighter Networks."
London: International Centre for the Study of Radicalisation and Political
Violence.

CBC News. 2013. "'Toronto 18' member Ali Mohamed Dirie reportedly
died in Syria." 25 September. http://www.cbc.ca/news/world/
toronto-18-member-ali-mohamed-dirie-reportedly-died-in-syria-1.1868119.

– 2014. "John Maguire, Ottawa man fighting for ISIS, urges attacks on
Canadian targets in video." 7 December. http://www.cbc.ca/news/world/
john-maguire-ottawa-man-fighting-for-isis-urges-attacks-on-canadian-
targets-in-video-1.2863655.

Conway, Maura. 2012. "From al-Zarqawi to al-Awlaki: The Emergence and
Development of an Online Radical Milieu." *CTX: Combating Terrorism
Exchange* 2(4): 12–22.

Conway, Maura. 2017. "Determining the role of the Internet in violent extremism and terrorism: Six suggestions for processing research." *Studies in Conflict & Terrorism* 40(1): 77–98.

Cottee, Simon. 2015. "'The Cyber Activists Who Want to Shut Down ISIS." *The Atlantic*, 8 October.

Crenshaw, Martha, and Gary LaFree. 2017. *Countering Terrorism: No Simple Solutions.* Washington: Brookings Institution Press.

Dabiq, issue 15, p. 70; 4, 9; 5, 37.

Davies, Garth, Christine Neudecker, Marie Ouellet, Martin Bouchard, and Benjamin Ducol. 2016. "Toward a Framework Understanding of Online Programs for Countering Violent Extremism." *Journal for Deradicalization* 6: 51–86.

Ducol, Benjamin. 2015. "Comment le jihadisme est-il devenu numérique?" *Sécurité et stratégie* 20(1): 34–43. https://doi.org/10.3917/sestr.020.0034.

Ducol, Benjamin, Martin Bouchard, Garth Davies, Marie Ouellet, and Christine Neudecker. 2016. "Assessment of the State of Knowledge: Connections between Research on the Social Psychology of the Internet and Violent Extremism." TSAS working paper 16-05, Canadian Network for Research on Terrorism, Security, and Society.

Fisher, Ali. 2015. "Swarmcast: How Jihadist Networks Maintain a Persistent Online Presence." *Perspectives on Terrorism* 9(3): 3–20.

Forcese, Craig. 2007. *National Security Law: Canadian Practice in International Perspective.* Toronto: Irwin Law.

Forcese, Craig, and Kent Roach. 2015a. *False Security: The Radicalization of Canadian Anti-Terrorism.* Toronto: Irwin Law.

– 2015b. "Criminalizing Terrorist Babble: Canada's Dubious New Terrorist Speech Crime." *Alberta Law Review* 53(1): 35–84.

Gill, Paul, Emily Corner, Maura Conway, Amy Thornton, Mia Bloom, and John Horgan. 2017. "Terrorist Use of the Internet by the Numbers." *Criminology and Public Policy* 16(1): 99–117. https://doi.org/10.1111/1745-9133.12249.

Gladstone, Rick. 2015. "Behind a veil of anonymity: Online vigilantes battle the Islamic State." *New York Times*, 24 March.

Hegghammer, Thomas. 2016. "The Future of Jihadism in Europe: A Pessimistic View." *Perspectives on Terrorism* 10(6): 156–70.

Huey, Laura, Johnny Nhan, and Ryan Broll. 2012. "'Uppity Civilians' and 'Cyber-Vigilantes': The Role of the General Public in Policing Cyber-Crime." *Criminology and Criminal Justice* 13(1): 81–97. https://doi.org/10.1177/1748895812448086.

Huey, Laura, and Hina Kalyal. 2015. "'Questions about Dawlah: DM me, plz.' The Sock Puppet Problem in Online Terrorism Research." *Sociology Publications*, paper no. 33, 1–19.

Huey, Laura, and Hillary Peladeau. 2016. "Cheering on the Jihad: An Exploration of Women's Participation in Online Pro-Jihadist Networks." TSAS working paper no. 16–07, TSAS, Canadian Network for Research on Terrorism, Security, and Society.

Inspire, no. 10 (2013), 24; 14 (2015), 9; 17 (2017), 92.

Klausen, Jytte. 2015. "Tweeting the Jihad: Social Media Networks of Western Foreign Fighters in Syria and Iraq." *Studies in Conflict and Terrorism* 38(1): 1–22. https://doi.org/10.1080/1057610X.2014.974948.

Lia, Brynjar. 2009. *Architect of Global Jihad: The Life of Al-Qaeda Strategist Abu Mus'ab Al-Suri.* Oxford: Oxford University Press.

Lemieux, Anthony, Jarret M. Brachman, Jason Levitt, and Jay Wood. 2014. "Inspire Magazine: A Critical Analysis of Its Significance and Potential Impact through the Lens of the Information, Motivation, and Behavioral Skills Model." *Terrorism and Political Violence* 26(2): 354–71. https://doi.org/10.1080/09546553.2013.828604.

Leung, Marlene. 2015. "Ottawa students fight ISIS with satirical YouTube series." *CTV News*, 17 March. http://www.ctvnews.ca/canada/ottawa-students-fight-isis-with-satirical-youtube-series-1.2283318.

Lohlker, Rudiger, ed. 2013. *Jihadism: Online Discourses and Representations.* Goettingen: Vienna University Press.

Maher, Shiraz. 2016. *Salafi-Jihadism: The History of an Idea.* New York: C. Hurst & Co.

Matusitz, Jonathan. 2015. *Symbolism in Terrorism: Motivation, Communication, and Behavior.* Lanham: Rowman and Littlefield.

Miller, Greg, and Scott Higham (2015) "In a propaganda war against ISIS, the US tried to play by the enemy's rules." *The Washington Post*, 8 May.

Neumann, Peter R. 2016. *Radicalized: New Jihadists and the Threat to the West.* London: I.B. Tauris.

O'Grady, Siobhán, and Elias Groll. 2015. "Quelle Horreur! France Unveils Anti-Jihadist Propaganda Campaign." *Foreign Policy*, 29 January.

Platt, Brian. 2017. "Terrorism bill aims to help prosecutors: Old legislation too vague to hold up in courts." *Ottawa Citizen*, 1 December.

Prucha, Nico, and Ali Fisher. 2013. "Tweeting for the Caliphate: Twitter as the New Frontier for Jihadist Propaganda." *CTC Sentinel* 6(6): 19–23.

Ramsay, Gilbert. 2013. *Jihadi Culture on the World Wide Web.* New York: Bloomsbury.

RCMP (Royal Canadian Mounted Police). 2009. *Youth Online and at Risk: Radicalization Facilitated by the Internet.* Ottawa.

– 2016. *Terrorism and Violent Extremism Awareness Guide.* Ottawa.

Resurgence, no. 2 (2015), 68.

Rumiyah, no. 9 (2017), 46.

Saltman, Erin, and Jonathan Russell. 2014. *White Paper – The Role of Prevention in Countering Online Extremism.* London: Quilliam Foundation.

Silverman, Tanya, Christopher J. Stewart, Zahed Amanullah, and Jonathan Birdwell. 2016. *The Impact of Counter-Narratives: Insights from a Year-Long Cross-Platform Pilot Study of Counter-Narrative Curation, Targeting, Evaluation, and Impact.* London: Institute for Strategic Dialogue.

Standing Committee on Public Safety and National Security. 2017. *Protecting Canadians and Their Rights: A New Road Map for Canada's National Security.* 42nd Parl., 1st Sess.

Stern, Jessica, and J.M. Berger. 2015. *ISIS: The State of Terror.* New York: HarperCollins.

Torres, Manuel R., Javier Jordán, and Nicola Horsburgh. 2006. "Analysis and Evolution of the Global Jihadist Movement Propaganda." *Terrorism and Political Violence* 18(3): 399–421. https://doi.org/10.1080/09546550600751990.

Torres Soriano, Manuel R. 2012. "Between the Pen and the Sword: The Global Islamic Media Front in the West." *Terrorism and Political Violence* 24(5): 769–86. https://doi.org/10.1080/09546553.2011.643934.

United Kingdom. 2006. *Terrorism Act 2006.* http://www.legislation.gov.uk/ukpga/2006/11/pdfs/ukpga_20060011_en.pdf.

– 2015. "Report online material promoting terrorism or extremism." https://www.gov.uk/report-terrorism.

von Behr, Ines, Anais Reding, Charlie Edwards, and Luke Gribbon. 2013. "Radicalisation in the digital era: The use of the Internet in 15 cases of terrorism and extremism." RAND Corporation.

Van Ginkel, Bibi T. 2015. *Responding to Cyber Jihad: Towards an Effective Counter Narrative.* The Hague: International Centre for Counter-Terrorism.

VICE News. 2014. "The Canadian Jihadist." 25 September. https://www.vice.com/en_ca/article/vdpxq9/the-canadian-jihadist-678.

Veilleux-Lepage, Yannick. 2016. "Paradigmatic Shifts in Jihadism in Cyberspace: The Emerging Role of Unaffiliated Sympathizers in Islamic State's Social Media Strategy." *Journal of Terrorism Research* 7(1): 36–51. https://doi.org/10.15664/jtr.1183.

Weimann, Gabriel. 2009. "Terror on Facebook, Twitter, and YouTube." *Brown Journal of World Affairs* 16(2): 45–54.

– 2014. *New Terrorism and New Media.* Washington, D.C.: Commons Lab of the Woodrow Wilson International Center for Scholars.

Weiss, Caleb. 2014. "Islamic State Spokesman Again Threatens West in New Speech." *Long War Journal*, 21 September. http://www.longwarjournal.org/archives/2014/09/islamic_state_spokesman_again.php.

Wilner, Alex, and Brandon Rigato. 2017. "The 60 Days of PVE Campaign: Lessons on Organizing an Online, Peer-to-Peer, Counter-radicalization Program." *Journal for Deradicalization* 12: 227–68.

Winter, Charlie. 2015. *The Virtual Caliphate Understanding Islamic State's Propaganda Strategy*. London: Quilliam Foundation.

Winter, Charlie, and Jordan Bach-Lombardo. 2016. "Why ISIS Propaganda Works." *The Atlantic*, 13 February. https://www.theatlantic.com/international/archive/2016/02/isis-propaganda-war/462702.

Zelin, Aaron Y. 2013. *The State of Global Jihad Online: A Qualitative, Quantitative, and Cross-lingual Analysis*. Washington, D.C.: New America Foundation.

PART TWO

Security and Counterterrorism

6 Counterterrorism Security Planning in Canada: From Imperialism to International Terrorism

DOMINIQUE CLÉMENT

Counterterrorism planning in Canada has a long history, from spying on Irish revolutionaries in the 1850s to the current War on Terror. In fact, there are many parallels between current and past practices around security policing. For this reason, it is worthwhile placing current debates in their historical context. Most Canadians are unaware of this history. Many of the recent initiatives designed to deal with the threat of domestic and international terrorism were, in fact, used in the past to deal with threats to national security. Yet in many cases, these practices or laws have since been condemned as unnecessary and excessive restrictions on civil liberties.

This chapter documents three stages in the evolution of national security planning in Canada. It is based on extensive archival research as well as security planning documents released under the Federal Access to Information Act. Analyses of this information demonstrate that during the first stage, from the period before Confederation until the early years of the Cold War, security planners were preoccupied with threats directed against Britain using Canada as a proxy. By the mid-twentieth century, however, fears of communist espionage and subversion dominated national security planning. The final stage began in the 1970s with a shift toward domestic and international terrorism. I argue that these stages, while distinct, have shared several qualities: planning in a global context; targeting immigrant communities; dependence on foreign intelligence-gathering agencies, notably British and American; and responding to national security threats with a heavy hand and some excessive force. Moreover, I argue that Canadians have demonstrated a remarkable tolerance of the restrictions on their civil liberties by the state in response to these threats.

Colony to Nation

Organized policing to infiltrate and undermine threats to the state began as early as the 1830s. In the aftermath of an abortive rebellion in the colonies, British authorities in Lower Canada appointed officials within the rural police force to collect intelligence in order to subvert political radicals. It was in the 1860s, however, that the government launched a sustained effort at covert policing. Fenians – Irish nationalists living in the United States – proposed using violence against Canada to pressure Britain to abandon Ireland. A small secret police force had been established in 1864 during the American Civil War to target military recruiters in neutral Canada. This force, which was expanded to more than fifty agents and assisted by British consular officials in American cities, was used to gather intelligence about the Fenians (Parnaby, Kealey, and Neargarth 2009; Whitaker, Kealey, and Parnaby 2012, 19–37).

Restrictions on civil liberties were a defining feature of the state's response to national security threats (Greenwood 1988, 292). Habeas corpus had been suspended in Lower Canada almost every year between 1793 and 1812 to protect the colony from American spies who might precede an invasion. The state's response to the Fenian threat was similarly extreme. Habeas corpus was suspended in 1866–67, and the Legislative Assembly invoked a post-rebellion statute called the *Lawless Aggression Act*, which, among other things, allowed for trials without a jury. Fifty-seven men suspected of Fenian sympathies were arrested and tried; twenty-two of them were convicted and hanged (Whitaker, Kealey, and Parnaby 2012, 29–30). A year later, police arrested and detained twenty-five men without charge during an investigation of the assassination of Thomas D'Arcy McGee, a former Fenian turned Canadian nationalist. The suspension of habeas corpus was "part of the humdrum business of Parliament" (Wilson 2009, 87, 98). McGee's assassination was also used as a pretext to establish the Dominion Police in 1868. As Whitaker and colleagues explain, the federal government had, by 1868, created the foundation for a permanent security service: "it boasted institutional support in the form of the newly minted Dominion Police, possessed a stable budget with the secret service fund, and depended more and more on the expertise of its own well-paid and highly placed agents than on the observations of well-connected imperial officials" (Whitaker, Kealey, and Parnaby 2012, 33).

When the North-West Mounted Police merged with the Dominion Police in 1920 to create the Royal Canadian Mounted Police (RCMP), the security service was still a minor component of the force. It depended on British embassies and staff to assist in intelligence gathering. The greatest threats were seen as domestic, not from abroad, and as directed against Britain. Among the primary threats identified during this period, for example, were Hindu nationalists, who, like the Fenians, might use violence against Canada as leverage against British control in India. An elaborate system of informants was established to monitor and report on the activities of immigrants from India (Hewitt 2002; Whitaker, Kealey, and Parnaby 2012, 38–59). This was only the beginning of what would be a long history of targeting immigrant communities and using immigration law to deal with potential threats (Iacovetta 2000; 2006).

The state's penchant for restricting civil liberties in response to national security threats remained apparent during the First and Second World Wars. The federal government suspended habeas corpus; imposed widespread censorship; declared numerous associations to be unlawful; broke strikes and barred newspapers from reporting on their actions; constrained due process to facilitate prosecutions; interned thousands of enemy aliens; and imposed conscription, which led to the jailing of thousands of men for desertion (Clément 2016b, 49–72). The state's security police expanded dramatically during the wars, but in truth, the RCMP still lacked the resources and expertise to identify genuine saboteurs or spies. Practices commonly associated with political policing had become routine by the interwar period: "secrecy, surveillance, intelligence gathering and sabotage; suspicion of immigrant groups and their 'foreign' ideologies; and coordination of covert activities with conventional uses of government power" (Whitaker, Kealey, and Parnaby 2012, 58). Far too often the state reacted against non-existent threats, for example, when it expelled Japanese Canadians during the Second World War.

However, the beginning of a profound shift in national security planning was under way by the First World War. The security service shifted its focus from threats to Britain to threats to the Canadian state posed by organized labour and the political left. In 1919, when workers in Winnipeg launched a massive general strike, the federal government responded by adding Section 98 to the *Criminal Code*. Instead of criminalizing a specific action, this unusual amendment made it illegal to belong to any political party that advocated the use of violence to influence economic policy or change government. The effect was to ban the Communist Party in Canada, which no other country in the Commonwealth had done (Mackenzie 1971–72, 474). In addition, complementary amendments to the *Immigration Act* created new powers to deport anyone who was not a citizen as well as individuals advocating the destruction of property or belonging to an organization promoting the overthrow of the government (Anderson 2013, 99–100). In effect, the government, abetted by a police force that was dogmatically anti-communist, had undermined a legitimate political movement. Nearly 7,000 people were deported in 1931 alone (Petryshyn 1982, 47). That same year, the leaders of the Communist Party of Canada were placed on trial under Section 98. Tim Buck, the General Secretary of the Communist Party of Canada, and his colleagues were found guilty and spent several years in jail (Molinaro 2017). Within a year, another 1,500 people had been prosecuted, and 355 convicted, for political crimes (Whitaker, Kealey, and Parnaby 2012, 122–6; Molinaro 2017).

By the mid-twentieth century, anti-communism had become normalized. The police saw the left as the greatest threat to national security. In Toronto in 1929, the police commission issued an edict banning all political meetings held in any language other than English. They also promised that any public places that rented space for "communist or Bolshevik" meetings would lose their licence (Petryshyn 1982, 43). When the Canadian Labour Defence League sponsored a theatre production that was critical of the government for imprisoning the leader of the Communist Party of Canada, the police shut it down (Petryshyn 1982, 53). During the Great Depression, the RCMP increased surveillance on workers' organizations to identify any communist links. In many cases, the police engaged in activities designed to undermine organizations representing workers and the unemployed. Meanwhile, the fledgling Canadian Radio Broadcasting Commission routinely denied communists airtime with the national broadcaster (Vipond 2010, 81–4). As one MP, speaking before the House of Commons, explained: "Sedition must be stamped out. It is all very well to talk of free speech, but to talk of Bolshevism and riots and overthrowing the Government is a different thing" (Mathieu 2010, 122).

The Cold War and Anti-Communism

Anti-communism would dominate security policing in Canada for a generation. This constituted a profound shift in security planning: communism replaced threats to Britain as the primary danger to national security. Whereas reliance on British civil servants stationed abroad made sense when the threat was thought to come from Fenians or Hindu nationalists, the danger posed by communism necessitated the expansion of domestic policing. For the RCMP in particular, events and developments such as the Winnipeg General Strike, the Communist Party of Canada, and the On-to-Ottawa Trek confirmed their fears of communist subversion and justified the expansion of surveillance, infiltration, arrest, and deportation.[1]

No event better symbolizes this new stage in security planning than Igor Gouzenko's defection in 1945 and the subsequent Royal Commission. A cipher clerk assigned to the Soviet Embassy in Ottawa, Gouzenko sought asylum using stolen documents that provided evidence of a Soviet espionage network (Whitaker and Marcuse 1994; Clément 2000; 2001; Lambertson 2005; Knight 2005). The defection was without precedent, and the RCMP had little experience with defectors. True, the RCMP and its security service had grown since the late 1930s, when the Intelligence Section had only three officers. But it was rather unsophisticated compared to other countries and was often ridiculed by other members of the force as well as being "something of an aberration" (Whitaker, Kealey, and Parnaby 2012, 148–9, 255).

The state's response was, again, excessive. During a top-secret meeting with three cabinet members in September 1945, the prime minister approved an order-in-council authorized under the *War Measures Act* to provide the RCMP with emergency powers. For several months, the RCMP investigated Gouzenko's allegations but took no action. In February 1946, however, when a journalist publicly revealed the defection, the prime minister appointed two Supreme Court of Canada justices to lead a Royal Commission to investigate the alleged espionage network. The RCMP used the order-in-council to detain dozens of suspected spies and hold them incommunicado in tiny cells under twenty-four-hour suicide watch. The suspects were subjected to repeated interrogations before they were brought before the commission. Habeas corpus was suspended, and the suspects were denied access to lawyers. In effect, the government used wartime powers during peacetime to circumvent due process. The suspects' "testimony" was later used in court. All of the detainees were traumatized, but few were convicted. It was one of the worst abuses of state power in Canadian history (Clément 2000, 2001; Knight 2005).

Curiously, rather than focus on the threat from the Soviet Union, the Royal Commission's report highlighted the dangers of internal subversion (Canada 1946).[2] It confirmed the state's fear of communist subversion and provided the justification for a massive program of security screening for civil servants, immigrants, and defence industry employees. People were denied employment without appeal. There were also several purges, most notably within the National Film Board. Numerous refugee and citizenship applications were denied on the basis that the applicants were perceived security threats (Whitaker and Marcuse 1994).

Anti-communism had thus become the pretext for another surge in the state's capacity for policing national security threats. Domestic surveillance and security screening for civil servants required a dramatic increase in funding and staffing levels (Whitaker and Marcuse 1994; Hannant 1995; Hewitt 2002; Hewitt and Sethna 2012). The RCMP's Intelligence Section had become an independent department reporting directly to the commissioner in 1950. It was renamed, in 1956, the Security Intelligence Directorate and, later, the Security Service. The size of the directorate increased fiftyfold in the thirty years after 1945. By 1970, the RCMP's Security Service had 300 officers in Montreal alone, at a time when the Province of Quebec and City of Montreal's local anti-terrorism squads totalled only forty-five people.[3] Meanwhile, the RCMP and local police forces created vast databases of dossiers on individual citizens – the RCMP alone had at least 800,000 files (Canada 1981a). Surveillance went far beyond communist-affiliated organizations to include a wide range of associations, from women's groups to Aboriginal rights organizations.

Domestic and International Terrorism

The state's excessive response to a largely imagined threat in 1946 would have remained the worst abuse of civil liberties in peacetime had it not been for the October Crisis in 1970–71. The Front de libération du Québec (FLQ) had pursued its vision for an independent Quebec nation through violence, including bombings and thefts throughout the 1960s. Among the most infamous incidents were the bombings of the Montreal Stock Exchange, which injured twenty people, and of an army barracks that led to the death of a security guard (Clément 2008). In October 1970, when the FLQ kidnapped a British diplomat, and then kidnapped and murdered a provincial cabinet minister, the federal government invoked the *War Measures Act* and placed the Province of Quebec under martial law. Habeas corpus was suspended; hundreds were arrested and held incommunicado without access to a lawyer; and the police conducted thousands of arbitrary searches (Clément 2008). The state's response was disproportionate to the threat. Most of the detainees were never charged. Even the RCMP's commissioner acknowledged that the use of emergency powers was unwarranted (Whitaker 2003, 251).

The RCMP's obsession with communist subversives had produced an institutional culture that was slow to adapt to new threats. Elements within the force remained convinced that communism was still the dominant threat to national security (the Counter-Subversion Branch was commonly referred to as the Anti-Communism Branch) (Palmer 2009; Hewitt and Sethna 2012). The danger posed by violent separatists, however, compelled the RCMP to recognize the existence of a new type of threat. The next stage in national security planning was therefore a reactive response to a new threat that emerged during this period. In the aftermath of the crisis, the RCMP committed extensive resources to infiltrating and subverting domestic terrorist organizations.[4]

These developments coincided with preparations for the Montreal Summer Olympics, which further contributed to this shift in national security planning. The games, according to the Security Service, "provided an opportunity for the Force and the Security Service to participate in the planning and implementation of the largest security operations ever known in this country" (LAC 1976a). The need to plan for a massive international event on domestic soil forced the RCMP to better integrate international terrorism into its security planning. The RCMP was acutely aware that these games were unlike their predecessors: the massacre of eleven members of the Israeli Olympic team by a radical wing of the Palestinian Liberation Organization at the Munich games in 1972 had fundamentally altered security planning for Olympic games. Munich had, more than any other event, made visible the dangers of international terrorism. The period before the Montreal games had seen an increase in terrorism. There had been at least 4,340 terrorist attacks around the world between 1970 and 1976 (Global Terrorism Database). In the aftermath of the Munich massacre, major sporting events such as the World Cup and the Asian Games implemented highly visible security programs (Clément 2016). As the Security Service noted in its Final Report on the operation, "early in the planning stages, the spectre of international terrorism was perceived as the major threat to the Olympic Games" (LAC 1976a; 1976c).

The language used in the RCMP's archival records confirms that international terrorism was supplanting communism as the dominant threat to national security. Although the focus was on the Olympics, the security plan, which was developed over several years, included a comprehensive review of national security threats. It is noteworthy, therefore, that communism was almost never mentioned in that plan. The Security Service was especially concerned about Quebec separatists, Native extremists, and black nationalists (Clément 2016a, 9–11). Threat assessment reports also routinely referenced international terrorist organizations such as the Irish Republican Army, the Palestinian Liberation Organization, and groups originating in Cuba and Japan (LAC 1976b). There were also fears that Ukrainian, Chilean, or Haitian immigrants would use the games to protest governments back home, and that right-wing terrorist organizations such as the Ku Klux Klan would exploit the games to advance their cause. The almost complete lack of planning around communist subversives constituted a definitive break from a generation obsessed with Cold War threats.[5]

There were, however, limits to the RCMP's ability to plan a major international security operation. The federal government had never intended for its national police force to engage in external intelligence gathering. There were only four officers in the Counter-Intelligence Branch. As had been the case for more than a century, the RCMP depended on American and British assistance for intelligence on threats from abroad (Whitaker, Kealey, and Parnaby 2012, 19, 24, 207). The Security Branch also had minimal resources: a budget of $35 million out of a total RCMP budget of $237 million in 1975. There were only 18,198 RCMP employees spread across the country: one third were civilians, and a significant portion of the force was committed to front-line policing (LAC 1974–75). The security operation for the Olympics was therefore all the more impressive given these limited resources. A force of 17,224 was assigned to protect 6,000 athletes. The operation included the army, five police forces, and at least a half-dozen federal agencies (Clément 2016a). The federal government passed special legislation allowing the Minister of Immigration to deport anyone who *might* engage in violence during the Olympics. It was an unusual statute: the entire law was a single sentence that gave the minister unfettered authority to deport non-citizens and deny them the right to appeal (LAC 1976b). Even by global standards, the security plan for the Montreal Olympics was imposing,[6] yet there were no security incidents of note during the games (Clément 2016a).

The state's penchant for applying excessive measures to deal with threats to national security, from the Gouzenko Affair to the Montreal Olympics, rarely elicited a strong public response. The Liberal government in 1946 handily won re-election, and few people in the media criticized the suspension of civil liberties for accused communist spies. Even civil liberties activists held back: many liberal and social democrats were simply unwilling to defend communists.[7] In 1970, with the notable exception of several unions and civil liberties organizations in Vancouver and Toronto, Canadians supported the state's extreme measures (Clément 2008). Similarly, the security measures for the Olympics generated little public opposition. Even within Parliament, the government's political opponents rarely challenged the use of severe measures in response to national security threats.[8]

The War on Terror

Despite the lack of a sustained or widespread backlash against the state's national security policies, legislators were forced to respond to growing concerns surrounding the police's questionable practices.

In part, this was a result of the emergence of new social movements, including the New Left, which challenged authority and rejected Cold War conformity (Palmer 2009). As well, a new human rights movement was emerging, which resulted in the first human rights and privacy laws as well as a bill of rights, which was entrenched in the constitution in 1982 (Clément 2016b). At the same time, the RCMP's Security Service faced increased scrutiny. Their questionable and at times illegal practices became public in the 1970s (Canada 1981a, 1981b; Quebec 1980). These practices included opening people's mail, secretly raiding the offices of political parties (including the Parti Québécois), conducting widespread surveillance, and spreading disinformation among community groups (Canada 1981a, 1981b). A Royal Commission recommended separating the security service from the RCMP, which the federal government did in 1984 when it created the Canadian Security Intelligence Service (CSIS). CSIS, not the RCMP, would be responsible for gathering intelligence, and restrictions were placed on CSIS's operations (e.g., warrants would now be required for surveillance, and a civilian oversight committee was established). Furthermore, in 1988, the *War Measures Act* was repealed and replaced with the *Emergencies Act*. Unlike its predecessor, the *Emergencies Act* defined emergencies, required Parliamentary oversight, and acknowledged the need to protect civil liberties (Lindsay 2014; Tenofsky 1989).

Nonetheless, Canada's response to the terror attacks in the United States on 11 September 2001 has demonstrated that the state's approach to national security threats remains largely consistent with past practices. Ministers used provisions under the *Immigration Act* to issue security certificates, which allowed the police to detain and deport perceived security threats without charge. Five individuals were held indefinitely because they could not be deported to countries where they might be tortured. One person, Hassan Almrei, was imprisoned for eight years without charge (Ramraj et al. 2012, 528–9). The *Anti-Terrorism Act* gave police the power to detain suspected terrorists for three days without charge and to compel them to answer questions in a secret hearing. The same law created several new terrorism-related offences with strict penalties; allowed for greater electronic surveillance of Canadian citizens; criminalized motive by defining terrorism as seeking to advance political, religious, or ideological causes; and empowered the government to ban or revoke charitable status for any organization supporting terrorists at home or abroad (Roach 2007, 59; 2012a).

The War on Terror has, to be sure, had a profound impact on security planning in Canada. At the same time, the security police have been cognizant of the terrorism threat since at least the Montreal Olympics in 1976. In a curious historical parallel, much as the Montreal games were held in the aftermath of the Munich massacre, the Vancouver Winter Olympics in 2010 were held in the shadow of 9/11. In fact, there were several parallels between the two events. The security operation in Vancouver had an international component, involved restrictions on civil liberties, and did not generate extensive public opposition. Fears of both domestic and international terrorism were a defining feature of security planning in both operations. The most notable difference was the nature of the threat. The primary threats identified for the Montreal security operation had included hostage taking, occupation of a building, aircraft hijacking or accidents, bomb threats or suspicious parcels, crowd control, natural disasters, an attack on the queen, an epidemic or shutdown of a major utility, and a disaster in the metro system (LAC 1976d, 37). In Vancouver, threat assessments focused on bomb attacks, a chlorine spill, plane crashes, radioactive attacks on the transit system, organized crime, human trafficking, and a virus spread from cruise ships (Boyle, Clément, and Haggerty 2014).

The state imposed extensive measures to guarantee security for the Vancouver Olympics. The security operation in 2010 was essentially an expanded version of the precedent set in Montreal: research to identify domestic and external threats; a visible police and military presence; no-fly zones; new systems of identification and accreditation; intelligence gathering on domestic and international organizations; policing critical infrastructure, transit, and border crossings; and coordination among military as well as municipal, provincial, and national police (Boyle and Haggerty 2006; Boyle, Clément, and Haggerty 2014). The security operation in both Montreal and Vancouver included information sharing with foreign agencies; using Canadian embassies to gather intelligence; cooperation with foreign as well as domestic military and police services; and, especially by 2010, integration into a global network of major event security expertise and technology. Security plans were also defined by extensive surveillance, albeit the scale was much greater in Vancouver: police conducted more than 200,000 background checks and accredited almost 150,000 people, while installing more than 900 temporary surveillance cameras (Boyle, Clément, and Haggerty 2014).

The Vancouver Olympics raised several civil liberties issues.[9] Because Section 50 of the International Olympic Committee's charter forbids demonstrations as well as political expression on Olympic venues, the effect of the games was to prohibit legitimate dissent or protest in some public spaces. Also, security for major events routinely involves police harassing and infiltrating anti-Olympics activists, which was no less the case in Vancouver (Mickelburgh 2009a; 2009c; Boykoff 2014). The state increased its surveillance capacity using CCTV cameras. Criminal procedures in British Columbia as well as nearby provinces were delayed to enable the RCMP to shift personnel to security for the games (Mickelburgh 2009b). Day parole was suspended for prisoners in the region, and homeless people were harassed out of the downtown core (Hyslop 2010; Boykoff 2014). The city even went so far as to introduce a by-law restricting protests on municipal lands (Vancouver 2009). The province also amended the *Municipal Enabling and Validating Act* to give special powers to police to forcibly enter homes to remove signs (political censorship, including censorship of any criticism of the games or the International Olympic Committee, is required for hosting the games) (British Columbia 2009; Boykoff 2014). To be sure, these measures generated some opposition from civil liberties and other organizations in the province (Hyslop 2010). The British Columbia Civil Liberties Association described the city by-law as "bizarre, unnecessary and arbitrary restrictions on political expression" (British Columbia Civil Liberties Association 2011). Yet these restrictions did not generate widespread opposition. There was no sustained opposition from political leaders, media, or advocacy groups regarding these measures, which have become a routine aspect of Olympic games (Atkinson and Young 2005; Fussey, Coaffee, Armstrong, and Hobbs 2011).[10] Opposition was limited to a small number of advocacy organizations in Vancouver.

Conclusion

In some ways, the current war on terror is unique. There is no historical precedent for the focus on Islamic militants. It also coincides with an unparalleled level of surveillance and intelligence gathering, which has been made possible by new technologies. Yet this is simply a continuation of a long historical trajectory of counterterrorism planning in Canada.[11] There is an obvious international component. Immigrant communities, much like Hindus and Fenians a century ago, have been targeted for surveillance while the government uses immigration law to detain, deport, or bar suspected terrorists (Roach, 2012b; Whitaker, Kealey, and Parnaby 2012, 539–543). Counterterrorism is a global struggle involving multiple nations. It requires close cooperation and information sharing among intelligence agencies, most notably Britain and the United States. It has spurred increased domestic surveillance. The controversial amendments to the *Anti-Terrorism Act* in 2015 introduced an unprecedented new power – to "disrupt" potential terrorist activities – without a clear definition or proper oversight. In effect, the government legalized a practice that the RCMP had been condemned for using in the 1970s.[12]

The government's anti-terrorism policies have, to be sure, generated intense public opposition. A host of advocacy organizations, from civil liberties groups to those representing ethnic and religious minorities, have criticized the legislation. The 2015 amendments, in particular, have been especially controversial (Forcese and Roach 2015; CCLA 2015). At the same time, there remains, as has been the case in the past, some tolerance for these measures. A 2014 survey by the Angus Reid Institute found that only 27 per cent of respondents were concerned that proposed anti-terror legislation restricted civil liberties. The same survey found majority support for measures such as deportation, indefinite imprisonment, and the blocking of internet sites (Angus Reid Institute 2014).

Canada's history of counterterrorism planning demonstrates the state's penchant for imposing excessive measures to protect against threats to national security. Often, these powers have been disproportionate to the threat. Moreover, there has been a surprising tolerance among Canadians for limits on civil liberties. Legal reforms, such as the *Emergencies Act*, have placed some limits on policing and state power to better protect individual rights.[13] But these protections have not prevented the state from imposing restrictions on civil liberties based on perceived threats (Tenofsky 1989; Weinrib, 2001).

NOTES

1 As F. Murray Greenwood argues, legislators in Canada have historically "indulge[d] in drastic security legislation in times of crisis, real or apprehended, without much concern for civil liberties and with almost no critical examination of the invariably elastic language used" (Greenwood 1988, 292) These developments and events are covered by much of the literature cited above. The Winnipeg General Strike between 15 May and 25 June 1919 involved more than 30,000 workers and met fierce resistance from manufacturers and business owners. Fearing the spread of further strikes in Canada, the federal government intervened with legislative changes and through the North West Mounted Police. Strike leaders were arrested, and on 21 June, "Bloody Saturday," a police charge of strikers resulted in one death and twenty-nine further casualties. In 1935, with the "On to Ottawa" trek, more than 1,000 workers from Vancouver and other provinces travelled to Ottawa to protest the poor conditions in Depression Era camps.

2 To be sure, the security service considered the threat from the Soviet Union and internal subversion as closely linked. Even so, it is notable that there is no discussion in the report of foreign espionage or threats from abroad. The report makes no explicit connection between espionage and internal subversion.

3 Provincial and municipal anti-terror squads were not part of the federal RCMP Security Service. Rather, they were embedded in municipal and provincial police forces. Quebec Minister of Justice, *Rapport Sur Les Événements D'octobre 1970.*

4 This was as much a priority shift within the federal government as it was within the police force: the RCMP was fully aware of the FLQ threat, but the government had largely ignored the RCMP's warnings regarding the FLQ (Whitaker 2003, 250–1).

5 The Montreal Olympics also symbolized a new era in security policing, with new structures and technologies for gathering and organizing information. The RCMP amassed an immense amount of data on security threats and employed new technologies to provide that information to authorities at airports and other arrival points (see Clément 2016a).

6 On security planning and the Olympic Games, see Cottrell 2003; Sanan 1996; Toohey and Taylor 2008.

7 Even among lawyers, as one legal scholar notes, "what is remarkable about constitutional thought during the war is the pronounced absence of civil liberties concerns." (Adams 2009, 79).

8 The New Democratic Party did, however, raise some concerns within Parliament regarding the government's response to the October Crisis. A few Members of Parliament also spoke out during the Gouzenko Affair.

9 The British Columbia Civil Liberties Association's Micheal Vonn described the Olympics as an "anti-transparency device" and was highly critical of the lack of transparency around planning and budgets (Boykoff 2014, 71).

10 "As was the case with Montreal, there was no major security incident in 2010. In fact, although there were notable restrictions on civil liberties, the security plan allowed for peaceful protest. This was in stark contrast to trends in policing demonstrations and marches for anti-globalization protests. The G20 in Toronto, in particular, led to widespread police brutality of peaceful demonstrators. This was part of a broader trend since the 1990s of police using more extreme methods to control peaceful protest, such as the APEC summit in 1997 to the Montebello summit in 2007" (Beare, Des Rosiers, and Deshman 2015).

11 There is a historical parallel with the Conservative Party's proposal in August 2015 to criminalize travel from Canada to countries under the control of terrorist organizations. In 1937, the federal government, fearing that some of its citizens would travel to Spain to support the

communists in the civil war there, criminalized participation in the International Brigades. People convicted under the amended *Foreign Enlistment Act* could face $2,000 in fines and up to two years in jail. Soon after, the federal government passed on order-in-council explicitly banning travel to Spain.

12 The amendments further expanded the police's powers of preventative detention and as well as their power to collect information on citizens. *An Act to enact the Security of Canada Information Sharing Act and the Secure Air Travel Act, to amend the Criminal Code, the Canadian Security Intelligence Service Act and the Immigration and Refugee Protection Act and to make related and consequential amendments to other Acts,* Statutes of Canada, 2015.

13 There are provisions in Canada's anti-terrorism legislation designed to protect individual rights. For instance, there are provisions to protect free speech (no restrictions on the press) as well as freedom of association (membership in a group is not made illegal), and there are greater immunity protections. Kent Roach (2012) argues that Canada's approach is more restrained than in some other countries such as Australia.

REFERENCES

Adams, Eric. 2009. "The Idea of Constitutional Rights and the Transformation of Canadian Constitutional Law, 1930–1960." PhD dissertation, University of Toronto.

Anderson, Christopher G. 2013. *Canadian Liberalism and the Politics of Border Control, 1867–1967.* Vancouver: UBC Press.

Angus Reid Institute. 2014. *Report: Homegrown Terrorism and Radicalization in Canada.* http://angusreid.org/homegrown-terrorism-radicalization-canada-overblown-serious-threat.

Atkinson, Michael, and Kevin Young. 2005. *Political Violence, Terrorism, and Security at the Olympic Games.* New York: Elsevier.

Beare, Margaret E., Nathalie Des Rosiers, and Abigail Deshman. 2015. *Putting the State on Trial: The Policing of Protest during the G20 Summit.* Vancouver: UBC Press.

Boykoff, Jules. 2014. *Activism and the Olympics: Dissent at the Games in Vancouver and London.* Vancouver: UBC Press.

Boyle, Phil, and Kevin D. Haggerty. 2006. "Spectacular Security: Mega-Events and the Security Complex." *International Political Sociology* 3(2): 257–74. https://doi.org/10.1111/j.1749-5687.2009.00075.x.

Boyle, Phil, Dominique Clément, and Kevin Haggerty. 2014. "Iterations of Olympic Security: Montreal and Vancouver." *Security Dialogue* 46(2): 109–25. https://doi.org/10.1177/0967010614543582.

British Columbia. 2009. *Miscellaneous Statutes Amendment Act*. Statutes of British Columbia, c.22.

British Columbia Civil Liberties Association. 2011. "BCCLA says 'Take Two' on City's political structures bylaw still violates rights." https://bccla.org/news/2011/04/bccla-says-take-two-on-citys-political-structures-bylaw-still-violates-rights.

Canada. 1946. *The Report of the Royal Commission to Investigate Facts Relating to and the Circumstances Surrounding the Communication, by Public Officials and Other Persons in Positions of Trust of Secret and Confidential Information to Agents of a Foreign Power*. Ottawa: Queen's Printer.

Canada. 1981a. *Freedom and Security under the Law*.

Canada. 1981b. *Certain RCMP Activities and the Question of Governmental Knowledge*, vol. 3. Ottawa: Queen's Printer.

CCLA (Canadian Civil Liberties Association). 2015. "Canadian Civil Liberties Association's response to anti-terrorism legislation." https://ccla.org/focus-areas/national-security/due-process-and-counter-terrorism.

Clément, Dominique. 2000. "The Royal Commission on Espionage and the Spy Trials of 1946–9: A Case Study in Parliamentary Supremacy." *Journal of the Canadian Historical Association* 11(1): 151–72. https://doi.org/10.7202/031135ar.

– 2001. "Spies, Lies, and a Commission, 1946–8: A Case Study in the Mobilization of the Canadian Civil Liberties Movement." *Left History* 7(2): 53–79 https://doi.org/10.25071/1913-9632.5454.

– 2008. "The October Crisis of 1970: Human Rights Abuses under the War Measures Act." *Journal of Canadian Studies* 42(2): 160–86. https://doi.org/10.3138/jcs.42.2.160.

– 2008. *Canada's Rights Revolution: Social Movements and Social Change, 1937–1982*. Vancouver: UBC Press.

– 2016a. "The Transformation of Security Planning for the Olympics: The 1976 Montreal Games." *Terrorism and Political Violence* 28(1): 27–51. https://doi.org/10.1080/09546553.2014.987342.

– 2016b. *Human Rights in Canada: A History*. Kitchener-Waterloo: Wilfrid Laurier University Press.

Cottrell, Robert C. 2003. "The Legacy of Munich 1972: Terrorism, Security and the Olympic Games." In *The Legacy of the Olympic Games 1984–2000*, ed. M. de Moragas, C. Kennett, and N. Puig. Lausanne: International Olympic Committee.

Forcese, Craig, and Kent Roach. 2015. *False Security: The Radicalization of Canadian Anti-Terrorism*. Toronto: Irwin Law.

Fussey, Pete, Joan Coaffee, Gary Armstrong, and Dick Hobbs. 2011. *Securing and Sustaining the Olympic City: Reconfiguring London for 2012 and Beyond*. Farnham: Ashgate.

Global Terrorism Database. https://www.start.umd.edu/gtd.

Greenwood, F. Murray. 1988. "The Drafting and Passage of the War Measures Act in 1914 and 1927: Object Lessons in the Need for Vigilance." In *Canadian Perspectives on Law and Society: Issues in Legal History*, ed. W. Wesley Pue and Barry Wright. Ottawa: Carleton University Press.

Hannant, Larry. 1995. *The Infernal Machine: Investigating the Loyalty of Canada's Citizens*. Toronto: University of Toronto Press.

Hewitt, Steve. 2002. *Spying 101: The RCMP's Secret Activities at Canadian Universities, 1917–1997*. Toronto: University of Toronto Press.

Hewitt, Steve and Christabelle Sethna. 2012. "Sex Spying: The RCMP Framing of English-Canadian Women's Liberation Groups during the Cold War." In *Debating Dissent: Canada and the Sixties*, ed. Lara Campbell, Dominique Clément, and Greg Kealey. Toronto: University of Toronto Press.

Hyslop, Lucy. 2010. "Winter Olympics on Slippery Slope after Vancouver Crackdown on Homeless." *The Guardian*, 3 February.

Iacovetta, Franca. 2000. *Enemies Within: Italian and Other Internees in Canada and Abroad*. Toronto: University of Toronto Press.

– 2006. *Gatekeepers: Reshaping Immigrant Lives in Canada*. Toronto: Between the Lines.

Knight, Amy. 2005. *How the Cold War Began: The Gouzenko Affair and the Hunt for Soviet Spies*. Toronto: McClelland and Stewart.

LAC (Library and Archives Canada). Royal Canadian Mounted Police (RCMP), RG 146, 1974–75, vol. 4874, f. Estimates-Supplement, Program Memorandum to Solicitor General.

– 1976a, vol. 4359, Final Report Security Service.

– 1976b, vol. 4367, f. Cabinet Committee on Security and Intelligence – Planning & Threats, Security Assessment, 20 February.

– 1976c, vol. 4359, f. Wallet Attachments, Final Report Security Service, 1976.

– 1976d, vol. 4358, f. Wallet, RCMP, National Security Plan, 1976.

Lambertson, Ross. 2005. *Repression and Resistance: Canadian Human Rights Activists, 1930–1960*. Toronto: University of Toronto Press.

Lindsay, John. 2014. "The Power to React: Review and Discussion of Canada's Emergency Measures Legislation." *International Journal of Human Rights* 18(2): 159–77. https://doi.org/10.1080/13642987.2014.889392.

Mackenzie, J.B. 1971–72. "Section 98, Criminal Code, and Freedom of Expression in Canada." *Queen's Quarterly* 1(1): 469–85.

Mathieu, Sarah-Jane. 2010. *North of the Color Line: Migration and Black Resistance in Canada, 1870–1955*. Chapel Hill: University of North Carolina Press, 2010.

Mickelburgh, Rod. 2009a. "Rights body upset over 'intimidating' security tactics." *Globe and Mail*, 13 June.

– 2009b. "Olympics likely to put Alberta justice on ice." *Globe and Mail*, 24 June.

– 2009c. "Stop harassing us, Olympic protestors tell police." *Globe and Mail*, 3 July.

Molinaro, Dennis. 2017. *An Exceptional Law: Section 98 and the Emergency State, 1919–1936*. Toronto: University of Toronto Press.

Palmer, Bryan, D. 2009. *Canada's 1960s: The Ironies of Identity in a Rebellious Era*. Toronto: University of Toronto Press.

Parnaby, Andrew, Gregory S. Kealey, and Kirk Neargarth. 2009. "'High-Handed, Impolite, and Empire-Breaking Actions': Radicalism, Anti-Imperialism, and State Security in Canada before the Great War." In *Canadian State Trials and Security Measures*, ed. Barry Wright and Susan Binnie. Toronto: University of Toronto Press, 2009.

Petryshyn, J. 1982. "Class Conflict and Civil Liberties: The Origins and Activities of the Canadian Labour Defense League, 1925–1940." *Labour/Le Travail* 10: 39–63. https://doi.org/10.2307/25140138.

Ramraj, Victor V., Michael Hor, Kent Roach, George Williams, eds. 2012. *Global Anti-Terrorism Law and Policy*, vol. 2. Cambridge: Cambridge University Press.

Roach, Kent. 2007."A Comparison of Australian and Canadian Anti-Terrorism Laws." *University of New South Wales Law Journal* 30(1): 53–85.

– 2012a. "Counter-Terrorism in and outside Canada and in and outside the Anti-Terrorism Act." *Review of Constitutional Studies / Revue d'études constitutionnelles* 16(2): 243–65.

Sanan, Guy. 1996. "Olympic Security Operations, 1972–1994." In *Terrorism and the 2000 Olympics*, ed. Alan Thompson. Sydney: Australia Defense Studies Centre.

Tenofsky, Elliot. 1989. "The War Measures and Emergencies Acts: Implications for Canadian Civil Rights and Liberties." *American Review of Canadian Studies* 19(3): 293–306. https://doi.org/10.1080/02722018909481455.

Toohey, Kristine, and Tracy Taylor. 2008. "Mega Events, Fear, and Risk: Terrorism at the Olympic Games." *Journal of Sport Management* 22(2): 451–69.

Vancouver. 2009. *2010 Winter Games By-Law No.9908*. City of Vancouver.

Vipond, Mary. 2010. "Censorship in a Liberal State: Regulating Talk on Canadian Radio in the Early 1990s." *Historical Journal of Film, Radio and Television* 30(1): 75–94. https://doi.org/10.1080/01439680903577284.

Weinrib, Lorraine E. 2001. "Terrorism's Challenge to the Constitutional Order." In *The Security of Freedom: Essays on Canada's Anti-Terrorism Bill*, ed. Ronald J. Daniels, Patrick Macklem, and Kent Roach. Toronto: University of Toronto Press.

Whitaker, Reg. 2003. "Keeping Up with the Neighbours? Canadian Responses to 9/11 in Historical and Comparative Context." *Osgoode Hall Law Journal* 41(2–3): 241–65

Whitaker, Reg, Gregory S. Kealey, and Andrew Parnaby. 2012. *Secret Service: Political Policing in Canada from the Fenians to Fortress America*. Toronto: University of Toronto Press.

Whitaker, Reg, and Gary Marcuse. 1994. *Cold War Canada: The Making of a National Insecurity State, 1945–1957*. Toronto: University of Toronto Press, 1994.

Wilson, David A. 2009. "The D'arcy Mcgee Affair and the Suspension of Habeas Corpus." In *Canadian State Trials: Political Trials and Security Measures, 1840–1914*, ed. Barry Wright and Susan Binnie. Toronto: University of Toronto Press.

7 Deterrence or Blowback? The Consequences of Canadian Intervention in Afghanistan

ERICA CHENOWETH AND LAURA DUGAN

The horrific acts in the United States have reminded us that terrorism is a global threat against which no nation is immune. It has also revealed that terrorist operations are increasingly decentralized and terrorist cells are made up of highly-motivated, highly-trained individuals. Together, with our allies, we will defy and defeat the threat that terrorism poses to all civilized nations.

– Prime Minister Jean Chrétien,
speech to Parliament, 25 September 2001

... this is in retaliation for Afghanistan and because Harper wants to send his troops to Iraq. Canada's officially become one of our enemies by fighting and bombing us and creating a lot of terror in our countries and killing us and killing our innocents. So, just aiming to hit some soldiers just to show that you're not safe even in your own land, and you gotta be careful.

– Michael Zehaf-Bibeau,
in a self-recorded video explaining his motive
for attacking Parliament Hill in Ottawa on 22 October 2014

In October 2001, Canada joined the United States and numerous other NATO allies in a joint mission to deprive al Qaeda of a safe haven from which to launch more 9/11-like attacks and, ultimately, to contain and defeat a Taliban insurgency. Jean Chrétien repeatedly explained that the decision to join the fight in Afghanistan was motivated by Canada's vital security interests. As the war carried on through two subsequent governments, the primary explanation for Canada's continued involvement in the war against al Qaeda and the Taliban in Afghanistan was to prevent jihadi-inspired terrorism from occurring on Canadian soil. A content analysis of hundreds of speeches by Canadian officials between 2001 and 2008 – ranging across the Chrétien, Martin, and

Harper governments – finds that 45 per cent of speeches explained that the war in Afghanistan would help keep Canadians safer at home (Boucher 2009, 726). The war effort transitioned to a training mission that finally wound down in March 2014, but the rise of the Islamic State in Iraq and the Levant (ISIL) in Syria and Iraq precipitated a renewed commitment by Stephen Harper's government to support Canada's allies in military operations against ISIL – a commitment maintained by his successor, Justin Trudeau.

On 20 October 2014, Martin Couture-Rouleau, an alleged sympathizer of ISIL, rammed his car into two Canadian soldiers in a shopping centre parking lot in Saint-Jean-sur-Richelieu, Quebec. After fleeing in his car, running it into a ditch, and charging a policewoman with a knife, police shot and killed him. Two days later, Michael Zehaf-Bibeau shot and killed Corporal Nathan Cirillo as he stood on ceremonial sentry duty at the Canadian National War Memorial. Zehaf-Bibeau then stormed the Parliament building, where police shot and killed him. Zehaf-Bibeau's purported motivation for the attack was retaliation for Canada's involvement in the war in Afghanistan, as well as its potential involvement in the growing war against ISIL.

These attacks raised the question of whether Canadians were actually safer after the country's extended intervention in Afghanistan. Some suggest that the government's already expanded powers – particularly its militaristic responses to terrorism over the previous decade – were responsible for the attacks. Others blame radical Islamic ideology – which we refer to as jihadism – as the culprit, while still others pin the blame on mental illness. A further group sees these attacks as signs that the Canadian government requires still greater powers with regard to anti-terrorism.

Yet even before these attacks, Canadians were questioning whether the war in Afghanistan had achieved its principal aims. Although the Canadian public demonstrated increasing ambivalence about the mission over time, by the end of Canada's official mission in Afghanistan in March 2014, an Abicus Data poll found that 79 per cent of Canadians felt that "very little has really been gained for all casualties and money spent fighting the war in Afghanistan" (Lilley 2014).

These debates within Canada speak to an ongoing dispute in the terrorism literature more generally: are coercive responses effective in reducing terror attacks, or do they tend to backfire? Some perspectives suggest that repressive measures are relatively effective at punishing and preventing subsequent terror attacks – what some would call the *deterrence thesis* (Bejan and Parkin 2015). Others hypothesize that repressive measures rarely remove the threat of future terror attacks, while potentially inflaming grievances and motivating future attacks – what some would call the *blowback thesis* (Choi and Piazza 2015; Johnson 2000).

How effective was Canada's Afghan mission in keeping Canadians safe at home? Does the pattern of Canadian involvement and subsequent terror attacks better fit the deterrence or blowback model? In this analysis, we employ a new dataset of Canadian actions in Afghanistan to empirically test the claim that Canada's operations in Afghanistan improved the security of Canadians at home. Specifically, we evaluate the impacts of Canadian government activity in Afghanistan on motivating jihadi-inspired extremist incidents in Canada.[1] We find that as Canada's coercive involvement in Afghanistan increased during the 2000s, the number of jihadi-inspired incidents increased at home. We also find that target-hardening measures – such as increased border controls and providing extra security at major events – were associated with an increase in extremist attacks rather than a decrease. These results provide greater support for the blowback thesis than the deterrence thesis. We conclude by identifying the limitations of our inquiry and suggesting steps for further research.

The Evidence: Event-Level Data on Canadian Government Actions and Extremist Attacks

To evaluate the validity of the deterrence and blowback theses in the Canadian case, we generated a unique dataset called the Government Actions in Terror Environments (GATE) – Canada dataset (Chenoweth and Dugan 2015). This dataset is the first of its kind to identify events-level[2] actions by the Canadian government toward various terror groups and the constituencies those groups purport to represent. We then match these data with data on extremist attacks in Canada drawn from the Global Terrorism Database (GTD), the Canadian Incident Database (CIDB) compiled by the Canadian Network for Research on Terrorism, Security and Society (TSAS), and the Equipe de Recherche sur le Terrorisme et l'antiterrorisme database (ERTA). We explain the collection and measurement processes for each of these datasets below.

Measuring Canadian Government Actions

GATE–Canada events include any publicly reported actions by Canadian federal actors relevant to terrorist organizations or their constituencies that threaten Canada.[3] The database therefore includes *all* Canadian actions toward substate actors from 1985 through 2013 defined only by the requirement that the actor be a member of the Canadian government and the target be a terrorist organization (e.g., al Qaeda) or its claimed constituency (e.g., Muslims). Because Canada has experienced terrorism from a variety of different groups since 1985, GATE–Canada includes government actions relevant to far right, anti-abortion, leftist, environmental, Muslim, Sikh, Tamil, and franco-phone separatist constituencies.

We collected these data by downloading articles from fifteen[4] international and Canadian anglophone news sources based on a defined search string[5] in Lexis-Nexis for the period 1 January 1985 to 31 December 2013. This resulted in more than fourteen million stories. We then used Textual Analysis by Augmented Replacement Instructions (TABARI), which searches the lead sentences and identifies observations that match the criteria of an extensive set of dictionaries designed to capture international and domestic activity (Schrodt 2006). Dropping duplicates, excluding irrelevant stories, and hand-coding each observation for accuracy resulted in 7,216 final observations.

During this process, we coded several additional variables. First, the Conciliatory–Repression scale, illustrated in Table 7.1, features distinctions in the intensity of the action as well as its relative placement of the action on a conciliation–repression spectrum. Table 7.2 provides examples of actions under each category.

Second, we coded the target type for each observation. *Discriminate* actions attempt to single out "guilty" or "suspected" parties from uninvolved parties. *Indiscriminate* actions directly affect uninvolved people (i.e., those who are not suspected of involvement in terrorist activity, or what we refer to as the broader population), even if the government only intends to affect a specific person or organization. For example, if the RCMP raided a workplace to capture a known terror suspect, the action was indiscriminate because other uninvolved persons could have been present. We also code as indiscriminate any actions that affect the broader population rather than just a terrorist group (e.g., Muslims in general as opposed to jihadi-inspired suspects).

Third, we coded the location of the action (e.g., in Afghanistan or in Canada). Finally, we coded a variable called *targhard*, which specifies whether the action increases protection around a terrorist target (e.g., increase in airport security) or decreases protection (e.g., removal of troops from a location). Most actions were unrelated to target hardening, but an important subset of actions related to efforts to increase or decrease protection.

Table 7.1. Seven-point guide for the conciliatory–repression scale

Category	Description	Examples
1 Accommodation	• Appeasing or surrendering • Making tangible, full concessions according to opponent's demands	• Signing self-government agreement • Granting independence
2 Conciliatory action	• Making tangible, material concessions short of full concessions • Taking tangible action that signals intention to cooperate or negotiate with opponent	• Paying a ransom • Providing economic aid to a population • Compensating aggrieved individuals • Releasing someone from prison or acquitting them
3 Conciliatory statement or intentions	• Expressing intention to cooperate or showing support • Verbal expression short of physical action	• Stating support for Afghan government negotiating with the Taliban • Praising aggrieved constituency • Making verbal commitment to conciliate
4 Neutral or ambiguous	• Infighting • Neutrally discussing an issue • No clear moves towards or away from resolution of conflict • Requires more context to determine whether it is conciliatory or repressive	• Infighting over how to respond to terrorist groups (or their constituencies) within the Canadian government • Any attempts to ask for help from a third party to resolve a conflict
5 Verbal conflict	• Expressing intent to engage in conflict or threaten • Declining to cease ongoing conflict; maintain the status quo during conflict • Verbal expression short of physical action	• Criticizing, blaming, or threatening aggrieved constituency • Denying government responsibility in conflict escalation
6 Physical conflict	• Taking physical or violent action aimed at coercing opponent • No apparent intention to kill	• Arresting a suspect • Convicting and sentencing a suspect • Withdrawing or withholding funds from a constituency
7 Extreme deadly repression	• Taking physical action exhibiting intent to kill • Engaging in torture or severe violence (such as severe beatings), which could kill someone	• Military operations involving lethal engagements with Al Qaeda affiliates in Afghanistan • Air strikes

Table 7.2. Examples of common actions in GATE-Canada for each scale item

1. Accommodation/full concessions	5. Verbal conflict
Sign land claim	Make pessimistic comment
2. Conciliatory action	Accuse Nazi war criminal
	Brush off abuse claims
Withdraw army	Push for more investigative freedoms
Cut controversial funding	Praise Alaska pipeline
Fine polluters	Condemn attack
Sign carbon treaty	
	6. Physical conflict
3. Conciliatory statement or intentions	Deploy troops
Urge support for minorities	Lift abortion restrictions
Apologize for mistake	Convict terrorist leader
Express support for gun owners	Approve energy project
Discuss green initiatives	Arrest
Offer to meet with Muslim leaders	
	7. Extreme deadly repression
4. Neutral or ambiguous	Kill Taliban fighters
Infight over	Launch assault mission
Fail to reach agreement	Bomb targets
Plan a visit	Raid
Aim to settle controversy	Engage in gun battle
Investigate attack	

The resulting dataset offers a day-by-day view of Canadian actions relevant to conflicts with various non-state actors inside and outside the country. For the purposes of our analysis, however, we aggregate these actions in several ways. First, we aggregate the data to produce counts of the number of conciliatory and repressive actions per month. Conciliatory actions are those with conciliatory–repressive scores of 1, 2, or 3. Repressive actions are those with conciliatory–repressive scores of 5, 6, or 7. The resulting dataset gives us daily, monthly, quarterly, and annual counts of conciliatory and repressive observations from 1985–2013. For our purposes, this article focuses exclusively on actions against al Qaeda, jihadi-inspired groups, or Muslims generally after 9/11.

Measuring Extremist Attacks

We compiled the dependent variable for this analysis using data from the GTD, CIDB, and ERTA. These data include domestic incidents, such as Zehaf-Bibeau's attack, and international ones, such as attacks on Canadian installations abroad. Due to the varying definitions of terrorism and political violence used by each of these databases, incorporating data from all of these sources enabled this project to include a wider array of incidents of political violence that occurred in Canada than any single source – what we refer to as extremist "incidents" or "attacks." This allowed us to corroborate data and fill in missing data across datasets.

To give readers a sense of the range of incidents included, consider the following five examples:

- 19 February 1986: Someone left an improvised explosive device at the front door of the Canadian Immigration Centre in Surrey, BC. A note found at the scene protested the openness of the Canadian government's immigration policies.
- 17 December 1991: The Billingsgate Fish Company Shop in Edmonton, Alberta, was set on fire following the vandalism of three fish trucks, which were spray-painted with the words "revenge" and "murder" and the acronym "ALF" (Animal Liberation Front).
- 4 January 1998: Five members of White Power and other white supremacist groups killed Nirmal Singh Gill, a caretaker at the Guru Nanak Sikh Temple in Surrey, BC.
- 1 November 2000: Two synagogues were attacked with Molotov cocktails in Edmonton, Alberta.
- 8 April 2007: A roadside bomb killed six Canadian soldiers in southern Afghanistan.

After combining the three datasets, we identified potential duplicates based on whether an event was described within two days within another dataset. We assumed that events that met this criterion but occurred in different locations were unique events. However, in cases where the location was the same or at least one was unknown, we determined duplicates based on whether the reported target, event type, and weapon were similar. After confirming cases like this, we coded these events as duplicates and removed one of the cases.

Using these methods, we identified thirty-eight duplicate events, yielding a final analytic sample of 957 events between 1 January 1985 and 31 December 2014. As Figure 7.1 shows, we sourced the vast majority (83.8%) of the attacks from the TSAS database. Most of the events we removed came from the GTD, with thirty-seven out of the original fifty-two GTD events (71.2%) determined to be duplicates.

Figure 7.2 depicts the number of attacks in each year, measured on the left axis, and the number of fatalities each year, measured on the right axis. The highest number of attacks in a single year was 85 (occurring in 2006). Outside of 1985, when terrorist attacks killed

Figure 7.1. Number of attacks per year by original data source

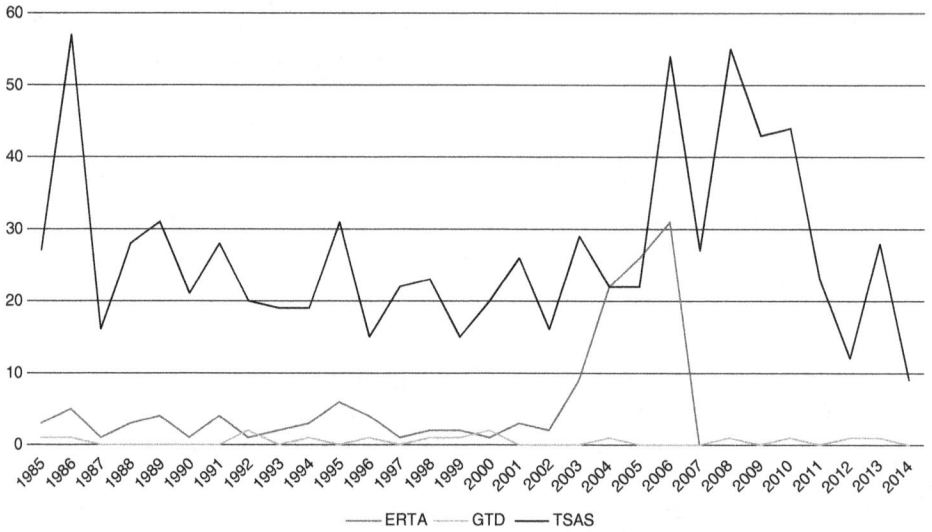

Figure 7.2. Number of attacks per year and number of people killed

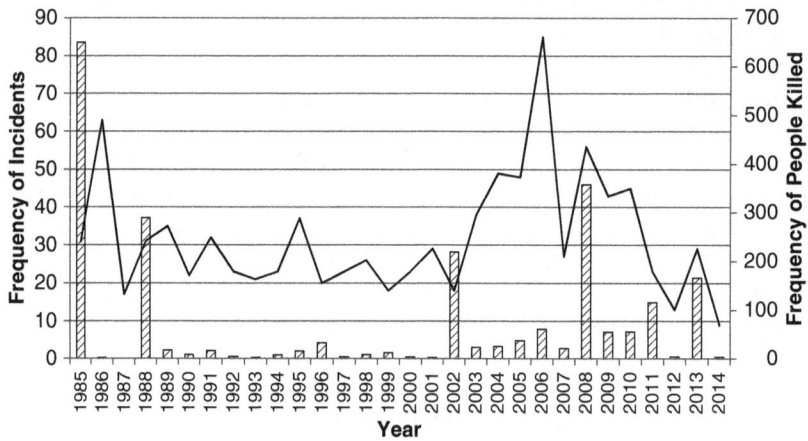

650 people (including 329 in the attack on Air India 182), the two years that resulted in the most people killed were 1988 ($f = 289$) and 2008 ($f = 358$).

We identified the primary ideological motivation for the attack based on the motivation variable from TSAS, the group that perpetrated the

Table 7.3. Frequency of attacks by attributed perpetrator

Constituency	Freq.	Percentage of total attacks	Percentage of attributed attacks
Anti-abortion extremist	15	1.57	3.55
Environmental extremist	54	5.64	12.80
General	2	0.21	0.47
Jewish extremist	3	0.31	0.71
Jihadi-inspired	109	11.39	25.83
Far right extremist	116	12.12	27.49
Separatist extremist	41	4.28	9.72
Leftist extremist	58	6.06	13.74
Write-In	17	1.78	4.03
Sikh extremist	5	0.52	1.18
Aboriginal extremist	1	0.10	0.24
Palestinian nationalist extremist	1	0.10	0.24
Missing	535	55.90	–
Total	**957**	**100.00**	**100**

attack according to the GTD, and the narratives attached to the ERTA database. The only exception to this was from the TSAS database, in which all attacks directed at targets labelled "Healthcare/Hospital/Abortion" were coded as anti-abortion. We derived the constituencies themselves from the GATE-Canada protocol, and the initial distribution of events attributed to a constituency can be seen below in Table 7.3. Figure 7.3 visualizes this distribution.

In all, 109 incidents were attributed to jihadi-inspired perpetrators, representing over 25 per cent of extremist events during the series. A total of 535 events within this dataset did not have an identified constituency, representing 55.9 per cent of the total number of events. Therefore, we could not assign an ideological motivation to the attack, and we code these as "unknown perpetrators."[6]

Thus, for the analysis below, we construct two dependent variables: (1) a strict measure, which counts only the number of attacks attributed to jihadi-inspired perpetrators; and (2) a weak measure, which counts the number of attacks attributed to jihadi-inspired perpetrators and the number of attacks with unknown perpetrators. We expect that the true number of jihadi-inspired attacks falls between the two estimates.

Figure 7.3. Proportion of attacks attributed to each perpetrator type[7]

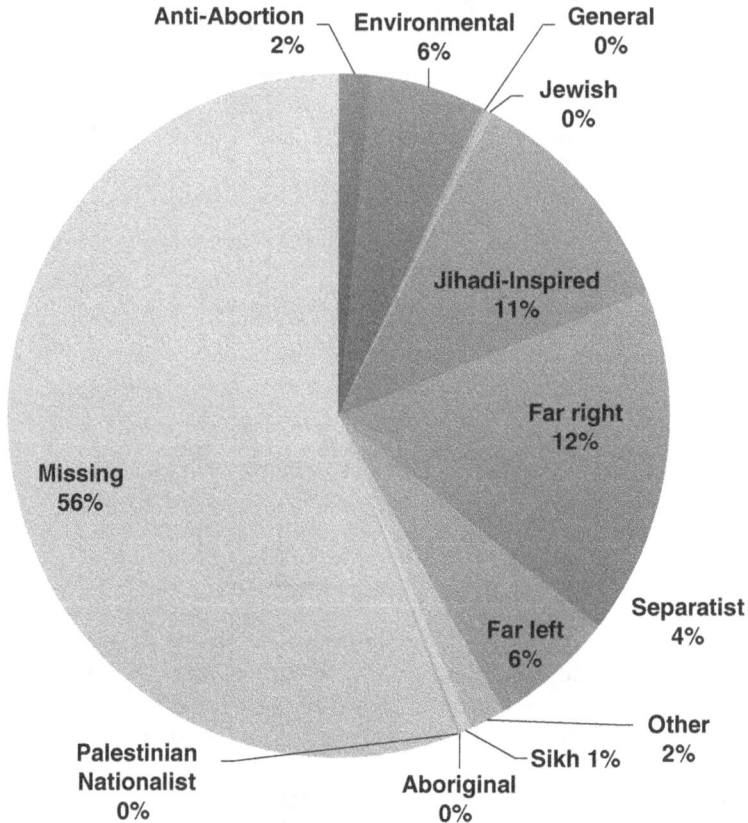

Trends from Canada's War on Extremism

In this section, we detail some descriptive data regarding the GATE–Canada data as well as trends in extremist attacks against Canadians attributed to jihadi-inspired groups at home and abroad. First, Figure 7.4 presents the distribution of GATE actions targeting different constituencies from 1985–2013.

Even though far right extremists tend to be the most common perpetrators of political violence in Canada (see Figure 7.3), the most common reported government actions related to Muslims. More than 35 per cent of Canada's actions from 1985 to 2013 were most relevant to Muslim constituencies. Actions relevant to jihadi-inspired groups include troop

Figure 7.4. Primary constituencies of Canadian government actions,
1985–2013 ($n = 7,612$)

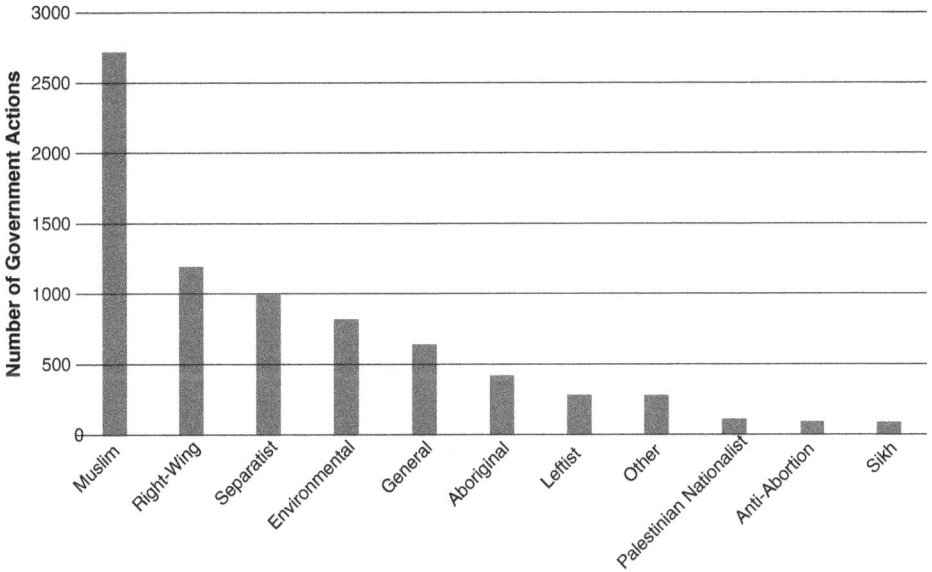

deployments in Afghanistan and arrests of homegrown jihadi-inspired
extremists, whereas actions relevant to Muslims as a whole include
decisions regarding religious rights such as the right to wear a hijab in
the classroom, refugee and immigration issues that relate to Muslims
who try to stay in Canada, and investigations into abuses of Muslims
(as in the Maher Arar case).

We classify "general" counterterrorism actions as those intended to
stop *any* terrorist activity. These actions, representing 8 per cent of the
actions, are less centred on the ideology of the perpetrator and more
focused on prevention. They include actions such improving security
at the border, bolstering aviation security, and adopting anti-terrorism
legislation that specifies particular targets.

Figure 7.5 presents the trends of GATE actions related to Muslims
over time, aggregated for simplicity. We mark actions coded as 1, 2, and
3 as conciliatory actions, and we mark actions coded as 5, 6, and 7 as
repressive actions (item 4 is omitted for simplicity). The solid black line
represents more conciliatory actions, and the dotted black line represents repressive actions.

Perhaps the most striking patterns relate to Canada's post-9/11
focus on Muslims and on extremism in general. Canada has clearly

Figure 7.5. Conciliatory and repressive actions by the Canadian government toward Muslim constituencies, 1985–2013

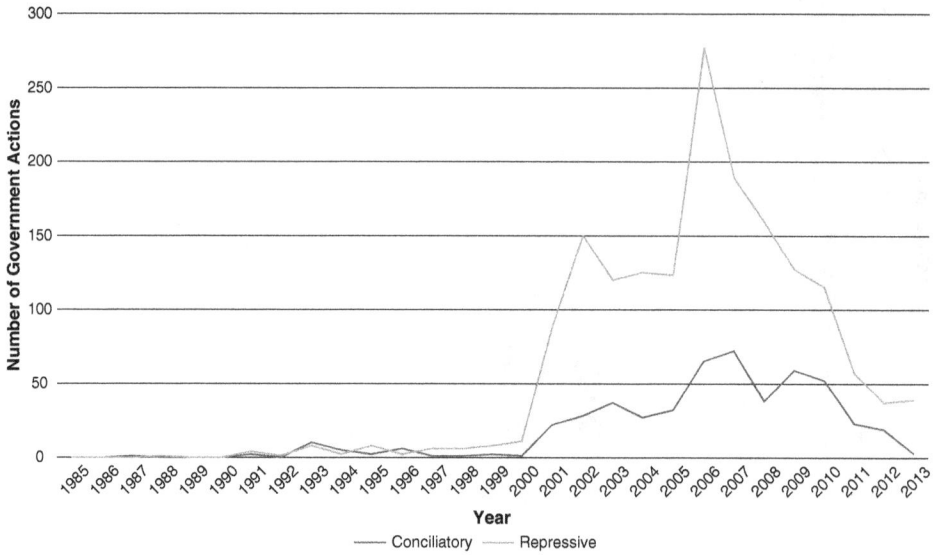

intensified its focus on jihadi-inspired terrorism, with a sudden increase in response to 9/11. Although the government has adopted some conciliatory actions toward Muslims in Afghanistan and at home, the dominant mode of Canadian actions toward this constituency has been repressive. The government has also increased general counterterrorism actions since 9/11 (not shown in the figure). These actions have generally been repressive or "threatening" and include improving border and aviation security, tightening financial regulations to eliminate funding to terror groups, issuing statements that Canada will not tolerate extremism of any kind, and adopting laws with a generalized focus on extremism as opposed to singling out particular constituencies. There has been no commensurate number of conciliatory actions (e.g., court cases ruling that certain elements of anti-terrorism laws are unconstitutional) for Muslims or for general constituencies.

We overlay the data on extremist attacks, measured on the right axis, on the GATE actions related to Muslims after 9/11, measured on the left axis. As Figure 7.6 illustrates, trends in such attacks closely parallel trends in repressive GATE actions. Similar patterns hold in Afghanistan (Figure 7.7).

Figure 7.8 shows the distribution of discriminate and indiscriminate actions related to Muslims in terms of whether the action was conciliatory or repressive. For Muslim constituencies, most actions

Figure 7.6. Canadian government actions related to Muslims and jihadi-inspired attacks, 9/2001–12/2013

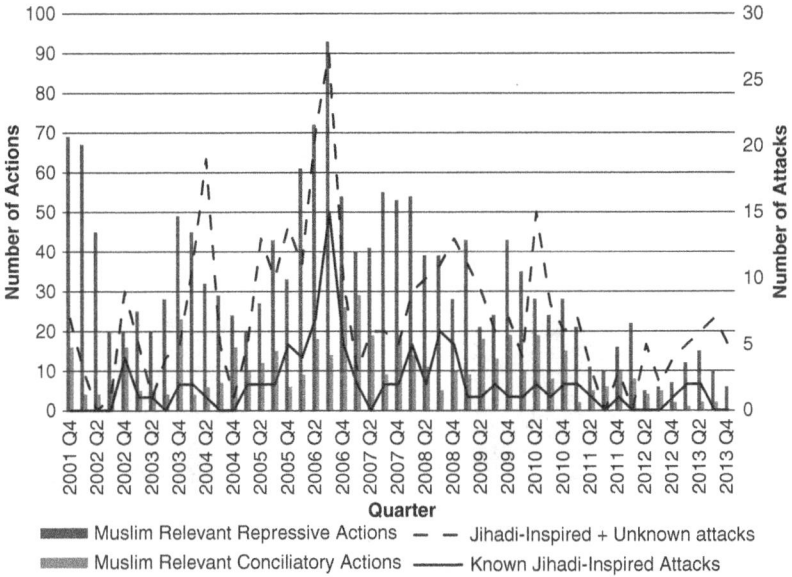

Muslim Relevant Repressive Actions — — Jihadi-Inspired + Unknown attacks
Muslim Relevant Conciliatory Actions —— Known Jihadi-Inspired Attacks

Figure 7.7. Canadian government actions in Afghanistan and attacks against Canadians in Afghanistan, 9/2001–12/2013

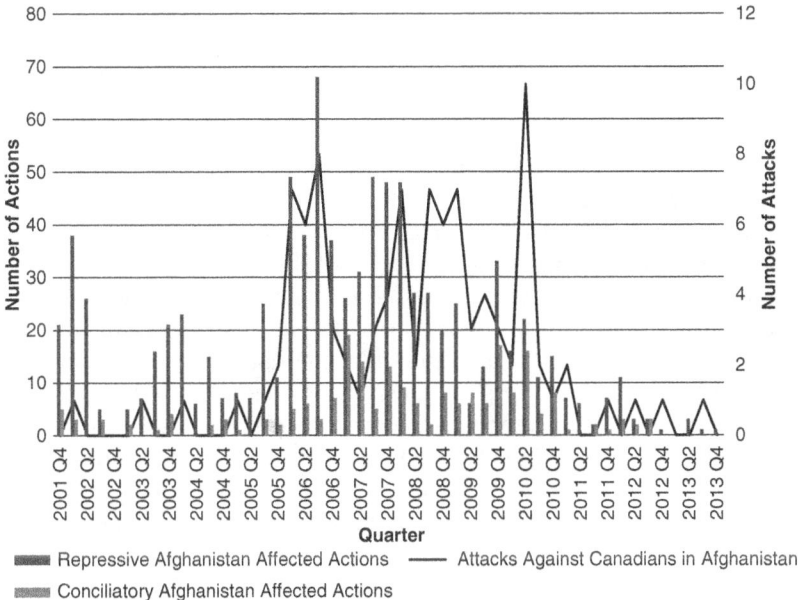

Repressive Afghanistan Affected Actions —— Attacks Against Canadians in Afghanistan
Conciliatory Afghanistan Affected Actions

Figure 7.8. Conciliatory and repressive discriminate and indiscriminate actions toward Muslim constituency, 1985–2013

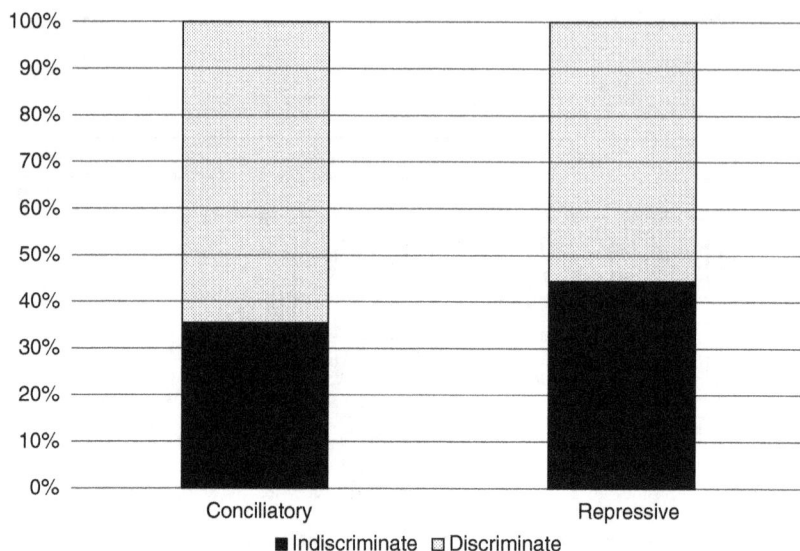

(whether conciliatory or repressive) directly affected terrorists or those suspected of terrorist acts. In other words, the majority of conciliatory actions toward Muslims have involved those specifically accused of terrorism-related activity (e.g., releasing a terror suspect from prison) rather than indiscriminate actions (e.g., providing more robust engagement programs with the Muslim community). Similarly, repressive actions have tended to involve specific suspects (e.g., arrests of terror suspects) as opposed to generalized repression (e.g., raids on Muslim community organizations).

We now compare actions in Canada with actions in the Afghanistan/Pakistan region. Figure 7.9 shows the distribution of conciliatory and repressive actions for each location. Most notable is that most actions are repressive; in fact, in the Afghanistan/Pakistan region, more than 80 per cent of the actions are repressive, compared to only 64 per cent in Canada. This is unsurprising, given that Canadians were engaged in military operations to combat al Qaeda terrorism and a Taliban-fuelled insurgency while in Afghanistan, whereas within Canada, politicians are the primary actors and draw upon a broader range of tools to resolve conflicts. Indeed, the military is responsible for nearly half the actions in Afghanistan/Pakistan but only 1 per cent of the actions in Canada.

Figure 7.9. Distribution of government actions at home and abroad, 1985–2013

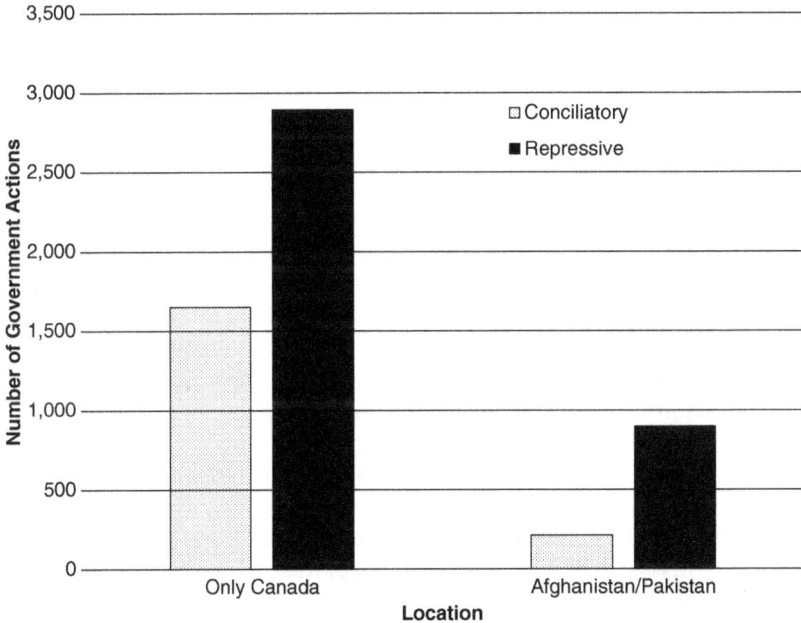

Having reviewed the descriptive statistics for the data, we now turn to an analysis of how these different actions have affected extremist violence by jihadi-inspired perpetrators in Canada.

Empirical Analysis: Did Canadian Action in Afghanistan Make Canadians Safer at Home?

We are primarily interested in whether Canadian actions in the Afghanistan conflict affected the frequency of jihadi-inspired incidents in Canada. We next explore two competing hypotheses – deterrence, and blowback. The deterrence thesis posits that repressive actions will reduce subsequent terror attacks and incidents by demonstrating that terrorism is too costly as a strategy, and that conciliatory actions will increase terror attacks and incidents by rewarding terror perpetrators with concessions (Bejan and Parkin 2015; Dugan and Chenoweth 2012). The blowback thesis posits that repressive actions will increase subsequent terror attacks by further angering terror groups and, potentially, the constituencies those groups purport to represent. The blowback thesis does not articulate specific expectations as to the effects of conciliatory actions.

As such, if the deterrence thesis is correct, we should expect to see a negative association between repressive actions in Afghanistan and subsequent jihadi-inspired attacks in Canada, and we should expect to see a positive association between conciliation and concessions in Afghanistan and subsequent jihadi-inspired attacks in Canada. If the blowback thesis is correct, we should expect a positive correlation between repressive actions in Afghanistan and subsequent jihadi-inspired attacks in Canada.

We evaluate these claims by aggregating our data into 148 monthly units between September 2001 and December 2013. The dependent variable is the number of jihadi-inspired incidents and attacks in the current month (see the discussion on the strict and weak measures above). We use appropriate statistical techniques to estimate the effects of government actions on terror attacks in the subsequent month.

The primary independent variables are (a) the number of conciliatory actions in the previous month and (b) the number of repressive actions in the previous month. Neutral or ambiguous actions are omitted. We also include several additional covariates: (c) dummy indicators for each government (Chrétien, Martin, and Harper, with Harper omitted from the model as the reference category) to account for potential variations across prime minister; (d) lagged indicators of jihadi-inspired attacks, lagging 1, 2, 3, and 4 months to account for the effect of earlier attacks; and (e) logged population size as the exposure variable. Table 7.4 contains descriptive statistics for the data.

Table 7.5 shows the results. The reported models evaluate the effects of repressive and conciliatory actions in Afghanistan on jihadi-inspired attacks in Canada. Model 1 details the relationship using the strict measure of the dependent variable, and Model 2 shows the association using the weak measure of the dependent variable. As we can see, the effect of conciliatory actions is not statistically significant. However, the effect of repressive actions is positive and statistically significant. It may surprise readers to learn that Paul Martin's government endured a higher number of attacks than Chrétien's or Harper's, possibly because of Canada's surge in involvement in the war in Afghanistan during Martin's term. Recall that we include attacks on Canadian troops in Afghanistan as part of the overall count (hence the escalation during Martin's tenure). We also see that the lag terms for prior extremist attacks by jihadi-inspired perpetrators were not strongly correlated with an increase in violence by such groups, although the one-month lag is correlated with an increase in the weak measure. Figures 7.10 and 7.11 illustrate the associations in Model 1 using the GAM smoother, which further supports the findings in Table 7.5.

Table 7.4. Descriptive statistics of covariates

Variable	N	Mean	Standard deviation	Min	Max
Jihadi-inspired attacks in Canada (strict measure)	148	0.142	0.142	0	3
Attacks by jihadi-inspired + unknown perpetrators in Canada (weak measure)	148	1.047	1.472	0	7
Lagged conciliatory actions in Afghanistan	148	1.439	1.910	0	8
Lagged repressive actions in Afghanistan	148	6.041	6.322	0	36
Lagged target-hardening actions in Canada	148	3.912	3.440	0	26

Table 7.5. Effect of actions in Afghanistan on jihadi-inspired extremist attacks in Canada

Variable	Model 1 (attacks – strict measure)	Model 2 (attacks – broad measure)
Conciliatory actions	−0.350 (0.243)	−0.064 (0.073)
Repressive actions	0.097* (0.049)	0.029 (0.019)
PM Chrétien	−1.087 (1.115)	−0.074 (0.325)
PM Martin	1.137+ (0.581)	0.709** (0.274)
Lagged jihadi-inspired attacks in Canada$_{t-1}$	0.313 (0.362)	0.142* (0.071)
Lagged jihadi-inspired attacks in Canada$_{t-2}$	0.514 (0.370)	0.059 (0.073)
Lagged jihadi-inspired attacks in Canada$_{t-3}$	−0.902 (0.552)	−0.003 (0.071)
Lagged jihadi-inspired attacks in Canada$_{t-4}$	0.006 (0.485)	−0.015 (0.074)
Constant	−13.005*** (0.529)	−10.869*** (0.228)
Observations	148	148

t-statistics in parentheses
+ $p<0.10$, * $p<0.05$,
** $p<0.01$,
*** $p<0.001$

Figure 7.10. Effect of repressive acts in Afghanistan on jihadi-inspired attacks in Canada, 9/2001–12/2013 (based on Table 5, Model 1)

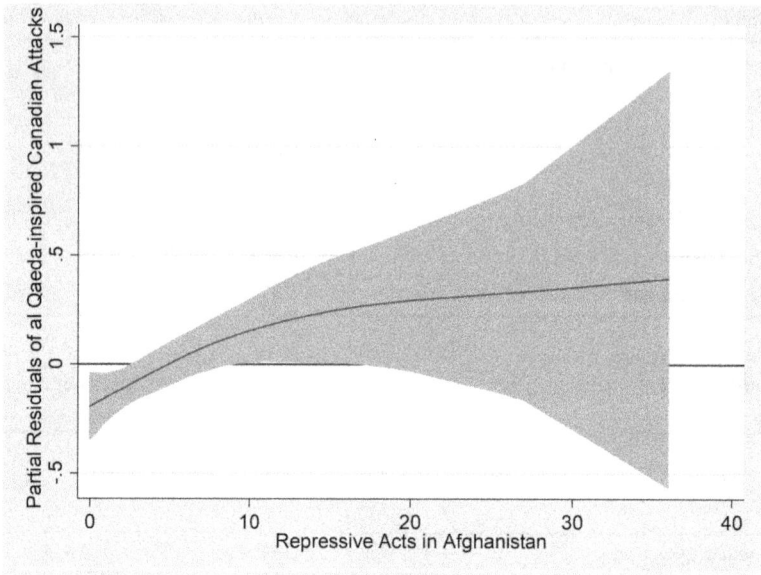

Figure 7.11. Effect of conciliatory acts in Afghanistan on jihadi-inspired attacks in Canada, 9/2001–12/2013 (based on Table 5, Model 1)

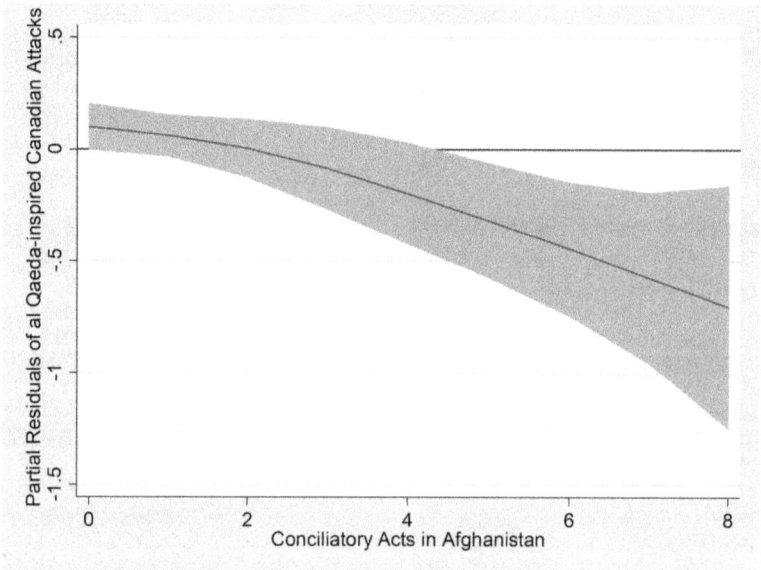

As a result, it seems clear that we can reject the deterrence thesis in this case. Canada's actions in Afghanistan do not appear to have deterred more attacks at home. Instead, we find a significant relationship between government actions in Afghanistan and the number of attacks perpetrated by jihadi-inspired individuals or groups against Canadians within Canada. As Canada's involvement in Afghanistan increased during the 2000s, the number of domestic counterterrorism actions also increased. This finding lends support to the blowback thesis.

Limitations and Next Steps

The results reported in Table 7.5 cast doubt on the notion that repressive government actions tend to deter future terrorist attacks. Instead, we find support for the notion that such responses – particularly militarized responses to terrorism abroad – have tended to elicit retaliatory attacks against Canadians at home.

The current study is limited in key ways. First, our current analysis uses fairly blunt measures of Canadian government actions. We aggregated the actions into repressive and conciliatory categories that are useful for testing basis hypotheses but do not provide specific information on the precise kinds of actions or policies that were the most inflammatory. The GATE data yield a number of potential directions for a more nuanced and informative analysis of the specific types of repressive and conciliatory actions that are most productive in reducing extremism, so future researchers could easily explore these issues. For instance, future researchers could further distil the data into which actors (politicians, military, police, or judiciaries) were implementing different policies as a way to differentiate between military, diplomatic, and criminal justice approaches to counterterrorism.

Second, our analysis did not distinguish between discriminate and indiscriminate actions – those that target terror suspects compared those aimed at the broader population. Prior studies indicate that this can be an important determinant of the longer-term political effects of different actions (Dugan and Chenoweth 2012). Our prior work on the Israeli–Palestinian conflict suggests that there are meaningful differences in the impact of counterterrorism actions depending on whether they help or harm the broader population that terror groups purport to represent. Specifically, therefore, future studies should evaluate whether repressive actions are more effective when they single out specific suspects instead of coercing the general population.

Third, our analysis is limited to the Canadian case and does not take into account the potential effects of other global players – such as the United States, other NATO partners, and the Afghan and

Pakistan governments themselves – in shaping which counterterrorism actions Canada adopted and the effects they had on the ground. Future research could collect and combine comparative data to give a fuller picture at the global context of Canadian counterterrorism and its effects. Our own current work includes versions of GATE for Israel, Turkey, Lebanon, Egypt, Algeria, and the United States. As future cases become available, it will be useful for researchers to conduct careful comparative studies across these various cases.

Regardless, in the meantime, our results should give pause to advocates of more forceful military action against terror groups abroad, such as military intervention against ISIL in Iraq and Syria. Since the invasion of Afghanistan following the 9/11 attacks, repressive military actions in Afghanistan have been correlated with a rise in jihadi-inspired incidents and attacks at home. Given other academic work that shows an association between foreign military engagements and an increase in targeting by terror groups (Choi and Piazza 2015; Johnson 2000), it is clearer *what not to do* than *what to do* to counter terrorism and violent extremism. However, knowing which measures are historically counterproductive can be a useful motivation for innovating new forms of action. With regard to countering terrorism and extremism, devoting concerted attention to other tools – such as intelligence, financial and economic instruments, and diplomatic action – might yield alternatives to repressive actions in ways that could ultimately improve the security of Canadians at home.

NOTES

1 By "incidents," we mean successful or foiled attacks, so long as the foiled attacks were concrete and under way at the time of their disruption. This is standard practice in the Global Terrorism Database and the Canadian Incident Database, since including plots under way yields a more accurate picture of the number of would-be perpetrators who attempt to carry out an attack. For simplicity, we use the terms "incidents" and "attacks" synonymously throughout this chapter.
2 Events are discrete actions. For example, arriving for a meeting is an event, but every word exchanged across the table is not; arresting a suspected terrorist is an event, but we did not count each day he or she was held in jail a daily event.
3 We used the same set of filters for actors and targets because sometimes TABARI coded them in opposite roles. For example, TABARI might mark al Qaeda as the actor and the US government as the target when the US

government is the actor and al Qaeda is the target. However, to avoid confusion in this report, we keep the actor/target distinction in the text.
4 The sources include Agence France-Presse (AFP), Associated Press (AP), the *Calgary Herald*, Canada Newswire, Canadian Government News, the *Edmonton Journal*, the Hali*fax Daily News*, the *Hamilton Spectator*, the *National Post* and *Financial Post*, the *Ottawa Citizen*, the *Gazette* (Montreal), the *Globe and Mail*, the *Toronto Star*, the *Vancouver Province*, and the *Vancouver Sun*.
5 The search string entered into Lexis-Nexis was: [canad! or ottawa or toronto or vancouver or montreal or edmonton or calgary or quebec or winnipeg or hamilton or ontario or yukon or alberta or nunavut or manitoba or saskatchewan or "british columbia" or "northwest territories" or "new brunswick" or "nova scotia" or "prince edward island" or "newfoundland and labrador" or inuit or cree or inuktitut or ojibway or "first nations" or metis].
6 The lack of perpetrator data in the CIDB-GTD-ERTA combined data is not unique; perpetrator data is a recognized gap across data sources.
7 We use a negative binomial estimation strategy, since our dependent variable is an event count with overdispersion. We also estimate the model using a generalized additive model (GAM) smoother to account for the possibility that the association is non-parametric. We also use the GAM models to visualize the association between the primary independent and dependent variables.

REFERENCES

Bejan, Vladimir, and William S. Parkin. 2015. "Examining the Effect of Repressive and Conciliatory Government Actions on Terrorism Activity in Israel." *Economics Letters* 133: 55–8. https://doi.org/10.1016/j.econlet.2015.05.016.
Boucher, Jean-Christophe. 2009. "Selling Afghanistan: A Discourse Analysis of Canada's Military Intervention, 2001–2008." *International Journal* 64(3): 717–33. https://doi.org/10.1177/002070200906400308.
Bronskill, Jim. 2015. "Parliament attack 'retaliation' for Canada's role in Afghanistan, Iraq." *Global News*, 6 March. http://globalnews.ca/news/1868053/live-rcmp-show-parliament-shooters-self-made-video-11-a-m-est.
Chenoweth, Erica, and Laura Dugan. 2015. "The Canadian Way of Counterterrorism: Introducing the GATE-Canada Dataset." *Canadian Foreign Policy Journal* 22(3): 316–30. https://doi.org/10.1080/11926422.2016.1144210.
Choi, Seung-Whan, and James A. Piazza. 2015. "Foreign Military Interventions and Suicide Attacks." *Journal of Conflict Resolution* 61(2): 271–97. https://doi.org/10.1177/0022002715576575.
Dugan, Laura, and Erica Chenoweth. 2012. "Moving beyond Deterrence: The Effectiveness of Raising the Expected Utility of Abstaining from Terrorism

in Israel." *American Sociological Review* 77(4) (September): 597–624. https://doi.org/10.1177/0003122412450573.

Ellis, James O. 2015. *The Canadian Incident Database.* http://extremism.ca, accessed 13 August 2015.

Enders, Walter, and Todd Sandler. 1993. "The Effectiveness of Antiterrorism Policies: A Vector Autoregression-Intervention Analysis." *American Political Science Review* 87(4): 829–44. https://doi.org/10.2307/2938817.

Johnson, Chalmers. 2000. *Blowback: The Costs and Consequences of American Empire.* New York: Metropolitan Books.

LaFree, Gary, and Laura Dugan. 2007. "Introducing the Global Terrorism Database." *Terrorism and Political Violence* 19(2): 181–204. https://doi.org/10.1080/09546550701246817.

Leman-Longlois, Stephane, and Jean-Paul Brodeur. 2005. "Terrorism Old and New: Counterterrorism in Canada." *Police Practice and Research* 6(2): 121–40. https://doi.org/10.1080/15614260500121096.

Lilley, Brian. 2014. "Harper looks back on Afghan mission." *Calgary Sun*, 31 March 31. http://www.calgarysun.com/2014/03/31/harper-looks-back-on-afghan-mission.

Schrodt, Philip A. 2006. "Twenty Years of the Kansas Event Data System Project. Unpublished manuscript, University of Kansas.

8 The Social Structure of Extremist Websites

MARTIN BOUCHARD,[1] GARTH DAVIES,
RICHARD FRANK, EDITH WU, AND KILA JOFFRES

Despite numerous developments in how extremist groups connect with their supporters online, the official website still serves a purpose as the public "face" of the group, its first opportunity to define its goals and its cause. Research on the content of terrorist groups' websites suggests that these groups use them in much the same way and for the same reasons that non-terrorist groups do: to provide information on their organizations, their missions, and their origins, and to try to generate awareness of the causes that motivate their existence (Seib and Janbek 2011; Davies et al. 2015; Weimann 2006).

There has been research on the content published by extremist groups on these websites (Seib and Janbek 2011; Davies et al. 2015; Weimann 2006), but rarely considered is the larger community in which these websites are embedded. This community can be defined in multiple ways, from individuals who follow and comment on (but do not necessarily support) events related to terrorist groups such as ISIS (Thomas et al. 2016), to entities such as the websites of terrorist organizations forming connections via hyperlinks to other websites and internet content they like, or publicly recognize as worthy of a visit (Bouchard, Joffres, and Frank 2014; Burris, Smith, and Strahm 2000). This chapter focuses on the latter type of community, in which the unit of observation is the website, as opposed to the individual. These communities are important, if only because part of the goal of these groups is to generate awareness of their cause among individuals who surf the Web and who would have been previously unaware of their existence or their activities. It follows that research efforts aimed at reproducing the exploratory behaviour of Web users has become necessary.

In this study, we select the official websites of four known extremist groups and map the networks of hyperlinked websites forming a virtual community around them. The networks are constructed using a custom-built webcrawler (TENE: Terrorism and Extremism Network Extractor), which searches the HTML of a website for all the hyperlinks inserted directing to other websites (Bouchard, Joffres, and Frank 2014). Following all of these hyperlinks out of the initial website of interest results in a network of websites forming a community that is more or less cohesive, more or less extensive, and more or less devoted to the same cause (Bouchard and Westlake 2016; Westlake and Bouchard 2016). When the official website of a group contains many hyperlinks toward external websites, this may indicate a more active community, and a more active social movement.

Two of the groups we have selected for this study are characterized as being driven by localized conflicts or grievances: the Revolutionary Armed Forces of Columbia (FARC), and the Popular Front for the Liberation of Palestine (PFLP). The other two are usually labelled as "left-wing" extremist ideologies: Earth First! (EF), and the Animal Liberation Front (ALF). The four groups were selected specifically for one or more of these reasons: (1) their presence on the list of terrorist organizations found in Canada's *Criminal Code*, Section 83.05; (2) the fact that they actively hyperlinked to related websites; and (3) the different communication strategies they used to make their cause and goals known to the public on their official webpage (Davies et al. 2015). With regard to the latter criterion, prior research has shown that the official website of an extremist group can be classified based on two central characteristics: (1) how violent it is, and (2) how actively it is calling for action. The official pages of both FARC and PFLP were classified as "passive, but containing violent content," whereas the official websites of EF! and ALF showed "active call[s] for action but [were] non-violent" (Davies et al. 2015). This study examines whether the social networks surrounding these official websites reproduce these patterns. Do the communities of hyperlinked websites display *more* or *less* violent extremist content than the official webpages of the extremist groups in our sample? A related question, given the context of this book more generally, is whether and how Canadian-related content is represented or discussed on these websites.

Virtual Communities: The Networks of Hyperlinked Websites

Criminal communities have long attracted the attention of researchers of traditional crime, particularly when it comes to criminal subcultures (Cohen 1955), but few empirical studies have traced the contours of these communities or subcultures. Change is evident in at least two areas of criminological research, both driven by scholars adopting network methods. The first area involves research on street gangs, where researchers adopting a network approach have been able to redefine more precisely what constitutes the core gang, its periphery, and the larger social structure around gang members (Bouchard and Konarski 2014; Morselli 2009; Papachristos 2006; Tremblay et al. 2016). The second area where the use of "communities" as a unit of analysis has become more prominent is research on cyberspace more generally (Haythornthwaite 2009; Wellman and Gulia 1999), but also on online social spaces amenable to the discovery of extreme narratives (Bouchard, Joffres, and Frank 2014; Chen 2012; Frank et al. 2015) or illegal behaviour (Bouchard and Westlake 2016; Westlake and Bouchard 2016).

In this chapter, our analysis focuses on one type of virtual community that is developing around the websites of extremist groups via the interconnected hyperlinks inserted on the site by their creators. A *hyperlink* connects one webpage or document to another and is activated by simply clicking on a highlighted word or part of the text. Together, these hyperlinks form a virtual network in which the primary units of analysis are the websites (rather than individuals) and the communities around them. Behind these sites are the individuals who create them and who produce content for them. But here the individual's decision to hyperlink is not analysed directly – rather, the presence of a hyperlink acts as a proxy for a website creator, who recognizes the existence of another website and potentially shares interests regarding its content. A series of reciprocal hyperlinks among multiple websites acts as a concrete signal of the development of a virtual community (Burris, Smith, and Strahm 2000). Burris and colleagues (2000) were among the first to exploit hyperlinks to build networks of websites sharing extremist content. As the literature indicates, we should not confuse these hyperlinks (the virtual community) with the strong ties we have with our loved ones. That said, the use of these hyperlinks to reproduce the virtual communities that are created around a common interest on the Web yielded an overview of the social structure of right-wing extremists online, a phenomenon that is difficult to observe otherwise (Burris, Smith, and Strahm 2000).

Very few studies built on the work of Burris and colleagues (2000). The research of the Dark Web Project (Chen 2012) does exploit the hyperlinked nature of terrorist websites and is perhaps the most systematic look into the content of terrorist websites. In 2005, Zhou and colleagues (2005) proposed a semi-automated methodology that would combine the efficiency of automatic data collection with the accuracy of manual collection for the purpose of identifying, classifying, and organizing extremist website data. Starting from a seed website, a webcrawler captures the hyperlinks found in the HTML of a Web domain and follows them through in order to create the network. The end result is a network of webservers, the webpages they contain, and the links among these webpages. The data retrieved on the internet by the webcrawler can then be used to map and analyse terrorist and extremist networks (Bouchard, Joffres, and Frank 2014). It is important to note that the entire process described in Chen and colleagues' (2012) research is automatic, with little input from the user. The merging of content and network analysis in researching these websites and forums is a work in progress. This chapter aims to contribute by using these tools to understand the social structure of extremist websites.

A Typology of Extremist Websites

We build on a recent study by Davies and colleagues (2015), who studied eight known extremist groups and created a typology of the different ways in which these groups used their official websites. The authors classified websites based on two central characteristics: (1) how violent they were, and (2) how actively they were calling for action. The typology is reproduced in Table 8.1.

The typology is comprised of four classifications, though only three were found in their study sample. The first type of website is labelled "fact-based" because it refers to websites that are mainly informational. As exemplified by the Liberation Tigers of Tamil Eelam (LTTE), these sites do not emphasize recruitment, but rather seek to make people aware of their cause, and explain it. Sites of this sort present relatively low levels of extremism and are not considered in the current study. Like the fact-based websites, the second type of website, "displays of violence," has a considerable informational component. In contrast to the first websites, however, these websites make more specific reference to violence, particularly justified defensive violence. Examples include the websites operated by FARC-EP and PFLP, both selected for inclusion in this study. The two other websites selected, ALF and Earth First! were classified by Davies and colleagues (2015) in the "join the cause" category. These websites are strongly geared toward recruitment but are less inclined to extremism than those sites displaying violent content. Though the authors haven't observed it, the "call for violence" category would explicitly condone or even encourage violent action to further the cause.[2]

The current study compares the networks of hyperlinked websites taken from the "displays of violence" and "join the cause" categories. Both the goals and the content of these groups' official websites have been shown to differ regarding how they approach recruitment as well as how much extremism-related content they publish. Unknown is whether these differences also affect the way they connect to the virtual world around them.

Table 8.1. Typology of recruitment websites – examples (adapted from Davies et al. 2015)

		Extremism	
		Non-Violent	Violent
Recruitment	*Passive*	Fact-based (Know us please) LTTE	Displays of violence (Support us because) FARC Shaheed Khalsa PFLP
	Active	Join the cause (Join us now) Aryan Nations LWK ALF Earth First!	Call to violence (Act now with us) (not found)

Data and Methods

This study is comprised of three distinct methodological elements: (1) the selection of seed websites for analysis; (2) the creation of a recruitment scale and an extremism scale to classify the websites; and (3) the use of a webcrawler to extract information on the websites and map their egocentric networks. The first two of these elements build on the Davies and colleagues (2015) study cited above, while the third element is new to the current chapter. We describe each of these steps below.

Finding Seed Websites

The seed websites used as the starting point for TENE were drawn primarily from the Government of Canada's "Listed Terrorist Entities."[3] As stated in Article 83.05 of Canada's *Criminal Code*, the *Anti-Terrorism Act* provides measures for the Government of Canada to create a list of entities that:

a) have knowingly carried out, attempted to carry out, participated in or facilitated a terrorist activity;
b) knowingly acted on behalf of, at the direction of or in association with an entity that has knowingly carried out, attempted to carry out, participated in or facilitated a terrorist activity.

The Public Safety Canada (PSC) website specifies that the listing process begins with criminal and/or security intelligence reports on an entity that disclose the reasonable grounds to believe that the entity fits the above criteria. "If the Minister has reasonable grounds to believe that the above test is met, the Minister may make a recommendation to the Governor in Council to place the entity on the list."[4]

Note that we make no judgment as to whether these organizations deserve to be listed. The information used by government officials to create the list is simply not available to researchers. Yet we needed a starting point to develop our sample of extremist groups, and this list is one of the few official documents publicly available to use as a sampling frame. It is in this spirit that we use the term "extremist organization/group" throughout this chapter. Our choices should also be seen in the spirit of a field that sometimes needs to broaden its focus of inquiry to include groups situated at the margins of what is considered to be "violent extremism," especially online (Conway 2017).

As of 5 August 2016, PSC listed fifty-four organizations on its website. The sample for this study included two groups on the PSC list: FARC, and PFLP. For both organizations, an English-based information website existed that could be analysed in the context of this study. We then expanded our list to encompass a broader range of extremist activities, with organizations known to be active in Canada. Two other groups were added at this second step: Earth First!, and the Animal Liberation Front.

To generate a list of seed websites for the webcrawler, we performed a Google search using search terms that included the entity's name and related terms. The goal was to find the official website for the group or websites affiliated with it in some manner. During these searches, any extremist website (related or unrelated) was recorded. The determination of a website as extremist was based broadly on the extremism scale described below (any website that scored 1–4 was included). To produce the seed websites, this list was narrowed down to two to three websites for each entity. This list included the official website (if found), the most popular website (i.e., the website that featured earliest in the search), and any related Canadian content. Often, the official and the most popular website were the same. These websites were then analysed in terms of their general characteristics (including an assessment of their level of extremism) and the extent to which they emphasized various elements of recruitment (more information on data collection procedures can be found in Davies et al. 2015).

Extremism and Recruitment Scales

The Website Extremism Scale

Taken from Davies and colleagues (2015), the extremism scale is based on variations around two dimensions. First, we examine whether the website actively encourages visitors to join the cause (or movement, or group). A website is considered "active" when it explicitly tries to elicit participation or motivates visitor to action. "Passive" websites merely provide information on the cause, without engaging directly with visitors regarding what they can do to support it. Second, we examine whether websites contain violent content. Websites deemed to contain violent content either have images/videos that clearly demonstrate acts of violence being perpetrated against or for the cause, or text expressing violent ideas against another group (e.g., hate speech).

Merging these two concepts creates a 4-point scale of extremism, as illustrated in Table 8.2 below. At the bottom of the scale (level 1) are websites that are informational only, with that information avoiding hate speech or clear presentations of violence ("fact-based websites"). Level 2 websites also avoid violence in the text or images presented, but they explicitly encourage visitors to actively support the cause by inviting them to donate, join their list of supporters, or get together at public events ("join-the-cause" websites). Websites can present material of a clearly violent nature without explicitly encouraging individuals into action ("displays-of-violence" websites). These would be level 3 websites, where the call for action is not explicit. Finally, level 4 websites are those that actively encourage individuals to actions, including violent actions, that support the cause ("call-to-violence" websites).

The Website Recruitment Scale

In addition, each website was evaluated on a number of dimensions related to recruitment. These evaluations were then summarized via a *recruitment scale*, which attempted to capture the nature of the presence of recruiting on a website. This was premised on the degree to which the website actively encouraged action on the viewer's part. The scale ranges from 0 to 3. At the lowest end, a score of 0 corresponds to "no recruiting presence." It indicates that the website displays no materials relevant to recruiting. The next level of recruitment presents what might best be considered the "first steps" toward recruitment. This "passive" recruitment suggests attempts to pique the curiosity of site

Table 8.2. Website extremism scale

	Violent	Non-violent
Active	Level 4: **Call-to-violence**	Level 2: **Join-the-cause**
Passive	Level 3: **Displays-of-violence**	Level 1: **Fact-based**

Table 8.3. Website recruitment scale

Score	Recruitment presence
0	None
1	Passive
2	Indirect action
3	Active

visitors. It includes the presence of public forums or opportunities to subscribe to newsletters or magazines. A score of 2 on the recruitment scale connotes "indirect action." At this level, visitors are encouraged to support the cause and the actions of others involved with the cause. However, this encouragement stops short of stimulating direct personal action. The clearest examples of indirect action are calls for donations. Finally, the highest range of the scale indicates "active" recruitment. It reflects encouragement toward direct action on the part of the potential recruit. This is the most varied of the recruitment categories and includes things such as links to membership forms, announcements of (or invitations to) events, and overt calls to action. The website recruitment scale is summarized below, in Table 8.3.

The Terrorism and Extremism Network Extractor (TENE)

This study has used a webcrawler that automatically collects and analyses online data. While some manual analysis is important, especially to understand the structure of websites and the content displayed in pictures and videos, sole reliance on manual analysis would have made many of our analyses impossible to do given the size of most of the websites under study (some of them had thousands of pages to analyse).

Webcrawlers are the tools used by all search engines to automatically navigate the internet and collect information about each website and webpage. Given a starting webpage, the webcrawler recursively follows the links out of that webpage until some user-specified termination conditions apply. During this process the webcrawler keeps track of all the links between other websites and (optionally) eventually follows and retrieves them as well. The content, as it is retrieved, is saved to the hard drive of the local user for later use.

The webcrawler used in this study has been labelled the Terrorism and Extremism Network Extractor (TENE). TENE is a customized computer program that automatically browses the World Wide Web for terrorism and extremism content. This approach is based on a combination of the groundbreaking work associated with the Dark Web Project (Chen 2012) at the University of Arizona, and previous research related to online child exploitation websites at Simon Fraser University (Westlake, Bouchard, and Frank 2011; Westlake and Bouchard 2015; 2016).

TENE is designed to download webpages from the Internet and recursively follow links from those webpages until it meets specific termination criteria (e.g., reaches a certain number of pages or websites). Having been given a set of limits and some starting criteria, such as the target webpages, the crawler retrieves a series of webpages and collects statistics on the content, keywords, images, and videos on each of the webpages stemming from that particular website. The captured dataset is then analysed (manually) for violent extremist content and processes of recruitment.

Figure 8.1 provides an overview of TENE. A TENE system can actually be distributed across multiple machines, depending on the resources available. In our lab, four computers are available to TENE, although the system usually only runs on two. Each machine is capable of running three instances of the TENE software, with each instance downloading 50 webpages at a time at a rate of approximately 25 each minute. At that rate, each instance can download approximately 36,000 webpages in a day, with the entire TENE system downloading approximately 432,000 webpages a day if all four computers are used.

As with any process, data collection through TENE needs a starting point. Each "job" has three parameters imposed to prevent it from perpetually crawling the internet and wandering into websites/webpages unrelated to violent extremists. First, a limit on the number of webpages retrieved must be included to keep the extraction process timely. For the crawls specified for this study, this limit n was set at 500,000. None of the crawls reached that amount. Second, the number of domains across which TENE collects data must also be specified. In this study, we collected data on the seed and its immediate neighbourhood (all sites connected to the seed via hyperlinks). Finally, a set of domains were specified that told the crawler that everything on that domain was not associated

Figure 8.1. TENE overview

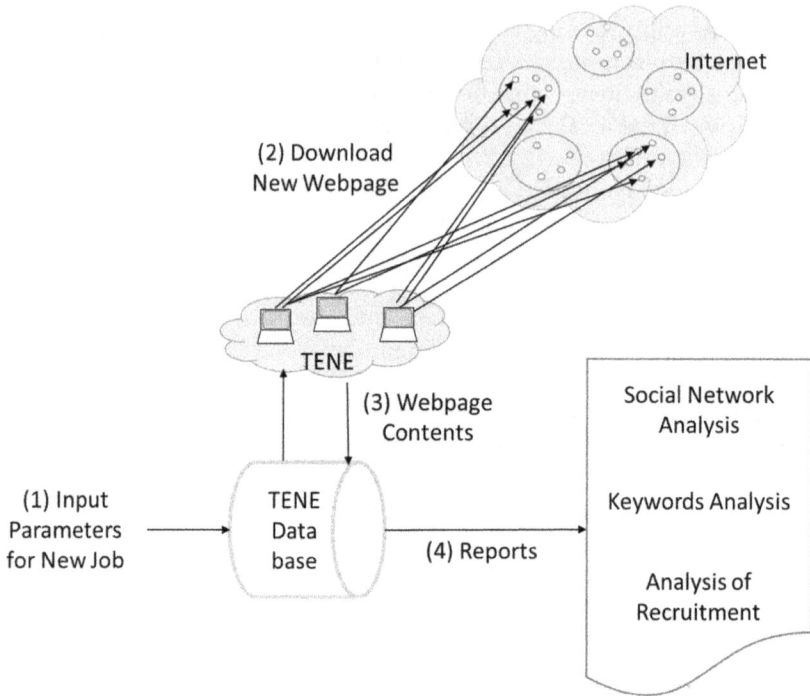

with extremism one way or another (*trusted* domains) and that it should not retrieve any webpage on those domains. Without this mechanism, TENE could wander into a search engine leading it completely off topic and making the resulting network irrelevant to the specified topic. The trusted domains during the data collection performed for this project included Google, Yahoo, Microsoft, Wikipedia, Doubleclick, Gizmodo, Adobe, Macromedia, W3schools, Adlog, and Doubleclick. Note that a set of keywords were defined in order to analyse website content, but those keywords were not used to evaluate whether a website should be retrieved or not. We collected data on all websites connected to the seed and only used keywords for content analysis purposes.

Results

The results are structured around analyses of the networks connected to the official websites of each organization. We assess the community around official websites in three ways. First, we describe the structure of the network using standard measures, such as size, density, and reciprocity.[5] Is it a sparse community of disconnected websites, or are the websites aware of one another, showing signs of cohesion? Second, we use community detection analyses to assess whether the network can be partitioned into multiple, more cohesive subgroups. The "faction" procedure (measure of fit – modularity) in the UCInet 6.617 software (Borgatti, Everett, and Freeman 2002) is used for this step. The faction algorithm aims to find the best subdivision of the network that can describe mutually exclusive, cohesive subgroups.[6] Finally, we use the extremism and recruitment scales to describe the communities uncovered to examine whether or not the official website surrounds itself with similar others.

FARC-EP

Figure 8.2 shows that FARC-EP's network is rather small (seven hyperlinks) and confined: it is comprised of its other formal websites and popular social networking platforms (Facebook, YouTube) that help disseminate the group's ideology in a consistent manner. Two of these websites, FARC-EP Peace Delegation and PAZ FARC-EP (Spanish version), are used to promote FARC's efforts with the Colombian government toward a peaceful accord, including to an English audience. This is not surprising, as FARC-EP Official's website consistently presents both the need for armed struggle and a desire for peace. The majority of the hyperlinks connect to other pages that are within the domain.

The faction algorithm identified two subgroups within this network: community one, consisting of the starting FARC-EP site and isolated (mostly social media) sites ($n = 5$; circles); and community two, on the left site ($n = 3$; squares), forming a dense cluster (subgroup density = 0.67) of closely related sites displaying passive recruitment content such as FARC-Peace.

Table 8.4 indicates that less than half of FARC-EP Official's hyperlinks are returned (reciprocity = 40%), which is still relatively high for this sample. Reciprocity is driven by community two: sites that are managed either by the same group or by related FARC webmasters. As shown in Table 8.4, the FARC-EP site is more extreme than its neighbours but less focused on recruitment. None of the websites in FARC's community contain content that suggests scores that are higher than passive recruitment efforts (0.625). This less direct approach to recruitment may imply that the acquisition of members and active supports are more likely to occur in person or via different

Figure 8.2. Egocentric network – FARC-EP

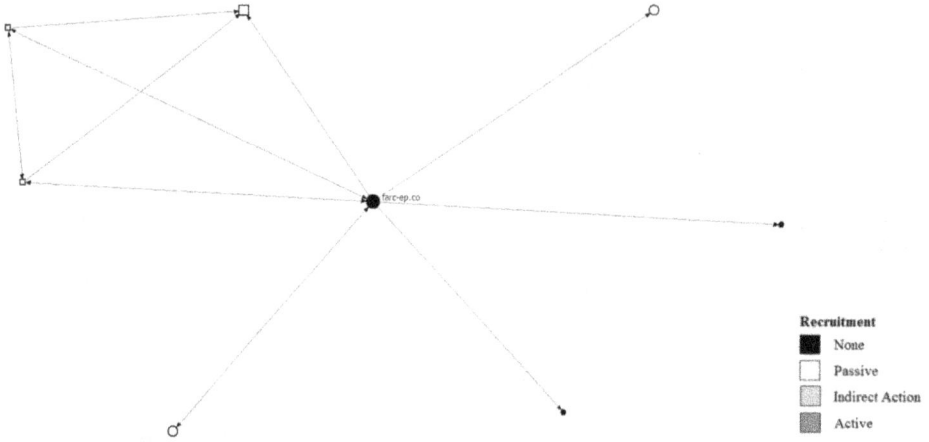

Note: Node shape based on subgroup membership; node size based on extremism scale – the larger, the more extreme.

Table 8.4. Network and other descriptive measures – FARC-EP

Network Name: http://www.farc-ep.co/	
Network size	8
Number of ties	14
Density	0.34
Reciprocity (% of ties reciprocated)	0.40
Number of subgroups	2
Extremism scale – Seed – Average full network	 3 1.63
Recruitment scale – Seed – Average full network	 0 0.63

channels. Given the objectives of FARC-EP, this implication is consistent with the organization's target audience. Its attention and efforts, as they apply to recruitment, are more efficiently spent rallying the Colombian community than revealing sensitive locations and contacts to the general public. As such, there is little to no reference to Canada on this website.

We also decided to explore the related site, FARC-PEACE, to better understand FARC's virtual community. The neighbourhood of FARC-EP Peace Delegation is comprised of its other official domains, which are predominantly in Spanish, as well as other organizations – within the legitimate as well as illicit domains – that share its socialist Marxist-Leninist ideology and rhetoric. The network suggests a high level of cooperation, or at least some communication, with other international organizations that cultivate extreme, politically left-wing ideologies. TENE reveals that the FARC-Peace website hyperlinks to other news and government agency domains that are not readily accessible manually. In particular, the program uncovers a disproportionate number of Chinese journalism and government websites ($n = 31$).

Figure 8.3 presents the egocentric network of the FARC Peace website, which at 50 sites is much larger than the official website examined above. Although the community is relatively large, the reciprocity measure remains high (0.326), suggesting a cohesive group (see Table 8.5). This can be better understood by investigating the three subgroups uncovered by the factions algorithm. Two of the subgroups found on the left side (squares and up triangles) consist mainly of interconnected Chinese (*.cn) websites. Community one (circles), on the right side, is composed of Spanish websites, including many common to the original FARC-EP network (Figure 8.2). This latter community is the only one to include extreme content as well as some form of (mainly) passive recruitment. Density is, of course, higher in any of these subgroups (0.21 or more) than in the network as a whole (0.16).

PFLP

The PFLP network, presented in Figure 8.4, is fairly sparse compared to those described above. This is reflected in the low density (0.08) as well as in a reciprocity score of 10.1 per cent overall (Table 8.6). The network can be divided in three subgroups, including a fairly cohesive (density = 0.23) subgroup of websites mostly devoted to Palestinian issues (up triangles).

The network is also slightly more oriented toward violent extremism and recruitment than what we have seen with FARC, with an average of 1.69 (Table 8.6). Yet the network includes 17 sites that scored zero on the scale, including popular social media websites such as Facebook, YouTube, and Twitter. Social media websites received the most links in the network, although they were among the least likely to reciprocate these links. The majority of the extremist websites

Figure 8.3. Egocentric network – FARC-EP/Peace

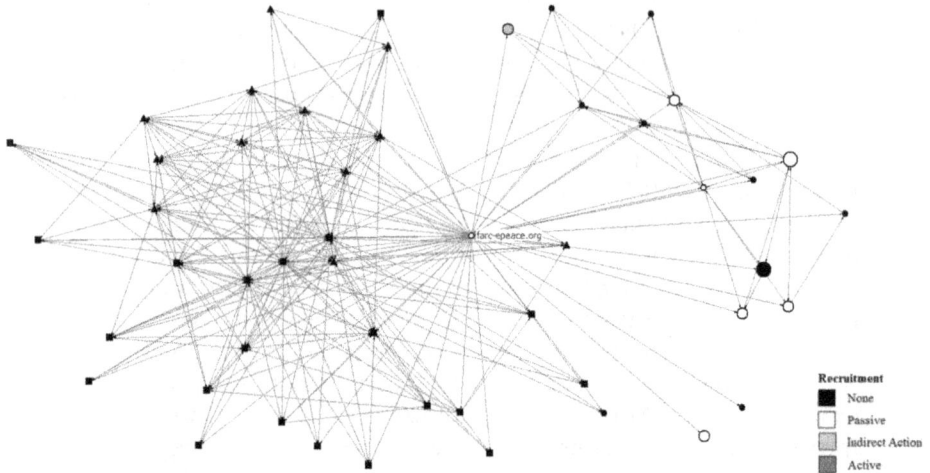

Note: Node shape based on subgroup membership; node size based on extremism scale – the larger, the more extreme.

Table 8.5. Network and other descriptive measures – FARC-EP/Peace

Network Name: http://farc-epeace.org/	
Network size	50
Number of ties	346
Density	0.16
Reciprocity (% of ties reciprocated)	33.0
Number of subgroups	3
Extremism scale	
– Seed	1
– Average full network	1.18
Recruitment scale	
– Seed	1
– Average full network	0.18

found in PFLP's network explicitly support the same cause, and most of them do so in a similar manner: by posting opinion pieces, articles, and images that serve as propaganda for the Palestinian cause. This propaganda is usually embedded among more neutral articles reporting on events in Palestine, and it generally takes the form of opinion

Figure 8.4. Egocentric network – PFLP

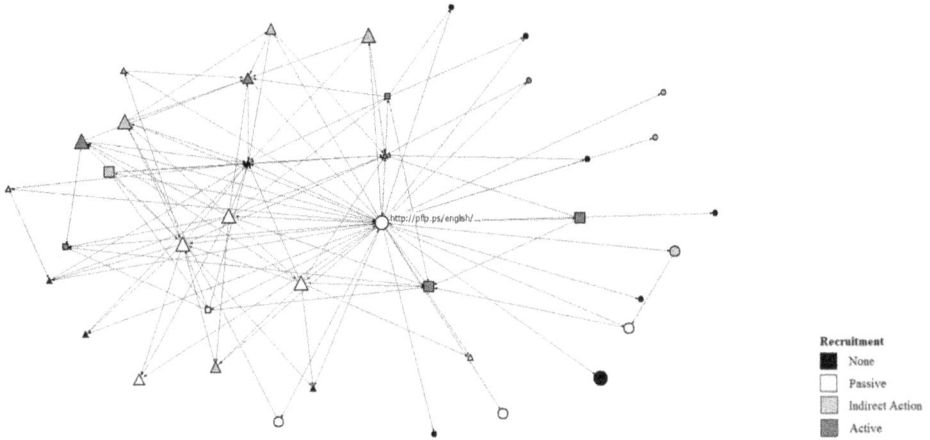

Recruitment
None
Passive
Indirect Action
Active

Note: Node shape based on subgroup membership; node size based on extremism scale – the larger, the more extreme.

Table 8.6. Network and other descriptive measures – PFLP

Network name: http://pflp – Popular Front for the Liberation of Palestine.ps/english/	
Network size	40
Number of ties	120
Density	0.08
Reciprocity (% of ties reciprocated)	10.1
Number of subgroups	3
Extremism scale – Seed – Average full network	 3 1.69
Recruitment scale – Seed – Average full network	 1 1.38

pieces or editorials. There is some reference to Canada, including with respect to ending the PFLP's terrorist designation in Canada, activists from Canada travelling to Gaza, and reports on Palestinian-related news in Canada. However, Canada is referenced most often in relation to its Indigenous population; the website draws parallels between the struggle of Aboriginals who confronted "state violence and land theft," and the Palestinian plight, with the PFLP "saluting

[Aboriginal] strugglers" and expressing "solidarity with the struggle of Native people in North America."

In terms of recruitment, the network as a whole scored fairly similarly to PFLP's website (PFLP = 1; network = 1.38). The slight discrepancy suggests that PFLP's efforts to encourage its users to join are less extensive than those of its neighbours. The main forms of recruitment involved subscriptions, links to join a website's social media pages (generally Facebook and Twitter), and options to contribute content to the website (generally articles).

ALF

We now move to two organizations whose websites displayed lower levels of violence, but were shown to be trying harder to recruit new members. The network of the official ALF website is shown in Figure 8.5; it is a sparse network with a low 4 per cent density and only 3 per cent of ties reciprocated. The decentralized nature of the network is driven by the ALF site's tendency to hyperlink a diversity of resources for vegetarian diets and for similar-minded organizations around the world. The factions algorithm uncovered three subgroups, including a relatively cohesive group (density = 17%, see up triangle on the right side of the network) consisting mainly of *.org animal rights websites from the UK. ALF is active in Canada, and its website contained numerous references to specific events in Canada (protest to "Deer Hunt Nov 21st, Ontario, Canada," "Vancouver Demonstration Against Animal Testing," "Canadian AR group hosts anti-fur demonstration," "Canada ARAs protest Circus," "1st International Animal Law Conference in Canada," and "Rights group aims to stop killing of Canada GMO pigs"). Animal rights-related information in a Canadian context is also provided ("The Sad State of Captive Elephants in Canada," strays in Canada, "Why is Canada murdering these bears?," "Animals keep dying, horribly ... Shhh ... this is Canada," "BROKEN WINGS: The Breakdown of Animal Protection in Canada," and "Canada Calf-Roping Under Fire by ARAs"). Articles on the activities of Canadian activists (stopping fur trucks, freeing captive animals) are also featured.

Table 8.7 shows that the average extremism score of the network is slightly higher (2.18) than ALF's (2). However, the theme for these extremist websites is clear: recruitment is important. The recruitment average for the network is slightly lower (2.35) than ALF's (3), but it remains relatively high compared to the networks described above. Most of the network websites are fairly similar to ALF, and all are

Figure 8.5. Egocentric network – ALF

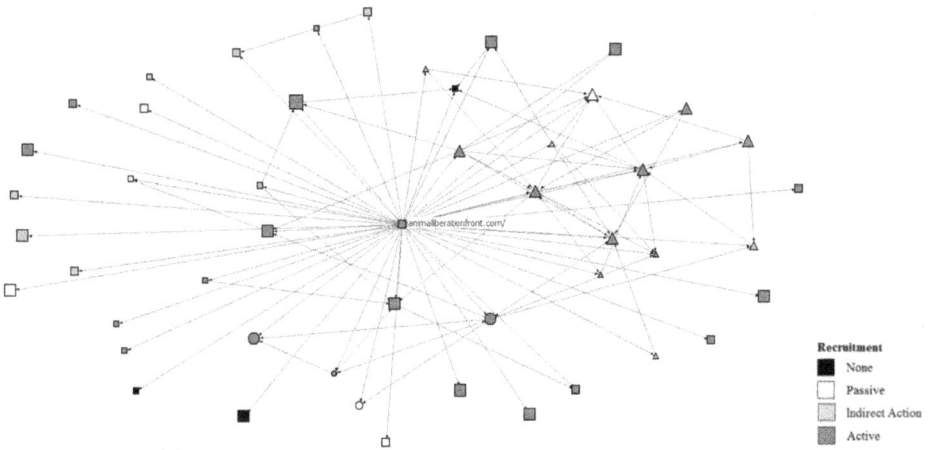

Note: Node shape based on subgroup membership; node size based on extremism scale – the larger, the more extreme.

Table 8.7. Network and other descriptive measures – ALF

Network name: http://www.animalliberationfront.com/	
Network size	50
Number of ties	100
Density	0.04
Reciprocity (% of ties reciprocated)	0.03
Number of subgroups	3
Extremism scale	
Seed	2
– Average full network	2.18
Recruitment scale	
– Seed	3
– Average full network	2.35

related to ALF's cause; they vary from animal liberation to vegetarian websites. Many discuss the mistreatment and torture of animals, with some including videos of factory animals or pictures of harmed animals. Some also discuss animal rights campaigns, imprisoned activists, vegan recipes, petitions to save animals, animal sanctuaries, and organic farms. A large portion of these websites are strongly oriented toward recruitment; most commonly, websites offer membership to the site and/or publicize demonstrations, protests, or campaigns against fur clothes, laboratory animals, or foods like foie gras. Some websites link to petitions, call for volunteers for events, include calendars for relevant events, and provide subscriptions for website and event updates. Many of these websites also make use of social media websites, such as Facebook, Twitter, and YouTube, to further engage individuals.

Earth First!

The last network we analysed is Earth First! Its community of hyperlinked websites is presented in Figure 8.6. Most of the network's websites are fact-based (updated with news and scholarly articles) or join-the-cause–based (with publicized events and encouragements to protect the environment). Many of the sites are translations of the original site, or websites overlapping in the cause they support. The word "earth," for example, is represented in a majority of the Web domains found in Figure 8.6. Canada is referenced many times on the site, largely in the context of current environmental concerns. Thus, "earth" appears often in reference to Canada's forests (particularly the boreal forest) and to clear-cutting or construction that is destroying forested areas. With respect to recruitment, Canadian conservancy and environmental groups are also mentioned (e.g., Youth for a Better World, Lifewater, Earth Save Canada, Toronto Atmospheric Fund, Canadian Environment Industry Association), and websites encourage individuals to join these groups or otherwise support them.

As shown in Table 8.8, this network is very similar in structure to ALF's: low density (5%), coupled with low reciprocity (6.7%). Based on the results of the factions analysis, this network is better described as being formed of five moderately dense subgroups, with density ranging from 10 to 25 per cent. These subgroups are visible through the various clusters organized around five different node shapes in Figure 8.6. The level of extremism is relatively low (1.66), at least compared to ALF's community of websites. The community found in the centre left of the graph (up triangles) displayed more violence than others, on average. These websites were often focused on specific, localized forests or issues. The story here, however, is also about recruitment: all subgroups have at least one website shown to be actively engaged in recruiting new members (dark-grey nodes). This makes the EF community much more homogeneous in content than we could have predicted, considering the otherwise low cohesion levels.

Figure 8.6. Egocentric network – Earth First!

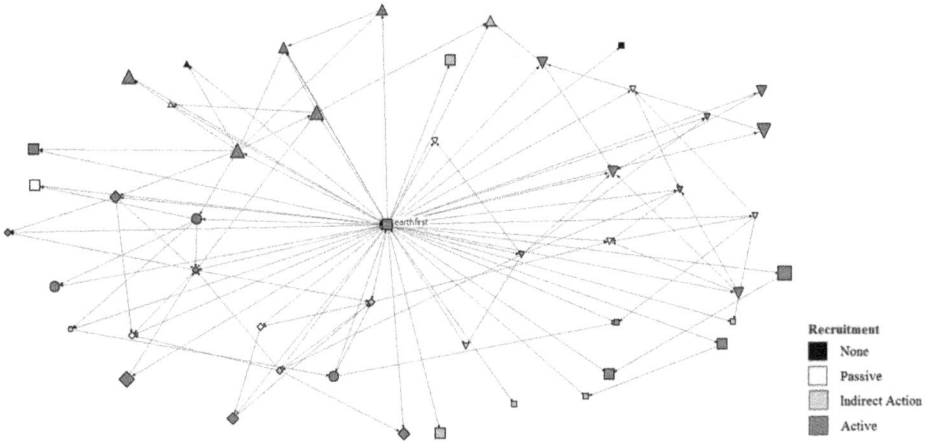

Recruitment
■ None
□ Passive
▨ Indirect Action
■ Active

Note: Node shape based on subgroup membership; node size based on extremism scale – the larger, the more extreme.

Table 8.8. Network and other descriptive measures – Earth First!

Network Name: http://www.earthfirst.org/	
Network size	50
Number of ties	111
Density	0.05
Reciprocity (% of ties reciprocated)	6.70
Number of subgroups	5
Extremism scale – Seed – Average full network	 2 1.66
Recruitment scale – Seed – Average full network	 3 2.32

Conclusions and Implications

This study examined the official websites of four organizations that are often associated with violent extremism, focusing on the community of other websites in which each is embedded. While these groups and their websites were not specialized on Canadian content, all sites analysed (except FARC's) either reference Canadian events, make analogies to Canadian-specific struggles, or encourage users to support Canadian groups associated with the cause. The communities we found are varied in structure, providing a window onto the variety of online strategies followed by these groups. For instance, FARC-EP is not using its Web platform to connect widely to the world, but the FARC-EP/Peace website is doing so. FARC-EP/Peace PFLP, ALF, and Earth First! all connect to a wide variety of related websites, but the social structure of these sites is best described through the various subgroups found within the network. These subgroups show the patterns of reciprocity in hyperlinking we expect of "communities."

This study has implications for research on extremism and violence in online settings. Automated tools such as our webcrawler TENE provide an extremely efficient method of collecting and classifying data. This study limited its focus to publicly available material, but nothing prevents anyone from using the webcrawler in password-protected areas of the Web (the "Deep Web"). It is easy to imagine TENE developing further to match specific research and policy interests in the future, including those related to specific groups active in Canada. There are two developments worth noting for the purpose of this chapter. First, programs like TENE can be paired with many other programs written in compatible languages to produce specific analyses, such as the nature of "sentiments" found in the narrative for a specific website. Our team manually analysed the content of websites and videos for sentiments in this study, but future research in this area will combine manual and automated analyses of sentiments in order to handle a more ambitious amount of text and detect violent narratives in unexpected or unexplored places on the Web. Second, a set of rules can be added to TENE so that it only follows the hyperlinks for reaching a certain type of website that corresponds to these rules or criteria. In the context of child pornography, for example, a version of the webcrawler was programmed to only follow hyperlinks if the website on the other end contained at least seven of a set of eighty-three keywords that the websites of interest typically contained (Westlake, Bouchard, and Frank 2011). This strategy proved impractical in the context of terror-related websites (Bouchard, Joffres, and Frank 2014), as both websites supporting terrorism-related violence and websites denouncing it typically use the same keywords – contextual analyses were therefore needed to determine the direction of sentiments. Furthermore, the variety of causes, motives, and content related to terrorism and extremism is such that a different set of keywords (and by extension, a different version of TENE) would be needed for each type of seed website. Future research in this area will combine the frequency of keyword use and the general sentiments on a website to establish a simple set of rules or criteria to allow TENE to analyse only those domains susceptible to containing violent narratives.

Beyond scoring websites on scales of extremism and recruitment, it was outside the objectives of this project to carefully analyse the content of the numerous websites hyperlinked to our seed websites. Yet doing so provides one of the most fruitful ways forward for future research in this area, and for policy as well. One reason is that the websites that were selected for analysis may not be the most salient ones for group members and sympathizers. The official website may simply be a sort of "online broker," an easy-to-find starting-point website for new recruits to get background/foundational information on the group, leading them to other more pertinent websites, online discussion groups not publicly accessible, and so on. The webcrawler allows for a quick scan of the online social environment around these official websites for the purpose of selecting perhaps an even better window into the online community associated with a specific extremist group. The power of networks in general lies in the influence they have on those connected entities, and in the ability for connected members to travel from one entity to the next. Online networks form communities that vary in their levels of both cohesion and activity (Bouchard and Westlake 2016; Westlake and Bouchard 2016). A violent extremist group whose online community is especially strong and cohesive should be prioritized over one where the online community is weaker. Future research in this area should systematically analyse key targeted websites as well as the networked community in which they are embedded for a more sophisticated assessment of threats, both current and future.

NOTES

1 Research for this chapter was partly funded by Public Safety Canada –
   Kanishka Program. The authors wish to thank Brett Kubicek and the
   anonymous reviewers, as well as the editors of this volume, for the useful
   comments made on earlier versions of the chapter. The corresponding
   author is Martin Bouchard, Simon Fraser University.
2 It would be important to replicate the study with a focus on ISIS. The 2015
   study by Davies and colleagues was designed before ISIS started making
   headlines in 2014.
3 http://www.publicsafety.gc.ca/cnt/ntnl-scrt/cntr-trrrsm/lstd-ntts/crrnt-
   lstd-ntts-eng.aspx.

4 http://www.publicsafety.gc.ca/cnt/ntnl-scrt/cntr-trrrsm/lstd-ntts/
   bt-lstng-prcss-eng.aspx, accessed 15 June 2014.
5 Density is the proportion of ties present in the network, based on the total
   number of ties that are possible. The higher the density, the more cohesive
   the network. Reciprocity occurs when a hyperlink to a site goes in both
   directions: from site A to site B, and from site B to site A. The higher the reciprocity, the more cohesive the network.
6 The overall fit (modularity Q) varied between 0.13 (FARC-EP) and
   FARC-EP (.30). The measure varies between 0 and 1 – the higher, the better
   the faction solution chosen fit the data.

REFERENCES

Borgatti, S.P., M.G. Everett, and L.C. Freeman. 2002. *Ucinet 6 for Windows:
    Software for Social Network Analysis*. Cambridge, MA: Analytic Technologies.
Bouchard, M., K. Joffres, and R. Frank. 2014. "Preliminary Analytical
    Considerations in Designing a Terrorism and Extremism Online Network
    Extractor." In *Computational Models of Complex Systems*, ed. V. Mago and
    V. Dabbaghian, 171–84. New York: Springer.
Bouchard, M., and R. Konarski. 2014. "Assessing the Core Membership of
    a Youth Gang from its Co-offending Network." In *Crime and Networks:
    Criminology and Justice Series*, ed. C. Morselli, 81–93. New York: Routledge.
Bouchard, M., and B. Westlake. 2016. « La détection de communautés au sein
    de réseaux criminels en ligne et ses implications pour les recherches en co-
    délinquance. » In *Les réseaux criminels*, ed. R. Boivin and C. Morselli, 209–30.
    Montréal: Les Presses de l'Université de Montréal.
Burris, V., E. Smith, and A. Strahm. 2000. "White Supremacist Networks on
    the Internet." *Sociological Focus* 33(2): 215–35. https://doi.org/10.1080/0038
    0237.2000.10571166.
Chen, W. 2012. *Dark Web: Exploring and Data Mining the Dark Side of the Web*.
    New York: Springer.
Cohen, A.K. 1955. *Delinquent Boys: The Culture of the Gang*. New York:
    Free Press.
Conway, Maura. 2017. "Determining the Role of the Internet in Violent
    Extremism and Terrorism: Six Suggestions for Progressing Research."
    Studies in Conflict and Terrorism 40(1): 77–98. https://doi.org/10.1080/10576
    10X.2016.1157408.
Davies, G., M. Bouchard, E. Wu, K. Joffres, and R. Frank. 2015. "Terrorist
    Organizations' Use of the Internet for Recruitment." In *Social Network,
    Terrorism and Counter-Terrorism: Radical and Connected*, ed. M. Bouchard,
    105–27. New York: Routledge.

Frank, R., M. Bouchard, G. Davies, and J. Mei. 2015. "Spreading the Message Digitally: A Look into Extremist Content on the Internet." In *Cybercrime Risks and Responses: Eastern and Western Perspectives*, ed. R. Smith, R. Cheung, and L. Lau, 130–45. New York: Palgrave Macmillan.

Haythornthwaite, C. 2009. "Crowds and Communities: Light and Heavyweight Models of Peer Production." *Proceedings of the 42nd Hawaii International Conference on System Sciences*. Los Alamitos: IEEE Computer Society.

Morselli, C. 2009. *Inside Criminal Networks*. New York: Springer.

Papachristos, A.V. 2006. "Social Network Analysis and Gang Research: Theory and Methods." In *Studying Youth Gangs*, ed. J.F. Short and L.A. Hughes, 99–116. Lanham: Altamira Press.

Seib, P.M., and D.M. Janbek. 2011. *Global Terrorism and the New Media: The Post–Al Qaeda Generation*. London and New York: Routledge.

Thomas, E., M. Bouchard, S. Hashimi, J. Mei, and R. Frank. 2016. "The Social Structure of Support: Examining the Co-evolution of a Terrorist Group and Its Online Followers." Public Safety Canada, Canadian Safety and Security Program (CSSP), CSSP-2014-CP-2018.

Tremblay, P., M. Charest, Y. Charette, and M. Tremblay-Faulkner. 2016. *Le Délinquant Affilié: La Sous-Culture des Gangs de Rue Haïtiens de Montréal*. Montréal: Liber.

Weimann, G. 2006. *Terror on the Internet: The New Arena, the New Challenges*. Washington, D.C.: U.S. Institute of Peace.

Wellman, B., and M. Gulia. 1999. "Net Surfers Don't Ride Alone: Virtual Communities as Communities." In *Networks in the Global Village*, ed. B. Wellman, 331–66. Boulder: Westview Press.

Westlake, B., and M. Bouchard. 2015. "Criminal Careers in Cyberspace: Examining Website Failure within Child Exploitation Networks." *Justice Quarterly* 1–28. https://doi.org/10.1080/07418825.2015.1046393.

Westlake, B., and M. Bouchard. 2016. "Liking and Hyperlinking: Community Detection in Online Child Exploitation Networks." *Social Science Research*, 1–14. https://doi.org/10.1016/j.ssresearch.2016.04.010.

Westlake, B., M. Bouchard, and R. Frank. 2011. "Finding the Key Players in Online Child Exploitation Networks." *Policy and Internet* 3(2): 1–32. https://doi.org/10.2202/1944-2866.1126.

Zhou, Y., J. Qin, G. Lai, E. Reid, and H. Chen. 2005. "Building Knowledge Management System for Researching Terrorist Groups on the Web." Paper presented at the Association for Information Systems – 11th Americas Conference on Information Systems: A Conference on a Human Scale, Omaha, 2524–36.

9 Terrorist Resourcing – Much More Than Money

JOHN M. SCHMIDT

When the September 2001 terrorist attacks in the United States occurred, it was clear that a considerable amount of preparation and at least some financial expenditure had preceded them. Questions were raised regarding both how the group that conducted the attacks managed to avoid detection and whether its activities should have been detected using financial or other types of intelligence (Roth, Greenburg, and Wille 2004). Concerns over the flow of money and the nexus with criminal organizations predates 9/11. In fact, by 2000, the international community had made substantial headway in establishing international and country-specific regimes to combat the laundering of the proceeds of (mostly) organized illegal-drug trafficking and fraud crime, with the creation of financial intelligence units (FIUs) and financial transaction reporting requirements for banks and other financial intermediaries. Canada, among the last major countries to so do, created the Financial Transactions and Reports Analysis Centre (FINTRAC) in July 2000 and passed the *Proceeds of Crime (Money Laundering) Act* (PCMLA) in October 2000.

As a consequence of the 2001 attacks on the United States, vigorous arguments were made in that country and elsewhere, including Canada, to bring financial transaction information and the anti-money laundering (AML) intelligence produced from it to bear on identifying and blocking terrorist financing activities. In contrast to the money laundering experience, Canada was among the first countries to take steps to amend its AML legislation to include a counterterrorist financing (CTF) component. It did this in December 2001, renaming the PCMLA so that it now became the *Proceeds of Crime (Money Laundering) and Terrorist Financing Act* (PCMLTFA).[1] Unfortunately, such legislative changes did little more than add terrorist financing (TF) as essentially a variation or subtype of money laundering (ML). It created the expectation that the same definitions, processes, models, and analytical strategies could be used to identify terrorist financing, identify those doing that financing, and seize the funds before they could be used. However, experience indicates that TF and ML are quite different, even though they use many of the same processes to accomplish their objectives. This chapter focuses upon those differences and illustrates that the current mindset for, and approach to, combating ML is insufficient to deal with TF. As will be discussed below, Canada's and other nations' domestic and international AML/CTF regimes have spent the past decade learning more about how TF operates and what they can do to counter it.

A few examples illustrate the range of terrorist financing activities:

1 Sometime during the mid-1990s, an intelligence report from a particular Middle Eastern country noted that the head of a certain terrorist cell had traded 2,240 kilograms of firewood for seven surface-to-air missiles of a specified type – that is, used something having considerable exchange value in the region to purchase the missiles.
2 As well as receiving training, weapons, and other equipment from India's Research and Analysis Wing and funds from supporters in Tamil Nadu, the Liberation Tigers of Tamil Eelam (LTTE) were well-known for seizing weapons and other equipment from killed Sri Lankan police and soldiers in the early and middle phases of the war (Wickremesekera 2016). In one media image of a row of dead Sri Lankan Army soldiers, it is clear that they had also been stripped of their boots and uniforms.
3 There have been many reports of Iran's Islamic Revolutionary Guard Corps–Qods Force shipping weapons by sea, air, and land to Hezbollah, Hamas, and other designated terrorist groups in recent years (Beck 2014; Abramowicz 2015; Pollak 2015). It is unclear whether the otherwise innocuous items, such as construction materials, used to disguise the shipments are intended for the same recipients.

These examples demonstrate that terrorist groups require many things, including weapons, food, information, and people, in order to develop, organize, and maintain themselves, and to carry out attacks. The need for various resources also applies, to a lesser extent, to lone (single or very small group) actors (often inappropriately referred to as "lone wolves"). While the above examples illustrate single steps in the process of obtaining such end-use goods, identifiable steps were taken before and after the resources, weapons, and materials were collected or delivered. Furthermore, only the second example mentions the provision of any money, although it is possible that money was involved at some point in each of the other two. However, money does not appear to be a factor in all cases. Thus, following the money, while often very important, can provide only a portion of the TF picture. The rest of that picture needs to be filled out with other types of information and a broader understanding of the problem.

This chapter takes a broader approach to understanding terrorist financing – or, more appropriately, "terrorist resourcing" – and develops a model for analysing it. The approach and model are based on a strategic intelligence assessment conducted by the author, using both classified and open-source information.[2] That assessment was subsequently published by Canada's Integrated Threat (now "Terrorism") Assessment Centre (ITAC) in late 2007 (ITAC 2007). In addition, the approach and the model were previously outlined to the Air India Inquiry in 2007 (Air India Inquiry 2010; Schmidt 2007).[3] This updated iteration builds upon work completed by the author and colleagues in the financial intelligence and broader counterterrorism arena since 2007.

The conceptual framework discussed here challenges the frequent public characterization of the relevant activities and their manifestations associated with "counterterrorist financing." Such characterizations tend to focus on financial transactions and on the role and products of financial intelligence units (FIUs) around the world as if they, alone, can solve the problem. This mischaracterization has been replicated internationally since the Financial Action Task Force (FATF) itself assimilated TF into its exiting AML mandate post-2001. At the operational level, and increasingly at the policy level, there is a maturing appreciation of the other elements that need to be fully considered and included in efforts to combat terrorists' and terrorist groups' efforts to obtain the things they need in order to do the things they do.

The terrorist resourcing concept and model discussed in this chapter have been used for analysing the activities of certain terrorist groups in both operational and academic environments (O'Halloran et al. 2016). In addition, the resourcing model has had some influence on Canadian and international policy discussions and decisions (Canada 2015; FATF 2013; 2015a). This chapter lays out the terrorist resourcing conceptual framework and model in order to provide the reader with a sound understanding of how the process works as well as a basis for analysing and countering terrorist resourcing activities. Because intentions absent capability pose no significant threat, it draws upon standard threat approaches that assess both the intent and capability of actors. Capability, which is the enabler of intentions, is a function of resources.

Therefore, effective efforts to eliminate or minimize the resources available to a potential threat actor directly reduce the threat.

Why Have a Model?

Some of the most influential scholars in international relations, such as Huntington (1996) and Mearsheimer and Walt (2013), have observed that simplified map(s) of reality – that is, theories, concepts, models, and paradigms – are required in order to understand the world. Absent these intellectual constructs, there is, as William James said, only 'a bloomin' buzzin' confusion.'[4] Good models help us learn, comprehend, investigate, and analyse. A good model also helps us develop and share our knowledge and understanding, identify gaps in our knowledge and understanding, frame questions, and know what to look for by providing a sound basis and framework for our search (Huntington 1996, 12).

For our purposes, the criteria for a good model for terrorist financing and related activities include:

- Does it provide a sound and straightforward basis for understanding the modelled system?
- Is it sufficiently flexible to cover all variations and adaptations in the modelled system without requiring additional elements for particular instances?
- Does it provide a basis for:
    o identifying gaps in observed activities;
    o predicting what we might see when we look for new information;
    o forecasting subsequent events from those that are seen; or
    o identifying emerging trends and methods?

The concepts and model presented in this chapter accommodate and make sense of the relevant knowledge derived from financial intelligence, or FININT, together with human intelligence (HUMINT), signals intelligence (SIGINT), imagery intelligence (IMINT), open-source intelligence (OSINT), and forensic analysis (Lowenthal 2012). They provide a basis for a clear and common strategic and practically applicable understanding of how terrorist financing and associated activities operate. Besides being instructive for those who are less knowledgeable about these activities, the concepts and model provide an effective framework for discussing those activities and deciding how to respond to them, both strategically and tactically, as part of an overall counterterrorism effort. In particular, they help us do the following: understand and contextualize specific cases and activities that we see; focus on vulnerable points, where the generation, movement, and use of funds and other relevant things are most identifiable, observable, and subject to disruption; and identify and address knowledge gaps and blind spots for FIUs and counterterrorism agencies. Ultimately, the concepts and model in this chapter help us ask the right questions in our analyses, investigations, and policy decision-making.

The Money Laundering Model

The conventional model for money laundering has three stages. According to the Financial Crimes Enforcement Network (FinCEN), the FIU based within the US Treasury Department (United States 2015):

> Money laundering is the process of making illegally-gained proceeds (i.e., "dirty money") appear legal (i.e., "clean"). Typically, it involves three steps: placement, layering and integration. First, the illegitimate funds are furtively introduced into the legitimate financial system. Then, the money is moved around to create confusion, sometimes by wiring or transferring through numerous accounts. Finally, it is integrated into the financial system through additional transactions until the "dirty money" appears "clean."

This model's structure was originally based on experience with cash-intensive illegal drug proceeds (Batchelor 2016). It is also applicable to proceeds from fraud and other white-collar crime, although almost always without the placement stage, because such funds are already within the financial system (IRS 2016). The placement–layering–integration (PLI) model overly simplifies the actual processes used by profit-motivated criminals. First, it is important to realize that criminal proceeds often include goods instead of money, or as well as money. Both present several options and challenges for the criminal. For goods, one option is simply to hold onto or even use them (e.g., a stolen motor vehicle) either for personal benefit or to commit further crimes. Stolen goods can also be sold to convert them into money.

Money, especially larger amounts, can of course be put through a PLI laundering process either by those who committed the initial ("predicate") crimes or by ML specialists, who are paid fees for doing so. Alternatively, the money can be recycled into the primary criminal enterprise (e.g., to purchase more drugs from wholesale markets) or simply spent by the criminals for everything from basic living expenses to such things as luxury goods and services. Criminals who take the latter course expose themselves to an increased likelihood of detection, which is the primary reason why they choose the ML path. Operational practitioners and criminal intelligence analysts understand this variability and that financial intelligence is but one contributing component to combating the process (IRS 2016). However, many organizations, officials, academics, and commentators still use the PLI model to try to describe and explain such activities, narrowly equating the proceeds of crime with the funds that are actually laundered. This has created its own mini-services and consultancy industry – for example, About Business Crime Solutions Inc (ABCSI) advises companies on money laundering and terrorism financing issues (ABCSI 2016). There is a mutually sustaining or even reinforcing relationship between profit-motivated crime and the disposition of its proceeds. Essentially, profit-motivated crime drives both the need and the opportunity to dispose of its proceeds. At the same time, the successful disposition of the proceeds enables profit-motivated crime to continue. Without one, the other would be meaningless.

Terrorist Financing

After September 2001, many responsible for AML policy and operations applied the PLI ML model to try to describe TF activities (FATF 2008). Others have since posited that the proper model for understanding terrorist financing is the inverse of that for money laundering – it entails turning good money to bad uses (International Federation of Accountants 2004). Officials have increasingly acknowledged that differences do exist between ML and TF (FATF 2008), yet it is still common to try and equate the two. This has led to acceptance of the idea that the best means of responding to terrorist financing is to increase financial transaction reporting requirements for banks and other entities and strengthen enforcement of those requirements (Sima 2015; Hutchings 2015).

The two frequently do intersect and share many of the same techniques, yet it is clear that terrorist financing is not the same as money laundering and that the PLI money laundering model does not effectively conceptualize the terrorist financing process (Lilley 2006a). Ryder concludes that the post-9/11 targeting of terrorist finances was "ill conceived, rushed and based on a 'money laundering' model or 'profit' driven model" that is not working (Ryder 2015, 182). Lilley, too, decried the emphasis on highly regulated financial transaction reporting as a singular attempt around the world to combat terrorist financing (Lilley 2006b). Drawing from the UN Security Council's Al-Qaida and the

Taliban Sanctions Monitoring Team, he noted that "[e]nhanced scrutiny by authorities of regulated financial systems and the lax controls at many borders continue to make the physical movement of cash and other forms of value attractive to terrorists as well as other criminals" (UNSC 2005, 21).

So, what is "terrorist financing"? Under the UN's International Convention for the Suppression of the Financing of Terrorism adopted by the General Assembly in Resolution 54/109 in December 1999, it is defined thus (United Nations 1999):

> Any person commits an offence ... if that person by any means, directly or indirectly, unlawfully and wilfully, provides or collects *funds* [emphasis added] with the intention that they should be used or in the knowledge that they are to be used, in full or in part, in order to carry out [a terrorist act].

According to the convention's definitions, "funds" means (financial) "assets of every kind ... including, but not limited to, bank credits, traveller's cheques, bank cheques, money orders, shares, securities, bonds, drafts, and letters of credit." The World Bank defines terrorist financing as "the *financial support* [emphasis added] in any form, of terrorism or of those who encourage, plan or engage in terrorism" (Schott 2006).

There are four key differences between terrorist financing and money laundering:

1 Their initial states are different – one is the possession of too much tainted money; the other is the need for the things that the funds can buy.
2 Money laundering occurs after a profit-producing criminal event has taken place, whereas terrorist financing and associated activities occur in anticipation of a terrorist action/event.
3 While the source of funds in money laundering is, by definition, illegal, the sources of funds for terrorist financing are much more complex and quite often legal.
4 Most importantly, the fundamental purposes and objectives of terrorist financing and money laundering are different. Money laundering is about the money, while terrorist financing is about the actions in support of which the funds can be applied.

In simple terms, acts of terrorism require resources. These resources, which may be money or other tradable or valuable goods or services, are the means to achieve terrorism, not ends in themselves.

Terrorist Resourcing

In reality, the process of resourcing terrorism need not involve money or other financial instruments at every step or even at all. Instead, it may involve goods or services, either those that can eventually be exchanged for other things or those the terrorists can actually use in their various activities. Even when money is involved, as it is to some extent in most cases, it does not necessarily go directly to the operational cell but is often spent somewhere upstream to acquire goods or services for use by the operational cell. We therefore need to shift our frame of reference from "terrorist financing" to the broader one of "terrorist resourcing" in order to begin to really understand what is happening.

This shift also requires official vocabulary and mindsets to change to reflect this situation. To be clear, "financing" is not a distinct activity, but rather is interwoven with the other elements of terrorist resourcing processes. Even those who try to limit the discussion to financial terms find themselves referring to relevant activities that go beyond simple financial ones (Sima 2015). While the broader criminal law in Canada, the United States, and Australia, as discussed below, goes beyond "financing," the specific AML/CTF laws in those countries and else-where do not. The FIUs are focused on financial transactions. For its part, the FATF has only recently acknowledged resourcing beyond financing (more as a consequence of financing), especially in its 2015 Gold Risk and ISIL reports (FATF 2015a; 2015b; 2015c). Even so, rec-ommended solutions still focus entirely on financial transactions and accounts, revealing that the mindset of the Task Force remains rooted in finance, not resources. For example, in its 2012 best practices docu-ment the FATF generally focuses on the monetary value, rather than also including the nature and potential end-usefulness of the goods themselves. The situation is changing, but slowly (FATF 2016). In addition, it suggests that the FATF considers this broader understand-ing little more than window dressing.

This resourcing conceptualization is largely consistent with that which we apply to ourselves, our families, our businesses, governments and their agencies, and so on, in planning and carrying out our own activities. We think not just in monetary terms but also in terms of com-plete packages of resource (including financial) requirements and the means and processes of satisfying them. Terrorists, terrorist organiza-tions, and profit-motivated criminals and groups do the same, although they are not bound in the same ways; they also use illegitimate means to achieve their resourcing ends whenever necessary for convenience, effectiveness, or security. Why, then, would we not consider the broader resourcing conceptualization to encompass such activities, instead of the limited "financing" one that is so prevalent?

Wittig (2011) writes that analyses of terrorist finance can suffer from "Western bias," despite the recognition that terrorism is a heterogeneous phenomenon that transcends geography, ideology, and cultures. The assumption that non-Western terrorists, even those targeting Western states, think and behave the same as Westerners amounts to cognitive dissonance. This has given rise to the official mantra that terrorist financing is primarily about the money. Wittig notes that this conceptualization, which underpins the global regime for combating terrorist finance, applies the seemingly commonsense reasoning that terrorists need to obtain, move, and spend money in order to operate. In addition, the assumption that the global financial system is the primary mechanism through which money flows leads to the belief that terrorists will suffer if domestic and international controls, laws, and norms block "terrorist money" from the financial system. As he concludes, the major implications of this are that counterterrorist financing regimes are often only marginally relevant to the realities of terrorist resourcing, and analysis of terrorist financing should more appropriately focus on flows of value ("value chains") and how they are accessed for effect by terrorist actors (Wittig 2011; see also Ryder 2015; Neumann 2017).

Those responsible for national and international counterterrorist financing policies and financial intelligence operations, as well as professional commentators, continue generally to portray and discuss "terrorist financing" simplistically; however, some countries' criminal legislative frameworks actually do contemplate the more complex "terrorist resourcing" conceptualization. Canada, the United States, and Australia, for example, articulate broader terrorist resourcing approaches in their respective criminal codes.

In Canada, Sections 83.02 to 83.04 of the *Criminal Code* define the relevant activities, all of which are indictable offences.[5] For example, Section 83.02 states:

> Every one who, directly or indirectly, wilfully and without lawful justification or excuse, provides or collects property intending that it be used or knowing that it will be used, in whole or in part, in order to carry out ... [terrorist activity] ...

Unfortunately, the heading for sections 83.02 to 83.04 is "financing of terrorism" and therefore nearly all publicly available documentation and discussion of the topic by the Department of Finance (responsible for Canada's AML/CTF policy) and FINTRAC disregard the more expansive *Criminal Code* sections and refer only to the PCMLTFA provisions. This, even though the latter rely on those *Criminal Code* sections when defining the terrorist activity financing offence.

The *Criminal Code* legislation in the United States is even more explicit. In Title 18, Sections 2339A and B describe the offence of providing "material support or resources" to terrorists or to a designated foreign terrorist organization, and Section 2339C prohibits the financing of terrorism.[6] Paraphrasing the first two sections:

> Whoever provides material support or resources or conceals or disguises the nature, location, source, or ownership of material support or resources, knowing or intending that they are to be used in preparation for, or in carrying out, [terrorist activities] ...
>
> "material support or resources" means any property, tangible or intangible, or service, including currency or monetary instruments or financial securities, financial services, lodging, training, expert advice or assistance, safe houses, false documentation or identification, communications equipment, facilities, weapons, lethal substances, explosives, personnel, and transportation, except medicine or religious materials ...

Relevant US criminal prosecutions and commentaries on them often reflect this broader characterization to some extent, although particular cases often seem to focus on the financial aspects or financial representation of other aspects in the criminal charges and evidentiary processes (Taxay 2014, 2; Taxay, Schneider, and Didow 2014, 9).

In Australia's *Criminal Code*, the relevant provisions are in Sections 102.2 to 102.8, 103.1, and 103.2.[7] Sections 103.1 and 103.2 talk about providing or collecting funds while "being reckless" as to whether the funds will be used to facilitate or engage in a terrorist act. Sections 102.2 to 102.8 identify the following other activities as criminal:

- 102.2 – directing the activities of a terrorist organisation,
- 102.3 – being a member of a terrorist organisation,
- 102.4 – recruiting for a terrorist organisation,
- 102.5 – training a terrorist organisation or receiving training from one,
- 102.6 – getting funds to, from or for a terrorist organisation,
- 102.7 – providing support or resources to a terrorist organisation, or
- 102.8 – associating with a member, promoter or director, intending that the support assist the terrorist organisation to expand or to continue to exist

Thus, Australian law, like its Canadian and US counterparts, has wide coverage that extends beyond the mere provision of funds.

Varying Resourcing Needs, Capabilities, and Mechanisms

Terrorist resourcing is a complex, highly variable, and highly adaptive set of systems. A variety of types of terrorist groups and individuals exist, including large, international, hierarchical organizations, and looser groups composed of cells and networks, as well as lone actors (Asal and Rethemeyer 2008; Kilberg 2012). Within such organizations and networks not all participants or supporters conduct acts of violence. More specialized roles exist, and for some of these people the only role is to fund and direct others, as instruments or surrogates, to carry out the actual terrorist activities. In addition, terrorist activities range from planned, organized, and highly specific, (e.g., Timothy McVeigh's 1995 Oklahoma City attack), to essentially random and opportunistic (e.g., Martin Couture-Rouleau's 2014 automobile attack on two Canadian Armed Forces soldiers in Saint-John-sur-Richelieu, Quebec). These differences result in different resourcing needs, capabilities, and mechanisms. Terrorist organizations' and individuals' resourcing methods are mixed; they are constantly evolving as new technologies and opportunities arise and as the international community takes more steps to frustrate existing methods. Existing methods continue to be used in new ways, and new ones emerge (FATF 2015c).

Thus the terrorist resourcing "trail" is not, as some have suggested (Schott 2006), like a single piece of string one can follow from its beginning to its end; rather, it is like a river system, with many tributaries and outflows, many obstructions and alternative routes, and many different things floating along its course. It can be a trickle or a torrent, depending on numerous factors. In other words, terrorist resourcing is a process that involves *many things* from *many sources* through *many channels* to *many recipients* for *many uses*. These "things" can include anything of value or of direct usefulness to the terrorists.

A 2012 examination of the open-source literature on a number of terrorist groups through the resourcing lens illustrated the range of inputs into terrorist activity (Myres 2012). The extent to which it may be intertwined with the legitimate financial, trade, and other activities of our society underscores the sheer scope of the problem. Although some changes have occurred since 2013, Figures 9.1 to 9.4 represent illustrative summaries and remain accurate in many respects. They indicate the similarities and differences in the resources, their sources, and their uses.

Similarly, Wittig (2011, 66) identifies critical resources used by terrorists (reproduced in Table 9.1) Here Wittig breaks the resources

Figure 9.1. Boko Haram resourcing chain

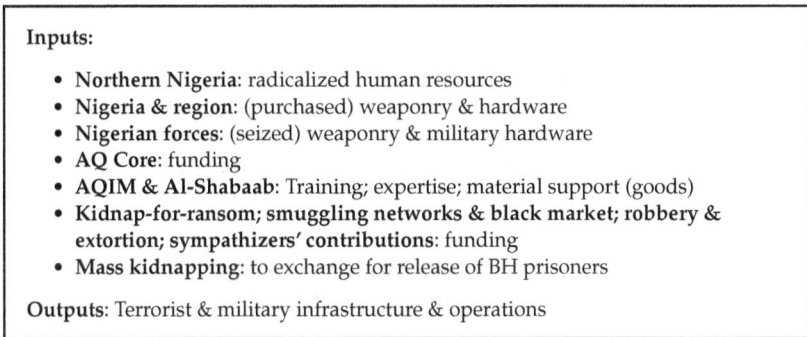

Inputs:

- **Northern Nigeria**: radicalized human resources
- **Nigeria & region**: (purchased) weaponry & hardware
- **Nigerian forces**: (seized) weaponry & military hardware
- **AQ Core**: funding
- **AQIM & Al-Shabaab**: Training; expertise; material support (goods)
- **Kidnap-for-ransom; smuggling networks & black market; robbery & extortion; sympathizers' contributions**: funding
- **Mass kidnapping**: to exchange for release of BH prisoners

Outputs: Terrorist & military infrastructure & operations

Figure 9.2. Hezbollah resourcing chain

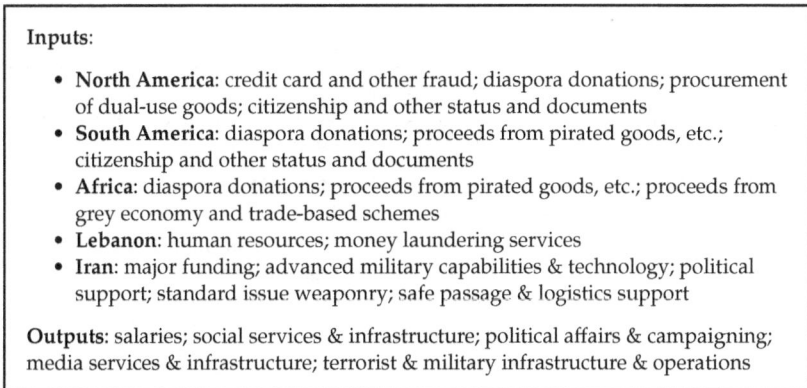

Inputs:

- **North America**: credit card and other fraud; diaspora donations; procurement of dual-use goods; citizenship and other status and documents
- **South America**: diaspora donations; proceeds from pirated goods, etc.; citizenship and other status and documents
- **Africa**: diaspora donations; proceeds from pirated goods, etc.; proceeds from grey economy and trade-based schemes
- **Lebanon**: human resources; money laundering services
- **Iran**: major funding; advanced military capabilities & technology; political support; standard issue weaponry; safe passage & logistics support

Outputs: salaries; social services & infrastructure; political affairs & campaigning; media services & infrastructure; terrorist & military infrastructure & operations

Figure 9.3. Islamic State of Iraq and Levant (ISIL) resourcing chain

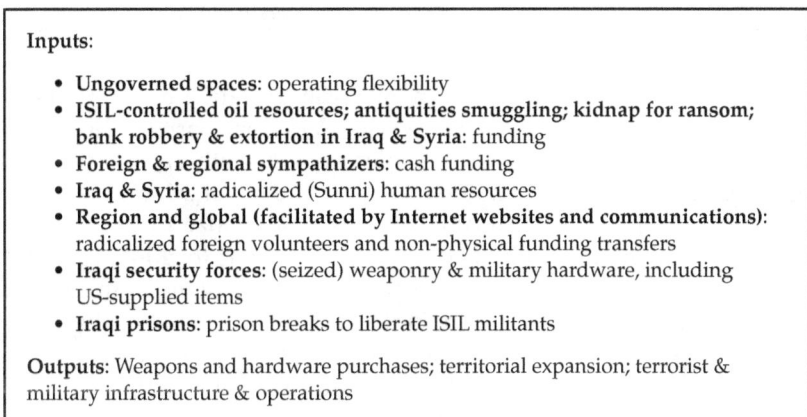

Inputs:

- **Ungoverned spaces**: operating flexibility
- **ISIL-controlled oil resources; antiquities smuggling; kidnap for ransom; bank robbery & extortion in Iraq & Syria**: funding
- **Foreign & regional sympathizers**: cash funding
- **Iraq & Syria**: radicalized (Sunni) human resources
- **Region and global (facilitated by Internet websites and communications)**: radicalized foreign volunteers and non-physical funding transfers
- **Iraqi security forces**: (seized) weaponry & military hardware, including US-supplied items
- **Iraqi prisons**: prison breaks to liberate ISIL militants

Outputs: Weapons and hardware purchases; territorial expansion; terrorist & military infrastructure & operations

Figure 9.4. Domestic small cell and lone actor resourcing chain

Inputs:

- **Job income; welfare; savings; personal loans:** funding
- **Petty crime; theft; robbery; street-level drug dealing; card fraud:** funding
- **Web forums; radicalization venues:** radicalized individuals
- **Commercial & industrial sites:** stolen commercial explosives and other hardware

Outputs: "Foreign fighters"; airline tickets; travel logistics; documents, etc.; accommodation; facilities; homemade explosives; vehicle rentals; guns

Table 9.1. Wittig's preliminary lexicon of terrorist resources

Category of resource	Selected examples	
	Material resources	Non-material resources
Military resources	Small arms, explosives, ammunition, dual-use explosive components (vehicles, cell phones, etc.)	Technical expertise, training services, "outsourced" operations, intelligence
Logistical resources	Vehicles, computers, telephones, radios, SIM cards	Transport, internet access, telephone service
Human resources	Fighters, supporters (donors, facilitators, middlemen), service providers (accountants)	Loyalty, obligation, inter-group relationships
Financial resources	Cash or its equivalents, marketable goods and commodities	Money services, banking services, influence over markets, business intelligence
Political resources	Propaganda material, websites	Propaganda material development and distribution, relationships, ideological support

down by category, and between material and non-material types (the latter generally labelled as "services" in this chapter). However, Wittig has not included such necessities as food, clothing, and shelter/accommodation, which demonstrates how the list of critical resources can change with the circumstances – as would that for a family, a business, or a national military. Even so, the shift to thinking about resources – not simply money – brings to bear a sharper focus that considers the terrorist, or group, in the context of its relationship with the wider society and other actors. For example, the Assad regime required oil and continued to purchase oil from ISIS even though the two were in conflict (Solomon 2016; Solomon, Kwong, and Bernard 2016), and even Western companies are alleged to have funded terrorism in Syria indirectly by paying intermediaries to prevent disruption of services (Atkins 2017).

The Terrorist Resourcing Model

Thus, a focus on money or finance is insufficient; a broader terrorist resourcing conceptualization is required. In addition, it is also clear that an effective framework or model for understanding and responding to such activities is required. This is the Terrorist Resourcing Model (TRM). It has five "stages" (distinguishable but interconnected processes): acquisition, aggregation, transmission to the terrorist organization, transmission to the terrorist cell, and conversion.

Acquisition

Acquisition is the initial identifiable movement of funds or goods into the terrorist resourcing process. It is the transition point between not-terrorist-oriented and terrorist-oriented processes. There are many types of acquisition activities. Examples of financial acquisition include voluntary donations by individuals and businesses to legitimate or sham charitable, religious, or community organizations; loans by individuals and businesses to terrorist front organizations; contributions by governments or their agents; contributions extorted from overseas expatriates; "taxes" or fees collected from a local populace; proceeds from criminal activities; proceeds from legal business or investment dealings; an individual's employment wages or welfare payments; and personal credit cards or bank loans.

Non-financial acquisition is the direct receipt or theft of either of two types of goods: those that are meant to be exchanged for money or other goods, such as precious metals or motor vehicles, and end-use goods, such as weapons, a motor vehicle to deliver an improvised explosive device, or food. Individuals involved in the acquisition stage, or who contribute the funds or goods, may or may not know their ultimate purpose – they may be totally unaware that the funds or goods will eventually be used to support terrorist activities.

Aggregation

In the aggregation stage the pooling of smaller amounts of funds or goods into larger ones occurs, usually by moving them to one or a few financial institution accounts or, for cash or physical goods, to one or a few locations. Aggregation can occur concurrently with or immediately following the acquisition stage, but it can also occur later in the process. It may be relatively simple or complex, or may not be needed at all, if the initial amount from a single source is sufficiently large. As with acquisition, those involved at the aggregation stage may not know the ultimate purpose of the funds or goods.

Transmission to the Terrorist Organization

After resources are acquired or aggregated, at some point they need to be sent or otherwise delivered to the terrorist organization. The transmission phase covers the movement of the funds or goods to the central terrorist organization (where one exists), to a location within its control, or to someone acting on its behalf. This stage necessarily brings the funds or goods into the full control of the terrorist organization. Transmission may occur in one or a number of steps and involve one or more individuals or organizations. It may even include a transfer from one terrorist organization to another. Transmission often includes at least one international movement of the funds or goods, including through electronic funds transfers, *hawala*-type exchanges, or bulk cash movements, or by the shipment or carriage of usually high-value exchange or end-use goods. The latter can be facilitated by legal or illegal means – for example, by smuggling or by use of otherwise legitimate trade systems. International trade is very often a major factor in the transmission of exchange and end-use goods. Trade-based transmission can take many forms, including the following: under- or over-invoicing (pricing) of goods being shipped; multiple invoicing for the same goods or trade services; misidentifying the goods on the bill of lading or mixing them in with the goods named on the bill of lading; delivery to recipients different from those identified on the bill of lading; disguising the destination country via transhipment, that is, by sending the shipment first to another country, from which the goods are then forwarded to their actual destination; movements through free trade zones; and use of shell or front companies.

FIUs and their partner agencies have some idea about the money that is moving in and out of their countries, due to electronic funds transfer reporting, cross-border cash movement and seizure reports, and suspicious activity reports. However, most countries know very little about the goods that are crossing their borders via trade channels, especially outwardly, in support of terrorist activities.

Transmission to the Operational Cell

Assuming that a formal terrorist organization receives the resources, a further stage is the delivery of the resources to the actual operational cell. This transmission phase involves the allocation of funds or goods by the terrorist organization and their delivery to the cells responsible for directly executing the organization's executive, attack, support, propaganda, training, intelligence, facilitation, or other activities. This stage can include use of the same types of transmission mechanisms as the third stage, although conditions will be different and often entail less sophisticated methods. If funds are transmitted at this stage, they are usually in somewhat smaller amounts than those transmitted in the third stage. Goods that are transmitted are generally end-use goods. Whatever the case, they are specific to the cell's operational requirements. A recent example would be the supply of resources by ISIS to suspected cells in India (Callimachi 2017).

Conversion

Money, financial equivalents, or goods may need to be exchanged for end-use goods or services to support or carry out the organization's activities. End-use goods and services include such things as weapons, travel, training, food, accommodation, and fraudulent documents. Conversion may also involve such activities as recruitment, propaganda, attack preparation, bribery of officials, or support for suicide bombers' families. Some groups – for example, ISIS, Hezbollah, and, before their military defeat in 2009, the LTTE – have used some of their resources for things like building hospitals or providing quasi-government services. Conversion can occur at any point during the terrorist resourcing process, following acquisition.

Translations and Storage

It is important to understand that conversion is only from something of value, be it funds or exchange goods, to end-use goods or services. There can be any number of exchanges between various types of funds and exchange goods during the stages of the process after acquisition and prior to conversion. These are "translations." A translation is not a stage in itself, but an element of the process that can occur at any point after acquisition and prior to conversion. Examples of a translation include the following: from one currency to another; from one type of monetary instrument to another; from money to exchange goods; from one type of exchange good to another; and from exchange goods to money. The purpose is to retain the value while moving it to the point at which it can be converted to end-use goods or services.

Storage can also occur at any point in the process. It is not a particular "stage," but rather a holding-point component of one of the stages. This does not mean it is insignificant, as both storage and a translation point can create opportunities for counterterrorist agencies to destroy, seize, or otherwise remove funds or goods (resources) from the terrorists.

Variations and Rules for the TRM

Not all five stages are present in every terrorist resourcing process, and they need not be in the order presented. While acquisition always occurs first, conversion may not need to occur and, when it does, may not be the final stage. For example, a variation might be from acquisition (of end-use goods), through transmission to the organization, to transmission to the cell, or even the singular acquisition of the end-use goods or services directly by the cell or lone actor.

To accommodate possible variations in the resourcing process, the TRM is flexible, though the model and the processes therein do stipulate to a set of fundamental rules. First, the acquisition stage is always required (it is the only stage that is) and is always first. Second, if the acquisition is of anything other than end-use goods or services, there must be a conversion stage. Third, if both transmission to the organization and transmission to the operational cell occur in a resourcing process, the former must precede the latter. And fourth, if the operational cell does not directly acquire the funds, goods, or services, then transmission to the operational cell is required.

It is, however, not always necessary to be able to observe or analyse the complete resourcing process in a particular case. Rather, the analyst might drill down through one or two stages to fully examine the detailed transactions and manoeuvres being used, or move up from specific transactions and other activities to identify their places in the model and work outward to find others.

Humans as Exchange and End-Use Goods

Another important consideration is that humans are included in the definitions of both exchange and end-use goods, and there have been many examples of both occurring. People play many roles in and on behalf of terrorist organizations, and those trying to defeat terrorist organizations (often) take steps to capture or eliminate such people or to frustrate their efforts. For example, in late November 2015, the United States-led coalition fighting Islamic State militants in Iraq and Syria killed the group's finance minister, Abu Salah, and two other senior leaders in air strikes. According to a US military spokesperson, Salah "was one of the most senior and experienced members of ISIL's financial network and he was a legacy Al Qaeda member" (Ali and Alexander 2015). The spokesperson noted he was the third member of the finance network who had been killed in as many months, adding that such targeted killings "exhaust[] the knowledge and talent needed to coordinate funding within the organization" (Ali and Alexander 2015). Numerous other examples of humans as end-use goods include efforts by ISIL to acquire doctors, engineers, and other professionals and administrative experts (BBC News 2014; Maloof 2015; Agron, 2015).

The use of humans as exchange goods is well documented. Kidnappings by the Taliban and others are prime examples: abductees have been converted into funds and into concessions such as the release of terrorists or changes to government policies. The ease and effectiveness of kidnapping has led to its increased use in many regions (Europol 2015). Boko Haram's kidnapping of 219 schoolchildren from a remote town in Nigeria's northeast in April 2014 is a well-known example of this problem. The following month, Boko Haram's leader, Abubaker Shekau, demanded that all Boko Haram prisoners in Nigeria, Cameroon, and Niger be released before he would order the return of the girls (Zenn 2014). Then in November 2014, Shekau said that the girls had all converted to Islam and been "married off" to Boko Haram members (Associated Press 2014). This is a good example of humans, initially acquired as exchange goods, being converted into end-use goods by the terrorist organization. While the goods (people), themselves, were not exchanged for something else, some transformative process changed their significance for the organization.

Another example is historical and illustrates that the model is not limited to contemporary terrorism: Patty Hearst. On 4 February 1974, the nineteen-year-old Hearst was kidnapped from her Berkeley, California, apartment by a left-wing terrorist group, the Symbionese Liberation Army (SLA). When the attempt to exchange Hearst for jailed SLA members failed, the group demanded that the captive's family distribute $70 worth of food to every needy Californian. In response, Hearst's father arranged the immediate donation of $6 million worth of food to the poor of the Bay Area. Soon after, the SLA refused to release Hearst because they deemed the food to have been of poor quality. On 3 April 1974, Hearst announced on an audiotape that she had joined the SLA and assumed the name "Tania." Later communications from her asserted that she was committed to the goals of the SLA. On 15 April 1974, she was photographed wielding an assault rifle while robbing a branch of the Hibernia Bank. In September 1975, she was arrested in a San Francisco apartment with other SLA members (FBI, n.d.).

Reversion

Following conversion, end-use goods normally remain as such until they are consumed or otherwise cease to be of use to the terrorists. However, there have been instances where end-use goods have under-gone "reversion" to exchange goods. The schoolchildren kidnapped by Boko Haram, mentioned above, are a good example. In August 2016, Boko Haram again showed the girls in a video and again demanded the release of Boko Haram fighters in exchange for them (BBC News 2016). End-use goods that retain some value can be given or sold to others, or otherwise exchanged for money, exchange goods, or other end-use goods or services. This does not necessitate yet another stage in the model, but only a loop-back generally within the conversion stage. It is essentially just another type of translation, although it may require intermediate steps to be completed. In any case, it is important to note that such actions can occur and thus have implications.

Conclusion

Capability, for all intents and purposes, equals the ability to obtain and use resources. As with ML, a driver–enabler relationship operates between resourcing and the activities it supports. Without terrorism, there would be no need for resourcing, but, without resourcing, ter-rorism would be impossible. Preventing terrorists from obtaining the resources they need, and using the information we have on resourcing activities to infer intent, presents an opportunity to frustrate or disrupt attacks before they take place. Military strategy very often includes attempts to cut opponents' supply lines and destroy the sources of those supplies, or to apply knowledge about them and their movements to infer an opponent's plans and strategies. By this means, one side can defeat even a superior force. This would also be an important aspect of an effective counterterrorism strategy. The TRM can be helpful in this regard. The resourcing of the Islamic State and the increased recogni-tion of the nexus between terrorism and criminality in Europe provide examples of resourcing that go well beyond simple money. In Canada and elsewhere the sheer scope of the terrorist resourcing process is not yet fully understood, nor is its complexity. This limits the ability to implement truly effective strategies, which (among other things) drive international cooperation against terrorism financing (Associated Press 2015). While there is evidence of a shift in operational environments related to an appreciation of resources, the discourse and mindset of the public and of elected officials still revolve around finance rather than resources.

The TRM is an end-to-end model, one that accommodates all steps and variations in the terrorist resourcing process – that is, up to the point that end-use goods are actually used. It is important to understand that not all five stages are necessarily present in all cases, nor do they occur in the linear order presented here. In fact, this feature has caused one group of authors to suggest a non-linear (not "stages," but "nested cells") approach that, they suggest, more readily reflects the variability of the process as well as the feedback links that can occur (O'Halloran et al. 2016). This approach and the model and concepts that describe it relate to the "river system" analogy whereby the terrorist resourcing process has many elements interacting in a self-reinforcing but constantly changing movement. Nevertheless, it is a directional process, with initiators and outcomes, a process that can be observed, and understood, in both general and specific cases. This offers counterterrorism officials an opportunity to anticipate and prevent violent terrorist acts, rather than having to wait until they have occurred to try to put the pieces together.

NOTES

1 Canada, *Proceeds of Crime (Money Laundering) and Terrorist Financing Act* (Canada 2000) http://laws-lois.justice.gc.ca/eng/acts/p-24.501/page-1. html.
2 Only open source or highly sanitized and generalized information is used in this chapter. It contains no direct references to classified or sensitive information.
3 Since the publication of the original ITAC document, this material has been presented and discussed in several Canadian and international classified and open conferences, briefings, and meetings, including in the US, the UK, Belgium, and Australia. It was also presented as expert testimony at Canada's Commission of Inquiry into the Investigation of the 1985 Bombing of Air India Flight 182 (Air India Inquiry 2010; Schmidt 2007).
4 The phrase "one great blooming, buzzing confusion" is attributed to William James, found on page 492 of his work *The Principles of Psychology*, published in 1890. James's works are summarized in the online *Stanford*

Encyclopedia of Philosophy, published in 2000 and revised in 2013: https://plato.stanford.edu/entries/james. Huntington, among others, makes use of James's quote in his *Clash of Civilizations* (1996, 12).

5 Canada, *Criminal Code* (Canada 1985), http://laws-lois.justice.gc.ca/eng/acts/C-46/.

6 United States, Title 18, U.S.C. Subsection 2339A, as well as Subsections 2339B and 2339C, relate to material support offences. See 18 U.S. Code § 2339A – Providing material support to terrorists; 18 U.S. Code § 2339B – Providing material support or resources to designated foreign terrorist organizations; and 18 U.S. Code § 2339C – Prohibitions against the financing of terrorism for further information. Available at Cornell Law School, Legal Information Institute (LLI) at https://www.law.cornell.edu/uscode/text/18/2339A and https://www.law.cornell.edu/uscode/text/18/2339B and https://www.law.cornell.edu/uscode/text/18/2339C.

7 For the Australian legislation, see the *Criminal Code Act 1995* – Schedule. The *Criminal Code* is available at the Australasian Legal Information Institute (AustLII), available at http://www.austlii.edu.au/cgi-bin/viewdoc/au/legis/cth/consol_act/cca1995115/sch1.html?context=1;query=terrorist. Sections Division 101 onward detail specific terrorist offences and procedures.

REFERENCES

ABCSI. 2016. "Money Laundering: A Three-Stage Process." About Business Crimes Solutions Inc., https://www.moneylaundering.ca/public/law/3_stages_ML.php.

Abramowicz, Sara. 2015. "Iranian weapons shipments to Hezbollah and Hamas have increased in the wake of the framework nuclear deal with the P5+1." United with Israel, 15 April, https://unitedwithisrael.org/iran-spreads-terror-as-it-ships-weapons-to-hamas-and-hezbollah.

Agron, A. 2015. "Wanted: Western Professionals to Join the Islamic State (ISIS)." *MEMRI Jihad and Terrorism Threat Monitor*, 15 May. http://www.memrijttm.org/wanted-western-professionals-to-join-the-islamic-state-isis.html.

Air India Inquiry. 2010. *Final report of the Commission of Inquiry into the Investigation of the Bombing of Air India Flight 182*, vol. 5: *Terrorist Financing*. http://www.publicsafety.gc.ca/lbrr/archives/cn33719-5-eng.pdf.

Ali, Idrees, and David Alexander. 2015. "Three Islamic State leaders killed in recent strikes – U.S. military." Reuters, 11 December. http://www.newsjs.com/url.php?p=http://uk.reuters.com/article/uk-mideast-crisis-leaders-idUKKBN0TT2BH20151211.

Asal, Victor, and R. Karl Rethemeyer. 2008. "The Nature of the Beast: Organizational Structures and the Lethality of Terrorist Attacks." *Journal of Politics* 70(2): 437–49. https://doi.org/10.1017/S0022381608080419.

Associated Press. 2014. "Nigerian schoolgirls kidnapped by Boko Haram married off, leader says." 1 November. http://www.cbc.ca/news/world/nigerian-schoolgirls-kidnapped-by-boko-haram-married-off-leader-says-1.2820648.

– 2015. "United Nations adopts plan to attack Islamic State's funding." *The Guardian*, 17 December. https://www.theguardian.com/world/2015/dec/17/united-nations-plan-islamic-state-funding-terrorist-group-al-qaida.

Atkins, Ralph. 2017. "LafargeHolcim faces French inquiry over Syrian scandal." *Financial Times*, 13 June. https://www.ft.com/content/6864b576-5055-11e7-bfb8-997009366969.

Australia. 1995. *Criminal Code Act 1995*. http://www.austlii.edu.au/au/legis/cth/consol_act/cca1995115/sch1.html.

Batchelor, Amanda. 2016. "22 people charged in Miami drug money laundering operation." 7 April. http://www.local10.com/news/22-people-charged-in-miami-drug-money-laundering-operation.

BBC News. 2014. "Isis leader calls on Muslims to 'build Islamic State.'" 1 July. http://www.bbc.com/news/world-middle-east-28116846.

BBC News. 2016. "Nigeria Chibok girls: Boko Haram video shows captives." 14 August. http://www.bbc.com/news/world-africa-37076644.

Beck, Atara. 2014. "Iranian weapons shipment to Gaza blocked by IDF." United with Israel, 5 March. https://unitedwithisrael.org/iranian-weapons-shipment-to-gaza-blocked-by-idf.

Callimachi, Rukmini. 2017. "Not 'lone wolves' after all." *New York Times*, 5 February, A1.

Canada. 1985. *Criminal Code* (R.S.C., 1985, c. C-46). http://laws-lois.justice.gc.ca/eng/acts/C-46.

– 2000. *Proceeds of Crime (Money Laundering) and Terrorist Financing Act* (S.C. 2000, c.17). http://laws-lois.justice.gc.ca/eng/acts/p-24.501/page-1.html.

– 2015. "Assessment of Inherent Risks of Money Laundering and Terrorist Financing in Canada." Department of Finance, Canada, July. http://www.fin.gc.ca/pub/mltf-rpcfat/mltf-rpcfat-eng.pdf.

Europol. 2015. "European Union Terrorism Situation and Trend Report." (TE-SAT) 2015, https://www.europol.europa.eu/sites/default/files/publications/p_europol_tsat15_09jun15_low-rev.pdf.

FATF. 2008. Terrorist Financing Typologies Report. 9 February. http://www.fatf-gafi.org/publications/methodsandtrends/documents/fatfterroristfinancingtypologiesreport.html, 34.

– 2013. Report: "Terrorist Financing in West Africa." October. http://www.fatf-gafi.org/publications/methodsandtrends/documents/tf-west-africa.html.

– 2015a. Report: "Financing of the Terrorist Organisation Islamic State in Iraq and the Levant (ISIL)." February. http://www.fatf-gafi.org/media/fatf/documents/reports/Financing-of-the-terrorist-organisation-ISIL.pdf.
– 2015b. "Money Laundering and Terrorist Financing Risks and Vulnerabilities Associated with Gold." Paris: FATF, and Sydney: APG.
– 2015c. "Emerging Terrorist Financing Risks." October. Paris: FATF.
– 2016. "Combating Terrorist Financing as Part of a Complete Strategy to Defeat ISIL and Prevent Terrorist Attacks." Address by Je-Yoon Shin, FATF President, to Chatham House Conference on Countering Terrorist Financing. 8 February, London. http://www.fatf-gafi.org/publications/fatfgeneral/documents/chatham-countering-terrorist-financing.html.
FBI. n.d. "Patty Hearst: Famous Cases and Criminals." https://www.fbi.gov/history/famous-cases/patty-hearst.
Huntington, Samuel P. 1996. *The Clash of Civilizations and the Remaking of World Order*. New York: Simon and Shuster.
Hutchings, Denise. 2015. "58 Red Flags for Terrorist Financing." *Verafin*, 26 May. https://verafin.com/2015/05/58-red-flags-for-terrorist-financing.
International Federation of Accountants. 2004. *Anti-Money Laundering*, 2nd ed. http://www.ifac.org/sites/default/files/publications/files/anti-money-laundering-2n.pdf.
IRS. 2016. "Examples of Money Laundering Investigations – Fiscal Year 2016." https://www.irs.gov/uac/examples-of-money-laundering-investigations-fiscal-year-2016.
ITAC. 2007. "A Terrorist Financing/Resourcing Model." ITAC document 07/29 – Revised, 28 August.
Kilberg, Joshua. 2012. "A Basic Model Explaining Terrorist Group Organizational Structure." *Studies in Conflict and Terrorism* 35(11): 810–30. https://doi.org/10.1080/1057610X.2012.720240.
Lilley, Peter. 2006a. "Terrorist Financing Is Not Money Laundering." White paper no. 20, Proximal Consulting, November 2006. https://www.proximalconsulting.com/s/WP20.pdf.
– 2006b. "Why the Terrorist Financing Model Is Inadequate." White paper no. 21, Proximal Consulting, November 2006. https://static1.squarespace.com/static/56699360dc5cb494f64d97f4/t/58079bafd482e9eb1f5d2154/1476893619588/WP21.pdf.
Lowenthal, Mark M. 2012. *Intelligence: From Secrets to Policy*, 5th ed. Los Angeles: CQ Press.
Maloof, Michael F. 2015. "ISIS recruiting engineers, doctors, accountants, reporters." *World Net Daily*, 15 February. 21 http://www.wnd.com/2015/02/isis-runs-help-wanted-ads-for-professionals.
Mearsheimer, John J., and Stephen M. Walt. 2013. "Leaving Theory Behind: Why Simplistic Hypothesis Testing Is Bad for International Relations."

European Journal of International Relations 19(3): 427–57. https://doi.
org/10.1177/1354066113494320.

Myres, Graham. 2012. "Investing in the Market of Violence: Toward a Micro-
Theory of Terrorist Financing." *Studies in Conflict and Terrorism* 35(10): 693–
711. https://doi.org/10.1080/1057610X.2012.712031.

Neumann, Peter R. 2017. "Don't Follow the Money." *Foreign Affairs* 96(4): 93–102.
https://www.foreignaffairs.com/articles/2017-06-13/dont-follow-money.

O'Halloran, Patrick J., Ali Ghanbar Pour Dizboni, Christian Leuprecht,
David Adelstein, Alexandra Green, and Matthew Porges. 2016. "Research
into How Resources Are Acquired, Moved, and Used to Support Acts of
Terrorism." TSAS, Canadian Network for Research on Terrorism, Society
and Security, working paper no. 16–10. July. tsas5.wpengine.com/wp-
content/uploads/2018/03/TSASWP16-10_OHalloranEtAl.pdf.

Pollak, Nadav. 2015. "Rethinking U.S. Strategy for Intercepting Iranian
Arms Transfers." Washington Institute – Policy Watch, 20 August.
http://www.washingtoninstitute.org/policy-analysis/view/
rethinking-u.s.-strategy-for-intercepting-iranian-arms-transfers.

Roth, John, Douglas Greenburg, and Serena Wille. 2004. "Monograph on
Terrorist Financing." Staff Report to the Commission. National Commission
on Terrorist Attacks upon the United States. http://govinfo.library.unt.
edu/911/staff_statements/911_TerrFin_Monograph.pdf.

Ryder, Nicholas. 2015. *The Financial War on Terrorism.* London and New York:
Routledge.

Schmidt, John. 2007. "Testimony of John Schmidt of the Integrated Threat
Assessment Centre (ITAC)," vol. 53, 27 September 2007, (approx.) 6640–70,
plus Exhibit P223, Commission of Inquiry into the Investigation of the
Bombing of Air India Flight 182, 2010. http://www.cpac.ca/en/programs/
inquiries-on-cpac/episodes/90000709.

Schott, Paul Allan. 2006. *Reference Guide to Anti-Money Laundering and
Combating the Financing of Terrorism. Second Edition and Supplement on
Special Recommendation IX.* Washington, D.C.: World Bank. https://
openknowledge.worldbank.org/handle/10986/6977.

Sima, Julie. 2015. "Countering terrorism financing through anti-money
laundering measures," *Global Risk Insights,* 9 December. http://
globalriskinsights.com/2015/12/countering-terrorism-financing-through-
anti-money-laundering-measures.

Solomon, Erika. 2016. "Isis oil: deal with traders nets jihadis badly
needed funds." *Financial Times,* February 26. https://www.ft.com/
content/0c6707f6-dc8e-11e5-8541-00fb33bdf038.

Solomon, Erika, Robin Kwong, and Steven Bernard. 2016. "Inside Isis Inc: The
Journey of a Barrel of Oil." *Financial Times,* 29 February. https://ig.ft.com/
sites/2015/isis-oil.

Taxay, Michael. 2014. "Trends in the Prosecution of Terrorist Financing and Facilitation." *United States Attorney's Bulletin* 62(5): 2–9.

Taxay, Michael, Larry Schneider, and Katherine Didow. 2014. "What to Charge in a Terrorist Financing or Facilitation Case in Terrorist Financing." *United States Attorney's Bulletin* 62(5): 9–15.

United Nations. 1999. *International Convention for the Suppression of the Financing of Terrorism*, article 2. http://www.un.org/law/cod/finterr.htm.

UNSC (UN Security Council). 2005. *Second report of the Analytical Support and Sanctions Monitoring Team appointed pursuant to resolution 1526 (2004) concerning Al-Qaida and the Taliban and associated individuals and entities.* S/2005/83 (15 February 2005) 21. http://www.un.org/en/ga/search/view_doc.asp?symbol=S/2005/83.

United States, Title 18, U.S.C. Subsection 2339A, https://www.law.cornell.edu/uscode/text/18/2339A.

United States, Title 18, U.S.C. Subsection 2339B, https://www.law.cornell.edu/uscode/text/18/2339B.

United States, Title 18, U.S.C. Subsection 2339C, https://www.law.cornell.edu/uscode/text/18/2339C.

United States. Department of the Treasury. 2015. "History of Anti-Money Laundering Laws." https://www.fincen.gov/history-anti-money-laundering-laws.

Wickremesekera, Channa. 2016. *The Tamil Separatist War in Sri Lanka*. London and New York: Routledge.

"William James." 2013. *Stanford Encyclopaedia of Philosophy*. https://plato.stanford.edu/entries/james.

Wittig, Timothy. 2011. *Understanding Terrorist Finance*. London: Palgrave Macmillan.

Zenn, Jacob. 2014. "Boko Haram and the Kidnapping of the Chibok Schoolgirls." Combatting Terrorism Center, 29 May.

PART THREE

Society, Terrorism, and Counterterrorism

10 Parliamentarians and Intelligence Accountability

SUSAN DECKER[1]

Calls for enhanced accountability for Canada's intelligence services have been getting louder throughout the last decade and a half (Whitaker and Farson 2009; Whitaker 2012). In Canada in recent times, demands for greater parliamentary scrutiny had once fallen on deaf ears;[2] but this has now changed, at least in part. On 16 June 2016, the government tabled Bill C-22, titled "An Act to establish the National Security and Intelligence Committee of Parliamentarians and to make consequential amendments to certain Acts." It would create a joint committee of Parliament to scrutinize national security and intelligence activities and examine related issues. Just over a year later, the bill received Royal Assent (Canada 2017). For the first time, a parliamentary committee has access to classified material.

The immediate history of Bill C-22 begins with the terrorist-inspired events in Canada, particularly in the fall of 2014 (see Tishler, Ouellet, and Kilberg in this volume; and Perry and Scrivens in this volume). Not unlike in the period following 9/11, the response of the government was to legislate, namely to expand the powers of the Canadian Security Intelligence Service (CSIS), reinforce opportunities for government departments to share information, and make explicit the power of the Federal Court to issue warrants with extra-territorial effect.[3] The ensuing legislation, Bill C-51, became *The Anti-Terrorism Act, 2015*, and generated intense debates (Forcese and Roach 2015b). Although public support for these measures was and continues to be solid (Angus Reid 2015a; 2015b; 2016; Clark 2016), a chorus of voices focused on the already existing accountability gap and the very real prospect that it would soon become a "canyon" (Forcese, Roach, and Sherriff 2015). The government of the time, under prime minister Stephen Harper, did not agree and offered only an increase in the budget of the Security Intelligence Review Committee (SIRC), the CSIS review body.

The legislative response to the tragic events of 2014 may have acted as a catalyst for a more vociferous discussion of intelligence account-ability.[4] However, prior to 2014 periodic attention had been paid to accountability issues in the context of national security, particularly in the aftermath of 9/11, as Canada's security agencies grappled with the prospect of a terror attack on Canadian soil. For example, the O'Connor and Iacobucci commissions of inquiry were both struck to address instances of information sharing that led to the mistreatment of sev-eral individuals in the period immediately following 9/11.[5] This was the beginning of an enduring concern about the dangers of informa-tion sharing, even with close allies. These concerns were exemplified in the case of Maher Arar, who was removed from the United States by the Americans and sent to Syria, where he was detained and tortured. There is also the case of Omar Khadr, a young Canadian who was also detained by the Americans, raising questions about the appropriate treatment of youth consistent with Canada's international obligations (SIRC 2009; Whitaker, Kealey, and Parnaby 2012). Similar concerns emerged over the use of security certificates to remove from Canada five men suspected of constituting threats to the security of Canada, which led to several protracted judicial processes that continue to this day. Finally, though unconnected to 9/11, an inquiry into the Air India bombing released its findings in the same period, and raised similar concerns about intelligence and about errors that may have contrib-uted to the failure to stop an attack that led to the deaths of 331 peo-ple in 1985 (Air India Inquiry 2010). Collectively, these and other cases signalled a need to enhance the accountability structures in place for Canada's intelligence and security agencies.

After 9/11 some important changes were also made to the under-pinnings of Canada's national security apparatus, including to how intelligence is used in judicial processes, through amendments to the *Immigration and Refugee Protection Act* (IRPA). Another major con-sequence of the post 9/11 period is the new mindset that modern anti-terrorism requires an integrated, whole-of-government approach with a corresponding emphasis on the sharing of information.[6] The *Security of Canada Information Sharing Act* (SCISA) – itself part of the Bill C-51 omnibus legislation – facilitates increased information shar-ing among seventeen departments and agencies. Taken together, these developments indicate that there has been sustained attention to accountability issues in recent years – issues such as the lack of a com-mittee of Parliament with a formal role in intelligence accountability. Yet no enhancements to accountability were made until very recently. In fact, until 2016 the only real change over the last decade was the dissolution of CSIS's Inspector General, a key internal institution of accountability.

The passage of Bill C-22 in June 2017 addressed this major deficiency: the absence of a committee of parliamentarians with access to classified material and with a specialized function to closely examine the mandates and operations of all government departments and agencies with national security responsibilities. The bill succeeded where multiple previous attempts to create such a committee of parliamentarians had failed.[7] That Canada was the only one of the "Five Eyes"[8] partners without such a mechanism had been a frequent lament of critics of Canada's system of accountability.

The creation of such a committee has gone some distance toward resolving another long-standing issue regarding accountability: the lack of a dedicated institution of accountability able to look at national security issues horizontally, and with full access to classified material. The Liberal government under Trudeau buttressed its response to the accountability "canyon" by tabling legislation on national security measures. Bill C-59 provided for the creation of the National Security and Intelligence Review Agency (NSIRA), which has the mandate to review any activity carried out in any federal department or agency that relates to national security or intelligence. Although important, the creation of NSIRA and its impact on accountability is beyond the scope of this chapter. Moreover, the creation of an expert review body with an expanded mandate, though a positive development, cannot and does not substitute for direct parliamentary involvement in intelligence accountability matters.

At the same time, there are other gaps with respect to national security accountability that the creation of this committee will not by itself resolve. These relate to the surveillance activities of the state, issues that have been given profile in the wake of the Edward Snowden disclosures, including in Canada (Geist 2015). As discussed below, such issues have the potential to languish or fester in the absence of an appropriate venue for more public forms of accountability. Absent a form of public accountability, the courts have become the chief avenue through which various interests seek change and accountability; one of the most high-profile cases has been initiated by the British Columbia Civil Liberties Association (BCCLA) with respect to the Communications Security Establishment (CSE) in the wake of Snowden's document dump (BCCLA 2015). Canada is not alone in facing legal challenges in the intelligence realm. In the UK, changes in 2013 to enhance parliamentary scrutiny of national security activities were meant, in part, to make the courts less attractive to the public as an avenue of accountability (HM Government 2011). If Canada's new parliamentary body is to establish itself as relevant and as a publicly accessible source of accountability, it should concern itself with such high-profile issues as soon as possible.

This chapter does not purport to address all of the many issues confronting Canada's system of accountability for national security. It will take as a given that these challenges exist and that the recent enhancements to the intelligence community through the passage of C-59 may have only exacerbated them. Instead, the goal of this chapter is to contribute to Canada's discussions on accountability by examining the experience of the UK for insights that may be instructive with respect to Canada's new committee of parliamentarians. The UK experience is particularly interesting given that it has been instituting sweeping changes to its own system of accountability through the recently enacted *Investigatory Powers Act* (IPA). Moreover, Canada shares much with the UK, including its parliamentary system and its membership in the Five Eyes, which itself suggests shared values and intelligence priorities.

In this chapter, the focus is on two aspects of the UK experience with accountability that deserve special attention by Canadian decision-makers. The first is the UK's Intelligence and Security Committee of Parliament (ISC), which appears to have served unofficially as an inspiration for the creation of a similar committee in Canada (McLeod 2016). I argue that Canada should pay careful attention to the evolution of the ISC in order to avoid the problematic aspects of its history, through careful institutional design and the posture of the committee itself with respect to its own independence. The second is the important changes that are happening in public expectations of accountability, in part as a result of the reach and scope of the new tools of counterterrorism. Acknowledgment of the important role played by institutions of accountability in maintaining the public trust is well represented in current UK discussions on accountability reform, but barely at all in Canadian discussions.[9]

The UK's Intelligence and Security Committee of Parliament (ISC)

The ISC was created pursuant to the *Intelligence Services Act* (ISA) in 1994. Its creation was notable because at that time, the activities of intelligence agencies in the UK[10] and elsewhere were not part of mainstream political discussions. In many ways, however, the history of the ISC is one of a gradual distancing from government structures and the equally gradual expansion of its role with respect to the review of intelligence operations.

The ISC had a mandate to examine the "expenditure, administration and policy" of the three intelligence services but not their operations under Section 10 of the ISA. Though this mandate is consistent with other departmental parliamentary select committees, the decision to constitute the ISC as a "committee of parliamentarians" and not a "parliamentary committee" is itself significant. Of greatest import is that parliamentary committees are creatures of Parliament and have more independence. By contrast, committees of parliamentarians like the ISC have a stronger relationship with the executive than with Parliament. In the UK this was especially pronounced during the ISC's earlier period, when it was co-located with the Cabinet Office, which also had effective control over the ISC budget.[11] ISC staff were drawn from the Cabinet Office. The ISC also lacked the authority of parliamentary committees to require that agencies provide information; instead, it could only *request* information. In addition, the committee was appointed by the prime minister with only a formal consultation with the opposition parties.

During its first few years, the public performance of the ISC reflected its narrow mandate in that, based on its annual reports, the ISC was seemingly quite deferential to the government, even offering in its first report to expressly avoid issues of controversy (Phythian 2007; Gill 2007). Similarly, in its early history the ISC was criticized for its failure to address substantial human rights concerns (Gill 2007; Phythian 2007). ISC reports made scant mention of any human rights–related issues until at least 2005, and only after the US treatment of detainees became known and the question of UK complicity was raised publicly, at which point the government requested that the ISC examine the issue (Gill 2007, 26). Far from bolstering its credibility, however, the subsequent ISC report was compared unfavourably with the Parliamentary Joint Committee on Human Rights report on the same topic (Leigh 2012). The Joint Committee eventually would accuse the ISC of accepting the account of the intelligence services "apparently without challenge" (Leigh 2012, 727).

Whether criticisms of the ISC were entirely founded is difficult to assess, especially in light of the limits of its mandate. Regardless, a perceived lack of independence, admitted even by the ISC (2010, 7), adversely affected its credibility (HM Government 2007, 32). As a consequence, changes were made in 2007 and again in 2009 to bring the procedures of the ISC more in line with those of other select committees, including that Parliament be more involved in the choice of ISC members.[12] The ISC also visibly distanced itself from the executive by moving out of the Cabinet Office to a separate location and taking control of its own budget. For the first time, and in a move to make the ISC more like other committees, provisions were also made for some of its hearings to be held in public (ISC 2009, 4–6).

These changes did not, however, restore confidence in the ISC, and by October 2011, the UK government released a paper in response to the lack of public confidence in the oversight of intelligence (HM Government 2011, 39). The ISC itself argued for radical changes (ISC 2012, 49–50).[13] Pursuant to the *Justice and Security Act* of 2013, the ISC was made a statutory committee of Parliament with greater powers and an expanded mandate, including to conduct retrospective reviews of operational activities related to matters of "significant national interest."[14] It was also given access to primary materials held by the security services. This preserved the ISC's reporting relationship to the prime minister on matters that were national security sensitive, while strengthening its links to Parliament. The act also made it mandatory for the agencies to provide material to the committee, subject only to a veto by a Secretary of State (ISC 2014, 14).

Will these changes "rescue" the reputation of the ISC? Only time will tell. Since their implementation, there have been visible changes in the ISC in the form of a wholesale turnover of its membership, including a new chair. Also, its more recent reports have been more decisive in tone (ISC 2014; 2015b), with the chair, Dominic Grieve, seemingly intent on asserting the authority of the ISC.[15] Grieve's first priorities for the committee included examining the legality of drone strikes and revisiting the issue of the UK's involvement with the United States with regard to rendition and detention (ISC 2015b). These suggest less focus on administrative or efficiency issues and a greater orientation to issues that touch on propriety and human rights. That said, upon the release of its report on drone strikes, the ISC expressed "profound disappointment" that the government had refused to provide all access to key information. Thus, the authority of the ISC to demand all relevant documentation continues to be called into question by the UK government.

Significance for Canada

The leading Canadian scholars on accountability have argued that the careful design of a committee of parliamentarians in Canada is essential to its future success, and that it should have "robust access to secret (as in classified) information, [and be] charged primarily with strategic issues, including an emphasis on 'efficacy' review – that is, focusing on the overall efficiency and effectiveness of Canada's S&I community, laws and policies" (Forcese and Roach 2015a, 3). The experience of the UK suggests two principal lessons in this regard. First, and most importantly, the relationship of the committee with the executive should be managed carefully by the committee. The perception of too close a relationship has the potential to undermine both the credibility and the authority of the committee. Second, an overemphasis on efficacy review may be ill-advised, especially initially, when the committee is establishing itself and its independence. A third aspect is ensuring that the committee is able to work effectively alongside the other principal mechanism in place related to intelligence accountability – NSIRA.

Executive vs Parliament

The relationship of the committee with the executive, and the formal linkages that exist between them, is of crucial importance. The ISC was created as a committee of parliamentarians with substantial links to the executive (in the form of the prime minister) and relatively weak links to Parliament. This meant that the usual parliamentary involvement in the selection of committee members was weakly construed until recent reforms; also, the ISC lacked the usual authority to demand responses from government. The decision to tether the ISC to the executive reflected the need to reconcile the democratic accountability of the intelligence services with the need to protect highly sensitive information. Moreover, the ISC was one of the first such committees with access to classified materials to be established.[16] It is not uncommon for similar committees in other jurisdictions to deviate from the procedures of other parliamentary committees. Thus, the compromise from full parliamentary scrutiny is a feature of other liberal democratic systems with like committees (Bochel, Defty, and Kirkpatrick 2015, 3). Nevertheless, there is variation regarding the extent to which the UK ISC deviates from other parliamentary committees in other nations, and even within its own history. The ISC's lack of authority during its early period is nowhere more visible than in the fact that the government denied it access to the classified reports of the commissioners responsible for overseeing the use of intrusive investigatory powers by British intelligence services.[17] As noted, however, the UK government continues to restrict the ISC's access to what it considers relevant documentation. However, that the ISC so publicly and assertively raised this represents an important departure from its past practices.

Significance for Canada

In Canada, strong views have been expressed intermittently about the wisdom of creating such a committee. It has been reasoned, for example, that it would not be appropriate for parliamentarians to be vetted and impossible for them not to be.[18] Others hold that Canadian parliamentarians would be hard pressed to avoid the temptation to exploit sensitive information for partisan purposes. In effect, they could not be trusted (Forcese and Roach 2015a, 4–25). The MacDonald Commission in the 1970s was the first to recommend a committee of parliamentarians, but this recommendation was rejected by the government of the day in favour of the SIRC model. The creation of SIRC was progressive at the time, but it was not a decision without consequences. Instead of a committee of Parliament with a mandate for multiple departments and agencies with responsibility for national security, as was proposed by MacDonald, SIRC became the first step toward a stove-piped review system. In fact, the review bodies as they existed until the creation of NSIRA – namely SIRC, OCSEC, CRCC – focused on specific agencies and not on the intelligence community as a whole. This reflects a Canadian proclivity for addressing accountability issues on a piecemeal basis, first through the creation of SIRC in 1984, then through the CRCC in 1988 and the OCSEC in 1996.

The received wisdom now is that integrated intelligence should be matched on the accountability side with integrated review. This is a view shared, virtually without exception, by those advocating for change in accountability (BCCLA 2016). In essence, as national security activity both requires and entails cooperation between the various agencies (i.e., the need to share), the stove-pipe model for review and accountability has prevented the review bodies from following "the thread" of an activity once it crossed over from one agency to another. A key recommendation by the O'Connor Commission in 2006 gave rise to the idea of a "super SIRC" that might cover the intelligence community as a whole (Wark 2015; O'Connor Inquiry 2006).

The National Security and Intelligence Committee of Parliamentarians (NSICOP), stood up in November 2017, is to be the first body to take an integrated approach to national security review. However, for it to succeed, and contribute perceptibly to accountability, the new committee will have to develop an appropriate distance from the executive. The history of the ISC and recent movements in both New Zealand and Australia together suggest that a gradual distancing from the executive is part of the trajectory of this type of committee.[19] For Canada, it would be far preferable for the committee to emulate the recent ISC than to be inspired by the earlier period of the ISC's history.[20]

The original bill tabled in June 2016 was anything but bold in this regard. As proposed, the NSICOP was to be a statutory committee of parliamentarians and not a parliamentary committee. This has been retained, and the Act explicitly states that "the committee is not a committee of either House of Parliament or of both Houses" (House of Commons 2017, 3). A further challenge was that originally it would be "appointed by and administratively housed within the executive branch" (Canada 2016). Agents of Parliament and the Parliamentary Budget Officer are also administratively housed within the Executive Branch.[21] The obvious difference is that agents of Parliament are a support to executive accountability to Parliament; they are not themselves democratically elected politicians. In other words, there was a troubling distance between the structure of the committee, as proposed, and its ultimate aim, which is to provide for parliamentary accountability of intelligence activities. The committee is appointed by the Governor in Council, "on the recommendation of the Prime Minister" (House of Commons, 2017, 3). Although this provides the committee with more independence that originally intended by the government, the structure still gives the prime minister an unusually strong role with respect to all committee members, including those not from the governing party. All members are to be appointed based on the recommendation of the prime minister and will hold office at the pleasure of the prime minister. The key position of committee chair will also be recommended by the prime minister, who will select from the members of the committee. By contrast, it is more usual for the chair to be selected by the committee members, albeit from among the members representing the governing party.

Moreover, though the committee has a mandate to review issues referred to it by a minister, other parliamentary committees and Parliament itself have no such ability to refer questions to the NSICOP. This is in contrast to the experience in other allied countries.[22] This misses altogether an opportunity to build linkages between the committee and Parliament, something that could usefully serve to reinforce the distance between NSICOP and the executive. The asymmetry of access to information between this committee and other parliamentarians already has the potential to be problematic, as was the case in the UK, where institutional rivalries existed and may continue to exist. There has been at least one instance of an ISC report being "revisited" by another parliamentary committee; the outcome of that revisit called into question the legitimacy of the ISC and its findings on the same issue.[23] Indeed, for this reason, the ISC's most virulent critics tend to be other committees in Parliament.[24] The absence of explicit linkages between NSICOP and Parliament may further compound these issues.

Overall, there is a risk that far from satisfying the need for parliamentary scrutiny of intelligence agencies, the committee will only breed cynicism among parliamentarians. The UK's experience suggests that the lacklustre performance of the committee and a perceived dependence on the executive diminished public confidence in intelligence oversight. In fact, recent criticism of the ISC has been vitriolic, with one NGO stating it had lost all confidence in the ISC (Liberty 2014, 29). Non-governmental organizations (NGOs) have called for reform and have accused the ISC of consistently "failing in its duty to challenge the intelligence agencies" (Investigatory Powers Review 2015, 191). Closer to home, the Home Affairs Committee has expressed its concern that weak oversight could adversely affect the credibility of Parliament itself (House of Commons 2014, 157). In Canada, every effort should be made to avoid this outcome, and this is where the experience of the UK suggests the need for NSICOP to adopt an assertive posture vis-à-vis the executive in the coming months and years.

Propriety vs Efficacy

A related issue concerns the committee mandate. In Canada, proponents have suggested a committee focused on efficacy issues, which tend to be more forward-looking and concerned with achieving improved outcomes. By contrast, the experience of the ISC suggests that a core function of parliamentary oversight should be a concern for propriety and human rights, lawfulness, or conformity with deeply held public values. As such, these have the most potential to be problematic for the government. A Canadian example would be the Afghan detainee issue, which dealt with Canada's obligations toward people under its authority. In the UK, rightly or wrongly, the ISC was perceived to be unwilling to pursue this type of controversial issue (Leigh 2012). This in turn undermined its credibility and ability to act as a public source of accountability.

Also, in any government, there are more opportunities to promote efficiency and effectiveness than exist to guard against impropriety. This is especially the case considering how rare it is that intelligence activities are brought before the courts. There is also now NSIRA, with a broad mandate and access more substantial than NSICOP. NSICOP, however, comprised primarily of elected representatives, may be better positioned to do justice to controversial issues, including public policy questions that touch on propriety, than NSIRA.

By contrast, there are multiple structures in place that address whole-of-government efficacy issues, including the Cabinet Committee on Intelligence and Emergency Management, chaired by the prime minister, and the Deputy Ministerial Committee on National Security. The National Security and Intelligence Adviser has a key role with respect to efficacy, as do the many interdepartmental working-level structures that on an ongoing basis monitor and make improvements in efficacy. In its final form, Bill C-22 provided a mandate to review the "legislative, regulatory, policy, administrative and financial framework for national security and intelligence" under Section 8(1)(a) (House of Commons 2017). While there is a place for enhanced parliamentary scrutiny of efficacy issues, there are structures in place occupied with efficacy concerns from the vantage point of the whole community. The committee is expected to liaise with the NSIRA; it is less clear how it will work with the machinery of government.

In addition, there is a role for efficacy concerns to be raised productively within existing parliamentary committees, those without access to classified materials. For example, the 2005 Subcommittee[25] on Public Safety and National Security review of the *Anti-Terrorism Act* featured eighty-eight witnesses and months of discussion, resulting in two reports with a long list of recommendations to improve the operation of the 2001 *Anti-Terrorism Act*. The ability of parliamentary committees to adequately review propriety issues – where so often the devil is in the details – with no access to classified operational information is more problematic, as we saw with respect to the Afghan detainee issue. Finally, there are also agents of Parliament who contribute to executive accountability. The Office of the Auditor General, for example, has done multiple performance audits on the implementation of large-scale government-wide counterterrorism and national security programs and initiatives.[26] Efficacy, in other words, need not be the central focus of this new committee of parliamentarians. At most, efficacy should be equal to considerations of propriety.

In fact, the committee has a threefold mandate. First, as noted above, it is to review legislative, regulatory, policy, administrative, and financial matters related to national security and intelligence. The committee is also to review any matter referred to it by a minister. Finally, the committee will have a mandate to review "any activity" by a department or agency relating to national security or intelligence. This mandate is not without restrictions. If the activity "is an ongoing operation and the appropriate Minister determines that the review would be injurious to national security," (House of Commons 2017, 4) it will be out of bounds for NSICOP.

This broad approach is in contrast to that of the ISC during its earlier and most problematic period; however, Bill C-22 in its final form still substantially restricts the committee's ability to review any activity if a minister determines it would be "injurious to national security." That potentially broad phrase carries significant implications. There are also substantial limitations on the committee's access to information, including, again, if the appropriate minister is of the opinion that the material would be "injurious to national security." The Act stipulates that the review body, now NSIRA, must be informed of the decision to withhold information, as well as the reasoning behind such decisions, yet those review bodies have no ability to remedy the refusal (i.e., they are not permitted to supply information that has been refused by the minister). The Act also denies the committee recourse to the courts in cases of disagreement, for the minister's decision is "final." As Forcese and others have noted, these limitations bring the committee's ability to be a "potent" reviewer of propriety into question (Forcese 2016). This may prove to be an unacceptable limitation that cannot be mitigated by the subsequent involvement of review bodies. Indeed, for the committee to avoid damage to its own credibility, it cannot appear to be incapable of being strong on propriety issues; thus it must be decisive in countering any limits on either its access or its remit.

Fortunately, attention has been paid to the linkages between review bodies and the committee that make explicit the expectation that both should "take all reasonable steps to cooperate with each other to avoid any unnecessary duplication" (House of Commons 2017). NSIRA has just been created, so it is not possible to anticipate where it may focus, nor how that focus will conflict (or not) with the priorities of NSICOP. A look historically at the review bodies may provide some clues, however. For SIRC, some of its thematic review work looked at issues of public interest, issues that may also attract the interest of the committee. The risk here is that the committee and a review body could arrive at different conclusions on a given question.

That said, the risk of duplication should not be overplayed, for NSICOP, with its more public-facing mandate, would presumably have an appetite for broader public policy issues. The ideal could be a system for determining whether the committee or a review body should seize a particular issue, based on appropriateness or other criteria. In the UK, it seems that a lack of communication between the expert bodies and the ISC diminished the system of oversight's overall effectiveness (RUSI 2015, 95).

The Public Side of Accountability

As the foregoing suggests, careful design of formal legal institutions of accountability is essential and will affect the authority of the institutions themselves, among other things. In the UK, there were problematic aspects of the design of the ISC that worked to undermine its authority. The recent experience in the UK also strongly underscores the need to infuse the system of accountability with a public dimension. In other words, it is not enough to merely reinforce the existing accountability structures or add new ones; it is necessary in a modern liberal democracy to reinforce the public dimension of those accountability structures. The UK's experience with making accountability for intelligence more accessible to the public has implications for NSICOP and Canada.

Openness and Transparency in the UK

In the UK, a striking feature of recent history is the extent of public engagement regarding intelligence matters by oversight bodies, including but not limited to the ISC. This openness is at least in part a by-product of the revelations found in documents released by Edward Snowden. But it is also a by-product of the new tools of counterterrorism, tools that exploit the large quantity of personal information that now exists as a function of modern communications. For intelligence, the digital society holds the promise to reduce intelligence failures, and perhaps to discover new links and "unknown unknowns" in the volumes of data. Modern communications, however, have brought intelligence activities to the door of masses of people like never before. In doing so, it is bringing into sharp relief the key accountability "dilemma" concerning national security. That is, whereas democratic societies expect openness regarding "what is being done in their name," the nature of national security is such that, for it to be effective, much information must be kept out of the public domain. This dilemma is not new, but the involvement of the interests of so many people *is*.

This fact was largely obscured from public view until Snowden opened up some of the most sensitive aspects of intelligence to hitherto unknown public scrutiny. It is debatable whether, before Snowden, there was a need for a renewed understanding of the proper scope of intelligence activities between the public and the state. But the situation was not left to develop on its own. Instead, Snowden forced a discussion, at least in some jurisdictions, including the UK, on the proper scope of intelligence activities and the extent of the public's right to know – if not the details, then at least the broad strokes of what the state was doing in its name.

For the ISC, this openness is most visible in *Privacy and Security: A Modern and Transparent Legal Framework* (ISC 2015c), a report that was compiled on the basis of fifty-six submissions and nineteen evidence sessions, featuring a range of witnesses, including academics and NGOs, many of whom were intensely critical of the government in general and of the ISC more specifically. Many sessions were held in public, with transcripts freely available, as were the written submissions. This is not novel for parliamentary committees in the UK and elsewhere, but it was exceptional for the ISC.

The ISC report, along with two other inquiries, was meant, inter alia, to contribute to the process around the Investigatory Powers Bill (IPB) by informing public debate on the UK's use of intrusive powers. By all accounts, the resulting ISC report succeeded in this regard. On the transparency front, the report included an unprecedented amount of information about the full range of intrusive capabilities used by the agencies, some of which were revealed for the first time. To take a concrete example, the catalyst for the decision by the prime minister to acknowledge the collection by the security services of "bulk personal data" was the ISC report (ISC 2015a; Privacy International 2016). Subsequent to this, the UK government provided a more thorough and public justification for the need for bulk interception in its document "Operational Case for Bulk Powers" (HM Government 2015). The IPB, which received Royal Assent in November 2016, according to one UK journalist provides the intelligence community with "the most sweeping surveillance powers in the western world [and] has passed into law with barely a whimper, meeting only token resistance ... from inside parliament and barely any from outside" (MacAskill 2016). Critics will maintain that the ISC did not go far enough, but this was a discussion pushed by the ISC and would have been impossible until recently.

Significance for Canada

Canada has a mixed record for openness and transparency in the area of intelligence. Whitaker argued in 2012 that "[s]tronger security has been accompanied by diminished accountability, and there is little reason to expect that this trend is going to be reversed in the immediate future" (140). Recent and significant changes in national security legislation, through the *ATA* (2015) in particular, generated a substantial public response, through the media and an engaged and knowledgeable community of interests, but without any real public consultations by government on the substance of the changes that were being proposed in the legislation (O'Malley 2015). This was a missed opportunity to do a signal check with the public with respect to key aspects of national security priorities. It was also in marked contrast to the UK's deliberations related to the IPB, where arguably far less radical changes prompted large-scale consultations.

In the UK, although it remains to be seen whether the ISC's recent openness to engage the public on intelligence issues represents a permanent change, the ISC is, in principle at least, available to provide a permanent venue or outlet for more public forms of accountability. That is also the position of the Independent Reviewer of Terrorism Legislation, which has a reputation for openness, thanks in part to the former Reviewer, David Anderson QC, who has been described as a "rare and crucial" source of accountability (Oxford 2016).

To some extent 2016 and the first half of 2017 have signalled a change in Canada. The debates over Bill C-22 were one manifestation of this. Another was the consultations on national security initiated in the second half of 2016 by the government that resulted in the *What We Learned Report* (Canada 2017). This was followed by the tabling of major new legislation on national security measures: Bill C-59. With NSICOP now on the statute, there will be a committee of parliamentarians. No Independent Reviewer of Terrorism legislation is envisaged, and currently no institution has a strong mandate to engage Canadians on intelligence issues. SIRC and OCSEC had long been criticized for being insufficiently open to the public (Wark 2015), but they had no mandate to consult with Canadians on accountability issues. It is not clear yet where NSIRA will land. The strongest push for openness and transparency has come recently from commissions of inquiry, led by retired judges. Commissions of inquiry, however, are exceptional, meaning they are not permanent avenues of accountability and can only be triggered by the government of the day. Parliament can create a subcommittee to examine a particular issue, but the issue of access to classified materials remains. However, the Standing Committee on Access to Information, Privacy, and Ethics reported on information sharing in national security (House of Commons 2017), indicating that other committees do venture into the national security world.

There are a number of national-security-related issues in Canada that are ripe for public discussion but, until the NSICOP, lacked a forum for discussion underpinned by classified information. Chief among these issues are the activities of CSE, given its profile following the Snowden revelations. Some attention was paid to this by Parliament, but that attention faded quickly and, arguably, before the issues were thoroughly exhausted.[27] As a result, questions linger. For example, CSE's metadata activities remain shrouded in secrecy despite substantial avowals in both the US and the UK. This raises concerns regarding whether those activities were sufficiently covered in the *National Defence Act*, which provides the authority for CSE. A similar question relates to whether CSE should be required to seek judicial instead of ministerial authorization for certain of its activities (Geist 2015). These are substantial public interest issues. Bill C-59 provided for a major overhaul of CSE with a new *CSE Act* and the establishment of an

Intelligence Commissioner to review ministerial authorizations related to CSE and aspects of CSIS's mandate. In that sense, it is possible public discussion will emerge in future years. However, as indicated by past governments and Canada's own history of public engagement related to intelligence issues, the level of transparency is at the behest of the government of the day in most cases, and reports from NSICOP, as noted, still position the prime minister as the arbiter of what is (and is not) released to the public.

Canada has thus far escaped the fate of the UK and the US, both of which have had discussions related to signals intelligence and other intelligence activities more or less forced upon them by the public interest as well as by legislatures reacting to the revelations. Canada would be well advised to avoid letting these questions go unanswered for too long, and ideally address them through the NSICOP. To not do so risks what Whitaker calls a "failure of official accountability" (2015), which he argues can lead to greater reliance on ad hoc inquiries, as we have seen, and on the courts, as is visible in BCCLA's civil suit, launched in 2013. Unless NSICOP changes the status quo, civil suits may become more common if interest groups determine that answers to pressing public interest questions are more likely to come from the courts than from mechanisms aimed at ensuring "official accountability." The failure of official accountability can also lead to an increase in "leakers" like Snowden, who at least profess to be driven by utilitarian motives (Whitaker 2015, 206). Indeed, Kent Roach writes that the "idea that illegal leaks can be considered as a legitimate part of a system of accountability is an uncomfortable thought, but it cannot be ignored" (2015, 194). Nevertheless, it does follow the trend that Aldrich and later Dover have called "regulation by revelation," leading to accountability from a culmination of investigative journalism, courts, whistle-blowers, and public pressure from NGOs (Aldrich 2009; Dover 2016).

For these discussions to be productive, however, there is a need for more transparency. Recent experience in the UK strongly underscores the role of the government in creating a culture of greater transparency. As noted, the ISC, at least with respect to bulk powers, has been instrumental here. In Canada, this has not been the trend, though that may change with a new committee and new legislation in coming years. As a committee, NSICOP must meet in private if it is deemed likely that protected information may be disclosed during the meeting. To a large degree, this will depend on the committee's commitment to openness, given that it will always be easier to meet in private lest a sensitive topic be discussed. It was not until 2007 that the ISC held any open sessions. Under the 2013 memorandum of understanding between the prime minister and the ISC, both "committed to enabling occasional evidence sessions in public on matters agreed by both parties" (ISC 2014, 17). Once established and in place, NSICOP should be motivated to be as transparent as possible in managing its proceedings. It should also make every effort to put as much information in the public domain as possible.

Conclusion

This chapter has examined elements of the UK experience with parliamentary involvement in intelligence accountability for insights of relevance to Canada. In Canada, after years of discussion and inaction, the current government has delivered on its campaign promise to establish a committee of parliamentarians. In that regard, the UK's experience with the ISC offers some salient lessons. First, it suggests that the extent to which a committee contributes to robust accountability, and is seen to contribute to it, depends at least in part on its institutional design. Second, the ISC illustrates what others have admonished: that a committee of parliamentarians is a necessary but not sufficient condition of robust accountability (BCCLA 2016).

When the decision was made in Canada thirty years ago to create SIRC instead of a committee of parliamentarians, it represented at the time some of the best and most forward-thinking accountability for intelligence. SIRC was created, after all, more than ten years before the ISC was established. In a new era there are new challenges for accountability. With the establishment of NSICOP and NSIRA, Canada has an opportunity to again fashion itself after the best of thinking on accountability, taking into account the important experiences of others. With respect to the parliamentary element of accountability, this means a committee of parliamentarians that is muscular enough to demand access to information, that is independent in its ability to control the information it releases, and that is seen to be, and is, independent. The final form of NSICOP appears to fudge some of these issues, so how it establishes itself as an independent actor is likely to be important in future years. In addition, the committee should interpret its broad mandate to ensure, among other things, that the rule of law is respected just as the activities of intelligence agencies remain nimble in the face of evolving threats. At face value, the committee does appear to have a mandate broad enough to permit this level of attention.

Canada's deliberations on accountability are taking place at a time when there has been a subtle but detectable shift in thinking on accountability for intelligence agencies, translating into expectations of greater transparency among the public. Some argue that this shift is being driven by the breaking down of traditional notions of privacy and national security as a function of the digital age. Others, like Wark (2015), argue that attention to intelligence issues in the post 9/11 period created a strong appetite for more transparency. Others still, such as Aldrich (2009), suggest it might equally be an outcome stemming from revelations and the ensuing public pressure for transparency and accountability. Regardless, the expectation of greater openness is extant. For the new committee, after so many years and several failed attempts, public expectations will be very high: perhaps unreasonably so. If the committee does not make itself visible, or worse, avoids controversial questions, the history of the ISC shows that it will be difficult to restore its reputation in the public's imagination. At the time of writing, NSICOP had just released its first Annual Report, which was lauded for including fully vetted declassified reports containing substantial detail. Only time will tell whether NSICOP will continue to push for greater transparency, or whether it will succeed in providing an outlet for public discussion in Canada on national security matters. Its first Annual Report, however, provides perhaps the first glimmers of optimism.

NOTES

1 The views expressed in this chapter reflect solely those of the author and not those of the author's employer, the National Security Intelligence Review Agency (NSIRA).
2 For example, although accountability gaps were raised during deliberations on the *Anti-Terrorism Act (2001)* after 9/11, nothing was done. Still more discussions on accountability took place as the consequences of post-9/11 reactions came home to roost, most visibly in the work of the Arar Commission, which addressed the extraordinary rendition of Canadian citizen Maher Arar.
3 These are the *Anti-Terrorism Act* (2015) and the *Protection of Canada from Terrorists Act* (2015).
4 "Accountability" is used here as it is by Wesley Wark, who prefers it to alternatives because it encompasses the whole system of accountability, which involves multiple institutions and perspectives – including those of parliamentarians – that scrutinize the activities of intelligence and security agencies (Wark 2015).
5 The O'Connor Inquiry related to the treatment of Maher Arar and produced the three-volume *Report of the Events Relating to Maher Arar* (2006). The Iacobucci Inquiry was not a public inquiry; rather, it was a

closed-door inquiry assigned the task of examining events leading to the detentions of three Canadians, Ahmad El Maati, Muayyed Nureddin, and Abdullah Almalki, in Syria and Egypt. A public version of a confidential report was released in October 2008 (Iacobucci 2008).

6 *Final Report of the National Commission on Terrorist Attacks Upon the United States* (2004), known as the "9/11 Commission Report."

7 Several bills have been introduced in Parliament, all of which provide for a committee of parliamentarians with responsibility for national security: Bills C-81 (November 2005), C-447 (May 2007), and C-352 (March 2009). To that end, in the 2015 mandate letter to the Minister of Public Safety, the prime minister directed the minister to "[a]ssist the Leader of the Government in the House of Commons in the creation of a statutory committee of Parliamentarians with special access to classified information to review government departments and agencies with national security responsibilities."

8 The Five Eyes refers to a relationship among the intelligence agencies of the US, the UK, Australia, New Zealand, and Canada. The agreement, which dates to the Second World War, originally included the UK and the US. It eventually expanded to include the other Anglo-American states: Canada, Australia, and New Zealand.

9 In fact, the McDonald Commission recommended the creation of a Joint Parliamentary Commission and a review body to cover all federal agencies (except the RCMP) engaged in the clandestine collection of intelligence. Others have maintained that the design of institutions matters (Wark 2015).

10 These are the Security Service (also known as MI5), the Secret Intelligence Service (SIS), and the Government Communications Headquarters (GCHQ).

11 The Cabinet Office is a member of the Intelligence Community. Pursuant to the *Justice and Security Act* (2013), the ISC has a mandate with respect to the Joint Intelligence Organisation in the Cabinet Office.

12 Specifically, on 17 July 2008 the House of Commons passed the following resolution: "That this House endorses the proposals for the reform of practice and operation of the Intelligence and Security Committee as set out in paragraphs 235–244 of The Governance of Britain White Paper Cm 7342-1, including provision for nomination of the members of the Committee drawn from the House of Commons to be based in future on proposals made by this House." ISC, Annual Report 2007–2008, (Cm 7542), para 13.

13 Many definitions of "oversight" can be found in the literature. Generally, the term "oversight" implies a measure of supervision of activities in real time. This is distinct from "review," which is an *ex post facto* process of retrospective scrutiny with no effective control over the outcome of

intelligence activities being scrutinized. The use of the term "oversight" here is in reference to its use in the UK to describe all mechanisms of accountability for intelligence.

14 See the UK *Justice and Security Act* (2013), Section 2.

15 Dominic Grieve is known to be a staunch supporter of the European Convention on Human Rights and for his genuine commitment to civil liberties. He was awarded a Lifetime Achievement Award for his work on civil liberties and the rule of law in 2014 by Liberty, a well-respected UK civil liberties organization.

16 Among the Five Eyes, for the sake of comparison, the Australian Parliamentary Joint Committee on Intelligence and Security was established in 2001 and New Zealand's Intelligence and Security Committee was created in 1996. The US system was established in 1975–76.

17 These are the Intelligence Services Commissioner and the Interception of Communications Commissioner. See Gill (2011).

18 Thus C.E.S. Franks argued in 1979 that "Parliament would likely argue that a requirement for security clearances for MP's by a security service is an unacceptable intrusion into parliamentary privilege." Cited in MacDonald (2011, 39).

19 In Australia, a bill has been introduced by the Senate Leader of the Opposition that calls for substantial changes in the remit of the Parliamentary Joint Committee on Intelligence and Security (PJCIS), including that it be empowered to conduct own-motion enquiries, even in operational matters. It also calls for the Inspector General to provide its reports to the committee, a practice that is not currently followed. *Parliamentary Joint Committee on Intelligence and Security Amendment Bill* (2015).

20 In fact, along with the UK ISC, the February 2016 *Report of the First Independent Review of Intelligence and Security in New Zealand* recommends changes to the statutory mandate of the Intelligence and Security Committee (ISC) in New Zealand that would, in effect, provide greater independence for the ISC with respect to the composition and size of the committee membership. The review also recommends that "the ISC be authorised to request (but not require) the Inspector-General to inquire into any matter relating to the Agencies' compliance with the law, including human rights law, and into the propriety of particular activities of the Agencies. This would include operationally sensitive matters." Report available at http://www.parliament.nz/resource/en-nz/51DB-HOH_PAP68536_1/64eeb7436d6fd817fb382a2005988c74dabd21fe. A similar discussion is happening in Australia. See Senate debates, Thursday, 3 March 2016, Bills, Parliamentary Joint Committee on Intelligence and Security Amendment Bill 2015, Second Reading.

21 The following are Agents of Parliament: the Auditor General, the
    Information Commissioner, the Commissioner of Official Languages,
    the Public Sector Integrity Commissioner, the Commissioner of Lobbying,
    the Chief Electoral Officer, and the Privacy Commissioner.

22 Linkages with Parliament can be stronger in other jurisdictions. For exam-
    ple, New Zealand's Intelligence and Security Committee (ISC), which is
    also a statutory committee and not a committee of Parliament, also con-
    siders legislation or other matters relating to the agencies referred to it by
    Parliament, though not any matter that is operationally sensitive or that
    falls within the jurisdiction of the Inspector General. As in the UK, the
    New Zealand ISC has a mandate to examine the policy, administration,
    and expenditures of the agencies. The same is true in Australia, namely,
    that the Joint Parliamentary Committee on Intelligence and Security can
    review matters referred to it by Parliament.

23 This is the 2009 Parliamentary Joint Committee on Human Rights (JCHR)
    report into the UK's involvement in rendition and mistreatment overseas,
    which was much more critical of the government than was the ISC report.
    As well, the ISC report on the 7/7 bombings did not stand up well against
    Lady Justice Hallett's Coroner's Report from the inquest into the 7/7
    bombings, which reported that "[t]he ISC may have inadvertently been
    misled and thus ... its reports may not have sufficiently addressed some of
    the central issues before it." Quoted in Liberty's written submission to the
    Investigatory Powers Review.

24 For example, in its 2009 report on UK involvement in mistreatment, the
    JCHR criticized the ISC's 2007 report on the same topic. The joint commit-
    tee said the report "should be a wake-up call to ministers that the current
    arrangements [of the Intelligence and Security Committee] are not satisfac-
    tory." Available at http://www.parliament.uk/business/news/2009/08/
    committee-calls-for-independent-torture-allegations-inquiry.

25 This was a Subcommittee of the Standing Committee on Justice, Human
    Rights, Public Safety and Emergency Preparedness.

26 See, for example, the spring 2013 audit on the use of funds under the
    Public Security and Anti-Terrorism (PSAT) Initiative, http://www.oag-
    bvg.gc.ca/internet/English/parl_oag_201304_e_38212.html, and espe-
    cially the March 2004 report on the 2001 Anti-Terrorism Initiative that
    discussed a number of significant operational deficiencies stemming from
    interdepartmental cooperation: http://www.oag-bvg.gc.ca/internet/
    English/parl_oag_200403_03_e_14895.html.

27 See, for example, the transcript of the appearance of the CSE Chief and
    the Director of CSIS before the Senate Standing Committee on National
    Security and Defence, 3 February 2014. Available at http://www.parl.
    gc.ca/content/sen/committee/412%5CSECD/51162-e.HTM.

REFERENCES

Air India Inquiry. 2010. *Air India Flight 182: A Canadian Tragedy*, vol. 1:
    The Overview. Ottawa: Public Works and Government Services Canada.
Aldrich, Richard J. 2009. "Regulation by Revelation? Intelligence,
    Transparency and the Media." In *Spinning Intelligence: Why Intelligence
    Needs the Media, Why the Media Needs Intelligence*, ed. Robert Dover and
    Michael S. Goodman, 13–37. New York: Columbia University Press.
Angus Reid. 2015a. "Bill C-51: Strong support for proposed anti-terror
    legislation, but additional oversight wanted too." http://angusreid.org/
    wp-content/uploads/2015/02/2015.02.19-C51.pdf.
– 2015b. "Bill C-51: Support declines after months of protest, but strong
    majority still backs anti-terror legislation." http://angusreid.org/wp-
    content/uploads/2015/05/2015.05.25-Bill-C-51.pdf.
– 2016. "Security vs. privacy: Canadians want more accountability, but
    accept trade-offs on civil liberties." http://angusreid.org/wp-content/
    uploads/2016/03/2016.03.18-Security.pdf.
BCCLA (BC Civil Liberties Association). 2015. "Stop illegal spying – case
    details British Columbia Civil Liberties Association." https://bccla.org/
    stop-illegal-spying/protect-our-privacy-case-details.
– 2016. "The necessary components of an effective and integrated national
    security accountability framework for Canada." Letter from BCCLA to
    the Minister of Public Safety Ralph Goodale. 9 March. https://bccla.org/
    wp-content/uploads/2016/03/2016-03-09A-Letter-to-Minister-Goodale_
    consultation-on-C-51.pdf.
Bochel, Hugh, Andrew Defty, and Jane Kirkpatrick. 2015. "New Mechanisms
    of Independent Accountability: Select Committees and Parliamentary
    Scrutiny of the Intelligence Services." *Parliamentary Affairs* 68(2): 314–31.
Canada. 2016. "Government of Canada 'Backgrounder' on the National
    Security and Intelligence Committee of Parliamentarians (NSICOP)."
    http://news.gc.ca/web/article-en.do?nid=1085649; https://www.
    canada.ca/en/leader-government-house-commons/news/2016/6/
    national-security-and-intelligence-committee-of-parliamentarians.
    html?=undefined&wbdisable=true.
– 2017. Statement by Ministers Goodale and Chagger: "Bill C-22 is Granted
    Royal Assent." https://www.canada.ca/en/public-safety-canada/
    news/2017/06/statement_by_ministersgoodaleandchaggerbillc-
    22isgrantedroyalass.html.
Clark, Campbell. 2016. "Trudeau gains favour on security." *Globe and Mail*,
    18 March.
Dover, Robert. 2016. "Regulation by Revelation: The Opportunities and
    Challenges of Information Control in an Intelligence Era." *SAIS Review of
    International Affairs* 36(2): 103–111. https://doi.org/10.1353/sais.2016.0023.

Forcese, Craig. 2016. "10 minute primer: Detailed overview: Proposed National Security and Intelligence Committee of Parliamentarians (mandate and challenges)." 28 June. http://craigforcese.squarespace.com/national-security-law-blog.

Forcese, Craig, and Kent Roach. 2015a. "Bridging the National Security Accountability Gap: A Three-Part System to Modernize Canada's Inadequate Review of National Security." TSAS Canadian Network for Research on Terrorism, Security, and Society, working paper no. 16–04, April 2016.

– 2015b. *False Security: The Radicalization of Canadian Anti-Terrorism*. Toronto: Irwin Law.

Forcese, Craig, Kent Roach, and Leah Sherriff. 2015. "Bill C-51 backgrounder #5: Oversight and review: Turning accountability gaps into canyons?" SSRN, 1 March. https://papers.ssrn.com/sol3/papers.cfm?abstract_id=2571245.

Geist, Michael, ed. 2015. *Law, Privacy, and Surveillance in Canada in the Post-Snowden Era*. Ottawa: University of Ottawa Press.

Gill, Peter. 2007. "Evaluating Intelligence Oversight Committees: The UK Intelligence and Security Committee and the 'War on Terror.'" *Intelligence and National Security* 22(1): 14–37. https://doi.org/10.1080/02684520701200756.

– 2011. "Response and recommendation regarding chapter 3: Non-judicial oversight." Submission to Justice and Security Green Paper Cm 8195, October 2011. http://webarchive.nationalarchives.gov.uk/20140911100308/http://consultation.cabinetoffice.gov.uk/justiceandsecurity/wp-content/uploads/2012/51_Peter%20Gill%20-University%20of%20Liverpool.pdf.

HM Government. 2007. Governance of Britain Green Paper. Ministry of Justice. July. London: HMSO.

– 2015. "Operational Case for Bulk Powers." https://www.gov.uk/government/uploads/system/uploads/attachment_data/file/504187/Operational_Case_for_Bulk_Powers.pdf.

House of Commons. 2014. "Home Affairs Committee – Seventeenth Report Counter-Terrorism UK parliament." 30 April. https://publications.parliament.uk/pa/cm201314/cmselect/cmhaff/231/23102.htm.

– 2017. *An Act to establish the National Security and Intelligence Committee of Parliamentarians and to make consequential amendments to certain Acts*.

Investigatory Powers Review. 2015. "A Question of Trust – Report of the Investigatory Powers Review (June)." Written submissions (H-V). https://terrorismlegislationreviewer.independent.gov.uk/wp-content/uploads/2015/06/Submissions-H-Z.pdf.

ISC. Annual Reports: 2007–2008, Cm 7542, March; 2009–2010, Cm 7844, March; 2010–11, Cm 8114, para 274; 2010–11, Cm 8114, July, para 274; 2011–2012, Cm 8403, July; 2013–14, HC 794, para 2; see also Annex A of ISC, Annual Report 2013–14, "A Memorandum of Understanding Agreed Between the

Prime Minister and the Intelligence and Security Committee of Parliament (ISC)," paras 18–19.

– 2014. "Report on the Intelligence Relating to the Murder of Fusilier Lee Rigby." November.

– 2015a. "Privacy and Security: A Modern and Transparent Legal Framework." 12 March.

– 2015b. "Work priorities statement." 29 October.

Leigh, Ian. 2012. "Rebalancing Rights and National Security." *Intelligence and National Security Intelligence and National Security* 5(27): 727. https://doi.org/10.1080/02684527.2012.708525.

Liberty. 2014. "Liberty's submission to Investigatory Powers Review." November. https://www.liberty-human-rights.org.uk/sites/default/files/Liberty%20 submission%20to%20the%20Review%20of%20Communications%20Data%20 and%20Interception%20Powers%20%28Nov%202014%29.pdf.

MacAskill, Ewan. 2016. "Extreme surveillance becomes UK law with barely a whimper." *The Guardian*, 19 November.

MacDonald, Nicholas A. 2011. "Parliamentarians and National Security in Canada." *Canadian Parliamentary Review*, Winter.

McLeod, Ian. 2016. "MP McGuinty to chair committee of parliament to monitor spying, security." *Ottawa Citizen*, 8 January.

O'Connor. Dennis. 2006. *Commission of Inquiry into the Actions of Canadian Officials in Relation to Maher Arar*, pt 2: *A New Review Mechanism for the RCMP's National Security Activities*. December.

O'Malley, Kady. 2015. "Bill C-51 amendments seem unconnected to committee process" *CBC*, 31 March.

Oxford. 2016. "David Anderson QC, Independent Reviewer of Terrorism Legislation, in conversation with associate professor Liora Lazarus, University of Oxford." 28 April. https://www.law.ox.ac.uk/events/david-anderson-qc-independent-reviewer-terrorism-legislation-conversation-associate-professor.

Phythian, Mark. 2007. "The British Experience with Intelligence Accountability." *Intelligence and National Security* 22(1): 75–99. https://doi.org/10.1080/02684520701200822.

Public Safety Canada. 2017. Report: "National Security Consultations: What We Learned." https://www.publicsafety.gc.ca/cnt/rsrcs/pblctns/2017-nsc-wwlr/index-en.aspx.

Privacy International. 2016. "REVEALED: Privacy International releases trove of documents that proves staggering reach of surveillance agencies." 20 April. https://privacyinternational.org/press-release/1249/revealed-privacy-international-releases-trove-documents-proves-staggering-reach.

Roach, Kent. 2015. "Permanent Accountability Gaps and Partial Remedies." In *Law, Privacy and Surveillance in Canada in the Post-Snowden Era*, ed. Michael Geist. Ottawa: University of Ottawa Press.

RUSI (Royal United Services Institute). 2015. *A Democratic License to Operate: An Independent Report on Surveillance.* Caxton Hill: Stephen Austin and Sons.

SIRC. 2009. "CSIS's Role in the Matter of Omar Khadr Security Intelligence Review Committee." SIRC study 2008-05. 8 July. http://www.sirc-csars.gc.ca/opbapb/2008-05/index-eng.html.

UK. Ministry of Justice. Green Paper: *Governance of Britain.* July. London: HMSO. July.

– 2011. Green Paper: *Justice and Security.* October. London: HMSO.

UK Home Affairs Committee. 2014. Seventeenth Report: *Counter-Terrorism,* 30 April. http://www.publications.parliament.uk/pa/cm201314/cmselect/cmhaff/231/2310.pdf.

Wark, Wesley. 2015. "Once More into the Breach," 30 March. http://canada2020.ca/once-more-into-the-breach.

Whitaker, Reg. 2012. "The Post-9/11 National Security Regime in Canada: Strengthening Security, Diminishing Accountability." *Review of Constitutional Studies* 16(2): 139–58.

– 2015. "The Failure of Official Accountability and the Rise of Guerrilla Accountability." In *Law, Privacy, and Surveillance in Canada in the Post-Snowden Era,* ed. Michael Geist. Ottawa: University of Ottawa Press.

Whitaker, Reg, and Stuart Farson. 2009. "Accountability in and for National Security." *IRPP Choices* 15(9).

Whitaker, Reg, Gregory S. Kealey, and Andrew Parnaby. 2012. *Secret Service.* Toronto: University of Toronto Press.

11 Who's a Terrorist? What's Terrorism? Comparative Media Representations of Lone-Actor Violence in Canada

BARBARA PERRY AND RYAN SCRIVENS

In early June 2014, twenty-four-year-old Justin Bourque terrorized the city of Moncton, New Brunswick, for more than twenty-eight hours. The community remained on lockdown as law enforcement agencies hunted for the suspect, who was armed with a high-powered rifle and a shotgun. The anti-authoritarian survivalist had targeted RCMP officers, killing three and injuring two (CBC News 2014). Less than five months later, on 20 October 2014, Martin Couture-Rouleau targeted two Canadian Armed Forces members in a parking lot outside the Integrated Personnel Support Centre (IPSC) in Saint-Jean-sur-Richelieu, Quebec. The officers were deliberately run down in a vehicular attack; one was killed, the other injured. Couture-Rouleau then fled the scene and was later shot and killed by officers after a high-speed pursuit. Days after, yet another lone-actor attack was committed on Canadian soil, this time on Parliament Hill in Ottawa. On 22 October 2014, thirty-two-year-old Michael Zehaf-Bibeau drove to the National War Memorial, where he fatally shot a Canadian soldier on ceremonial sentry duty. Zehaf-Bibeau later died in a shootout with parliament security officials in the nearby Centre Block parliament building. While there were striking similarities across all three incidents, it is also readily apparent that they were treated very differently in the press. Indeed, there was a rush to identify Couture-Rouleau's and Zehaf-Bibeau's actions both as "terrorist incidents." Curiously, though, this was not the case for Bourque. It is this contrast that we explore in this chapter.

Questions around media coverage of domestic terrorism, particularly that associated with the extreme right, have received little academic attention. An extensive review of the research literature found that most discussions were embedded in broader analyses of right-wing extremism, and hence largely in passing (e.g., Guterman 2013; Hamm 2007; Kurtulus 2011; Ross 1995; Simi 2010). Exceptions include Chermak and

Grunewald's (2006) examination of the factors that influenced whether an incident was presented in the news media as a terrorist incident. Winter (2010) described how domestic extreme-right terrorism has been characterized and indeed overlooked in political, media, and public discussions in the United States, and Falkheimer (2014) conducted a case study on the media coverage of the right-wing terrorist attacks in Norway in 2011. There have certainly been no comparative analyses of images of violent right-wing extremism and Islamist extremism. The closest scholars have come is to assess disparities in media coverage across categories of terrorism; their finding has been that regardless of the categories included in the analysis, terrorism related to Islam or jihadists garners the most attention (Kearns, Betus, and Lemieux, 2019; Mitnik, Freilich, and Chermak, 2018). Thus, we have conducted a media analysis of three separate Canadian lone-actor terrorist attacks as covered by the nation's principal newspapers: the *Toronto Star*, the *Globe and Mail*, and the *National Post*. Online news articles were culled for the day of each event and the three days following. Our intent in gathering the reports within this narrow time frame was to capture the media's immediate reactions to and representations of the incidents. The purposive sample included 204 news articles. Of these, 70 reported on the Bourque attack (29 from the *Toronto Star*, 21 from the *Globe and Mail*, and 20 from the *National Post*); 43 focused on the Couture-Rouleau attack (9 from the *Toronto Star*, 14 from the *Globe and Mail*, and 20 from the *National Post*); and 91 reported on the Zehaf-Bibeau attack (30 from the *Toronto Star*, 29 from the *Globe and Mail*, and 32 from the *National Post*).[1]

What distinguishes our approach from the above-mentioned studies is the uniquely short time frame within which three significant attacks were committed in Canada; this provided both inspiration and an opportunity to conduct an in-depth qualitative – and comparative – analysis of media responses to the events. Here we uncovered some very distinct trends. In the aftermath of these targeted acts of terror, each incident was exploited to amplify a climate of fear. However, this anxiety was shaped very differently, in that the Bourque incident was used to reproduce the more conventional fear of crime, while representations of the other two attackers were crafted so as to deepen a more specific fear of terrorism. Despite some pronounced similarities in the incidents, which we delineate below, Bourque was not identified as a lone-actor terrorist or even a violent right-wing extremist. Instead, the incident was immediately acknowledged across news sources as an ambush against police officers, a "multi-person shooting," or, at best, a "murderous rampage." Directly following the two other incidents, however, a distinct tone began to flood the newscast headlines, one that stood in stark contrast to the stories constructed about Bourque. Front-page terms such as "terror attack," the "war on terror," and "radicalization" began to shape the ensuing media profiles of the alleged perpetrators.

There is not much to distinguish the three lone-actor attacks from one another. Given the description of Bourque's leanings noted below, he was just as clearly motivated by his ideological stance as were Couture-Rouleau and Zehaf-Bibeau by theirs. Nonetheless, while these three separate events shared characteristics that arguably constitute "acts of terrorism," both the media and political representations of these events were skewed in terms of who was defined as a terrorist. Two lone-actor attacks, allegedly inspired by radical Islam, were framed as acts of terrorism, while the other, allegedly motivated by radical-right ideologies, was identified as simply a "cop-killing." The disparate representations of Bourque's attack on the one hand, and those of Couture-Rouleau and Zehaf-Bibeau on the other, suggests, as Mythen and Walklate contend, that representations of "the terrorist threat have been ambiguous, patchy and ill conceived" (2006, 14). Specifically, such constructions in the Canadian context have been narrowly defined and are highly dependent on the standard trope of Islamist extremism, thus excluding more common domestic forms of violence associated with right-wing extremism.

Our analysis begins with a brief consideration of how terrorism is defined. Then we set the larger context of the analysis through a discussion of how all three incidents were used to invoke a rhetoric of fear and anxiety. The three attacks provided ample fodder for journalists and their sources to proclaim the "end of innocence" for the historical sense of security of Canadians. However, it is also the case that Bourque's assault was framed very differently than those of Couture-Rouleau and Zehaf-Bibeau. After that, we turn to a more explicitly comparative assessment of the media framing of the three incidents in relation to the socially constructed notion of "terrorism." Here we explore the persistent tendency to individualize Bourque's motives and actions while insisting that Couture-Rouleau and Zehaf-Bibeau were part of a much broader threat linking international and home-grown terrorists. We conclude by considering how each of the incidents subsequently shaped discourse around changes in policy and practice.

What Constitutes Terrorism?

To make our case, we must measure the incidents themselves against standard definitions of "terrorism." This is a challenge, since the question of what constitutes terrorism remains highly contested among academics as well as practitioners in the field. Controversies continue to flare up around the term, and scholars disagree about its meaning (Hoffman 2006; Easson and Schmid 2011). In part, these definitional differences arise from how international judicial systems govern terrorism (Young 2006). The definition adopted in Canada refers to an act committed "in whole or in part for a political, religious, or ideological purpose, objective or cause with the intention of intimidating the public ... with regard to its security, including its economic security, or compelling a person, a government or a domestic or international organization to do or to refrain from doing any act." Canada's *Criminal Code* also identifies terrorist activities with risks posed to the health and safety of the public, death of and bodily harm to individuals, significant property damage, and interference or disruption of essential systems, facilities, or services (Department of Justice 2015). By these standards, we argue, there are prima facia grounds for interpreting all three incidents considered here as acts of terrorism. Furthermore, our comparative study of the 200-plus media articles on the attacks and our assessment of the initial reporting within the seventy-two hours of each incident indicate that the attacks were treated differently. We then examine the implications of these differences for counterterrorism policy and practice.

"It could have been worse": Spreading the Fear of Terrorism

If there is one area in which reporting was consistent across all three cases, it was in the use of the incidents to evoke fear – fear of the unknown, fear of what might have been, fear of what could be. Thanks largely to the popularity of analyses grounded in the notion of "moral panic" (Cohen 2002), it is by now a truism in criminology that the often exaggerated and distorted framing of social issues via political and media rhetoric amplifies the threat and thus the fear attached to those issues. The perpetuation of the fear of crime has become a staple of news media. While typically applied to crime generally, Altheide (2006) argues that the "fear" paradigm has been extended to terrorism in much the same way. Indeed, it might be said that the culture of fear to which we have all become so accustomed in the context of crime was readily available to be exploited in the case of the particular class of violent crime known as terrorism.

The fear that inevitably surrounds the spectres of violence and terrorism is harnessed first and foremost through the selection of language and the emotive tone of that language. The relative danger posed by the three events was characterized in very distinct terms: Bourque's attacks were seen as a shooting spree, but those of Couture-Rouleau and

Zehaf-Bibeau as terrorism. Bourque's assault was described variously
as a "rampage," a "massacre," or more simply as the "Moncton shooting." Couture-Rouleau's attack was, in the immediate aftermath, often
referred to as a "hit and run," and later as "lone wolf terrorism," or
the "Quebec terror." And finally, Zehaf-Bibeau's assault on Parliament
Hill was described as an "assault on Canada." The fear associated with
Bourque, then, was not of the terrorist, but of the traditional bogey-
man of the violent criminal – unpredictable, random, and crazed. That
associated with Couture-Rouleau and Zehaf-Bibeau was the fear of the
religious zealot willing to kill for a cause.

The evocation of fear is further employed in the highly emotive language used throughout the media reports. The examples are legion, so
we provide only a small sampling to illustrate the point. Interestingly,
all three incidents were described as holding a city or a nation "under
siege" and "under lockdown," such that the threat was constructed
as imminent, ongoing, and paralysing. It suggested that communities
were surrounded on all sides by hostile forces wreaking havoc and
barring movement. This, even though each incident involved only
one assailant, with rather "primitive" weapons, including, in the two
"terrorism" cases, a vehicle and a pump-action rifle. One could almost
sense the writer holding his breath as he announced, upon Bourque's
arrest, that Moncton was now "free from unknown terror, free from
their locked homes, free to finally roam their streets again" (A39).[2]
Another writer painted the following picture of Zehaf-Bibeau: "The
homegrown insurgent ambushing the homegrown warrior – in the
shadow of the Peace Tower – to kill and be killed, wreaking havoc and
tragedy in a blaze of twisted glory" (C7).

It is not just the violence itself that is characterized in such awe-
inspiring terms. So too are the assailants, who are portrayed in ways that
distinguish them from the norm, that separate us from them. Bourque
is described as an "armed lunatic" and a "radical angry remake of a
cop-killing Rambo." One of the most blatant examples of the application of binary thinking is Barbara Kay's diatribe in the *National Post*,
titled "The unique anguish of a terrorist's mother": "Two men died
in Ottawa on Wednesday. One was evil and guilty. One was good
and innocent. Some murderers' parents deserve our contempt – I am
thinking of the perverted values governing entire Islamist-dominated
regions – because they actually encourage and rejoice in their sons'
homicidal martyrdom" (B48). Here, Kay draws upon the familiar and
standard tropes that characterize Islamic culture as wholly war-like and
evil. Taking a cue from former US president George W. Bush, media

reports invoke the dichotomy of Islam and the West, "uncivilized" and "civilized," cruel and kind.

That Couture-Rouleau and Zehaf-Bibeau were understood – by the selected news outlets in the study – as converts to Islam leaves them open to these negative characterizations. However, the fact that they were also both Canadian-born men – indeed, one was white – posed challenges for this typical framing of the Islamic (and typically brown) other. These were not foreign threats but true "home-grown" killers. How, then, to fit them into the familiar trope of Muslim-as-terrorist? For Rouleau, this was accomplished through the use of his chosen name – Ahmed. This adopted "foreign" name is what set him apart as not really Canadian. Journalists also favoured other aliases – "Ahmed the convert"; the "AlCanadi moniker commonly used by foreigners that have gone to fight with Islamic terror groups like al-Qaeda and ISIS" – again highlighting his apparent rejection of his Canadian heritage (B2).

Zehaf-Bibeau, in some respects, represented an easier challenge. The first half of his hyphenated name, after all, was neither Anglo nor French, but Libyan. His otherness is traced through his patrilineal heritage. His father, we are frequently reminded, was Libyan and "fought in Libya," suggesting some nefarious activity on his part. By virtue of his Middle Eastern roots, we can be comforted that Zehaf-Bibeau's susceptibility to radicalization can be located elsewhere. In spite of being born in Canada, he can safely be identified with a foreign culture that is "not like ours."

There are a number of other strategies by which the print media have played on public paranoia, especially with respect to the two violent Islamists. One of these is the almost staccato repetition of language and themes that drums into the audience an impending sense of doom. Single words and phrases, describing both the acts and the actors, arise regularly – "lone wolf," "home-grown terror," "shooting spree," "shooting rampage," "radicalized," and "attack on Canada's values" are among these terms. Over the three days of media reporting following each incident, this litany was repeated in quick succession. The repetition was a reminder of the immediacy and intensity of the threat.

Another common refrain, restricted to descriptions of Couture-Rouleau and Zehaf-Bibeau, was the use of the term "convert." This is key to the *us versus them* binary noted above; in addition, it serves as a reminder of the dangers associated with the "descent into extremism" (B15) and the "zeal of the convert" (B8). Writing of Canada's involvement in the War on Terror, the *Star*'s Haroon Siddiqui reiterates the rationale for this decision, asserting that "if we don't go after the Muslim terrorists there, they would come here to your neighbourhood. It turns out that the 'they' are here – 'they' are part of us, going round the bend after being 'self-radicalized' by the internet or for other reasons" (B8). As in this article, readers are reminded again and again of the threat "they" pose, now that violent Islamists have come to us. What is not addressed, however, is the threat posed by the right-wing home-grown terrorists in our midst.

In his treatise on the intersection of terrorism and the politics of fear, Altheide (2006) highlights the trope of communal suffering, whereby "sorrow, suffering, empathy, and pain were merged with ... fear and vengeance" (119). Consequently, sweeping references to the impacts of the three attacks were widespread and common. The themes of "terrorizing" – though not terrorism in the case of Bourque – of horror, of paralysis, of widespread fear, are liberally sprinkled across news reports about the attacks. So too are allusions to the specific harms inflicted on the family members and friends of the victims. Interviews and excerpts from public statements highlight the grief that is understandably felt by those close to the victims. Their pain is shared with the readers, as in a story from the *Toronto Star* that describes one victim's young, pregnant wife and young son, further quoting her sister: "These two little guys, or girl – we don't know yet what it is going to be – will never know their dad ... This is the kind of nightmare you never wake up from" (A13). Such assertions – as frequent as they are – make the families' pain our pain. They ask readers to imagine themselves in the same situation.

That all three attacks involved only one perpetrator but were nonetheless the source of collective hand-wringing is symptomatic of the common tendency among media outlets to distort threats, especially of violence, and in this case terrorism (Altheide 2006). All three events were treated by the media so as to exaggerate the magnitude and intensity of the events. This involved a number of interrelated strategies. As we discuss in more detail below, similar incidents are frequently bundled together, and this gives the appearance of an "epidemic" of violence and threat. Conflating Bourque's shooting with a series of police killings and mass murders positions such violence as a "regular" occurrence. Bourque is not, however, typically associated with other terrorist attacks, although there is little doubt that he, too, was "radicalized," albeit around right-wing extremism. In contrast, Couture-Rouleau and Zehaf-Bibeau are connected to each other and to myriad other reputed terrorists. Indeed, the vast majority of articles beginning on the day of the Ottawa attack (22 October) referred to both in the same breath – in spite of repeated assurances that "there is nothing to link the two."

A *Toronto Star* report asks, "Was there any link between Zehaf-Bibeau and Martin Couture-Rouleau, the man who murdered the soldier in Quebec? On the face of it, it's hard to imagine that two attacks on soldiers in three days can be mere coincidence" (C5). However, news reports ensured that they would continue to be linked in our minds by the two attributes they shared: temporality and radicalization. The regular recitation of similar incidents leaves the reader with a sense of an extensive web of terrorism reaching even into Canada. Mythen and Walklate (2006) highlight the impact of this, arguing that "interconnected expressions of fear carry greater weight than those which appear in isolation. The recurrent hot potato of the 'terrorist scare,' passed from politicians to the public via the mass media, is unlikely to lessen public anxiety, nor to induce opposition to the hardening of domestic security" (389).

The public anxiety is churned up by another distortion device: the claim that Couture-Rouleau and Zehaf-Bibeau's attacks, specifically, signalled "the end of innocence" for Canada. These attacks were, it seems, Canada's 9/11. Indeed, one downtown worker who experienced the attack on Parliament Hill was quoted as saying, "It's really weird. I feel the same today as I did on Sept 11 [2001]. I was working that day here, there were people stuck here from the U.S. and security on Parliament Hill. It's the same kind of weird feeling" (C45). The proximal linking of the assaults by two men was constructed as a watershed moment for Canada, such that "terrorism became a perspective, an orientation, a discourse for 'our time,' the 'way things are today,' and 'how the world has changed'" (Aly and Green 2010, 79). Aly and Green (2010) remind us that "the fear of terrorism is not isolated nor strictly limited to the fear of terrorists per se but is more broadly associated with a perceived state of terror, a kind of new world order in which insecurity, suspicion and the manipulation of fear for political purposes are the norm" (79).

It is an exaggeration to suggest that two separate lone-actor attacks constitute an imminent and ongoing threat. Yet this certainly did not stop journalists from making such claims. Rather than presenting them as the anomalies they are, Couture-Rouleau and Zehaf-Bibeau's attacks are underscored as transformative moments. A new "trend" is said to have emerged, one that will inevitably grow into a regular occurrence that will keep us living in fear. This "pervasive threat," writes Altheide (2006), "is given credibility by events that are interpreted as part of an unfolding and very uncertain schema for the future" (127). Interestingly, Bourque's murder of three police officers was not framed in this way. The risk was, rather, confined to law enforcement and described as a reminder of "just how dangerous a job it can be" (A66).

"[He's] not a terrorist, but he terrorized"

That Canadian politicians, law enforcement officials, and security intelligence agencies have overlooked – if not publicly denied – the threat of right-wing extremism in Canada (Perry and Scrivens 2016) is reflected in how the nation's primary news sources reported on three lone-actor attacks in 2014. It was apparent that the majority of news sources disregarded a number of key characteristics of each attack and each attacker, and instead constructed countless stories to meet their own rigid profile of a terrorist, as well as ones that met the social threshold of who ought to be defined as a national threat. Even though an array of journalists reported how Bourque *terrorized* a community – some even describing the event as the "shooter's reign of terror" (A26) or "Moncton's three days of terror" – news sources did not identify it as an act of terrorism. One *Toronto Star* article that discussed all three attacks went so far as to blatantly deny the association, stating that "Justin Bourque was not a terrorist, but he terrorized" (Shephard 2014). Such media portrayals are a stark reminder that "no matter how seemingly heinous an act, there are invariably at least some individuals who will not see it as terrorism" (LaFree and Dugan 2004, 55).

Both Couture-Rouleau and Zehaf-Bibeau were immediately and consistently referred to as terrorists and as radicalized individuals. This was underscored, for example, by liberally sprinkled quotes from security and intelligence personnel who confirmed that Couture-Rouleau was on the national security radar screen. He was "known to federal authorities including our Integrated National Security Investigations team in Montreal who, along with other authorities, were concerned that he had become radicalized," according to an RCMP officer (B1). Similarly, "The Mounties' say the investigation into Martin Couture-Rouleau began last June when they saw on his Facebook account he was 'radicalizing' himself" (B7).

In search of a "suitable" motive behind the three separate attacks, as well as one that fit with the news reports and social construct of the terrorist threat, all three news sources turned to the suspects' internet activity for answers. Through Bourque's Facebook account, journalists and reporters uncovered that the suspect was a loner, a gun rights activist, and a paranoid survivalist, all of which are identifiable signs of a potential right-wing extremist. Yet this was rarely acknowledged. Reports also described how, shortly before the attack, he posted lyrics from the heavy metal band *Megadeth* on his Facebook profile (A35; A59), the insinuation being that he may have been motivated – or in part influenced – by the music, not by an ideological commitment to far-right ideals.

Couture-Rouleau's Facebook profile included anti-Semitic rhetoric, various passages from the Quran, and comments regarding the war in Syria and the rise of ISIS as well as the righteousness of Islam in comparison with Christianity. Also, a look at his Twitter account revealed that he was following a number of users who advocated for and were fighting alongside ISIS, and he was profiled as a Muslim convert who had "radicalized himself" through online ISIS propaganda. In a similar fashion, one source told the *National Post* that Zehaf-Bibeau had recently viewed online incitement messages from violent Islamists, including a post by a Canadian jihadist who urged his followers to "carry out attacks on Canada" (C50). The online activities of Couture-Rouleau and Zehaf-Bibeau were read as adding credence to their identification as terrorists. Yet the ideologically laden online sentiments of Bourque were not interpreted similarly as indicative of radicalization.

For insight into possible motives, news sources also interviewed the family members, friends, and acquaintances of the perpetrators. Here, similar motivational patterns began to emerge across the three incidents. Bourque, for example, was identified as a marksman and hunter who lived in a trailer park, and a number of reports suggested that he was depressed and unstable and that he could not maintain meaningful employment (A26; A35). He was characterized as a gun enthusiast on a mission, but certainly not a terrorist. This, in spite of reports that he was obsessed with global conflict and conspiracy issues, anti-authoritarianism, and anti-police ideologies. Only a very small number of reports associated the Moncton attack with an act of terror. The *National Post*, for example, noted that the perpetrator's motive was anti-authoritarian and described the initial ambush as stereotypical of the anti-governmental Freeman-on-the-Land movement (see Hofmann in this volume). The report quoted Dr Arntfield, an expert on police killings, as saying that given Bourque's evident targeting of police, "it's domestic terrorism, is what it is ... an attack against the state for ideological purposes" (A55). Similarly, another *National Post* article published a statement linking Bourque's motivation to extremist ideologies: "The account paints a picture of a guns right extremist with anti-police views" (A59). But these articles were exceptions to a much broader pattern that emphasized Bourque's instability rather than his ideologically charged motives.

Interviews with Couture-Rouleau's and Zehaf-Bibeau's friends and family also revealed two alienated men who may have shown signs of severe depression, yet much more detail about their backgrounds was publicized than in the Bourque case. Framing the incidents as terrorism-related might well have prompted more immediate attention to the background of Couture-Rouleau and Zehaf-Bibeau, but the interest was also likely an effort to paint a clearer picture of terrorists on Canadian soil. For example, Couture-Rouleau was allegedly "normal" one day, then changed the next day and converted to Islam. Sources described how he grew a full beard, wore a head covering, and became obsessed with practising his new religion: fundamentalist Islam (B36; B37). Journalists published stories – involving interviews with the suspect's parents – about how he turned to the internet, where he became consumed with news headlines and the teachings of Islam (B2; B22). One of Couture-Rouleau's neighbours noted that he had been brainwashed by online radicals (B15), and a friend reported that the suspect wanted to be a martyr and committed the attack to reach paradise. The unknown friend recalled: "He [Couture-Rouleau] became an extremist. He wanted to go fight jihad ... The caliphate called all the Muslims on earth to fight. He listened to what they had to say and he did his part here" (B1).

The profile of domestic terrorists continued to take shape as journalists published extensive pieces featuring interviews with Zehaf-Bibeau's friends. Sources told reporters that the suspect did not to appear to have extremist views or an inclination toward violence, but that he occasionally displayed a disturbing side, including references to a devil inside of him (C25; C44). Volunteers and residents at the shelter in which Zehaf-Bibeau stayed also told reporters that the suspect was battling with drug addictions and struggling with his faith, describing how the man "seemed very extreme" and isolated (C53; C85). As journalists across all news sources continued to emphasize the suspect's tattered adult life, his drug addiction and psychological torment, and his Islamic faith, the general consensus was that Zehaf-Bibeau had recently converted to Islam yet was also battling with a severe drug addiction. His parents also told *Toronto Star* columnists that their son was "lost and did not fit in" (C13), and the suspect's mother told the *National Post* that her son's actions were not driven by ideological or political motives but were instead a "last desperate act" from someone who was unwell and felt trapped (C108). However, by the time all of the pieces of the puzzle were placed together, the majority of news reports constructed a story of a terrorist attack, prioritizing Zehaf-Bibeau's radicalization over his history of mental health issues – a direct contrast to the treatment of Bourque's motives.

The final strategy by which media outlets sought to draw lines between terrorist and not-terrorist was by linking each attack to other historical acts of violence. For example, the Quebec attack was frequently associated with national and international acts of terror. News accounts consistently described how Couture-Rouleau's profile was similar to those of a number of Canadians who had travelled to the Middle Eastern countries to support terrorist-related activities

(B13; B17; B36; B46). Reporters noted that just one month prior to the Quebec attack a spokesman for ISIS had urged its supporters to strike back in Canada, the implication being that this group or its ideology had inspired Couture-Rouleau to engage in an act of terror (B30; B34). A number of *National Post* journalists even made direct comparisons to the 2013 murder of British serviceman Lee Rigby, who was brutally assaulted by two Islamists (B30; B43). This same news source identified two other Islamist groups in Canada, one of them being the Toronto 18, a group that had plotted to set off truck bombs at a Canadian military base, the CSIS office in Toronto, and the Toronto Stock Exchange (B30).

After the Ottawa attack, a flurry of questions surfaced regarding whether it was in some way connected to the soldiers who had been run over in Quebec just a few days before. The language journalists used tended to associate these two separate attacks, suggesting they were either part of a string of terrorist threats motivated by pseudo-religious ideologies, or emblematic of a new threat from individual home-grown jihadists (B46). One *Toronto Star* journalist asked: "Are we dealing with troubled individuals who have 'self-radicalized' with Islamist ideology on their own, so-called lone wolves? Or are they part of a network? And if they are part of a wider organization, what might others be planning?" (C5). These linkages and the assumptions underpinning them gained traction in most accounts of the event. Reporters were not convinced that the events were mere coincidence, especially since both perpetrators were understood to be Islamic converts and the two had much in common, according to a *Globe and Mail* news source. Journalists also reported that ISIS had claimed responsibility for Ottawa attack, and ISIS followers were actively posting messages on the Web claiming that Canada had got a taste of its own medicine.

Just as with the Quebec attack, all three outlets associated the Ottawa shooting with a large number of terrorist attacks, both national and international, the assumption being that it had been politically inspired. The *National Post*, for example, immediately profiled the man as a "home-grown terrorist," though it admitted knowing little about him (C76). Zehaf-Bibeau's name was included in a number of discussions about how a "typical" terrorist might recruit new members, and about how terrorists rationalized their own behaviour, even though at the time there was no solid link connecting the man to a particular terrorist group or ideology. For example, the *Toronto Star* outlined, in detail, terrorism in the twenty-first century, ranging from the attacks in London, Madrid, and Bali (C7) to the Toronto 18 plot (C2). Also, the Ottawa attack was associated with a massive car bomb in Baghdad during the same week and with a trio of car bombs that had been detonated in other parts of Baghdad just days prior. Reporters noted, "this is the war Canada has joined" (B26).

Remarkably, both the *Globe and Mail* and the *National Post* made reference to the Montreal École Polytechnique massacre of fourteen women in 1989, despite the distinctly different motives and death tolls. Interestingly, the Montreal massacre was also compared to the Moncton attack, but in that context, it was described as a school shooting and not as an act of terrorism (A49). A couple of news reports also compared Bourque's shootings to the Boston Marathon bombing (A17; A43) and Anders Breivik's attacks in Norway (A55). However, they stopped short even in those contexts of classifying Bourque's attacks as terrorism. Far more common were the parallels drawn between the ambush that killed four RCMP officers in Mayerthorpe, Alberta, in 2005 (A14; A15; A31; A69), the murder – also in Moncton – of two municipal police officers by kidnappers in 1974 (A10; A57), and police shootings in general (A32). Again, Bourque was constructed simply as a "cop-killer," his actions divorced from the broader far-right mentality that shaped his actions.

Combined, these diverse representations underscore how the post-9/11 campaign against terrorism has been so engrossed with the threat posed by Islamist terrorists and jihadi extremists that it has swept the threat posed by the domestic extreme right under the proverbial rug (Leighton 2004; Reader 2014; Winter 2010). Notwithstanding the obvious ideological motives that underpinned the Moncton attack, the designation of "terrorist" has been reserved for "the other" – in particular, Muslims. The imagery and sentiments these news stories share remind us that terrorism is indeed a social construct, grounded in the notion of the "terrorist other," discussed in the opening section of this analysis (Chermak and Gruenewald 2006; Guterman 2013; Hamm 2007; Tuman 2010; Winter 2010). Foreign outsiders, both visibly and ideologically, qualify as "terrorists" if they are perceived as a threat to the hegemonic order and as acting against an idealized image of a nation. The state, the media, and the public strategically ignore certain political movements in the name of legitimizing the governing ideology and egalitarian credentials of a nation, while simultaneously constructing images that demonize foreign or international political movements (Simi 2010; Winter 2010).

Suggested Reforms

The various narratives described above implant fear in the public psyche. Yet they have an additional utility in that such discourse also conditions us for a "politics of fear" that "characterizes social life as dangerous, fearful, and filled with actual or potential victims. This symbolic order invites protection, policing, and intervention to prevent further victimization" (Altheide 2006, 117). Indeed, the circulation of an "imminent threat" narrative can also enable a controlling narrative around state objectives (Mythen and Walklate 2006, 389). Consequently, media coverage of terrorism typically includes commentary on the way forward in responding to putative threats. A *Globe and Mail* journalist puzzles over this very issue: "[I]t's left to us to make sense of these incidents and decide on a response. Should it be tough new legislation? More intrusive surveillance? Walling off Parliament? Greater security measures at government facilities? The list of potential measures is long" (B20).

The list was indeed long, as journalists and their sources suggested a variety of appropriate reforms. Again, this was much more so with respect to the radical Islamic than the radical-right attacks. Indeed, there were very few suggestions for policy reform in the aftermath of Bourque's murder of three RCMP officers. Rather, suggested "remedies" tended to revolve around individualistic interventions, such as psychiatric assessment. Just one article referenced gun control reform (A20). There were no explicit calls for "deradicalization" or "counter-radicalization" strategies directed at right-wing extremism. Since Bourque's attack was seen as a "simple" criminal act committed by an unstable individual, rather than an act of terrorism, there were no links to be drawn to such approaches.

In plain contrast, hundreds of column inches were devoted to policy reform in the aftermath of the crimes of Couture-Rouleau and Zehaf-Bibeau, with particular emphasis on enhanced security measures and counter-radicalization initiatives. In part, this reflected a media filtering of statements coming from policy-makers. In line with his ongoing predilection for harsh responses to the threat of terrorism, then–prime minister Stephen Harper was quick to call for enhanced powers for CSIS in its "war on terror." In line with the mantra that our world "has changed forever," there were frequent claims that "Canada may have to change" (B17). In particular, we were urged to "think security" (Mythen and Walklate 2006). Then–Prime Minister Harper and his "law and order" team exploited the attacks by Couture-Rouleau and Zehaf-Bibeau in an attempt to garner support for yet more legislative intrusions on fundamental rights.

Yet the newspapers examined here were *not* unfailingly supportive of Harper's position. A final theme that stands out as noteworthy because it deviates from the broader pattern is the unexpected yet frequent media calls for a "reasoned" and "measured" response to terrorism. Though they shared responsibility for elevating the level of fear, the same media sources sometimes rejected politicians' calls for heightened security measures. Indeed, one article characterized Harper's proposed response as "simplistic," claiming instead that "[p]olicies based only on the criminalization of young people who fall into the black hole of Islamic radicalization may not be enough. More laws and increased policing powers can't do it all" (C64). Assessments like these argue for proportionality between the risk and the reaction. They recognize that the attacks were conditioned as much by mental health issues as by ideology. In this, at least, there are some parallels in how Bourque, Couture-Rouleau, and Zehaf-Bibeau were all viewed. A *Globe and Mail* article exploring the link between "ideology and pathology" characterizes all three men as mentally unstable – it is this trait that left them vulnerable to self-radicalization, so it is this trait that should be the focus of treatment. These killers "are creatures of mind and movement, illness and ideology, despair and determination. We may not be able to stop them all, but we may recognize them in our midst, and find a way to reach out" (C63). Thus a number of articles point toward counter-radicalization programs already in place elsewhere, citing for example Denmark's and Germany's approaches. These are cited optimistically as ways to "unglue the bonds between pathology and ideology, to separate the troubled mind from the very bad idea" (C63).

Conclusion

Our analysis of these three cases in 2014 suggests that media rhetoric on extremism and terrorism in Canada is decidedly one-dimensional. Islamic religious and ethnic groups draw the attention of media outlets, much more so than another very real political threat from the far right (Tanner and Campana 2014; Bérubé and Campana 2015; Perry and Scrivens 2019; Perry and Scrivens, 2016). Events such as 9/11, the bombings in Bali, Madrid, and London, and the Paris and Brussels attacks have marked a new era in which discussions of extremism, terrorism, and weapons of mass destruction, for example, are singularly focused on Islam. Considerable attention and resources are devoted to highlighting the threat posed by violent Islamists, both globally and domestically. In contrast, there is very limited acknowledgment of a different kind of "home-grown" threat: the extreme right.

In 2014, Martin Couture-Rouleau, who ran over and killed a Canadian Armed Forces member in Quebec, and Michael Zehaf-Bibeau, the Parliament Hill shooter of a Canadian soldier, were roundly characterized as terrorists, while Justin Bourque, the Moncton shooter of five RCMP officers, was perceived as a "cop-killer" who had mental health issues. Similarly, militant groups such as al Qaeda and ISIS are considered terrorist entities, but extreme-right groups such as Hammerskins or Blood & Honour are not. At best, they are deemed "three-man wrecking crews" or "losers without a cause," thereby minimizing the relative threat posed by the latter (Perry and Scrivens 2019). Recent reports from CSIS, however, reveal that more lone-actor attacks have come from right-wing extremists than from Islamist extremists (Boutilier 2015).

Overlooking such activities has limited our understanding of the historical threat posed by the far right. Drawing on a three-year study involving in-depth interviews with Canadian law enforcement officials, community organizations, and right-wing activists (active and former), as well as analyses of open-source intelligence (e.g., website analysis, court records, news reports, and a social media scan), our own work (Perry and Scrivens 2016; 2019) has established that right-wing extremism remains a persistent threat and that its proponents have been responsible for far greater harm in Canada over the past decade than have violent Islamists. However, this trend has been largely dismissed by news media outlets, law enforcement officials, and policy-makers. Our offering in this volume should be read as a call to reconsider the questions raised in the title: Who's a terrorist? What's terrorism?

NOTES

1 A number of these articles also featured discussions of the Couture-Rouleau and Zehaf-Bibeau attacks in the same report.
2 For the purposes of organization and legibility, individual news source references are numbered in-text and correspond to a list separate from the bibliography.

REFERENCES

Altheide, D.L. 2006. "Terrorism and the Politics of Fear." *Cultural Studies Critical Methodologies* 6(4): 415–39. https://doi.org/10.1177/1532708605285733.

Aly, A., and L. Green. 2010. "Fear, Anxiety, and the State of Terror." *Studies in Conflict and Terrorism* 33(3): 268–81. https://doi.org/10.1080/10576100903555796.

Bérubé, M., and A. Campana. 2015. "Les violences motivées par la haine. Idéologies et modes d'action des extrémistes de droite au Canada." *Criminologie* 48(1): 215–34. https://doi.org/10.7202/1029355ar.

CBC News. 2014. "Justine Bourque: Latest revelations about man charged in Moncton shooting." 5 June. http://www.cbc.ca/news/canada/new-brunswick/justin-bourque-latest-revelations-about-man-charged-in-moncton-shooting-1.2665900.

Chermak, S., and J. Gruenewald. 2006. "The Media's Coverage of Domestic Terrorism." *Justice Quarterly* 23(4): 428–61. https://doi.org/10.1080/07418820600985305.

Cohen, S. 2002. *Folk Devils and Moral Panics: The Creation of the Mods and Rockers*. Hove: Psychology Press.

Department of Justice. 2015. "Memorializing the victims of terrorism: Definitions of terrorism and the Canadian context." http://www.justice.gc.ca/eng/rp-pr/cj-jp/victim/rr09_6/p3.html.

Easson, J.J., and A.P. Schmid. 2011. "Appendix 2.1." In *The Routledge Handbook of Terrorism Research*, ed. A.P. Schmid, 99–157. New York: Routledge.

Falkheimer, J. 2014. "Crisis Communication and Terrorism: The Norway Attacks on 22 July 2011." *Corporate Communications: An International Journal* 19(1): 51–63. https://doi.org/10.1108/CCIJ-08-2012-0053.

Guterman, K. 2013. "The Dynamics of Stereotyping: Is a New Image of the Terrorist Evolving in American Popular Culture?" *Terrorism and Political Violence* 25(4): 640–52. https://doi.org/10.1080/09546553.2013.814506.

Hamm, M. 2007. *Terrorism as Crime*. New York: NYU Press.

Hoffman, B. 2006. *Inside Terrorism*, rev. ed. New York: Columbia University Press.

Kearns, E., A. Betus, and A. Lemieux. 2019. "Why Do Some Terrorist Attacks Receive More Media Attention Than Others?" *Justice Quarterly*. DOI: 10.1080/07418825.2018.1524507.

Kurtulus, E.N. 2011. "The 'New Terrorism' and Its Critics." *Studies in Conflict and Terrorism* 34(6): 476–500. https://doi.org/10.1080/1057610X.2011.571194.

LaFree, G., and L. Dugan. 2004. "How Does Studying Terrorism Compare to Studying Crime?" In *Terrorism and Counter-Terrorism: Criminological Perspectives*, ed. Mathieu Deflem, 53–74. New York: Elsevier.

Leighton, P. 2004. "The Challenge of Terrorism to Free Society in the Global Village." In *Terrorism and Counter-Terrorism: Criminological Perspectives*, ed. Mathieu Deflem, 199–218. New York: Elsevier.

Mitnik, Z.S., J.D. Freilich, and S.D. Chermak. 2018. "Post-9/11 Coverage of Terrorism in the New York Times." *Justice Quarterly*. DOI: 10.1080/07418825.2018.1488985.

Mythen, G., and S. Walklate. 2006. "Criminology and Terrorism: Which Thesis? Risk Society or Governmentality?" *British Journal of Criminology* 46(3): 379–98. https://doi.org/10.1093/bjc/azi074.

Perry, B., and R. Scrivens. 2016. "Uneasy Alliances: A Look at the Right-Wing Extremist Movement in Canada." *Studies in Conflict and Terrorism* 39(9): 819–41. http://dx.doi.org/10.1080/1057610X.2016.1139375.

Perry, B., and R. Scrivens. 2019. *Right-Wing Extremism in Canada*. Cham, Switzerland: Palgrave.

Reader, I. 2014. "Beating a Path of Salvation: Themes in the Reality of Religious Violence." In *Religious Radicalization and Securitization in Canada and Beyond*, ed. P. Ramadat and L. Dawson, 34–63. Toronto: University of Toronto Press.

Ross, J.I. 1995. "The Structure of Canadian Terrorism." *Peace Review* 7(3–4): 355–61. https://doi.org/10.1080/10402659508425901.

Shephard, M. 2014. "Tracking down 'lone wolf' terror an elusive target." *Toronto Star*, 24 October. https://www.thestar.com/news/world/2014/10/24/tracking_down_lone_wolf_terror_an_elusive_target.html.

Simi, P. 2010. "Why Study White Supremacist Terror? A Research Note." *Deviant Behavior* 31(3): 251–73. https://doi.org/10.1080/01639620903004572.

Tanner, S., and A. Campana. 2014. *The Process of Radicalization: Right Wing Skinheads in Quebec*. TSAS Working Paper. Vancouver: Canadian Network for Research on Terrorism, Security, and Society. https://www.tsas.ca/publications/the-process-of-radicalization-right-wing-skinheads-in-quebec.

Tuman, J.S. 2010. *Communicating Terror: The Rhetorical Dimensions of Terrorism*, 2nd ed. Los Angeles: Sage.

Winter, A. 2010. "American Terror: From Oklahoma City to 9/11 and After." In *Discourse and Practices of Terrorism: Interrogating Terror*, ed. B. Brecher, M. Devenney, and A. Winter, 156–76. Oxford: Routledge Critical Terrorism Studies.

Young, R. 2006. "Defining Terrorism: The Evolution of Terrorism as a Legal Concept, International Law and Its Influence on Definitions in Domestic Legislation." *Boston College International and Comparative Law Review* 29(1): 23–105. https://lawdigitalcommons.bc.edu/iclr/vol29/iss1/3.

News Article Citations

Justin Bourque

A10. Gallant J. 2014. "Moncton: A generally peaceful city, but with a history of police killings." *Toronto Star*, 5 June. http://www.thestar.com/news/canada/2014/06/05/moncton_a_generally_peaceful_city_but_with_a_history_of_police_killings.html.

A13. [*Star* staff]. 2014. "Moncton Shooting: Slain Mountie Leaves Behind Pregnant Wife and Young Son." *Toronto Star*, 5 June. http://www.thestar.com/news/canada/2014/06/05/moncton_shooting_slain_mountie_leaves_behind_pregnant_wife_and_young_son.html.

A14. Woods, A. 2014. "Moncton shooting suspect Justin Bourque arrested." *Toronto Star*, 6 June. http://www.thestar.com/news/canada/2014/06/06/moncton_shooting_suspect_justin_bourque_arrested.html.

A15. Gallant, J., and P. Edwards. 2014. "The moment Justin Bourque was captured: An RCMP officer describes the scene." *Toronto Star*, 6 June. http://www.thestar.com/news/canada/2014/06/06/rcmp_name_officers_killed_in_moncton_suspect_justin_bourque_unarmed_when_arrested.html.

A17. Edwards, P. 2014. "Eye-witness account of Moncton arrest." *Toronto Star*, 6 June. http://www.thestar.com/news/canada/2014/06/06/eyewitness_account_of_moncton_arrest.html.

A20. Charach, R. 2014. "After the Moncton shooting, a public safety wish list." *Toronto Star*, 6 June. http://www.thestar.com/opinion/commentary/2014/06/06/after_the_moncton_shootings_a_public_safety_wish_list.html.

A26. Woods A., and T. Alamenciak. 2014. "In Moncton, a search for a killer that paralyzed the city." *Toronto Star*, 7 June. Retrieved from http://www.thestar.com/news/canada/2014/06/07/in_moncton_a_search_for_a_killer_that_paralyzed_a_city.html.

A31. Canadian Press and Globe Staff. 2014. "Manhunt for Moncton shooting suspect continues." *Globe and Mail*, 5 June. Retrieved from http://www.theglobeandmail.com/news/national/police-hunt-suspect-in-moncton-after-people-shot/article18996151.

A35. Ha, T.T. 2014. "Suspect in Moncton shooting talked about going out 'with a bang.'" *Globe and Mail*, 5 June. http://www.theglobeandmail.com/news/national/suspect-in-moncton-shooting-talked-about-going-out-with-a-bang/article18999247.

A39. O'Kane, J. 2014. "'Moncton spirit' strong at vigil for fallen officers." *Globe and Mail*, 6 June. http://www.theglobeandmail.com/news/national/moncton-spirit-strong-at-vigil-for-fallen-officers/article19061397.

A43. Carlson, K.B., and J. Friesen. 2014. "From shooting to arrest: Moncton's two days of horror." *Globe and Mail*, 6 June. http://www.theglobeandmail.com/news/national/witnesses-describe-events-in-moncton-from-a-community-in-lockdown/article19037668.

A49. Renzetti, E. 2014. "It goes against journalistic instinct, but we should deny killers their glory." *Globe and Mail*, 7 June. http://www.theglobeandmail.com/globe-debate/it-goes-against-journalistic-instinctbut-we-should-deny-the-killers-their-glory/article19059262.

A55. Brean, J. 2014. "Moncton shooting accused may be a classic 'pseudo-commando' with anti-government Freeman ideology." *National Post*, 5 June. http://news.nationalpost.com/news/canada/moncton-shooting-accused-may-be-a-classic-pseudo-commando-with-anti-government-freeman-ideology.

A57. Hopper, T. 2014. "Moncton shooting manhunt quickly became one of Canada's largest police operations." *National Post*, 5 June. http://news.nationalpost.com/news/canada/moncton-shooting-manhunt-has-quickly-become-one-of-canadas-largest-police-operations.

A59. Visser, J. 2014. "Moncton shooting leaves city on lockdown – Justin Bourque at large." *National Post*, 5 June. http://news.nationalpost.com/ news/canada/moncton-shooting-manhunt-continues-as-city-remains-under-siege-with-gunman-on-the-loose.

A66. Montgomery, S. 2014. "Justin Bourque arrested after massive Moncton manhunt that lasted more than 24 hours." *National Post*, 6 June. http:// news.nationalpost.com/news/canada/justin-bourque-captured-accused-of-killing-three-rcmp-officers-in-moncton-on-wednesday.

A69. Canadian Press and Postmedia News. 2014. "Justin Bourque appears in Moncton court, charged with three counts of murder for shooting of RCMP officers." *National Post*, 6 June. http://news.nationalpost.com/news/ canada/justin-bourque-appears-in-moncton-court-charged-with-three-counts-of-murder-for-shooting-of-rcmp-officers.

Martin Couture-Rouleau

B1. Woods, A. 2014. "Martin Rouleau 'Died like he wanted to.'" *Toronto Star*, 20 October. http://www.thestar.com/news/canada/2014/10/20/ martin_rouleau_died_like_he_wanted_to.html.

B2. Woods, A. 2014. "Canadian soldier killed in suspected terror attack identified." *Toronto Star*, 21 October. http://www.thestar.com/news/canada/ 2014/10/21/soldier_run_down_in_possible_quebec_terror_attack_dies.html.

B7. The Canadian Press. 2014. "Federal government raises Canada's internal threat level." *Toronto Star*, 21 October. http://www.thestar.com/news/canada/ 2014/10/21/federal_government_raises_canadas_internal_threat_level.html.

B8. Siddiqui, H. 2014. "Killing of two soldiers raise troubling questions: Siddiqui." *Toronto Star*, 22 October. http://www.thestar.com/opinion/ commentary/2014/10/22/killings_of_two_soldiers_raise_troubling_ questions_siddiqui.html.

B13. [Editorial]. 2014. "Martin-Couture-Rouleau, and the challenge of someone who hasn't broken the law – yet." *Globe and Mail*, 21 October. http://www.theglobeandmail.com/try-it-now/?articleId=21216003.

B15. Peritz, I., T.T. Ha, and L. Perreaux. 2014. "Martin Couture-Rouleau's shift into extremism played out on social media." *Globe and Mail*, 21 October. http://www.theglobeandmail.com/news/national/ extremism-in-canadas-borders/article21217185.

B17. [Editorial]. 2014. *Globe and Mail*, 22 October. "After the attack, we're still Canada." http://www.theglobeandmail.com/globe-debate/editorials/ after-the-attack-were-still-canada/article21248043.

B20. Wark, W. 2014. "Canada's best response: Move forward." *Globe and Mail*, 22 October. http://www.theglobeandmail.com/globe-debate/canadas-best-response-move-forward/article21251894.

B22. Perreaux, L. 2014. "After convert Couture-Rouleau's killing, Quebec mosque eager to 'live and let live.'" *Globe and Mail*, 22 October. http://www.theglobeandmail.com/news/national/after-converts-killing-quebec-mosque-eager-to-live-and-let-live/article21217878.

B26. Martin, P. 2014. "There are consequences to joining the war against the Islamic State." *Globe and Mail*, 24 October. http://www.theglobeandmail.com/try-it-now/try-it-now-world-insider/?contentRedirect=true&articl eId=21283314.

B30. Bell, S. 2014. "Soldier dies after being run down in suspected terror attack near Montreal." *National Post*, 20 October. http://news.nationalpost.com/news/canada/driver-who-ran-into-canadian-soldiers-near-montreal-was-known-to-counter-terrorism-officials-rcmp.

B34. [*National Post* Staff, the Canadian Press, and Postmedia News]. 2014. "Saint-Jean-sur-Richelieu attack was 'clearly linked to terrorist ideology,' safety minister says." *National Post*, 21 October. http://news.nationalpost.com/news/canada/saint-jean-sur-richelieu-attack-was-an-unacceptable-act-of-violence-against-canada-public-safety-minister-says.

B36. Blackwell, T. 2014. "Was Quebec attack on soldiers really terrorism, or just the violent actions of a disturbed man?" *National Post*, 21 October. http://news.nationalpost.com/news/canada/was-quebec-attack-on-soldiers-really-terrorism-or-just-the-violent-actions-of-a-disturbed-man.

B37. Magdger, J. 2014. "Man allegedly behind attack on Canadian soldiers was known to police, active on social media, radicalized." *National Post*, 21 October. http://news.nationalpost.com/news/canada/man-allegedly-behind-deadly-attack-on-canadian-soldiers-was-known-to-police-active-on-social-media-and-radicalized.

B43. Hamilton, G. 2014. "A new reality for Canada's military members: They can become targets at home and overseas." *National Post*, 22 October. http://news.nationalpost.com/news/canada/quebec-soldiers-ordered-to-avoid-public-places-in-military-uniform-after-ottawa-shooting.

B46. Blackwell, T. 2014. "Radicalized young people feel like 'a speck of dust in an uncaring universe' before joining extremists like ISIS." *National Post*, 22 October. http://news.nationalpost.com/news/canada/na1023-tb-radicalization.

B48. Kay, B. 2014. "The unique anguish of a terrorist's mother." *National Post*, 23 October. http://news.nationalpost.com/full-comment/barbara-kay-the-unique-anguish-of-a-terrorists-mother.

Michael Zehaf-Bibeau

C2. Shephard, M. 2014. "Islamic State's call for domestic attacks has troubled security officials." *Toronto Star*, 22 October. http://www.thestar.com/news/canada/2014/10/22/islamic_states_call_for_domestic_attacks_has_troubled_security_officials.html.

C5. [Editorial]. "Tough questions will come after the Ottawa shooting." *Toronto Star*, 23 October. http://www.thestar.com/opinion/editorials/2014/10/23/tough_questions_will_come_after_the_ottawa_shooting_editorial.html.

C7. DiManno, R. 2014. "Canada is no haven from extremism." *Toronto Star*, 23 October. http://www.thestar.com/news/canada/2014/10/23/canada_is_no_haven_from_extremism_dimanno.html.

C13. [thestar.com]. 2014. "Ottawa killer's parents apologize for 'pain, fright, chaos.'" *Toronto Star*, 23 October. http://www.thestar.com/news/canada/2014/10/23/ottawa_killers_parents_apologize_for_pain_fright_chaos.html.

C25. Woods, A., and D. Bruser. 2014. "What propelled Michael Zehaf-Bibeau on path to radicalization." *Toronto Star*, 24 October. http://www.thestar.com/news/canada/2014/10/24/what_propelled_michael_zehafbibeau_on_path_to_radicalization.html.

C44. Freeze, C., and L. Perreaux. 2014. "Suspected killer in Ottawa shootings had religious wakening." *Globe and Mail*, 22 October. http://www.theglobeandmail.com/news/national/suspected-killer-in-ottawa-shootings-had-a-disturbing-side/article21252419.

C45. Wingrove, J., S. Chase, B. Curry, and J. Mahoney. 2014. "Attack on Ottawa: PM Harper cites terrorist motive." *Globe and Mail*, 22 October. .http://www.theglobeandmail.com/news/national/parliament-shooting/article21217602.

C50. Bell, S. 2014. "Ottawa shooter read posts by ISIS convert calling for 'Jihad in Canada.'" *National Post*, 23 October. http://news.nationalpost.com/news/canada/ottawa-shooter-read-posts-by-isis-convert-calling-for-attacks-on-canada.

C53. White, P., and L. Perreaux. 2014. "Ottawa gunman was drug addict, acquaintances at shelter say." *Globe and Mail*, 23 October. http://www.theglobeandmail.com/try-it-now/?articleId=21273168.

C63. Saunders, D. 2014. "When troubled young men turn to terror, is it ideology or pathology?" *Globe and Mail*, 24 October. http://www.theglobeandmail.com/news/national/lone-wolf-ideology-or-pathology/article21293910.

C64. [Editorial]. 2014. "Tougher laws are not the only way to stop radicalization." *Globe and Mail*, 24 October. http://www.theglobeandmail.com/globe-debate/editorials/tougher-laws-are-not-the-only-way-to-stop-radicalization/article21293639.

C76. Hopper, T., and M. Hurley. 2014. "Michael Zehaf-Bibeau, the accused Ottawa gunman: A Quebec man with a criminal past." *National Post*, 22 October. http://news.nationalpost.com/news/canada/alleged-ottawa-shooter-apparently-had-criminal-past-in-quebec-was-repeatedly-brought-in-on-drug-charges.

C85. Henderson, P. 2014. "Ottawa shooting suspect taught two young men about Islam while living at homeless shelter, witnesses say." *National Post*,

23 October. http://news.nationalpost.com/news/canada/ottawa-shooting-suspect-taught-two-young-men-about-islam-while-living-at-homeless-shelter-witnesses-say.

C108. Huan, D. 2014. "Ottawa shooting by Michael Zehaf-Bibeau was 'last desperate act' of a mentally ill person, his mother writes." *National Post*, 25 October. http://news.nationalpost.com/news/canada/michael-zehaf-bibeau-mother-says-killing-was-last-desperate-act-of-a-mentally-ill-person.

12 National Security: Exclusion and Isolation among Muslims in Canada

PATTI TAMARA LENARD AND BALJIT NAGRA

This chapter reports recent research directed at understanding Muslim Canadians' experiences with counterterrorism policy in Canada over the last fifteen years. Our hypothesis was uncontroversial: we expected to find that Muslim Canadians felt targeted and vilified by these policies. The belief among Muslims that they face pervasive discrimination in Canada – that they are second-class citizens of this country – is well documented (Helly 2004; Poynting and Perry 2007; Rousseau et al. 2011; Nagra and Peng 2013; Nagra and Maurutto 2016). It has been widely acknowledged in academic literature that Canada's counterterrorism policies and practices have a disproportionate impact on Canadian Muslims, yet little is known about how Canadian Muslims actually perceive and experience these policies. In a bid to fill this gap, we interviewed ninety-five Muslim community leaders living in five major Canadian cities.

Our research had two objectives. First, we aimed to give voice to the leaders of marginalized communities, and second, we aimed to contribute to the larger project of generating a better sense of how the pursuit of national security has impacted Canadian Muslim communities. We begin with an account of our research methodology, along with a detailed account of our research subjects. As detailed below, our research questions were wide-ranging. We asked interview respondents to comment on a host of policies adopted and defended in the name of security, as well as on their interactions with the agencies tasked with carrying out these policies. We asked about the reinvigoration of security certificates, changes to immigration policy and airport and border security, and so on. Here we report on only some of our results.

The findings discussed in this chapter represent the themes and patterns that emerged from our research, and the quotations selected reflect commonalties in the interviewees' experiences. We begin with their attitudes toward the Canadian Security Intelligence Service (CSIS) because of its central and expanded role in protecting national security; our interviewees' experiences are overwhelmingly negative and to a considerable degree shape their concerns with regard to counterterrorism strategy in Canada. We then identify three specific worries that our respondents returned to repeatedly over the course of our interviews.[1] In particular, they worry that counter-terrorism policies (1) "Muslimize" the problem of terrorism; (2) by simultaneously "homogenizing" Muslim communities and stigmatizing individual Muslims; and (3) consequently fail to address the root causes of terrorism. Our results suggest two problematic consequences: a sense among Muslim Canadians that their Charter rights are not being fully protected, and, consequently, a sense that they are being treated as second-class citizens in their own country.

Research Methodology and Sample

From May 2014 to September 2015, we conducted a qualitative research study to explore the impact of counterterrorism policies on Muslim communities in Canada. We interviewed 95 community leaders living in five major Canadian cities: Toronto (26 interviews), Vancouver (16), Ottawa (20), Montreal (15), and Calgary (18). Using an extensive interview questionnaire as our guide, we asked about experiences with, and concerns about, Canada's counterterrorism laws and practices, as well about the impact these have on Muslim Canadian communities. Interviewees were asked general questions about Canada's counterterrorism initiatives as well as specific questions about certain policies and laws such as the Passenger Protect List, airport and border security, Bill C-24 (the *Strengthening Canadian Citizenship Act*), the expanded use of security certificates, investigations by CSIS, and wide-ranging changes to immigration and citizenship policies such as the use of immigration measures as a means of counterterrorism, the problematization of immigration in security terms, and citizenship revocation debates related to national security (Whitaker, Kealey, and Parnaby 2012, 532–5; Huot et al. 2016; Clément in this volume).[2] Interviewees were encouraged to elaborate where they were able, and they were given an opportunity to identify additional issues and concerns. We identified Muslim community leaders as those who could speak to their communities' experiences with Canada's counterterrorism policies. These people included those who played prominent roles in Muslim organizations and mosques, as well as those who were actively involved in Muslim community organizations, including *imams*, youth leaders, and members of women's groups. In addition, we spoke with Muslim academics and lawyers with specific knowledge of the larger community's experiences with Canada's counterterrorism laws and practices. It is important to mention here that our interviewees included not only those in elite positions but also those who were active in their communities in other capacities. We chose to speak to leaders among the Muslim communities across Canada, hypothesizing that they would be well-placed to identify general trends and worries among Muslims in Canada. We reasoned that because they were active in their communities, they would have special insight into Canadian Muslims' experiences with counterterrorism measures. It is possible, however, that our selection strategy introduced some bias, in that we spoke with people who are more likely to have had first-hand experience with Canadian counterterrorism efforts, and thus who are more likely to report distrust of the Canadian state. While we cannot reject this possibility out of hand, and correspondingly cannot say that the views reported here are representative of Canadian Muslims as a whole, it is worth noting that our results are consistent with other research on the Muslim experience in Canada (Harris 2017; Nagra 2017; Zine 2012).

We contacted Muslim organizations and mosques to ask their leaders to speak with us, relying on snowball sampling to identify additional candidates for interviews. Each of our semi-structured, in-depth interviews lasted approximately one hour. Interviews were audio-recorded, transcribed, coded thematically, and then analysed using the N-VIVO qualitative analysis software program. We guaranteed anonymity to those who spoke to us (interviewees quoted below are identified by where they live and the number of their interview), although some interviewees waived confidentiality (and therefore are identified below by their name and position). Seventy per cent of our 95 interviewees were male and 30 per cent were female. During our recruitment procedures we strived for a sample that was equally representative of both genders. However, at present, leadership positions in Muslim organizations appear more often to be held by men. Our interviewees ranged in age from 23 to 74, and their average age was 45. Just over 90 per cent of our interviewees were Canadian citizens; 8 per cent were permanent residents; and 1 per cent fell into the category of Protected Persons. The vast majority of our sample was well-educated and middle-class. Nearly all of our interviewees (97%) had some form of post-secondary education: doctoral or professional degree (32%), master's degree (23%), undergraduate degree (35%), college diploma (8%), high school diploma (2%). Our interviewees represented the diversity of Islam. Interviewees came from a variety of ethnic backgrounds such as

Indian, Pakistani, African, Egyptian, Syrian, Bosnian, Lebanese, Middle Eastern, Palestinian, Bangladeshi, Fijian, Sri Lankan, and European. When we asked our interviewees to identify the Muslim sect to which they belonged, 38 per cent chose not to answer. Among those who did answer, 59 per cent identified as Sunni and 3 per cent as Shia.

Research Results: The Muslim Response to the Pursuit of Counterterrorism in Canada

CSIS Investigations and Broken Trust

Among the starting assumptions of our study was that trust among citizens, and between citizens and the state, is an essential ingredient to the proper functioning of democratic states, especially in diverse societies like Canada (Lenard 2008; 2012). So when state agencies – that is, agencies that are taken to act in the name of the state – engage in activities that undermine trust relations, trust in the overall state is at risk of being undermined as well. Using this frame, we asked our respondents their views on a range of agencies that might well be understood as representing the Canadian state.

One of the main changes brought about through successive waves of counterterrorism legislation in Canada has been the expansion of CSIS's powers (Roach 2011). We therefore asked in particular about our respondents' experiences with CSIS, because its expanded powers had made it a central player in counterterrorism in Canada.[3] Where they occur, overwhelmingly, interactions with the agency are reported in negative terms.[4] Our interviewees repeatedly voiced concerns regarding these investigations – more specifically, regarding the ways in which they believed that Muslims were their particular targets. A striking 87 per cent of our interviewees thought CSIS especially targeted Muslim communities, and 37 per cent had personally had a negative experience with CSIS officials. Additionally, 70 per cent of our interviewees knew someone who had a similar experience. One interviewee, who worked as an imam at a mosque, told us the following:

> So sometimes what happens you know a lot of times Muslims feel that there is a sense of just excessive focus on Muslims, excessive targeting on Muslims. You'll see CSIS agents always calling you know Muslim *imams* but they would not do that to church ministers or Jewish rabbis. And the Jewish rabbis I was talking to them in Hamilton and only one of them has ever received a call from CSIS agents in the last ten years. And where I as a (new) *imam* have received calls from at least five different CSIS agents.

A lot of times it is just feels that they are watching Muslims, the mosques and the Muslim communities. We know about people in the mosque that have been approached by CSIS and these people have been offered you know financial compensations in order to collect information within the community and to record interactions with people. So I have witnessed that myself actually. You don't see that you know in a church or in a rabbi congregation. That shows that Muslims are definitely targeted in terms of just focus by CSIS. (Toronto 22)

Faisal Kutty, a prominent Muslim lawyer who is active in Muslim communities and who has been a founding member of some Muslim organizations, corroborates this impression:

I've seen through my own legal offices. The way CSIS carry out their investigations. What kind of targeting they carry, what kind of surveillance they carry out. Who they are interested in? What are they wasting their resources on? At our office we get a call at least once a week from someone that is Muslim saying that CSIS wants to talk to me. About what? All they just want is to get information. They just want to talk about other people. In some cases, Muslims are asked to be informants against their friends, against their community. They are asked to go and spy on their communities. CSIS will deny these things and national security will deny all the stuff but it is clear to me what is happening. Their denials don't really carry much weight because I have seen it with my own eyes. There are a lot of clients that I have that have been approached by CSIS to do some spying for them. One of my clients was approached by CSIS basically to go to the Muslim community to go, just to keep an eye on things. Other clients have actually worked for CSIS as informants in expectation that they would get favourable treatment and like security clearance. They'll tell them, "We know you need security clearance for a job and we don't have a problem, but we'll make it a lot easier if you help us out." (Faisal Kutty, lawyer, Toronto)

Overall, interviewees expressed concern about the scrutiny and surveillance of Muslim communities by CSIS. They indicated that by recruiting Canadian Muslims to spy on one another, CSIS was creating a climate of fear and distrust in their communities. There was also fear that Friday sermons at mosques were being monitored and that cameras were being placed outside mosques by CSIS. Some interviewees mentioned that some Muslims had stopped coming to mosques to pray because they feared this would put them on CSIS's radar. Our interviewees felt that those who are visibly Muslim (e.g., those who wear the hijab or other traditional Muslim clothing) or who are actively involved within their communities are more likely to be placed under surveillance or to be approached to work as a CSIS spy. For instance, one interviewee said that "*imams* now feel that dealing with CSIS agents had become one of their regular duties." Another *imam* in our study was contemplating leaving his position in order to avoid any further dealings with CSIS.

Furthermore, there were concerns that simply travelling to the Middle East could result in unwelcome attention from CSIS. One interviewee offered the following general explanation of how Muslim Canadians have experienced CSIS powers:

> After 9/11 it became an excuse to control Muslims more than anybody else. You know Muslims, their life, their movement, everything is being watched. We are being watched twenty-four hours a day. They know who we are. They know where we live. They know who we call. They know who our friends are. They know how much money we have in the bank. They know where we go on holidays. They know where we do our shopping. Is that the life that we want when everything is supposed to be equal? Why only Muslims? They do not pay attention to the Filipinos or the Chinese or the Europeans, who are so free in this country. (Vancouver 12)

Overall, we identified a persistent fear among Muslims that they are being surveilled, or at risk of being surveilled, by CSIS, simply by engaging in day-to-day activities like praying, dressing in "Muslim-appearing" garments, and travelling, domestically and across borders. Thus they believe they face an ongoing and heightened risk, compared with what non-Muslim Canadians experience, of being labelled a terrorist or a terrorist threat. We will return to the possible impacts of these negative interactions with state agencies below, when we consider the diminishing level of trust reported between Muslim Canadians and the Canadian state.

"Muslimization" of Terrorism

It is not surprising to learn that 90 per cent of our respondents generally believed that Canada's counterterrorism policies targeted Muslim communities, and disproportionately so. Much prior academic scholarship, in Canada and elsewhere, has identified similar sentiments (Bahdi 2003; Bhabha 2003; Thobani 2007; Hanniman 2008; Razack 2008; International Civil Liberties Monitoring Group 2010; Khan 2012). In our work, we heard repeatedly that Canada's strategies for pursuing counterterrorism were extremely "biased against Muslims." In particular, our respondents complained that the discourse surrounding the adoption and defence of these policies permitted an easy conflation of Islam with terrorism. Indeed, 94 per cent of our respondents were concerned about the initiatives taken by the Canadian government to counter terrorist threats. Among their concerns was the equation of "terrorism" with Islam. They believed that the discourse surrounding the adoption and implementation of counterterrorism measures permitted and encouraged Canadians to believe that Muslim identity is synonymous with terrorism (see also Khan 2012). One respondent described the situation as follows:

> I think the Muslimization of the problem of terrorism is a big concern for the Muslim community. In the RCMP documents for example which deal with counterterrorism and counter-radicalization, they make it very clear that it's a Muslim problem, that it's not a problem with extreme political groups from all different ideologies. Research from the United States has demonstrated white supremacist and right-wing groups have perpetrated the majority of terrorist incidents in the United States. Last year there were many mass murders in the United States that killed far more people, and only one of those was committed by a Muslim and that was the Boston bombing. Yet, the overwhelming narrative about terrorism is that [it] is a Muslim problem and that [it] is these Muslims "who have come to northern America, who don't understand our values of democracy and they hate us for our freedoms and they are religiously programmed to spread terror in this land." By Islamizing the problem of terrorism they portray a very visibly identifiable minority group as being the primary threat to Canada, engineering more racism against ... already vulnerable minority groups. From both perspectives of security and racialization, it is an extremely problematic discourse. (Toronto 14)

One interviewee pointed out that the conflation of terrorism with Muslim religiosity was obvious in the terminology commonly used by governments, politicians, and the media:

> One could say we are just being paranoid. But it's very clear when you look at the terminology that is being used. For example, the words "radical jihadism" or "Islamic terrorism" as opposed to the word terrorism. That's very clearly indicating that we are talking about Muslims. (Ottawa 14)

Interviewees also mentioned that whenever someone who was Muslim engaged in acts of violence, it was automatically considered to be an act of terrorism, while the same principle did not hold for other communities (see Perry and Scrivens in this volume). Here is one of our interviewees expressing this view:

> What is terrorism? Right now terrorism means you need to be Muslim and you need to commit a murder or a mass attack. That's what terrorism is in their [the government's] definition. The Charleston shooter walks into a church and he shoots nine people, he's not a terrorist. He's a lone wolf. He's a white supremacist. He will never fit the criteria of being a terrorist with respect to this law. But if you look at the official definition of terrorism, it's the use [of] violence to intimidate and to push ideological, religious, or political views on to a population. For me you are specifically singling out the Muslim population when you only label them as being "terrorists." (Montreal 12)

Our interviewees also questioned Canada's aggressive pursuit of counterterrorism, when no major attacks have transpired in Canada, and wondered why in particular the Canadian government chose a discourse that appeared specifically intended to generate fear of Canada's Muslim citizens.[5]

The result of what our interviewee above referred to as the "Muslimization" of terrorism is that the government is signalling to Canadians that their Muslim neighbours are potentially dangerous and worthy of suspicion, in ways that make individual Muslims vulnerable to racism and discrimination. This worry was expressed by 69 per cent of our respondents. One respondent expressed a variation on this view:

> I feel like by adopting these measures they have directly contributed to increasing the amount of stigmatization, and racism and intolerance, and the Muslim community is suffering. They have singled out the Muslim community in a way that I frankly find completely disgusting. (Montreal 13)

Another respondent echoed concerns about the negative effects of counterterrorism policies in tandem with anti-Muslim discourse, seeing this as deeply problematic:

> There is a huge sacrifice for Muslims. There will be much, much more increase[d] racism towards Muslims. Because if the government is telling you to hate Muslims in the sense that they are terrorist[s], that because of

them all these horrible security laws are coming into place, which Canadians hate. So you'll automatically start hating Muslims. The government is
doing nothing to stop it, not one single statement of support for Muslims.
So how would you feel? (Calgary 10)

Similar worries were expressed by others. One respondent told us that
state policies were "breeding cultures of fear about Islam," were "dehu-
manizing Muslim communities," and "definitely affected how society
views them."

The Homogenization of Muslims in Canada

Our interviewees thought this conflation between Islam and terrorism
resulted in Muslim communities being blamed for the actions of a few.
In particular, the discourse adopted by the government (and repeated in
the media) signalled that "Muslims" were a homogeneous group. That
discourse failed to acknowledge that Islam is in fact a religion practised
in a variety of different ways by individuals who differ by race, culture,
ethnicity, country of origin, and depth of religious commitment, among
many other factors. Our respondents were critical of this "homogenizing," which they believed aided in casting Muslims in a negative light.
One interviewee told us:

> I think that anyone who is educated, anyone who is involved in policy
> should recognize ... that Muslims are a pluralistic community, a very
> diverse people. And that those who are not integrated are no different
> from other people who are marginalized in this society. Yes, they do have
> the common background as Muslims, but they're marginalized for other
> reasons, often it's racial, often it's economic, and these issues should be
> dealt with by social policy and social justice policy. That is not accepted,
> unfortunately, when it comes to issues of anti-terrorism and security leg-
> islations, they do not cover those aspects because they like to create the
> monolithic image of the terrorism Muslim. This is the issue that we have.
> (Ottawa 2)

The particular impact of this "homogenization" is this: overall, our
interviewees felt that Muslims were being equated with individuals
who commit acts of violence, and thus were collectively being held
responsible and accountable for the actions of a very small number
of individuals. This homogenization and subsequent vilification was
blamed not only on counterterrorism practices but also on the political discourse used to defend these measures, on the media, and on

the pre-existing stereotypes about Muslims within society and more generally across North America (Sides and Gross 2013; Helly 2004; Khalema and Wannas-Jones 2003). For example, one interviewee said this:

> So you are already living in an anti-Muslim climate and on top of that you feel that you are discriminated against in one way or the other, at work, or at school at times, and then you see throughout the day every single day in the media being told that Muslims are the source of all the evil in the world and to top it all off you get a slap from the government pretty much through their extremely biased and one-sided counterterrorism and foreign policies. (Toronto 16)

This portrayal of Muslims and Islam was particularly disturbing to our interviewees, for they viewed their religion as positive and beautiful. One interviewee said this:

> People that commit violence I am against that too because Islam does not teach that. Islam does not say go kill people. So you can't judge the whole Muslim community for it. People just need to know that it's not their religion, it's the person that really doesn't have full knowledge of the religion and misinterprets a few things or like they get brainwashed. But at the same time you can't just pinpoint just the Muslims, because there [are] other people with other religions that do the same things. (Calgary 13)

Our interviewees strongly believed that this way of portraying Islam has a detrimental effect on Muslim communities. They expressed the belief that the pursuit of counterterrorism and its surrounding discourse made them vulnerable to hate crimes, especially in public spaces, in the form of both verbal and physical abuse.

This vilification of Muslim communities is thought to have made Muslim women particularly vulnerable to abuse and violence. One interviewee from Vancouver, for example, mentioned that many Muslim women he knows, who wear the hijab, have experienced significant verbal and physical abuse on public transportation. In fact, 47 per cent of our interviewees indicated knowing someone who had faced some form of discrimination against Muslims (including verbal or physical abuse, and hurtful comments about Islam and Muslims, as well as employment discrimination). These reports are well-corroborated in additional work (Nagra and Peng 2013; Poynting and Perry 2007; Jamil and Rousseau 2012; Rahmath, Chambers, and Wakewich 2016) and in the frequent media reports of violence and abuse directed at Muslim citizens (CBC News 2012; 2015; IQRA 2009; Paling 2016).

Not Addressing the Root Causes of Terrorism

In his influential work, Edward Said argued that the Western world has historically approached Islam with hostility and fear and has thus perceived Muslims as anti-Western, anti-democratic, barbaric, and irrational (1997). Our interviewees corroborated this impression. For example, one interviewee said:

> It [counterterrorism] seems to be motivated based on a lot of fear and misunderstanding. I don't really think that we have a major radicalization problem in Canada. I think that it is based on the politics of fear and the politics of ignorance and it seems to be stigmatizing one specific community. (Montreal 16)

Our interviewees' experiences reveal the ongoing prevalence of these perceptions of Islam in Canadian society more generally.

Additionally, many of our interviewees thought that this strong focus on Muslim communities was misdirected and did not actually address the root causes of terrorism. For instance, one interviewee stated:

> There have been so many debates about adopting the proper policies to counterterrorism but no one has asked the question, what were we doing in countries like Syria and Iraq in the first place? You go back to 2003, the year the United States had invaded Iraq, and you just look at the country now – it has been completely shattered. So I think the US and the Canadian government[s] are directly responsible for a lot of the stuff that has been happening right now ... The causes of terrorism are the foreign policies of the US and Canadian government[s,] [which] support dictatorship and oppression of Muslim communities. (Montreal 13)

Overall, our interviewees thought that in the "war on terror," the social, political, and economic factors that could lead to acts of political violence were being ignored in favour of cultural explanations that blamed Islam. They found this to be problematic and short-sighted, and many believed that in order to truly to stop terrorism, a more historical, comprehensive, and reflexive perspective was required. Adopting this perspective would require a sustained examination of the role that Western nations have played in destabilizing Muslim countries and the role that poverty and the consequent social and economic marginalization might play in fuelling terrorism. They also pointed out that the current narrative of the "war on terror" too often overlooks that worldwide, most victims of terrorism are Muslims. In other words, they perceived a double-edged unfairness: Muslims are blamed for acts of political violence even as they are overwhelmingly the victims of this violence. By way of illustration, one interviewee told us:

> Out of what I have seen in this government so far ... every policy is focused to disgrace Muslim, to isolate [the] Muslim community, whether it is Bill C-24 or Bill C-51, or anti-terrorism laws earlier after the tragedy of 9/11. Even though Muslims are suffering through the hands of terrorism, more than any other community. It is not that the Christians are not suffering, or Jews are not suffering, or other minorities are not suffering, but compare the number of deaths. Who are more dead? Muslims. Whether it is in Iraq, or Syria, Afghanistan, or Pakistan or anywhere else, Muslim heritage has been destroyed by these terrorist groups. Muslim culture has been destroyed by these terrorists. But Mr Steven Harper government is targeting the victims instead of going after the terrorists. I mean ISIL, ISIS, and all these terrorist organizations are creat[ed] by the West. And they are blaming Islam, they are blaming Muslim[s], they are targeting ordinary Canadian Muslims out of suspicion. (Calgary 11)

Diminished Citizenship and Undermined Trust in an Era of Counterterrorism

The data we have reported above suggest that Canadian Muslims believe they are being victimized by counterterrorism policies and practices in Canada and by the associated discourse, which they believe stigmatizes Islam and its adherents. Muslim Canadians are witnessing the public portrayal of their religion as irrationally violent and barbaric, and this public portrayal has real-life consequences for them. While nearly all participants acknowledge that one of the state's jobs is to protect its citizens from a whole host of ills, including terrorism, many participants believe that the strategies that have been pursued unfairly target Muslims and their communities in ways that are stigmatizing. Above, we reported their sense that this environment is one in which Muslim Canadians are increasingly facing overt acts of racism and discrimination. This climate has two particularly worrying consequences: one is that Muslim Canadians believe that their Charter-protected right to religious freedom is being undermined, and the other is that the trust on which democratic institutions rely is being eroded. These two consequences are related, as we shall explain in this final section.

The Canadian Charter of Rights and Freedoms protects all citizens' right to practise religion freely in Canada. The right to practise religion freely necessarily requires an environment in which one is not vilified for doing so. Yet as noted above, our interviewees worry that the stigma attached to Islam compromises their ability to practise their religion. In particular, our interviewees noted that many Muslims are afraid to express their Muslim identity and religiosity. One interviewee describes this fear as follows:

> Muslims may fear practising their rights as Muslims. So that fear can cause them to maybe stop wearing the hijab for example or stop praying in school for example, or maybe fasting in the month of Ramadan, or any of their rights, or any of the religious practices that they want to practise but they might fear, they might not do it because of how it might affect their life. (Calgary 6)

This sentiment was expressed in multiple ways. Some worried that Muslims are no longer free to pray in public, to display Muslim identity markers, to wear the hijab or niqab, to go to the mosque and attend Muslim events, or to grow a beard. There is a significant fear that it is dangerous to appear to be Muslim, particularly a practising Muslim, in public spaces. Doing so opens one up to discrimination and abuse, which, respondents believed, is often tolerated by Canadians and Canadian state agencies.

Research demonstrates that citizens' trust relies on the belief that the state will protect their rights when they come under threat (Pettit, 1997). Where this protection cannot be assured, trust is at risk; the trust that citizens have in their state *relies* on their confidence that their rights will be protected when they come under threat. So it is particularly worrying when the state is perceived to be responsible for fostering an environment in which the protection of citizens' rights cannot be taken for granted. Our research demonstrates that this is among the dangers posed by the present state of, and discourse surrounding, Canadian counterterrorism policy.

The majority of our interviewees (55%) indicated that their trust in the Canadian state (and its agencies) had been undermined. One respondent explained that counterterrorism policies have functioned to "create a lack of confidence in the government and it is just not [a]

good feeling." Another respondent, who works at a Muslim organization, was even more explicit:

> We've completely lost trust in our government. Completely. We're living
> in a fear. We're a non-profit organization and there [are] so many of us
> that have charitable statuses. We live in constant fear that our charitable
> statuses will go away if we start speaking of the political oppression that
> we're feeling as Muslims. So these are some things that need to change
> immediately, that there should not be any repercussion[s] on your chari-
> table status; just because you are speaking out against your government's
> repressive measures on you. (Calgary 10)

Although the vast majority of our interviewees (91%) held Canadian
citizenship, they reported that they often did not feel welcome in
Canada. Sixty-eight per cent of our interviewees indicated that their
communities felt alienated and marginalized in Canada in the present
national security environment. One respondent observed:

> It's hurting the community, it's alienating significant portions of the popu-
> lation, including myself. It creates this feeling of being outside and inside
> at the same time. Like as a Canadian citizen, part of the effect of these laws
> is to make you feel a little bit outside, like you're not fully inside the Cana-
> dian community because you're partially outside. And obviously, the laws
> are not affecting me directly, personally, like I haven't been charged with
> a terrorism offence. But when you do see the very racialized aspects of it,
> you feel that there's something about the law that [is] clearly targeting the
> [Muslim] community. (Toronto 12)

Seventy-two per cent of our interviewees thought that Canadian
citizenship had become diminished for Canadian Muslims, precisely
because their rights were not viewed as worth protecting:

> I think most Canadians have a very strong feeling of appreciation for the
> bundle of rights and protections that come with Canadian citizenship. But
> suddenly, after 9/11, Muslims are left asking themselves, is my bundle
> worth as much as other people's bundles? What does my Canadian citi-
> zenship mean? And we've seen it get stripped away. (Faisal Bhabha, law
> professor, Toronto)

Overall, Muslim Canadians do not believe they are being treated as
equal citizens.

Conclusion

Our research raises important concerns and questions about how counterterrorism practices and policies operate in Canada. Our findings highlight some of the ways in which the Muslim community feels wronged by counterterrorism strategies pursued by the Canadian government since 2001. Muslims in Canada believe that terrorism has been "Muslimized," that is, that Canadians are being led – by political actors and by the media – to believe that being Muslim is synonymous with being a terrorist. They believe, additionally, that counterterrorism activities initiated by the government specially target Muslim communities in ways that fail to address the root causes of terrorism. Our interviewees reported that as a result of these experiences, they and their communities felt stigmatized, alienated, and marginalized in Canada. This contributed to their belief that their religious freedom was not protected by the Canadian state, and thus that their citizenship was perceived to be, and treated as, less valuable by the Canadian state. As a result, the trust between Muslim Canadians and the Canadian state has been undermined.

Our interviewees repeatedly called for their communities to be treated "equally before the law," citing the government's "responsibility toward all Canadians." They spoke passionately about the dangers Muslim Canadians faced, noting that "people that are Muslim or look Muslim should not be isolated from equal protection of the law" and "that Muslims should not be presumed guilty until proven innocent." Unfortunately, this is not how the Muslim Canadians we interviewed believed they were being treated in Canada. As Faisal Bhabha, a law professor at York University, says, for Canadian Muslims "national security means the security of others, not of us."

NOTES

1 We are *not* claiming that the expanded CSIS powers are solely, or uniquely, responsible for the attitudes we report here. We are simply observing that, at least as our respondents experience the national security environment in Canada, CSIS is the subject of considerable frustration.
2 A full summary of our results can be found in the final report prepared for Public Safety Canada: http://www.academia.edu/24765979/Securitizing_Muslim_Canadians_Evaluating_the_Impact_of_Counter-terrorism_National_Security_and_Immigration_Policies_Since_9_11.

3 Its role has become even more central, and more controversial, since the passage of Bill C-51, the *Anti-Terrorism Act, 2015*, but these changes took place after our interviews were completed.
4 Lest we be accused of making a larger claim about interactions with security agencies here, note that our research report identifies interactions with other agencies (notably the RCMP) as considerably less negative.
5 Some of our interviews were concluded before the October 2014 attacks in Canada.

REFERENCES

Bahdi, Reem. 2003. "No Exit: Racial Profiling and Canada's War against Terrorism." *Osgoode Hall Law Journal* 41 (2/3): 293–318.
Bhabha, Faisal. 2003. "Tracking 'Terrorists' or Solidifying Stereotypes? Canada's Antiterrorism Act in Light of the Charter's Equality Guarantees." *Windsor Review of Legal and Social Issues* 16: 95–136.
CBC News. 2012. "Woman's hijab pulling called a hate crime." *CBC News*, 9 March. http://www.cbc.ca/news/canada/ottawa/story/2012/03/09/ottawa-hijab-pull-kingston.html.
– 2015. "6 anti-Muslim incidents in Ontario since Paris attacks." *CBC News*, 21 November. http://www.cbc.ca/news/canada/toronto/hate-crimes-ontario-paris-attacks-1.3328660.
Hanniman, Wayne. 2008. "Canadian Muslims, Islamophobia, and National Security." *International Journal of Law, Crime and Justice* 36(4): 271–85. https://doi.org/10.1016/j.ijlcj.2008.08.003.
Harris, Kathleen. 2017 "Hate crimes against Muslims in Canada up 60%, StatsCan reports." *CBC News*, 13 June. http://www.cbc.ca/news/politics/hate-crimes-muslims-statscan-1.4158042.
Helly, Denise. 2004. "Are Muslims Discriminated against in Canada since September 2001?" *Canadian Ethnic Studies* 36(1): 24–48.
Huot, Suzanne, Andrea Bobadilla, Antoine Bailliard, and Debbie Laliberte Rudman. 2016. "Constructing Undesirables: A Critical Discourse Analysis of 'Othering' within the Protecting Canada's Immigration System Act." *International Migration* 54(2): 131–43. https://doi.org/10.1111/imig.12210.
International Civil Liberties Monitoring Group. 2010. *Report of the Information Clearinghouse on Border Controls and Infringements to Travellers' Rights.* http://www.travelwatchlist.ca/updir/travelwatchlist/ICLMG_Watchlists_Report.pdf.
IQRA. 2009. "London Muslims worried over hate crime." *IQRA Magazine*, 16 November. http://iqra.ca/2009/london-muslims-worried-over-hate-crime.

Jamil, Uzma, and Cécile Rousseau. 2012. "Subject Positioning, Fear, and Insecurity in South Asian Muslim Communities in the War on Terror Context." *Canadian Review of Sociology* 49(4): 370. https://doi.org/10.1111/j.1755-618X.2012.01299.x.

Khan, Sheema. 2012. "Politics over Principles: The Case of Omar Khadr." In *Omar Khadr: Oh Canada*, ed. J. Williamson, 51–66. Montreal and Kingston: McGill–Queen's University Press.

Khalema, N., and J. Wannas-Jones. 2003. "Under the Prism of Suspicion: Minority Voices in Canada Post September 11." *Journal of Muslim Minority Affairs* 23(11): 25–39. https://doi.org/10.1080/13602000305928.

Lenard, Patti Tamara. 2008. "Trust Your Compatriots, but Count Your Change: The Roles of Trust, Mistrust and Distrust in Democracy." *Political Studies* 56(2): 312–32. https://doi.org/10.1111/j.1467-9248.2007.00693.x.

– 2012. *Trust, Democracy, and Multicultural Challenges*. University Park: Pennsylvania University State Press.

Macklin, Audrey. 2014. "Citizenship Revocation, the Privilege to Have Rights, and the Production of the Alien." *Queen's Law Journal* 40(1): 1–54. https://doi.org/10.2139/ssrn.2507786. https://doi.org/10.2139/ssrn.2507786.

Nagra, Baljit. 2017. *Securitized Citizens: Canadian Muslims' Experiences of Race Relations and Identity Formation Post 9/11*. Toronto: University of Toronto Press.

Nagra, Baljit, and Paula Maurutto. 2016. "Crossing Borders and Managing Racialized Identities: Canadian Young Muslim's Experiences of Security and Surveillance." *Canadian Journal of Sociology* 41(2): 165–94. http://dx.doi.org/10.29173/cjs23031.

Nagra, Baljit, and Ito Peng. 2013. "Has Multiculturalism Really Failed? A Canadian Muslim Perspective." *Religions* 4(4): 603–20. https://doi.org/10.3390/rel4040603.

Paling, Emma. 2016. "Hate crimes against Muslims double in Canada (and it's not a coincidence)." *Huffington Post*, 14 April. http://www.huffingtonpost.ca/2016/04/14/anti-muslim-hate-crimes-c_n_9692890.html.

Pettit, Philip. 1997. *Republicanism: A Theory of Freedom and Government*. Oxford: Oxford University Press.

Poynting, Scott, and Barbara Perry. 2007. "Climates of Hate: Media and State Inspired Victimisation of Muslims in Canada and Australia since 9/11." *Current Issues in Criminal Justice* 1(2): 151–71. https://doi.org/10.1080/10345329.2007.12036423.

Rahmath, Sabaha, Lori Chambers, and Pamela Wakewich. 2016. "Asserting Citizenship: Muslim Women's Experiences with the Hijab in Canada." *Women's Studies International Forum* 58 (September–October): 34–40. https://doi.org/10.1016/j.wsif.2016.06.001.

Razack, Sherene. 2008. *Casting Out the Eviction of Muslims from Western Law and Politics*. Toronto: University of Toronto Press.

Roach, Kent. 2011. *The 9/11 Effect*. Cambridge: Cambridge University Press.

Rousseau, Cécile, Ghayda Hassan, Nicolas Moreau, and Brett D. Thombs. 2011. "Perceived Discrimination and Its Association with Psychological Distress among Newly Arrived Immigrants before and after September 11, 2001." *American Journal of Public Health* 101(5): 909–915. https://doi.org/10.2105/AJPH.2009.173062.

Sides, John, and Kimberly Gross. 2013. "Stereotypes of Muslims and Support for the War on Terror." *Journal of Politics* 75(3): 583–98. https://doi.org/10.1017/S0022381613000388.

Thobani, Sunera. 2007. *Exalted Subjects: Studies in the Making of Race and Nation in Canada*. Toronto: University of Toronto Press.

Whitaker, Reg, Gregory S. Kealey, and Andrew Parnaby. 2012. *Secret Service: Political Policing in Canada from the Fenians to Fortress America*. Toronto: University of Toronto Press.

Zine, Jasmin. 2012. "Stolen Youth: Lost Boys and Imperial Wars." In *Omar Khadr Oh Canada*, ed. J. Williason, 390–449. Montreal and Kingston: McGill–Queen's University Press.

13 When "Soft Security" Is Smart: On the Importance of Building Strong Community–Police Relationships in the Context of National Security

SARA K. THOMPSON AND SANDRA BUCERIUS

In Canada, as in other nations, counterterrorism strategies are generally separated within a binary typology that classifies them as "hard" (top-down models that rely on coercive legislative, military, or law enforcement strategies) or "soft" (non-coercive, community-oriented measures that emphasize a preventative, proactive, and partnership approach to security issues) (Hopkins Burke 2004; Innes 2005; Spalek 2009). The term *countering violent extremism* (CVE) is used to describe "soft" security strategies – preventative measures that aim to engage with persons and communities perceived to be vulnerable to recruitment into violent extremism before their radicalization begins or in its early stages. In the wake of increasing concerns over "home-grown terrorism," CVE strategies have become an important means through which to "build resilience against terrorism" (Public Safety Canada 2013).

CVE approaches aim to engage and empower local agencies and organizations to build collective resilience to violent radicalization through a variety of programs and initiatives that include community education; outreach and engagement efforts aimed preventing the emergence of conditions, attitudes, and behaviours that may contribute to violent radicalization; the provision of psychosocial supports to those who are assessed to be most at risk of radicalizing to violence; and rehabilitation programs that aim to help radicalized persons disengage from extremist networks, desist from violent action, and reintegrate into society (for an overview of the spectrum of CVE activities, see Harris-Hogan, Barrelle, and Zammit 2016; Mastroe and Szmania 2016). Often, local police services play a significant role in the development, implementation, and subsequent operation of CVE approaches, in part due to their operational capacity and their familiarity and existing relationships with the communities they serve (Waxman 2008, 7). For CVE approaches to be effective, however, they require a foundation of positive and (to the extent possible) trusting relationships with local communities (Spalek 2010), which, the research on inter-agency collaboration suggests, can be difficult when criminal justice agencies are involved as key players (Prothro-Stith 2004; Pardo, Gil-Garcia, and Burke 2006). Factors that can undermine the establishment of positive, trusting relationships include the biased execution and alienating effects of hard security strategies (see Spalek 2009; Lenard and Nagra's chapter in this volume) and the targeted way in which CVE policies and programs have often been implemented – that is, they largely identify immigrant and second-generation immigrant youth as vulnerable, "at risk" populations (Richards 2011; Ragazzi 2016).

One way to work toward advancing the perceived legitimacy and capacity for success of CVE strategies and programs is to take a "bottom up" approach that documents the experiences and perceptions of those directly affected. Doing so can help practitioners and policymakers understand key issues of concern, along with dimensions of CVE policy and practice that garner (or not) community support and legitimation (Briggs, Fieschi, and Lownsbrough 2006). To that end, drawing on in-depth interviews with 419 Somali-Canadian youth and young adults (age 16 to 30) in Toronto and Edmonton, we examine concerns over radicalization to violent extremism in the community, and experiences with and perceptions of local police services, as well as how those experiences may shape community members' willingness to cooperate with police in the context of national security. This information has enabled us to identify a set of recommendations that are grounded in the knowledge of young Somali Canadians in Toronto and Edmonton, whose lived experiences provide a deeper and wider local understanding of the security issues that face their communities and may therefore provide important insights into how those issues may best be addressed.

This chapter proceeds as follows. The first section outlines the security concerns that have shaped political and public discussions about the Somali diaspora in Canada over the past few years. In particular, we provide some background information on al Shabaab, a Somali-based terrorist organization that has actively recruited diaspora members from Canada, some of whom have travelled overseas to fight alongside the group in Somalia. In the second section, we outline our research orientation and methodological approach and provide contextual information about the Somali diasporas in Toronto and Edmonton. Next, we discuss our findings with respect to study participants' perceptions of and experiences with police, and why those perceptions matter in terms of countering violent extremism. Drawing on our interview material, we conclude by offering some general recommendations regarding whether and how the stronger relationships between Somali Canadian communities and the police required to implement effective CVE measures in both cities may be established.

Security Concerns – Background Information

In recent years, Somali Canadians (and members of Somali diasporas elsewhere) have found themselves at the centre of heightened security concerns surrounding the proliferation of al Shabaab's international recruitment networks. The Harakat al Shabaab al Mujahidin – commonly known as al Shabaab – emerged as a radical youth wing of the now defunct Islamic Courts Union (ICU) and has been waging jihad against "enemies of Islam" ever since. In the latter half of 2006, al Shabaab took over vast swaths of territory in central and southern Somalia, but a sustained military campaign in recent years, coupled with growing internal divisions, has weakened the group significantly (Rembold et al. 2013; Mueller 2016; Stanford University 2016). This lack of success in Somalia has prompted the development of a more transnational/global jihadist ideology; in the wake of its designation as a terrorist organization by the United States in 2008 (Canada followed suit in 2010), al Shabaab has targeted or called for attacks on Western interests both within and outside of Somalia (for example, in February 2015, al Shabaab posted an online video encouraging sympathizers to attack a list of shopping malls in Western countries, including the West Edmonton Mall in Edmonton, Alberta). It has also deployed a concerted recruitment strategy that targets young Muslims in Somali diasporas around the globe. In 2012, al Shabaab and al Qaeda formalized their long-standing organizational ties, announcing their merger in an online video; and in October 2015, Abdul Qadir Mumin, a high-ranking member of al Shabaab, became one of a small but increasing number of defectors to declare his pro-ISIS allegiance. Mumin's move is one of the more prominent among a growing number of defections, which disproportionately appear to involve younger members of al Shabaab, who, many argue, may find ISIS more relevant and appealing (Kriel and Duggan 2015).

Security experts commonly cite a number of mutually beneficial reasons for these formalized mergers, including their capacity to increase operational and recruitment reach (Kriel and Loposo 2015). Taken together, then, the emergence and growth of al Shabaab, along with the group's recent mergers and affiliations with other jihadist franchises, and Somalia's status as a "diasporised nation" (Menkhaus 2009, 10), have raised concerns about how young people of Somali origin may be vulnerable to terrorist ideology and recruitment. In 2011, it was estimated that "twenty Canadians and perhaps dozens more" had been radicalized and left the country, and concerns over the success of al Shabaab's reach into Canada were such that the group was deemed to be the "number one threat to Canada's national security" (CBC News 2011). Security concerns have intensified in the wake al Shabaab's growing affiliation with jihadi groups like ISIS, which appear to hold particular appeal among younger recruits from many Western nations. Indeed, since 2012, a number of young Somali Canadian men appear to have left cities like Calgary, Edmonton, and Toronto to take up arms in Syria (and not Somalia) alongside ISIS (Sawa, Seglins, and McDonald 2014; Anzalone 2015; Tucker 2015; see also Dawson and Amarasingham, in this volume).

As we will discuss below, young Somali Canadians perceive themselves to be the subject of intense police scrutiny on a day-to-day basis, which they argue is tied to the neighbourhoods in which they live (for our Toronto sample), high levels of crime and violence in their community, and stereotypical understandings on the part of police that associate being Black and Somali with "being up to no good." Members of the Somali diaspora in Canada also report that in response to concerns over the purported threat that Somali Canadians pose to national security, they have come under increased scrutiny by border control and national security agencies. For example, many of our study participants described racial profiling at land and air border crossings; being visited by the Canadian Security Intelligence Service (CSIS) and the RCMP Integrated National Security Enforcement Teams (INSETs) for the purposes of information gathering; and being the explicit subjects of programs and messaging campaigns aimed at countering violent extremism (CVE). Our data show that young Somali Canadians report generally antagonistic relationships with the police, as well as low levels of support for aggressive "hard security" approaches to dealing with security-related issues. But the data also show that young Somali Canadians in Toronto and Edmonton are deeply concerned about radicalization to violence among young people in their communities, and they articulate a desire for more and better community-based policing initiatives and those that are grounded in a softer and more holistic approach (Thompson and Bucerius 2014; Jossee, Bucerius, and Thompson 2015).

Methodology and Sample

We identified community-based participatory methodologies as the most appropriate research orientation for this project, based on a curriculum developed by researchers at the University of Washington: "The intent in CBPR is to transform research from a relationship where researchers *act upon* a community to answer a research question to one where researchers *work side by side* with community members to define the questions and methods, implement the research, disseminate the findings and apply them" (CBPR Curriculum 2006, http://depts.washington.edu/ccph/cbpr/u1/u11.php).

Participatory research methods are particularly useful in interactions with vulnerable populations, because such methods give them the opportunity to assist in the development of research goals and research questions, as well as appropriate and culturally sensitive instruments, methodologies, and dissemination strategies. They also provide crucial assistance in data analysis and interpretation, as well as in the formulation of recommendations that stem from the research findings. Our research team was diverse and comprised of research assistants of both Somali Canadian and non–Somali Canadian background. (Over time, we discovered that being an outsider to the community often opened up interesting and somewhat different insights into the community – for more on these and related issues regarding insider/outsider status, see Bucerius 2013.) We designed our interview instrument in continuous consultation and collaboration with Somali Canadian research assistants, to ensure that interview questions were both culturally appropriate and meaningful.

We approached our research from a critical realist perspective (Maxwell 2013), aiming to elicit and understand how our research participants construct their individual and shared meanings around our phenomena of interest (Lauckner, Patterson, and Krupa 2012, 6). This essentially means that we treated our participants' perceptions, intentions, experiences, and feelings as real – although unobserved – phenomena (Maxwell 2013). We view our study participants' understanding of their reality (such as the meaning of their experiences) as being shaped by their own perspectives and standpoints; thus, we assume that participants actively construct the reality in which they participate (Charmaz 2001).

We digitally recorded all interviews. Once the interviews were transcribed, we established a coding scheme that captured key themes and categories that emerged from the data. In coding the first twelve interviews according to our coding scheme, we used three different coders; this helped us establish inter-coder reliability and make final adjustments to our coding scheme. From there, we used NVIVO 10 (a qualitative data analysis software tool) to code and organize the remaining interview material.

Sampling Strategy and Characteristics

In recruiting study participants in both cities, we used "respondent driven sampling" (RDS) – a sampling method that allows for the recruitment of larger samples within a relatively short time frame. This method is often used for researching hidden or hard-to-reach populations – that is, groups that are small relative to the general population and for which no exhaustive list of population members is available.

In essence, RDS combines "snowball sampling" (i.e., getting individuals to refer people they know, and these individuals in turn refer people they know, and so on) with a mathematical model that weights the sample to compensate for the fact that the sample was collected in a non-random way. As such, it builds on intra-group connections – new participants are more likely to participate in the study because they are introduced to and become familiar with the research through someone they trust (Heckathorn 1997). RDS uses two types of structured incentives: a first one for completing the interview (in our case, $30), and a second one for recruiting new participants into the study to be interviewed ($10 per recruited participant, with a maximum of two recruits per person).

In total, we conducted interviews with 118 Somali Canadian youth and young adults (16 to 30) in Toronto and 301 in Edmonton. Achieving gender parity in our sample in Toronto proved to be very difficult, but in the end, we managed to interview fifty females and sixty-eight males (42% and 58% of the total sample, respectively). In Edmonton, we achieved gender parity. The interview questionnaire contained more than seventy questions, and the average interview was just over one hour in length.

After completing the data collection and analysis, we held a focus group (and several smaller meetings) with our community-based research assistants and other community partners (excluding law enforcement) in both cities, for assistance in interpreting our findings, identifying best practices, and developing policy recommendations. During these meetings, we also devised a dissemination strategy that would bring those findings back to the community – largely in the form of research reports, as well as public talks and meetings.

The Somali Diasporas in Toronto and Edmonton: Contextual Information

The Somali diaspora in Toronto is the biggest of its kind in Canada. The 2011 National Household Survey estimates that there are 44,996 Somalis currently living in Canada, but the Canadian Somali Congress believes the figure is actually closer to 200,000, with the majority living in the Toronto area (D'Aliesio 2011; Statistics Canada

2011). Though some Somalis immigrated to Canada prior to the 1990s, the great majority came as refugees in the early 1990s, following civil unrest and political instability in Somalia. Many settled in Rexdale, a low-income neighbourhood in Toronto's northwest corner. Edmonton houses the third-largest diaspora group in Canada (after Ottawa). While a great number of Somali Canadians live in northeast Edmonton, many members of the community live in neighbourhoods spread out across the city.

The Somali communities in Toronto and Edmonton have received considerable negative media attention in recent years, due to what are thought to be disproportionately high levels of gun-, gang-, and drug-related homicides involving young Somali men (Berns McGown 2013; Millett 2014; Fellin 2015). More recently, this coverage has portrayed members of Canada's Somali diaspora as a threat to national security. More specifically, study participants point to media coverage that explicitly links the Somali community with crime as well as national security concerns, as evidenced by media headlines and commentaries – such as "Violence plagues the Somali diaspora" (D'Aliesio 2014) – that describe these concerns as a consequence of "failings of the Somali community" (Warmington 2013). Many news accounts explicitly use Somali ethnicity to describe young men charged with violent crime and/or terrorism-related offences (e.g., MacLeod 2009; Pagliaro 2013). Many study participants perceive that such media portrayals have criminalized their community in the public imagination, so that they are widely viewed as "the usual suspects" when it comes to violent offending in general and concerns over national security in particular.

In Edmonton, in addition to the negative media attention discussed above, two events shaped public opinion about the Somali Canadian community during our study period. In 2014, a community leader, Mahamad Accord, publicly released a letter he had written to then–prime minister Stephen Harper in which he (Accord) discussed concerns about increasing radicalization in the Edmonton Somali community. The following year, al Shabaab posted an online video encouraging sympathizers to attack a list of shopping centres around the world, including the West Edmonton Mall. This highly publicized call for action once again drew negative attention to Edmonton's Somali Canadian community; it also reinforced a perceived link between the community and al Shabaab. This, even though the Edmonton Police Service, the provincial government, and the RCMP all immediately released statements that they perceived the threat to be low and were therefore not imminently concerned about any threat to national security or community safety.

Research Findings: Experiences of Discrimination

As a consequence of media portrayals that perpetuate more general stereotypes associated with their communities, young Somali Canadians
in Toronto and Edmonton perceive themselves to be a highly stigmatized group. We asked our participants a range of questions about
experiences of discrimination in the cities where they live as well as in
Canadian society more generally. In particular, we tried to situate discrimination within the personal biographies of our participants, asking
them where discrimination took place and who the major players in
these experiences were. We also asked about the context for discrimination, probing for school experiences, experiences in the labour market,
experiences with police, and experiences in "general society." While the
elimination of discrimination is a social good in its own right, it also
has important implications for public safety. This is because criminological and other research has long demonstrated that experiences of
discrimination, and the effects discrimination can have on one's sense
of belonging and "perceptions of injustice" (Matsueda and Drakulich
2009) in a given society, may prompt *some* members of affected communities to find an alternative place of belonging through "illegitimate
avenues," including radical groups (Borum 2004; Wortley and Tanner
2008; Lyons-Padilla et al. 2015).

Interview respondents reported feeling discriminated against for
a number of often interrelated reasons, including the neighbourhood in which they lived (for our Toronto sample – neighbourhood
context played no role for our Edmonton sample[1]) and stereotypical
popular perceptions that Somali people are violent or involved in
crime and/or terrorism, as well as on the basis of race and religion.
Common sites and situations where discrimination was experienced
included the educational system, the labour market, and at the hands
of police and border officials. Experiences of discrimination that were
shared by study participants often differed on the basis of gender:
male participants typically described experiences of discrimination by the police, while females were more likely to describe being
discriminated against by school guidance counsellors or strangers.
Discrimination experienced by female participants also and often
centred on wearing the hijab; they therefore had a unique vantage
point in terms of discerning how religious visibility contributed to
their discrimination. Many women remarked on how wearing the
hijab (which often began in their early teen years) was a watershed
moment in their lives in terms of their interactions with the wider
society. Participants reflected on incidents when they were wearing

a hijab and people made comments about their need to be "liberated" now that they were in Canada. One participant described an experience in elementary school when her hijab was removed by the teacher, who told her she was not allowed to wear it because it meant she was "just trying to be different from everybody else." Other individuals described being stared at on the streets, and being criticized for wearing a hijab.

Interview participants in both cities commonly reported experiencing discrimination for a variety of reasons, in a variety of contexts, and with a variety of different "others." However, Somali Canadians in Edmonton report less overall discrimination than our sample in Toronto – and in Edmonton, schools and employment situations are mentioned more frequently than police when it comes to discrimination experiences (in Toronto, the police were cited by the overwhelming majority of male study participants as the primary source of discrimination).[2] One of our Edmonton participants, who had previously lived in Toronto, offered an explanation as to why this may be the case: "Edmonton also has the Aboriginal population. They seem to be at the bottom of the ladder here. In Toronto, Somalis are at the bottom of the ladder." This explanation is consistent with research that suggests that where a particular group is placed on socially constructed racial/ethnic hierarchies matters for experiences of prejudice and discrimination (Snellman and Ekehammer 2005; Snellman 2007) and that those groups who are ascribed positions at lower rungs of the social ladder may suffer the brunt of prejudicial attitudes and behaviours. This is not to say that groups ascribed other, higher positions on the social hierarchy do not experience prejudice and discrimination, but rather that their experiences may sometimes be less acute.

We also asked study participants about key issues facing their communities. Violence, including the high number of homicides, was identified as one of the biggest issues that Somali Canadians in both Toronto and Edmonton are currently facing (for an in-depth discussion of this issue, and what study participants in both cities thought about causes and possible solutions, see Thompson and Bucerius 2014; Bucerius and Thompson 2016). Radicalization to violent extremism was also identified as a key issue of concern among a majority of study participants in both Toronto and Edmonton, particularly in the wake of a small number of well-known cases in which young Somali Canadians appear to have left Canada to take up arms with al Shabaab and, more recently, ISIS.[3] Furthermore, as will be discussed in the following section, perceptions of the police among our sample are generally negative, which, according to the literature, may reduce the likelihood that people will contact and cooperate with the police if and when they become concerned about behaviour changes and the possible radicalization of people in their midst (Tyler, Schulhofer, and Huq 2010; Lashley et al. 2016; Madon, Murphy, and Cherney 2016).

Experiences with and Perceptions of Police in Toronto and Edmonton

The majority of young Somali Canadians we interviewed in both cities reported having experienced negative and discriminatory treatment from police officers and knowing many other community members who had experienced negative treatment as well. As was the case with experiences of discrimination more generally, it appears that negative experiences with police were particularly acute in Toronto. Indeed, our young Somali Canadian participants in Toronto typically characterized their interactions with police as negative. Male interview participants were particularly likely to identify police officers as a source of discrimination, especially in the context of stop-and-search activity. The gendered nature of police attention was something that our female participants recognized as well: "I feel like it is worse for the guys more so than the girls. 'cause no one really, no cop like when I'm driving, no cop would ever pull me over but like my brother gets pulled over ... like ... maybe like every day."

Female respondents also reported gender-specific experiences of discrimination with law enforcement, largely related to the wearing of religious attire and in the context of land and air border crossings. The gendered nature of discrimination by law enforcement notwithstanding, male and female participants reported similar effects, and they commonly described feeling angry and embarrassed. They feel that such activity places them in the spotlight and draws even more negative attention to their community. The majority of study participants also reported feeling mistreated and disrespected in these encounters: "It's little things like that that, you know, like it gets you so agitated, and this happens every day ... Police officers grab, grab you harass you, 'Hey I know you're doing this, hey I know you're doing that,' it's just the same thing, day after day" (male, 24 years).

When we asked why they thought members of their community are subject to such intense police scrutiny, male respondents most frequently connected stop-and-search activity to the fact that they are black and Somali. Female participants, by contrast, thought that their encounters with law enforcement are most often connected with the fact that they are Muslim. In the vast majority of cases, our study participants reported that no charges were ultimately laid against them, despite police officers' assumption that they were "up to no good." This is consistent with the larger literature on racial profiling, which demonstrates that a disproportionate focus on members of racialized groups (compared to whites) is more likely to lead to the erosion of police–community relations than it is to the detection of criminality (Cole and Lambert 2001; Harris 2002).

Perceptions of the police in both cities were also shaped by the perceived high number of unsolved homicides involving Somali Canadian victims. As one study participant in Toronto stated: "There's a lot [of murders] and like none[4] of it's been solved, it's, and it's like do these people not matter, it's like why isn't anything being done" (female, 19 years). Another echoed these concerns: "Are Somali murder victims not worthy victims in the minds of the police? Is that the problem here?" Many respondents in both cities discussed this perceived lack of investigation and explicitly or implicitly expressed the need for further police investigation of the killings. While many respondents in Edmonton (not Toronto) believed the police are doing the best they can, the majority of them believed the police are not doing a *good enough job*, particularly of investigating the murders of young Somali males. These respondents often suggested that if the victims were white the police would be putting in more effort. Overall, our female respondents tended to be more critical of the police than were male respondents in this regard.

Our data reveal that many Somali Canadian adolescents and young adults are also wary of police activity and surveillance of their community members and within their neighbourhoods (particularly in Toronto), which they perceive to be arbitrary, overly invasive, and discriminatory. For them, then, there is a fundamental and very problematic contradiction in their experiences of being simultaneously "over-policed and under-protected" (Kushnick 1999). Along with negative experiences more generally, this perceived "hypocrisy" plays an important role in shaping perceptions of police legitimacy among study participants in both cities:

> Fuck the police, man. They're only too happy to come down here to hassle us, to arrest us, but they don't give a shit about us otherwise. Last summer there were shots fired right outside our window, and my mom called 911 – the police didn't even bother to show up. Betcha that wouldn't happen in rich, white neighbourhood, now would it? (Male 19 years, Toronto)

Why Perceptions of the Police Matter in the Context of CVE

There is an extensive literature that examines perceptions of police legitimacy and why those perceptions matter. Simply put, the criminological literature demonstrates that those who believe that the police execute their duties in an effective, impartial, and respectful manner are more likely to trust in and cooperate with them when necessary (Jackson et al. 2011; Tyler 2011). Cooperation involves a wide range of behaviours, from complying with an officer's request to reporting crimes, cooperating in investigations, sharing information, and/or actively contributing to crime prevention (McClusky, Mastrofsky, and Parks 1999; Tyler 2011). The converse is also true: if, because of negative experiences with the police, people do not perceive that they execute their duties in an effective, impartial, and respectful manner, they are less likely to cooperate. So, too, are people who have vicarious negative experiences – that is, those who learn about negative experiences with police from trusted friends or family members (Schuck and Rosenbaum 2005; Weitzer and Tuch 2005).

Recent research has also found that perceptions matter when it comes to the likelihood of cooperation with police in the context of terrorism (Tyler, Schulhofer, and Huq 2010; Lashley et al. 2016; Madon, Murphy, and Cherney 2016). More specifically, perceptions of police legitimacy have been found to increase "general receptivity toward helping the police in anti-terror work, and the specific willingness to alert police to terror related risks in a community" (Tyler, Schulhofer, and Huq 2010, 1). Community cooperation is crucial to the detection and mitigation of such risks, given that people are often radicalized to violence in private settings – for example, through some combination of face-to-face and online interaction with like-minded individuals, both of which tend to take place in settings that reduce the detection capacity of police and intelligence services (such as homes, cars, and other private places) (Precht 2007; Mullins 2010). Indeed, community members may serve as "trip wires" that first identify radicalizing/radicalized young people and bring them to the attention of community leaders and/or national security officials. Community-based trip wires are often activated via "leakage" – the tendency among radicalized individuals to broadcast their views and intentions to commit violent acts in advance, typically to friends, family, acquaintances, and/or community members (Alexander and Kraft 2007; Silver et al. 2017). As such, the cultivation of trust and relationships between communities and government agencies that will facilitate the sharing of this information is crucial to the mitigation of threats. And there is reason to be optimistic that such partnerships can be established. This is because overall, in both cities (and despite differing levels of perceived police legitimacy), study participants want to see an emphasis on community policing and community outreach, instead of traditional "hard" approaches to issues related to crime, violence, and violent extremism in the Somali Canadian community. As one participant in Toronto argued:

> In my opinion, the police are trying to work with us, trying to build a relationship, okay, which is a lot more than they've ever done before. So I appreciate that, you know? ...
>
> We need the police to work with us, not talk at us, or down to us. We need them to recognize that we [Somali Canadians] want to be part of the solution, not part of the problem. We're worried about the gang-bangers and the drug-dealers and the jihadists, too, yo. That's not what our community is about – never has been, never will be. But if we want to stop the violence, we've got to work together, man. And that means Somalis giving the cops a chance, and the cops giving us a chance. We got to start over.

In Edmonton, study participants echo the desire for greater community engagement. It is important to remember that our respondents in both cities are marginalized youth and young adults – people who, as research shows, typically report negative experiences with and perceptions of the police (Rankin 2009; Wortley and Owusu-Bempa 2009). And this is indeed the case with our samples: in both cities – but particularly in Toronto – study participants articulated the widespread belief that the police are biased and overly aggressive in their dealings with young Somali Canadians. Nevertheless, there appears to be a considerable (and perhaps surprising) desire for more and better community outreach and engagement by the police – but outreach that is sensitive to the community's needs and concerns and that is characterized by a partnership rather than a "top down" approach. The reasons behind this sentiment were perhaps best expressed by a study participant in Edmonton: "We don't want to be part of the problem, but part of the solution. Gotta put an end to the violence, we need to assume some responsibility here for ourselves, we need to advocate for our community and start working with the police instead of against them. It's time to move forward."

Moving Forward

We asked study participants in Toronto and Edmonton how their respective police services might go about improving the quality of outreach and engagement efforts in Somali Canadian communities. They had a lot to say, and the following section provides an overview of select recommendations made by study participants in both cities (for an in-depth discussion of "Items for Change" and "Recommendations," see Thompson and Bucerius 2014; Bucerius and Thompson 2016).

One way to improve community–police relationships would be to hire more Somali police officers (the Toronto and Edmonton Police Services currently have only a small number of Somali Canadian officers), though study participants who are interested in a policing career identified economic and systemic barriers to their success in the recruitment process.[5] In the meantime, it was recommended that both police services hire Somali civilian employees to work with officers in the design, implementation, and day-to-day operations of community outreach initiatives.

A related suggestion highlighted the importance of identifying and engaging women (particularly mothers) and youth/young adults who can speak on behalf of their respective segments of the community – people whose voices are often not heard by those who enforce the law and craft policy. Indeed, research shows that the voices of those whose identities lie at the margins, those who occupy disempowered positions, are particularly likely to be overlooked by practitioners and policy-makers (Paterson and Panessa 2008; Spalek et al. 2012; Shahrokh and Wheeler 2014). Yet it is precisely these people who are among those with the greatest potential to serve as "positive change agents" within their communities. Indeed, criminological research has long demonstrated that women – particularly girls, wives, and mothers – carry significant authority in their relationships with boys and men and can play important roles in influencing their offending trajectories and their choice to desist from criminal offending (Patillo 1998; Laub and Sampson 2001). As one participant in Edmonton laid out: "There are so many super smart young women out here. They built the basketball league for example. All girls. They are running the homework club. All girls. They have all the ideas to make positive changes, the community just has to start listening to them." Furthermore, given the strength of peer group influence, youth and young adults – male and female – are in a key position to shape the attitudes and behaviour of their peers – or, at the very least, be aware of and inclined to draw behavioural changes indicative of radicalization to the attention of the appropriate authorities (Williams, Horgan, and Evans 2015). Given that radicalization to violent extremism disproportionately involves young people, youth and young adults should be centrally involved in the development of CVE strategies, initiatives, and messages/narratives that will resonate with their peers.

However, the young people we spoke with articulated the need for "safe spaces" in which honest dialogue may take place without fear of reproach. A common issue identified by study participants in Toronto and Edmonton was that many self-proclaimed Somali Canadian community leaders – who make themselves available to government and police agencies as representatives of their communities – are older men, many of whom are viewed as out of touch with the day-to-day realities experienced by young people and women in the community. As one participant stated: "We want a piece of the pie. We're currently not at the table, we're just on the menu." Many indicate their hope that, moving forward, asset mapping of the community will be more representative and include people whose voices have not been heard.

One way that young people could be more directly engaged with the police, according to study participants, would be through the establishment of a youth Chief's Advisory Council, similar to the councils that exist for older community leaders. During such council meetings, community leaders and the police exchange their thoughts on problems the community is currently facing and that they are mutually trying to problem-solve. This often includes a debate over topics that relate to police work in the Somali community, such as negative experiences that community members are having with the police and how they might be mitigated in the future. Many of our younger Somali Canadian participants expressed concern that the issues that are plaguing young people were not being appropriately recognized by older community leaders. While a certain degree of disconnect between younger and older generations likely exists in all communities, this disconnect appears to be particularly salient in the Somali Canadian community, as one of our participants described: "It's a respect thing. It's difficult to speak up in front of our elders, especially when they are all male and we are young women. It's a taboo. So, it's a gender thing, and a clan thing, and a hierarchy thing. I would say it's a culture thing, actually." Having the opportunity to discuss the issues of young people directly with police members and not having to communicate through their elders, many reported, would offer the means to address this problem.

Another recommendation that our participants highlighted was the need for police to communicate with community leaders before potential negative news about the community becomes public knowledge through media coverage. This would allow community leaders to prepare their community for the news that will ultimately spread around; it would also prepare the community for any negative backlash as a consequence of media coverage. As an example of good police communication with the community, our participants mentioned the announcement of a video that circulated on the internet in which al Shabaab supposedly called for an attack on West Edmonton Mall. Before any information about this video became public, the Edmonton Police Service contacted the Muslim community to give them enough lead time to prepare public statements that denounced al Shabaab and its call for attacks.

Study participants in both cities also had a number of ideas about what the police should *not* be doing in the context of CVE. In particular, many lamented the existence of targeted approaches to crime prevention in general and CVE in particular that focus explicitly on Somali Canadian communities. Such programs and initiatives, they argue, have the very real potential to more deeply entrench existing stereotypes, further marginalize and alienate Somali Canadians, and reduce the likelihood that positive and trusting police–community relationships can be established.

Conclusion

This chapter has focused on the importance of incorporating "soft security" approaches into CVE policy and practice. More specifically, our data highlight the demand in Toronto and Edmonton for community-based initiatives based on engagement and partnership work between police officers and members of Somali Canadian communities. Yet community support for such initiatives hinges greatly on the quality and quantity of "hard security" approaches that are also being deployed in the name of national security. To date, there appears to be an overemphasis and overreliance on "hard security" measures; less time, effort, and funding has been earmarked for "softer" measures. The deployment of hard and soft security strategies is not, nor should it be understood as, an either/or decision – both are necessary and important. However, in order for counterterrorism strategies to be effective and sustainable, hard security approaches must be supplemented and balanced with preventative approaches that address the so-called root causes of terrorism. As Spalek (2009, 6) points out:

> "[H]ard" policing strategies have had significant consequences upon individuals' lives, leading to ostracisation from their wider communities, family breakdown and job losses. Moreover, these "hard" tactics can significantly undermine any attempts that police make to engage with Muslim communities as experiencing anti-terror laws in this way may reduce individuals' motivations to engage with state authorities.

Much in contrast to popular stereotypes, our data show that young Somali Canadians do not reject "hard security measures" for dealing with violent radicalization – if anything, they are *more* concerned about identifying and attending to radicalized individuals than the average non–Somali Canadian person. As a young man from the Somali community in Edmonton pointed out: "The last thing we want is more negative attention. We have already had enough of that. If there are Somali Canadians who support ISIS or any other terrorist group, I'd say: deal with them. They have nothing to do with us."

To which a female participant added: "The community cannot afford to stay silent on this. We cannot afford it."

These sentiments exemplify study participants' concerns when radicalized individuals are of Somali Canadian background, because such people draw negative attention to the community and more deeply entrench popular stereotypes about it. Thus, the participants articulate widespread support for hard security measures in dealing with such individuals. These considerations notwithstanding, when it comes to the prevention of radicalization to violence, young Somali Canadians in both Toronto and Edmonton articulate a clear preference for collaborative, softer measures that involve cultivating new and better relationships with local police services. Many of the young people we interviewed reported that such initiatives have the potential over time to create stronger partnerships between the community and the police, as well as to provide opportunities for mutual understanding. These relationships, which need to be built and fostered in "good times," before potential problems arise, will ultimately determine the extent to which community–police partnerships will be effective in navigating the "bad times."

NOTES

1 This is not surprising, given the geographic distribution of Somali Canadian households in both cities: in Toronto, a disproportionate number of Somali Canadians are concentrated within a small number of highrise buildings in the Rexdale area. In Edmonton, though there are small concentrations of Somali Canadian households – such as in the Dickensfield or 118th Avenue areas – they tend to be much more widely dispersed throughout the city's neighbourhoods. Most of the reported "neighbourhood discrimination," it must be noted, was a result of the more frequent and unwelcome police encounters that our participants had in the neighbourhoods where they resided, as opposed to discrimination *against* residents of particular neighbourhoods by those from other neighbourhoods. Indeed, many of our participants felt that young Somali Canadian men in particular received inordinate/discriminatory police attention.

2 While our data cannot speak to why study participants reported fewer
   discrimination experiences in all sectors of society in Edmonton (compared
   to Toronto), our focus group discussions (conducted after the survey and
   interview data were collected) may offer some insight in this regard. This
   study was conducted before the economic downturn in Alberta, which
   began in 2015, and it is conceivable that the overall employment situation,
   which was better than in Ontario when we conducted the Toronto study,
   influenced participants' perceptions of their position and opportunities
   for success in Canadian society. Indeed, the majority of study participants
   described that they are confident they would secure employment upon
   graduation, with the tar sands being seen as a "last resource that is always
   there." The school system itself may play a role as well. In cities where
   private school education is available, parents have the option of remov-
   ing their child from the public system if they are not satisfied with the
   perceived quality of education therein (provided, of course, they have the
   means to pay private school tuition costs). The city of Edmonton does not
   have many private schools – parents generally choose between the public
   and Catholic school systems – and this appears to have had positive implications for these two systems. That is, in the absence of options for private
   education in Edmonton, many parents have mobilized to advocate on
   behalf of their children and, in so doing, have improved the overall quality
   of education in their local schools. At the same time, it is easier to attend
   schools "out of boundary" in Edmonton; in fact, many of our participants
   reported choosing to not attend the neighbourhood school because their
   parents perceived a different school (outside of the neighbourhood) to be
   of higher quality. Interestingly, some of the most diverse schools in the city
   are the top performing (e.g., Mountpleasant Elementary School, Westbrook
   Elementary School), despite the fact that the average income of the parents at these schools is lower than for many other schools in Edmonton.
   On average, our participants were less likely to attend schools that had a
   majority of Somali Canadian students, in contrast to the Toronto study, and
   they were less likely to report that their school was a "bad school." Lastly,
   the Edmonton Police Service appears to be a very community-oriented
   service that focuses on building strong relationships with community members, and this may affect the quality of policing delivered in Edmonton and
   shape perceptions of discrimination in that city.
3 For example, in 2009, twenty-two-year-old University of Toronto student
   Mohamed Elmi Ibrahim, a second-generation Somali Canadian, left Canada
   to fight alongside Al Shabaab in Somalia. The following year, a eulogy
   posted on the extremist group's website reported that Ibrahim had died
   in combat. See also the Dawson and Amarasingham chapter in this volume for a discussion of four Somali Canadians from Edmonton – Omar

Abdirahman, brothers Hamza and Hersi Kariye, and their cousin Mahad Hersi – who died fighting with ISIS in Syria.

4 While the statement that "none of the homicides have been solved" is exaggerated (some homicides in the Somali Canadian community in both cities have been solved), the participant is stating the widespread perception of many members of Somali Canadian communities. It should be noted that perceptions are often more important than reality when it comes to how social actors evaluate their surroundings and position in society (Maxwell 2013).

5 For example, potential police recruits must undergo a series of standardized screening tests, which are conducted by an independent organization called Applicant Testing Services (ATS). The cost to each potential recruit is $330, with additional fees for rescheduling and retesting. For many Somali Canadian young adults, these fees are prohibitive. Study participants who were interested in policing as a career indicated that waiving of these fees, or the implementation of some sort of bursary system to assist in the payment of these fees, would increase the likelihood that lower-income Somalis would apply. Another barrier to employment with police organizations involves background checks for recruits who were not born in Canada. Many Somali Canadians came to Canada as refugees, and background information that dates back to their early years in Somalia is often not available, which results in a potential recruit's disqualification from the process. It was therefore recommended that police organizations train recruitment officers who specialize in processing applications of potential recruits who require background checks that involve additional and sometimes unique considerations.

REFERENCES

Alexander, Y., and M.B. Kraft. 2007. *Evolution of US Counterterrorism Policy.* Westport: Praeger.

Anzalone, Christopher. 2015. "Canadian Foreign Fighters in Syria and Iraq." https://www.ctc.usma.edu/posts/canadian-foreign-fighters-in-iraq-and-syria.

Berns-McGown, Rima. 2013. "'I am Canadian': Challenging Stereotypes about Young Somali-Canadians." IRPP Study no. 38. Montreal: Institute for Research on Public Policy.

Borum, Randy. 2004. "The Psychology of Terrorism." *Mental Health Law and Policy Faculty Publications* 571.

Briggs, R., C. Fieschi, and H. Lownsbrough. 2006. *Bringing It Home: Community-Based Approaches to Counter-Terrorism.* London: Demos.

Bucerius, Sandra. 2013. "Becoming a Trusted Outsider – Gender, Ethnicity, and Inequality in Ethnographic Research." *Journal of Contemporary Ethnography* 42(6): 690–721. https://doi.org/10.1177/0891241613497747.

Bucerius, Sandra, and Sara K. Thompson. 2016. "Final Report: The Somali Experience in Alberta: Hypermarginalization and 'Places of Belonging.'" Prepared for Public Safety Canada, Strategic Policy Division, Ottawa.

CBC News. 2011. "Somali terrorists now number one security threat to Canada." 26 January. https://www.youtube.com/watch?v=8oHOYjFw48E.

CPPR Curriculum. 2006. http://depts.washington.edu/ccph/cbpr/u1/u11.php.

Charmaz, K. 2001. "Qualitative Interviewing and Grounded Theory Analysis." In *Handbook of Interview Research*, ed. Jaber F. Gubrium and James A. Holstein. Thousand Oaks: Sage [ebook].

Cole, D., and J. Lambert. 2001. "The fallacy of racial profiling." *New York Times*, 13 May.

D'Aliesio, Renata. 2011. "Young Somali-Canadians drawn to activism." *Globe and Mail*, 23 September. http://www.theglobeandmail.com/news/toronto/young-canadian-somalis-drawn-to-activism/article4256817.

– 2014. "Project Traveller and the Dixon City Bloods." *Globe and Mail*, 17 May. http://www.theglobeandmail.com/news/toronto/project-traveller-and-the-dixon-city-bloods/article18737689/?page=all.

Fellin, Melissa. 2015. "The Impact of Media Representations on Somali Youth's Experiences in Educational Spaces." *Landscapes and Violence* 3(3): art. 5.

GCTF (Global Counterterrorism Forum). 2009. "Good practices on community engagement and community-oriented policing as tools to counter violent extremism." https://www.thegctf.org/documents/10162/159885/13Aug09_EN_Good+Practices+on+Community+Engagement+and+Community-Oriented+Policing.pdf.

Harris, D.A. 2002. *Profiles in Injustice: Why Racial Profiling Cannot Work.* New York: New Press.

Harris-Hogan, Shandon, Kate Barrelle, and Andrew Zammit. 2016. "What Is Countering Violent Extremism? Exploring CVE Policy and Practice in Australia." *Behavioural Sciences of Terrorism and Political Aggression* 8(1): 6–24. https://doi.org/10.1080/19434472.2015.1104710.

Heckathorn, D. 1997. "Respondent Driven Sampling: A New Approach to the Study of Hidden Populations." *Social Problems* 44(2): 174–99. https://doi.org/10.2307/3096941.

Hopkins Burke, Roger. 2004. *Hard Cop, Soft Cop: Dilemmas and Debates in Contemporary Policing.* Devon: Willan.

Innes, Martin. 2005. "Why 'Soft' Policing Is Hard: On the Curious Development of Reassurance Policing, How It Became Neighbourhood Policing, and What this Signifies about the Politics of Police Reform." *Journal of Community and Applied Social Psychology* 15(3): 156–69. https://doi.org/10.1002/casp.818.

Jackson, J., et al. 2011. "Developing European Indicators of Trust in Justice." *European Journal of Criminology* 8(4): 267–85. https://doi.org/10.1177/1477370811411458.

Jossee, Paul, Sandra Bucerius, and Sara Thompson. 2015. "Narratives and Counternarratives: Somali-Canadians on Recruitment as 'Foreign Fighters' to al-Shabaab." *British Journal of Criminology*. 6 March. https://doi.org/10.1093/bjc/azu103.

Kriel, Robyn, and Briana Duggan. 2015. "Al-Shabaab Faction Pleads Allegiance to ISIS." http://www.cnn.com/2015/10/22/africa/al-shabaab-faction-isis/index.html.

Kriel, Robyn, and Lilian Loposo. 2015. "In Video, Somali ISIS Members Court Al Shabaab." http://www.cnn.com/2015/05/22/world/somalia-isis-al-shabaab-video/index.html.

Kushnick. L. 1999. "Stephen Lawrence, Institutional and Police Practices." *Sociological Research Online* 4(1). http://socresonline.org.uk/4/lawrence/kushnick.html.

Lashley, Myrna, Sara K. Thompson, Ghayda Hassan, Serge Touzin, Michael Chartrand, and Sadeq Rahimi. 2016. *Cultural Competence and Canada's Security: Can Perceptions of Cultural Competence Be Beneficial in Assisting Police and Security Officers in Ensuring Canada's Security?* Final Report prepared for Public Safety Canada, Strategic Policy Division, Ottawa.

Laub, J.H., and R.J. Sampson. 2001. "Understanding Desistance from Crime." *Crime and Justice* 28: 1–69. https://doi.org/10.1086/652208.

Lauckner, H., M. Paterson, and T. Krupa. 2012. "Using Constructivist Case Study Methodology to Understand Community Development Processes: Proposed Methodological Questions to Guide the Research Process." *The Qualitative Report* 17: 1–22.

Lyons-Padilla, Sarah, M.J. Gelfand, H. Mirahmadi, M. Farooq, and M. van Egmond. 2015. "Belonging Nowhere: Marginalization and Radicalisation Risk among Muslim Immigrants." *Behavioural Science and Policy* 1(2): 1–12. https://doi.org/10.1353/bsp.2015.0019.

MacLeod, Ian. 2009. "Radical Somali Canadians Potential Threat." *Ottawa Citizen*, 31 October.

Madon, N.S., Kristina Murphy, and Adrian Cherney. 2016. "Promoting Community Collaboration in Counterterrorism: Do Social Identities and Perceptions of Legitimacy Mediate Reactions to Procedural Justice Policing?" *British Journal of Criminology* 56(5). https://doi.org/10.1093/bjc/azw053.

Mastroe, Caitlin, and Susan Szmania. 2016. "Surveying CVE Metrics in Prevention, Disengagement, and DeRadicalization Programs." Report to the Office of University Programs, Science and Technology Directorate, Department of Homeland Security. College Park: START.

Matsueda, R.L., and K. Drakulich. 2009. "Perceptions of Criminal Injustice, Symbolic Racism, and Racial Politics." *Annals of the American Academy of Political and Social Science* 623(1). https://doi.org/10.1177/0002716208330500.

Maxwell, J. 2013. *Qualitative Research Design*. New York: Sage.

McCluskey, J.D., S.D. Mastrofsky, and R.B. Parks. 1999. "To Acquiesce and Rebel: Predicting Citizen Compliance with Police Requests." *Police Quarterly* 2(4): 389–416. https://doi.org/10.1177/109861119900200401.

Menkhaus, K. 2009. "Violent Islamic Extremism: Al-Shabaab Recruitment in America." Testimony before the US Senate Homeland Security and Governmental Affairs Committee, Washington, D.C.

Millett, Kris. 2014. *Project Traveller and the Criminalization of Somali Canadian Youth.* http://www.academia.edu/8998705/Project_Traveller_and_the_Criminalization_of_Somali_Canadian_Youth.

Mueller, Jason C. 2016. "The Evolution of Political Violence: The Case of Somalia's al-Shabaab." *Terrorism and Political Violence*, 1–26. https://doi.org/10.1080/09546553.2016.1165213.

Mullins, Sam. 2007. "Homegrown Terrorism: Issues and Implications." *Perspectives on Terrorism* 1(3). http://www.terrorismanalysts.com/pt/index.php/pot/article/view/12/html.

Owusu-Bempa, Akwasi. 2014. *Black Males' Perceptions of and Experiences with the Police.* PhD diss., Centre of Criminology and Socio-Legal Studies, University of Toronto.

Pagliaro, Jennifer. 2013. "Turf of Alleged Gang in 'Dixon City' has Long, Violent History." *Toronto Star*, 18 June. http://www.thestar.com/news/crime/2013/06/14/turf_of_alleged_gang_in_dixon_city_has_long_violent_history.html.

Paterson, B., and C. Panessa. 2008. "Engagement as an Ethical Imperative in Harm Reduction Involving At-Risk Youth." *International Journal of Drug Policy* 19(1): 24–32. https://doi.org/10.1016/j.drugpo.2007.11.007.

Patillo, Mary. 1998. "Sweet Mothers and Gangbangers: Managing Crime in a Black Middle-Class Neighbourhood." *Social Forces* 76(3): 747–74. https://doi.org/10.1093/sf/76.3.747; https://doi.org/10.2307/3005693.

Pardo, TA., J.R. Gil-Garcia, and G.B. Burke. 2006. "Building Response Capacity through Cross-Boundary Information Sharing: The Critical Role of Trust." In *Exploiting the Knowledge Economy: Issues, Applications, Case Studies*, ed. P. Cunningham and M. Cunningham. Amsterdam: IOS Press.

Precht, Tomas. 2007. *Homegrown Terrorism and Islamic Radicalization in Europe: From Conversion to Terrorism.* Research report prepared for the Danish Ministry of Justice. http://www.justitsministeriet.dk/sites/default/files/media/Arbejdsomraader/Forskning/Forskningspuljen/2011/2007/Home_grown_terrorism_and_Islamist_radicalisation_in_Europe_-_an_assessment_of_influencing_factors__2_.pdf.

Prothrow-Stith, D. 2004. "Strengthening the Collaboration between Public Health and Criminal Justice to Prevent Violence." *Journal of Law, Medicine, and Ethics* 32(1): 82–8. https://doi.org/10.1111/j.1748-720X.2004.tb00451.x.

Public Safety Canada. 2013. *Countering Violent Extremism.* http://www.publicsafety.gc.ca/cnt/ntnl-scrt/cntr-trrrsm/cntrng-vlnt-xtrmsm/index-eng.aspx.

Ragazzi. F. 2016. "Suspect Community or Suspect Category? The Impact of Counter-Terrorism as 'Policed Multiculturalism.'" *Journal of Ethnic and Migration Studies* 42(5): 724–41. https://doi.org/10.1080/1369183X.2015.1121807.

Rankin, Jim. 2009. "Minorities' View of Police Worsens." *Toronto Star*, 6 November. https://www.thestar.com/news/gta/2009/11/06/minorities_view_of_police_worsens.html.

Rembold, F., S.M. Oduori, H. Gadain, and P. Toselli. 2013. "Mapping Charcoal Driven Forest Degradation during the Main Period of Al Shabaab Control in Southern Somalia." *Energy for Sustainable Development* 17(5): 510–14. https://doi.org/10.1016/j.esd.2013.07.001.

Richards, A. 2011. "The Problem with 'Radicalization': The Remit of 'Prevent' and the Need to Refocus on Terrorism in the UK." *International Affairs* 87(1): 143–52. https://doi.org/10.1111/j.1468-2346.2011.00964.x.

Sawa, Timothy, Dave Seglins, and Jeremy McDonald. 2014. "Canadians with Alleged Terrorist Links." http://www.cbc.ca/news/canada/canadians-with-alleged-terrorist-links-1.2839246.

Schuck, Amie, and Dennis P. Rosenbaum. 2005. "Global and Neighborhood Attitudes toward the Police: Differentiation by Race, Ethnicity and Type of Contact." *Journal of Quantitative Criminology* 21(4): 391–418. https://doi.org/10.1007/s10940-005-7356-5.

Silver, James, Paul Gill, and J.G. Horgan. 2017. "Foreshadowing Targeted Violence: Assessing Leakage of Intent by Public Mass Murderers." *Aggression and Violent Behaviour* 38: 94–100.

Snellman, A. 2007. "Social Hierarchies, Prejudice, and Discrimination." *Digital Comprehensive Summaries of Uppsala Dissertations from the Faculty of Social Sciences* 32: 54. http://uu.diva-portal.org/smash/get/diva2:170901/FULLTEXT01.pdf.

Snellman, A., and B. Ekehammar. 2005. "Ethnic Hierarchies, Ethnic Prejudice, and Social Dominance Orientation." *Journal of Community and Applied Social Psychology* 15(2): 1–12. https://doi.org/10.1002/casp.812.

Spalek, Basia. 2009. *Community Policing within a Counter-Terrorism Context: The Role of Trust When Working with Muslim Communities to Prevent Terror Crime*. http://works.bepress.com/cgi/viewcontent.cgi?article=1000&context=basia_spalek.

– 2010. "Community Policing, Trust, and Muslim Communities in Relation to 'New Terrorism.'" *Politics and Policy* 38(4): 789–815. https://doi.org/10.1111/j.1747-1346.2010.00258.x.

Spalek, Basia, Zubeda Limbada, Laura Zahra MacDonald, Dan Silk, and Raquel Da Silva. 2012. *Impact of Counter-Terrorism on Communities Methodology Report*. London: Institute for Strategic Dialogue. https://www.counterextremism.org/resources/details/id/208/impact-of-counter-terrorism-on-communities-methodology-report.

Shahrokh, T., and J. Wheeler. 2014. *Knowledge from the Margins: An Anthology from a Global Network on Participatory Practice and Policy Influence*. Brighton: IDS.

Stanford University. 2016. *Mapping Militant Organizations: Al Shabaab.* http://
web.stanford.edu/group/mappingmilitants/cgi-bin/groups/view/61.

Statistics Canada. 2011. *2011 National Household Survey: Data Tables.* www12.
statcan.gc.ca.

Thompson, Sara, and Sandra Bucerius. 2014. "Final Report: Collective Efficacy
and Cultural Capital: Building and Fostering Resilience in Different Ethnic
Communities." Prepared for Public Safety Canada, Strategic Policy Division,
Ottawa.

Tucker, Erika. 2015. "Terrorism charges laid against Canadian ISIS fighter."
Global News. http://globalnews.ca/news/2239099/terrorism-charges-
laid-against-canadian-isis-fighter.

Tyler, T.R. 2011. "Trust and Legitimacy: Policing in the USA and Europe." *European
Journal of Criminology* 8(4): 254–66. https://doi.org/10.1177/1477370811411462.

Tyler, T.R., S. Schulhofer, and A. Huq. 2010. "Legitimacy and Deterrence Effects
in Counterterrorism Policing: A Study of Muslim Americans." *Law and Society
Review* 44(2): 365–401. https://doi.org/10.1111/j.1540-5893.2010.00405.x.

Waxman, Matthew. 2008. *Police and National Security: American Local Law
Enforcement and Counter Terrorism after 9/11.* Columbia Public Law and Legal
Theory working paper, Columbia Law School, New York. http://lsr.nellco.
org/cgi/viewcontent.cgi?article=1049&context=columbia_pllt.

Warmington, Joe. 2013. "Somali Canadian leaders have some nerve blasting
police." *Toronto Sun*, 18 June. http://www.torontosun.com/2013/06/18/
somali-canadian-community-leaders-have-some-nerve-blasting-police.

Weitzer, Ronald, and Steven A. Tuch. 2005. "Racially Biased Policing:
Determinants of Citizen Perceptions." *Social Forces* 83(3): 1009–30. https://
doi.org/10.1353/sof.2005.0050.

Williams, Michael, John Horgan, and William P. Evans. 2015. "The Critical Role
of Friends in Networks for Countering Violent Extremism: Towards a Theory
of Vicarious Help Seeking." *Behavioural Sciences of Terrorism and Political
Aggression* 8(1): 1–21. https://doi.org/10.1080/19434472.2015.1101147.

Wortley, S., and A. Owusu-Bempah. 2009. "Unequal before the Law:
Immigrant and Racial Minority Perceptions of the Canadian Criminal Justice
System." *Journal of International Migration and Integration* 10(4): 447–73.
https://doi.org/10.1007/s12134-009-0108-x.

Wortley, Scot, and Julian Tanner. 2008. "Respect, Friendship, and Racial
Identity: Justifying Gang Membership in a Canadian City." In *Street Gangs,
Migration, and Ethnicity*, ed. Frank van Gemert, Dana Peterson, and Inger-
Lise Lien. New York: Routledge.

14 Conclusion

JEZ LITTLEWOOD, SARA THOMPSON,
AND LORNE DAWSON

No state has experienced another terrorist attack comparable to 9/11, but attacks continue worldwide and mass casualty attacks have occurred in Western democratic states. These include the Madrid train bombings in March 2004, the July 2005 attacks on the London public transport system, the coordinated attacks that struck Paris in November 2015, and the series of attacks that occurred in 2016 in Western Europe, particularly in Belgium, France, and Germany, as well as the attacks in the UK in 2017. Right-wing terrorism also has (re)emerged, most notably with the attack in Norway in 2011, and as data from the United States (START 2017) and Europe (Ravndal 2016) make clear, this threat is more pervasive than is commonly recognized.

Canada has not escaped terrorism or the attention of al Qaeda and ISIS. Law enforcement has thwarted at least six plots involving Canadians, and the courts have completed terrorist prosecutions against more than twenty individuals. In recent years this country has experienced two lethal lone-actor attacks inspired by jihadist ideology (October 2014); it has also witnessed a failed bombing attack by an individual (Aaron Driver) as well as a vehicle ramming attack in Edmonton (2017) that was at least inspired by ISIS. In addition, 190 Canadians have travelled abroad to fight for or otherwise support various terrorist and extremist groups; this number includes more than 100 who are understood to have joined jihadist groups in Syria, Iraq, Somalia, and elsewhere. Other, more amorphous kinds of terrorism are also evident, as sadly illustrated by the lethal mass shooting at Quebec City's Islamic Cultural Centre in January 2017 and by the vehicle attack on pedestrians in Toronto in April 2018. So while we have experienced less terrorism than some other nations, the threat of it is still very real, and it remains a chronic problem.

This is the predominant interpretive trope used to frame the Canadian situation, and on the whole it is accurate. The danger faced by Canadians is here to stay, and in fact it could get worse, given the plight of the many thousands of people displaced and stricken by conflict elsewhere in the world and the concomitant rise of far-right movements. The threat of terrorism has become a fact of life, and its significance is shaping a new, securitized popular consciousness with ramifications for many aspects of public policy and daily life. This volume has sought to sample the new research that Canadians, and some others, are conducting on terrorism and counterterrorism in Canada, and to examine the implications in terms of crafting a more singularly Canadian response to this new reality. Security officials in Canada, like those in most Western nations, face the challenge of determining how best to address the threat without sacrificing the very values, rights, and principles that terrorists want to undermine. This involves recognizing that the threat is proving to be both diverse and resilient; it mutates and adapts to changes in both the globalized systems and the local societal conditions it exploits (McCoy and Knight 2015).

Although counterterrorism in democratic states often involves strategies that have international components, in some respects all counterterrorism must equally be cognizant of the local effects on a given community or geographic region. Governments have the primary responsibility for ensuring the safety and security of the state and its citizens in the face of an increasingly complex, heterogeneous, and dynamic threat. The requirement to respond to terrorism entails short-term imperatives that can be in tension with long-term objectives. One dominant aspect of post-9/11 counterterrorism illustrates this interplay of competing priorities, namely the choice by a number of Western democratic states to focus most of their resources on fighting the terrorists overseas rather than at home. While counterterrorism is never simply about domestic versus international options, military operations abroad have been approved, framed, and perpetuated based on such dichotomous thinking. Yet few now doubt that the invasion and occupation of Afghanistan, and then Iraq, contributed significantly to the increase in terrorism back home. As Chenoweth concluded in her study of trends in counterterrorism actions by governments, including against al Qaeda–inspired terrorism between 2001 and 2013: "we can say with some confidence that since 1968, advanced democracies have generally not suffered from high levels of chronic terrorism unless they were interfering in other countries' affairs through military intervention or occupations, or unless they had ongoing and unresolved territorial conflicts" (Chenoweth 2013, 370).

On the one hand, then, Canada must act in concert with its international allies in waging the so-called war on terrorism. Canadian forces will continue to help allies fight terrorist groups and insurgencies in their countries. Under the conditions of increased globalization, everyone recognizes that the terrorist threat is truly transnational. In addition to military action, close and consistent cooperation is necessary between nations in terms of gathering and sharing intelligence, pursuing investigations and prosecutions, and coordinating an array of other counter- and preventive measures. Many procedural hurdles have yet to be cleared in this regard, and appropriate safeguards against the misuse of intelligence and the abuse of power need to be implemented and enforced.

Yet at the same time, as is often remarked, all terrorism is ultimately local (Rosenblatt 2016). Even with the infusion of ideas, ideologies, and narratives that are transnational, local conditions and experiences are important in determining who will and will not transition from holding radical and extremist beliefs to acting violently on them (McCoy and Knight 2015; Dawson and Amarasingam in this volume).

More precisely, as previous work on terrorism and securitization in Canada has urged, we need to think about terrorism as a "glocal" phenomenon (Bramadat and Dawson 2014). Surveys show that most Canadians are still inclined to "believe that conflicts are imported from abroad and that the domestic incidents of terrorism are a function of international influences" – whether jihadist, far-right, or leftist in nature (Jedwab 2015, 41, see also 46–7). This misperception is understandable, as Clément's chapter delineates, since that is how we have been conditioned to think of Canada's struggles with security threats. This mode of thinking is also emblematic of older and simpler ways of conceiving the process of globalization, ones still influential in populist politics throughout the world. From this vantage point, terrorism is one collateral consequence of a shrinking world; it represents an aspect of international politics and foreign culture creep that Canadians and others in the West need to resist and suppress. Alternative approaches to globalization, however, recognize that we can no longer draw a simple contrast between what is global and what is local, and it is misleading to think in terms of patterns of specific international actions and nationalist reactions. Rather, globalization entails the co-creation and co-presence of the global and the local, or universalizing and particularizing tendencies in the economic, political, and sociocultural systems (Robertson 1995). Furthermore, local conditions exercise a tempering effect on global pressures and development; global products and ideas are chosen, consumed, and modified in line with local needs, preferences, and social conditions. Yet most things that eventually go global start local, in the hotbeds of creativity or turmoil in societies that are being transformed by global pressures.

The contributors to this volume have focused on the local context of terrorism and counterterrorism in Canada, or better, the glocal context and processes conditioning the Canadian grasp of the issues. Much of the work is foundational in nature. The volume provides a better understanding of the Canadian encounter with terrorism (Tishler, Ouellet, and Kilberg; Clément) and contemporary manifestations of extremism in Canada (Dawson and Amarsingam; Hofmann; Bérubé and Ducol; and Bouchard et al.). Contributors examine the challenges of engaging with the communities most affected by extremism and efforts to counter it (Lenard and Nagra; Thompson and Bucerius). Other chapters assess aspects of the Canadian government's response to terrorism (Chenoweth and Dugan; Decker; Schmidt) as well as how it is treated by the media (Perry and Scrivens). Much more could be done, and we are cognizant that these studies are just a beginning.

This volume is intended to be a snapshot of the Canadian situation fifteen years or so after 9/11. Given the extraordinary rate at which every aspect of terrorism is evolving today, conventional academic publishing timelines and practices cannot keep pace. Consequently, much of the book is more about the past – admittedly the near past – than the present. There are dangers, however, in focusing on the present and the most recent past. Among these are too-strong a focus on the last attack, on particular kinds of groups and ideologies, and on specific means of attacks and their targets, as well as perceptions that the threat manifests itself in certain locations. Comprehension of the complex realities of terrorism and counterterrorism, however, depends on knowing about much more than what is happening today. It requires an understanding of the past, an awareness of emerging trends and continuities, and an appreciation of multiple and conflicting data points or events that do not point in a single, clear direction. In other words, context – historical, sociocultural, technological, and geographical – is everything. The Canadian context is what we have sought to provide readers of this volume, but inevitably some attempt must be made to indicate what can be gleaned from this collection about the near future.

When travelling in Europe, it is not uncommon for Canadian scholars of terrorism to be asked: Why has Canada experienced so much less terrorism? Why have there been fewer plots, attacks, and deaths? No real answer to that question is readily available. In fact, it is not even clear if the premise of the question is correct, or whether it merely reflects the limited attention that Canadian cases of terrorism have received in the international media (see Mullins 2013). Regarding jihadism, when pressed for an answer, experts might revert to some combination of factors, such as Canada's selective immigration practices, engrained national commitment to multiculturalism and heritage as a nation of immigrants, as well as the fact that Muslim immigrants have, on the whole, fared well in Canada. Muslims who have immigrated to this country in recent decades appear to be much more successfully integrated into society here than they are in such places as the UK or France. Combining two sources of survey data and a set of interviews with community leaders, a recent study concludes that "despite concerns in the community over discrimination and divisive areas of policy (e.g., security), Canadian Muslims are well integrated socially" (McCoy, Kirova, and Knight 2016, 21). It appears that the second generation of Muslim immigrants is poised to experience significant upward mobility through their educational accomplishments, but regrettably, statistically at this point, "Muslims [have taken] the place of Blacks as the most disadvantaged group" in Canada (Beyer 2014).

This answer more or less assumes, however, in line with many European analyses, that jihadist radicalization is driven primarily by frustration and anger born of poor social and economic prospects (Weggemans, Bakker, and Grol 2014; Coolsaet 2016). Whether this is actually the case, however, remains unclear (Rahimi and Graumans 2015; Deckard and Jacobson 2015; Dawson and Amarasingam 2017). In the face of discrepant evidence, the most logical conclusion is that different variables are relevant to various degrees in different circumstances. In other words, we should be careful in drawing inferences from the Muslim experience in the ethnic enclaves of Parisian *banlieues* for the radicalization of Muslim youth in the fairly privileged suburbs of Toronto (Dawson 2014), and vice versa. Context matters, and currently we know a lot more about the French situation than the Canadian one (Roy 2017; Kepel 2017). All of that said, the real challenge is to answer this question: Why do a very small but potentially significant number of young Muslims continue to radicalize toward violence when evidence points to the seeming unimportance of the obvious socio-economic factors thought to foster radicalism in Canada? And how does it happen, and in what circumstances? Much more work is required in this area, and in tackling that difficult question for other forms of violent extremism and terrorism as well.

So what does the near future hold in dealing with terrorism and counterterrorism? Moving forward, where primarily should attention be focused? We will briefly consider five issues: (1) the persistence of jihadist radicalization; (2) the perpetuation and growth of other forms of extremism; (3) the need to develop effective, community-based programs for countering all forms of violent extremism; (4) the accountability of Canadian security services; and (5) the role of new media in the radicalization process.

During 2017 a strong consensus was forming around the future of jihadism. First, the caliphate established by ISIS in Iraq and Syria was on its way to military defeat, yet ISIS would survive and persist as an insurgency in these countries and elsewhere (e.g., Afghanistan, Libya, and Yemen). Second, the fall of the territorial caliphate would be accompanied by a surge of terrorist attacks in Europe and elsewhere, as jihadists demonstrated that their cause was alive and still lethal. Third, the utopian dream of re-establishing an Islamic State would outlive the demise of the ISIS caliphate and continue to provide a powerful motivation for radicalization and violence. Fourth, the example set by the thousands of young men and women who had left to fight in Syria and Iraq for jihadist groups would be an ongoing source of inspiration, especially the example provided by the great many martyrs for the cause. Fifth, the thousands of surviving fighters returning home from the zones of conflict would pose a serious threat. Many would be intent on carrying on the fight, with a skill set enhanced by years of combat. They might do so under the direction of ISIS and other groups, or they might initiate attacks more independently as lone actors. Others would prove effective recruiters for a new generation of terrorists, and some would simply be disturbed and potentially dangerous. Sixth, while the notoriety achieved by ISIS had eclipsed the attention given to al Qaeda for a time, al Qaeda and its allies would continue to operate throughout the Middle East and Pakistan as well as in many parts of Africa and Southeast Asia. In its factional struggles with ISIS, al Qaeda would seek to launch attacks against Western targets, in order to maintain its competitive status (CSIS 2017 and CREST 2017). Military success in Iraq and Syria, then, would initiate a new phase of international terrorism, not end it.

Consequently, there is little reason to think that the threat posed by jihadism is going to dissipate much in Canada either. There may be reduced activity overall as fewer Canadians seek to travel overseas to fight for such groups. It is morally harder for individuals to steel themselves to perpetrate attacks on their fellow citizens, than it is to leave the country to take up arms against heretical tyrants abroad. The basic geopolitical and social-psychological conditions giving rise to jihadi radicalism, however, have not fundamentally changed (Hafez and Mullins 2015; Dawson 2017), and as the low-tech attacks, using vehicles and knives, carried out in England, Germany, and France in recent years indicate, angry and committed extremists will continue to pose a serious and largely unpredictable threat to public safety.

In thinking about these threats, however, we need to guard against the "Muslimization" of terrorism in Canada. It is notable that low-tech attacks using vehicles have been adopted by right-wing lone actors in the UK (Dodd and Rawlinson 2018) and the United States (Savage and Ruizag 2017); this sort of attack was responsible for the death of ten Canadians in Toronto even though at the time of this writing a terrorist link is not discernible. Other kinds of extremism, including those targeting Muslims, are present and potentially problematic. The study of the far right in Canada is, however, still in a nascent stage. Hofmann's chapter provides the first systematic assessment of one far-right movement that is on the government's radar, the Freemen-on-the-Land. At this point, he concludes, the group does not pose a serious threat to national security, but it is not completely benign either. Beyond the Freemen, the wider anti-authority movements in Canada have been responsible for at least twelve deaths, eight casualties, and three threats between 2005 and 2016 (Perry, Hofmann, and Scrivens 2017, 50–2). Individuals inspired by the world view of the Freemen-on-the-land killed or injured seven police officers in Canada between 2012 and 2015. So far, the strange mix of left-wing, anti-globalization, anti-government, and right-wing ideologies and grievances that fuel the Canadian Freemen has generated a loose-knit, highly factionalized, and decentralized movement. Many of the thousands of individuals involved, however, are very active locally and online. This situation is not dissimilar to that of other right-wing extremist, hate, and terrorist groups in Canada, as Perry and Scrivens (2016) document. The threat from the Canadian Freemen is directed against government officials and front-line law enforcement officers, but Hofmann cautions against complacency. In particular, he argues that the emergence of a charismatic leader or a precipitating event could trigger more violence and be the catalyst for more sustained terrorist activity by anti-government, far-right extremists in Canada. With justification, right-wing extremism is receiving more attention from security services in Europe and North America. The study of groups like the Freemen alerts us to the potential violence bubbling just beneath the surface of such anti-government groups and the need for Canada to remain vigilant about this threat.

It is now widely recognized that to counter violent extremism, time, energy, and money must be invested in prevention (Vidino and Hughes 2015; Harris-Hogan, Barrelle, and Zammit 2016; Thomas et al. 2017). Governments must partner with communities to implement awareness, training, and education programs; they must develop ways to divert youth, and others, from the path to extremism in the "pre-criminal space." Two chapters in this volume (Thompson and Bucerius; Lenard and Nagra) seek to bring to light, through interviews with more than 500 individuals in five Canadian cities (Toronto, Montreal, Edmonton, Ottawa, and Vancouver), the views of community leaders and youth in two of the groups most impacted by security measures in Canada in recent years. Both chapters highlight sectors of our society that seek to play an active, positive role in responding to terrorism. However, the authors find that Muslim community leaders and Somali youth, as a result of their experiences, perceive themselves as being suspect: as targeted for counterterrorism rather than employed as partners in countering terrorism. The evidence indicates that these people strongly desire to be viewed as equals before the law and to be treated as Canadians by the authorities rather than as "others" within Canadian society. Somali youth identified the building blocks for such partnerships, such as engagement with youth rather than simply with community leaders, engagement with women specifically, and the creation of safe spaces to have difficult conversations; they also suggested taking advantage of the influence of peers to promote resistance to the narratives of extremist groups. This suggests, as does other research, that the community itself is an asset, but one that is being underutilized or misunderstood by authorities, to the detriment of counterterrorism efforts (Jossee, Bucerius, and Thompson 2015).

The Canadian government has recognized this state of affairs and is moving to emulate more systematic approaches, such as the one taken by the PREVENT program in the UK, as well as initiatives in various cities in Europe (e.g., Aarhus and Berlin) and the United States (e.g., Boston, Los Angeles, Minneapolis). To this end, in June 2017 the government launched the Canada Centre for Community Engagement and Prevention of Violence (CCCEPV) (Public Safety Canada 2017). This is a significant improvement on the half-hearted community outreach efforts of the preceding Conservative government. But this office is in the very early stages of its work, and only a few community-oriented prevention programs have been initiated across Canada: for example, the Centre for the Prevention of Radicalization Leading to Violence in Montreal, Re-Direct in Calgary, and, in Toronto, a set of risk-driven, collaborative intervention mechanisms, known as "HUBs" or "situation tables." Overall, the situation is promising, but a tremendous amount of work remains to be done in developing more sound and systematic methods for detecting and engaging individuals at risk of radicalizing to violence, assessing the risk they pose, effectively intervening with them, and evaluating the overall efficacy of the programs created. The government has committed to assisting with this research through the new Community Resilience Fund, and to building and providing the resources needed to foster, guide, and financially support the kinds of grassroots community programs that are thought to be the preferred approach to this new social problem.

This "softer" approach to counterterrorism and countering violent extremism is not, however, without controversy. The politicization of terrorism and counterterrorism evident in the 2015 federal election returned in the fall of 2017 when the work of the CCCEPV coincided with the demise of the Islamic State and concerns over returning foreign fighters (Slaughter 2017). Political sparring presented counterterrorism in terms of simplistic "hard" versus "soft" approaches and created the impression that the choice was between incarceration and poetry readings. This simplistic discourse gained some traction despite the evidence that prevention, redirection, disengagement, and intervention programs had been considered by the previous Conservative government (Pressprogress, 2017); indeed, a wealth of historical data points to the efficacy of a multidimensional approach to terrorism (Foley 2013; Chowdhury and Fitzsimmons 2013; Lehrke and Schomaker 2016; Crenshaw and LaFree 2017).

All of this is happening against the backdrop of the continued "Muslimization" of the problem of terrorism in the public sphere. Canada's most recent *Public Report on the Terrorist Threat to Canada* states that the "main terrorist threat to Canada continues to stem from violent extremists inspired by groups such as Daesh and al-Qaida ... [but] ... Right-wing extremism is also a gowning concern" (Canada 2017b; 3). Given recent events worldwide, this is understandable, to a point, but it should not mask or downplay the threats posed by right-wing terrorism in Canada and other Western democratic states. Canadians must work harder to appreciate and acknowledge Muslim communities' real diversity. The stereotypical treatment of Canadian Muslims is detrimental to local relationships between communities and authorities and continues to feed the misperception in public discourse and the media that Canadian Muslims are all somewhat complicit in supporting extremism. As the chapter by Perry and Scrivens shows, violence perpetrated by an individual who is Muslim is probably linked to terrorism, whereas anti-government or anti-authority violence perpetrated by others, by "white" Canadians, is rarely labelled terrorism. Leaving aside the faulty assumption that all Muslims are non-white, the tendency to explain this latter type of violence as a "mass shooting" or the act of a "deranged individual," and not terrorism, shifts the blame away from the community (local, national, international, and virtual) as well as from the political and social milieu that may have influenced the violence.

This is a fundamental issue, and Canada is not the only country where it arises. In the media, white violence is rarely framed as terrorism unless specific evidence points to the fact, whereas violence by someone, or some group, presumed to be Muslim is rarely framed as not being terrorism. As such, the "Muslimization" of terrorism in Canada is not simply something that respondents to a particular research activity perceive; it is manifest in media discourse and public sentiment. To some extent this appears to be changing. The media representations and public debates about the murder of six Canadians in a Quebec mosque in 2017 by Alexandre Bissonnette point to frustration that he was not charged with terrorism offences (Roach 2017) as well as a growing concern about the rise of far-right groups (Lamoureux 2017; Montpetit 2017).

Overall, however, there remains an "us" versus "them" aspect to Canadian discourse and actions in the counterterrorism realm, as the work of Thompson and Bucerius, Lenard and Nagra, and Perry and Scrivens illustrate in this volume. While the authors, quite correctly, do not claim that all discourse and all counterterrorism is subject to this criticism, they bring to the fore the fact that prejudice exists and represents a very real challenge for the development of effective policies and programs in Canada. Left unattended, the "us versus them" public discourse about counterterrorism in Canada risks detrimental outcomes, for two reasons. First, already strong and inclusive communities find themselves unable to contribute to local-led, community-supported counterterrorism efforts because of the resentment they encounter, even though their input is essential to the prevention of violent extremism. Second, such real and perceived discrimination and suspicion fuels the narratives of both jihadi and right-wing terrorists and extremists, which posit (respectively) that Muslims are unwelcome in the West and that they pose a threat to our nation's social fabric and national security. One senior counterterrorism official in the UK noted vis-à-vis right-wing extremism that the "biggest concern for the country should [be] that violent Islamist extremism and violent right-wing extremism will feed off each other. Islamophobia is something we have to be really clear about in policing: hate is hate. And we should be very, very robust and have a zero tolerance towards hate crime" (Pantucci 2018).

Consultations on national security issues in 2016 in Canada underscored that a "growing level of distrust in key institutions involved in national security and law enforcement was clearly evident" (Canada 2017a). One aspect of this growing distrust relates to Canadian intelligence. Decker's chapter on parliamentary accountability for Canadian intelligence draws attention to the long history of distrust and suspicion regarding the work of intelligence agencies; so does does Clément's historical review of Canadian counterterrorism. Both authors point to the efforts to mitigate these concerns with new accountability regimes for intelligence. The *National Security and Intelligence Committee of Parliamentarians Act* (Bill C-22) received Royal Assent in June 2017, so Decker's overview of the UK's experience with a similar committee has become more salient. As Decker notes, there is a public side to the accountability mechanisms of this committee. If the Canadian committee replicates the early experience of the UK parliamentary committee and fails to address a number of difficult questions, complex problems, and sensitive national security issues because it is inopportune to do so or because of political pressure (real or perceived), trust in intelligence will continue to erode. The new NSICOP has had additional burdens placed upon it with the advent of quite radical proposals in the omnibus legislation of the *National Security Measures Act* announced mid-2017 (i.e., Bill C-59), and with the government's claims for a new era of transparency and disclosure in national security matters. Expectations for NSICOP remain high in terms of reviewing proprietary (lawfulness) issues of intelligence activity and the efficacy (efficiency and effectiveness) of the intelligence machinery of Canada. Should it stumble, or become captured by the executive or the machinery of government, concerns about intelligence activity, surveillance, and the practices of counterterrorism will continue to have a corrosive effect on public confidence overall. In that regard, NSICOP is part of the big picture of counterterrorism, and its success or failure may have important implications for the micro aspects of counterterrorism at the community and individual levels as well.

Finally, and as noted in our introduction, all terrorism exists within a political and social milieu, and understanding how extremist groups connect to the world to propagate their message, justify their actions, and seek support for their cause is an important aspect of counterterrorism in various ways. Technology and terrorism, as well as technology and counterterrorism, have a symbiotic relationship, but how technology affects both terrorism and counterterrorism is often difficult to determine with empirical evidence. What this means, and as demonstrated by two of the chapters in this volume, is that researchers have to turn to innovative methodologies in the digital realm. The use of webcrawlers to identify, understand, and possibly destabilize complex online communities is nothing new, but additional research must be undertaken. Furthermore, the foreign fighter phenomenon and the war in Syria have together served to intensify Canadian content and explicit Canadian connections to the jihadi digital realm. Canadians such as Shirdon have amplified their presence worldwide and in Canada through this medium, thus making Canadians more visible and Canada itself more prominent. Indeed, as Bérubé and Ducol note in their chapter, al Adnani's call to action, to kill disbelievers, specifically mentioned Canada. The reproduction of the call in *Dabiq* in September 2014 was closely followed by the two attacks in Canada in October 2014. As Chenoweth and Dugan note, a range of soft and hard countermeasures are evident in attempts by Canada, other states, and the private sector to remove, disrupt, and challenge online activities that support terrorism. Some involve individuals acting on their own – cyber-vigilantes – while others involve civil society groups, governments, and the international community. As with other counterterrorism measures, determining what works is a significant challenge. Moreover, as with so much in terrorism studies and the practice of counterterrorism, research on discrete aspects of the problem – in this case the Canadian dimension of the jihadi digital realm – provides an essential building block for determining an effective response to all forms of terrorism.

Taken together, the chapters in the volume identify numerous challenges facing Canada. Terrorism remains extant in the "peaceable kingdom" and continues to evolve. Both at home and abroad, Canadians are killed and injured by terrorists, and Canadians with connections to terrorism are operating around the world. The threat is not solely from one particular kind of terrorism or from a single group. As the contributors to this volume highlight, a deeper contextual understanding of both terrorism and counterterrorism is essential if the security of Canada and all Canadians is to be maintained and if the rights and liberties of our democratic society are to be protected, upheld, and strengthened. The backdrop of recent years, however, points to less nuance and more stridency in important portions of public discourse. Simple solutions to an extremely complex phenomenon risk undermining the efforts at the local, municipal, provincial, federal, and international levels that are evident in Canadian counterterrorism.

REFERENCES

Beyer, Peter. 2014. "Securitization and Young Muslim Males: Is None Too Many?" In *Religious Radicalization and Securitization in Canada and Beyond*, ed. Paul Bramadat and Lorne Dawson, 121–44. Toronto: University of Toronto Press.

Bramadat, Paul, and Lorne Dawson, eds. 2014. *Religious Radicalization and Securitization in Canada and Beyond*. Toronto: University of Toronto Press.

Canada. 2017a. "National Security Consultations: What We Learned Report." https://www.publicsafety.gc.ca/cnt/rsrcs/pblctns/2017-nsc-wwlr/index-en.aspx.

– 2017b. *Public Report on the Terrorist Threat to Canada.* https://www.publicsafety. gc.ca/cnt/rsrcs/pblctns/pblc-rprt-trrrst-thrt-cnd-2017/index-en.aspx.

Chenoweth, Erica. 2013. "Terrorism and Democracy." *Annual Review of Political Science* 16(1): 355–78. https://doi.org/10.1146/ annurev-polisci-032211-221825.

Chowdhury, Arjun, and Scott Fitzsimmons. 2013. "Effective but Inefficient: Understanding the Costs of Counterterrorism." *Critical Studies on Terrorism* 6(3): 447–56. https://doi.org/10.1080/17539153.2013.836307.

Coolsaet, Rik. 2016. "Facing the Fourth Foreign Fighter Wave: What Drives Europeans to Syria, and to Islamic State? Insights from the Belgian Case." Egmont – Royal Institute for International Relations (March).

Crenshaw, Martha, and Gary LaFree. 2017. *Countering Terrorism* Washington, D.C.: Brookings Institution Press.

CREST. 2017. *After Islamic State.* CREST Security Review (Spring), Centre for Research and Evidence on Security Threats. www.crestresearch.ac.uk.

CSIS. 2017. *What Comes after Daesh – Highlights from the Workshop.* Published by the Canadian Security Intelligence Service. www.csis-scrs.gc.ca.

Dawson, Lorne L. 2014. "Trying to Make Sense of Home-Grown Terrorist Radicalization: The Case of the Toronto 18." In *Religious Radicalization and Securitization in Canada and Beyond,* ed. Paul Bramadat and Lorne Dawson, 64–91. Toronto: University of Toronto Press.

– 2017. "Sketch of a Social Ecology Model for Explaining Homegrown Terrorist Radicalisation." International Centre for Counter-Terrorism. https://icct.nl/publication/sketch-of-a-social-ecology-model-for-explaining-homegrown-terrorist-radicalisation.

Dawson, Lorne L., and Amarnath Amarasingam. 2017. "Talking to Foreign Fighters: Insights into the Motivations for Hijrah to Syria and Iraq." *Studies in Conflict and Terrorism* 40(3): 191–210. https://doi.org/10.1080/10576 10X.2016.1274216.

Deckard, Natalie Delia, and David Jacobson. 2015. "The Prosperous Hardliner: Affluence, Fundamentalism, and Radicalization in Western European Muslim Communities." *Social Compass* 62(3): 412–33. https://doi. org/10.1177/0037768615587827.

Dodd, Vikram, and Kevin Rawlinson. 2018. "Finsbury Park attack: Man 'brainwashed by anti-Muslim propaganda' convicted." *The Guardian,* 1 February. https://www.theguardian.com/uk-news/2018/feb/01/ finsbury-park-van-attacker-darren-osborne-found-guilty-murder-makram-ali.

Foley, Frank. 2013. *Countering Terrorism in Britain and France* Cambridge: Cambridge University Press.

Hafez, Mohammad, and Creighton Mullins. 2015. "The Radicalization Puzzle: A Theoretical Synthesis of Empirical Approaches to Homegrown Extremism." *Studies in Conflict and Terrorism* 38(11): 958–75. https://doi.org/ 10.1080/1057610X.2015.1051375.

Harris-Hogan, Shandon, Kate Barrelle, and Andrew Zammit. 2016. "What Is Countering Violent Extremism? Exploring CVE Policy and Practice in Australia." *Behavioral Sciences of Terrorism and Political Aggression* 8(1): 6–24. https://doi.org/10.1080/19434472.2015.1104710.

Jedwab, Jack. 2015. *Counterterrorism and Identities: Canadian Viewpoints.* Westmount: Linda Leith.

Jossee, Paul, Sandra M. Bucerius, and Sara K. Thompson. 2015. "Narratives and Counternarratives: Somali-Canadians on Recruitment as Foreign Fighters to Al-Shabaab." *British Journal of Criminology* 55(4): 811–32. https://doi.org/10.1093/bjc/azu103.

Kepel, Gilles. 2017. *Terror in France: The Rise of Jihad in the West.* Princeton: Princeton University Press.

Lamoureux, Mack. 2017. "The Birth of Canada's Armed, Anti-Islamic 'Patriot' Group." 14 June. https://www.vice.com/en_ca/article/new9wd/the-birth-of-canadas-armed-anti-islamic-patriot-group.

Lehrke, Jesse Paul, and Rahel Schomaker. 2016. "Kill, Capture, or Defend? The Effectiveness of Specific and General Counterterrorism Tactics against the Global Threats of the Post-9/11 Era." *Security Studies* 25(4): 729–62. https://doi.org/10.1080/09636412.2016.1220199.

McCoy, John, Anna Kirova, and W. Andy Knight. 2016. "Gauging Social Integration among Canadian Muslims: A Sense of Belonging in an Age of Anxiety." *Canadian Ethnic Studies* 48(2): 21–52. https://doi.org/10.1353/ces.2016.0012.

McCoy, John, and W. Andy Knight. 2015. "Homegrown Terrorism in Canada: Local Patterns, Global Trends." *Studies in Conflict and Terrorism* 38(4): 253–74. https://doi.org/10.1080/1057610X.2014.994349.

Montpetit, Jonathan. 2017. "Does Canada take the threat of far-right extremism seriously?" CBC, 16 August. http://www.cbc.ca/news/canada/montreal/canada-far-right-extremism-csis-1.4248183.

Mullins, Sam. 2013. "'Global Jihad': The Canadian Experience." *Terrorism and Political Violence* 25(5): 734–76. https://doi.org/10.1080/09546553.2012.693552.

Pantucci, Raffaello. 2018. "A View from the CT Foxhole: Neil Basu, Senior National Coordinator for Counterterrorism Policing in the United Kingdom." *CTC Sentinel* 11(2): 10–14.

Perry, Barbara, David C. Hofmann, and Ryan Scrivens. 2017. "Broadening Our Understanding of Anti-Authority Movements in Canada." TSAS working paper no. 17-02. http://www.tsas.ca/wp-content/uploads/2018/03/2017-02_v2PerryFINAL.compressed.pdf.

Perry, Barbara, and Ryan Scrivens. 2016. "Uneasy Alliances: A Look at the Right-Wing Extremist Movement in Canada." *Studies in Conflict and Terrorism* 39(9): 819–41. https://doi.org/10.1080/1057610X.2016.1139375.

PressProgress. 2017. "Harper government identified 'mental health issues' as a root cause of terrorism, secret documents show." 14 December. http://pressprogress.ca/harper-government-identified-mental-health-issues-as-a-root-cause-of-terrorism-secret-documents-show.

Public Safety Canada. 2017. News release: "New Canada Centre for Community Engagement and Prevention of Violence supports local efforts." 26 June. https://www.canada.ca/en/public-safety-canada/news/2017/06/new_canada_centreforcommunityengagementandpreventionofviolencesu.html.

Rahimi, Sadeq, and Raissa Graumans. 2015. "Reconsidering the Relationship between Integration and Radicalization." *Journal for Deradicalization* 15/16(5): 28–62.

Ravndal, Jacob Aasland. 2016. "Right-Wing Terrorism and Violence in Western Europe: Introducing the RTV Dataset." *Perspectives on Terrorism* 10(3): 2–15.

Roach, Kent. 2018. "Why the Quebec City mosque shooting was terrorism." *Globe and Mail*, 19 April. https://www.theglobeandmail.com/opinion/article-why-the-quebec-city-mosque-shooting-was-terrorism.

Robertson, Roland. 1995. "Globalization: Time-Space and Homogeneity-Heterogeneity." In *Global Modernities*, ed. Mike Featherstone, Scott Lash, and Roland Robertson, 25–44. London: Sage.

Rosenblatt, Nate. 2016. "All jihad is local: What ISIS' files tell us about its fighters." *New America*. http://www.newamerica.org.

Roy, Olivier. 2017. *Jihad and Death: The Global Appeal of Islamic State*. New York: Oxford University Press.

Savage, Charlie, and Rebecca R. Ruizag. 2017. "Sessions Emerges as Forceful Figure in Condemning Charlottesville Violence." *New York Times*, 15 August, A14.

Slaughter, Graham. 2017. "Plan to deal with returning ISIS fighters sparks fiery exchange between Scheer, PM." *CTV News*, 28 November. https://www.ctvnews.ca/politics/plan-to-deal-with-returning-isis-fighters-sparks-fiery-exchange-between-scheer-pm-1.3698183.

START. 2017. "Ideological Motivations of Terrorism in the United States, 1970–2016" Background Report. November.

Thomas, Paul, Michele Grossman, Miah Shamim, and Kris Christmann. 2017. "Community Reporting Thresholds: Executive Summary." Center for Research and Evidence on Security Threats (CREST). https://crestresearch.ac.uk/resources/community-reporting-thresholds-executive-summary.

Vidino, Lorenzo, and Seamus Hughes. 2015. "Countering Violent Extremism in America." Center for Cyber and Homeland Security, George Washington University.

Weggemans, Daan, Edwin Bakker, and Peter Grol. 2014. "Who Are They and Why Do They Go? The Radicalisation and Preparatory Processes of Dutch Jihadist Foreign Fighters." *Perspectives on Terrorism* 8(4): 100–10.

Contributors

Amarnath Amarasingam is an Assistant Professor in the School of Religion at Queen's University in Canada. He is also a Senior Research Fellow at the Institute for Strategic Dialogue and an Associate Fellow at the International Centre for the Study of Radicalisation. His research interests are in radicalization, terrorism, diaspora politics, postwar reconstruction, and the sociology of religion. He is the author of *Pain, Pride, and Politics: Sri Lankan Tamil Activism in Canada* (2015), and the co-editor of *Sri Lanka: The Struggle for Peace in the Aftermath of War* (2016).

Maxime Bérubé is a Postdoctoral Fellow at Concordia University and the University of Waterloo. He is also sessional lecturer at the Université de Montréal, where he teaches on terrorism, counterterrorism, intelligence, and investigation strategies. His research interests include influence activities leading to violence, terrorism, social movements, and open source data analysis.

Martin Bouchard is Professor of Criminology at Simon Fraser University, where he runs the Crime and Illicit Networks (CaIN) Lab. He studies how social networks affect crime and criminal trajectories. He is the editor of *Social Networks, Terrorism, and Counter-Terrorism: Radical and Connected* (2015).

Sandra Bucerius is an Associate Professor of Sociology and Criminology at the University of Alberta. She is the author of *Unwanted – Muslim Immigrants, Dignity, and Drug Dealing* (2014) and publishes on issues related to immigration, ethnography, prisons, police, and drug dealers.

Erica Chenoweth is the Berthold Beitz Professor in Human Rights and International Affairs at Harvard Kennedy School and a Susan S. and

Kenneth L. Wallace Professor at the Radcliffe Institute for Advanced Study. She studies political violence and its alternatives.

Dominique Clément is a Professor in the Department of Sociology at the University of Alberta and a member of the Royal Society of Canada (CNSAS). He is the author of *Canada's Rights Revolution, Equality Deferred, Human Rights in Canada*, and *Debating Rights Inflation*. Clément has been a Visiting Scholar in Australia, Belgium, China, Ireland, and the United Kingdom. His websites, HistoryOfRights.ca and statefunding.ca, serve as research and teaching portals for the study of human rights and social movements.

Garth Davies is an Associate Professor in the School of Criminology at Simon Fraser University and the Associate Director of the Institute on Violence, Extremism, and Terrorism at Simon Fraser University. His current work involves developing a database for evaluating programs for countering violent extremism; the social psychology of radicalization; and the statistical modelling and projection of violent right-wing extremism. He has also been involved in the development of the Terrorism and Extremism Network Extractor (TENE), a Web crawler designed to investigate extremist activities on the internet, including the dark net.

Lorne L. Dawson is a Professor in the Departments of Sociology and Legal Studies and Religious Studies at the University of Waterloo. He is the Director of the Canadian Network for Research on Terrorism, Security, and Society (www.tsas.ca) and co-editor of *Religious Radicalization and Securitization in Canada and Beyond* (2014). His recent publications focus on Western foreign fighters in Syria and Iraq, the role of religion in motivating religious terrorism, and the social ecology of radicalization.

Susan Decker is a long-time practitioner of intelligence accountability in her capacity as Senior Research Adviser at the National Security and Intelligence Review Agency of the Government of Canada.

Benjamin Ducol, PhD, is research manager at the Centre for the Prevention of Radicalization Leading to Violence (CPRLV). He also is an Associate Professor with the School of Criminology at the University of Montreal and a Research Associate at the International Centre for Comparative Criminology (CICC).

Laura Dugan is Professor and Associate Chair in the Department of Criminology and Criminal Justice at the University of Maryland. She is a founding co-principal investigator for the Global Terrorism Database (GTD) and co-principal investigator for the Government Actions in Terrorist Environments (GATE) dataset. She is the co-author of *Putting Terrorism into Context: Lessons Learned from the World's Most Comprehensive Terrorism Database,* and has published more than sixty journal articles and book chapters.

Richard Frank is Assistant Professor in the School of Criminology at Simon Fraser University and Director of the International CyberCrime Research Centre (ICCRC). He has a PhD in Computing Science (2010) and another in Criminology (2013).

David C. Hofmann is an Assistant Professor in the Department of Sociology at the University of New Brunswick. His current research focuses on terrorist and criminal networks, Canadian right-wing extremism, and charismatic leadership.

Kila Joffres is a graduate student in Criminology at Simon Fraser University. Her research interests and publications examine the use of network analysis in policing, particularly for online child pornography and extremist networks.

Joshua Kilberg is an Adjunct Research Professor at the Norman Patterson School for International Affairs at Carleton University. He researches the organizational structures and leadership of terrorist groups and cyber-conflict. He holds a PhD in International Affairs from Carleton University and an MA in War Studies from King's College London (UK).

Patti Tamara Lenard is Associate Professor of Ethics in the Graduate School of Public and International Affairs, University of Ottawa. She is the author of *Trust, Democracy, and Multicultural Challenges* (2012) and is presently completing a manuscript focused on the moral principles that must guide counterterrorism activities in democratic states.

Jez Littlewood is a policy analyst based in Alberta. He worked previously on national security issues for more than two decades at a range of organizations, including the Norman Paterson School of International Affairs at Carleton University, the government of the United Kingdom, and the United Nations Office in Geneva.

Baljit Nagra is an Assistant Professor in the Criminology Department at the University of Ottawa. Her research focuses on the racial underpinnings of the "War on Terror," and she is the author of *Securitized Citizens: Canadian Muslims' Experience of Race Relations and Identity Formation Post-9/11* (2017).

Marie Ouellet is an Assistant Professor in the Department of Criminal Justice and Criminology at Georgia State University. Her research aims to understand how criminal groups emerge and evolve and how networks structure these processes.

Barbara Perry is a Professor in the Faculty of Social Science and Humanities at Ontario Tech University and the Director of the Centre on Hate, Bias, and Extremism. She has written extensively on hate crime. She is currently working in the areas of anti-Muslim violence, anti-Semitic hate crime, the community impacts of hate crime, and right-wing extremism in Canada.

John M. Schmidt is the founder of CANSYNTH. He practises and promotes the discipline of Synthesis in such areas as strategic intelligence, foresight, risk, and counterterrorist resourcing. He worked at FINTRAC (Canada's FIU) from 2000 to 2015, mostly in strategic intelligence, and was seconded to the Canadian Integrated Threat (now Terrorism) Assessment Centre from 2006 to 2011. He has a MSc in Psychology and has publications in several areas.

Ryan Scrivens is an Assistant Professor in the School of Criminal Justice at Michigan State University. He also is a Visiting Researcher at the VOX-Pol Network of Excellence, a Research Associate at the International CyberCrime Research Centre at Simon Fraser University, and the Associate Editor for Theses for *Perspectives on Terrorism*. His primary research interests include the use of the internet by terrorists and extremists, right-wing terrorism and extremism, hate crime, and computational social science.

Sara K. Thompson is an Associate Professor of Criminology at Ryerson University and Associate Director of the Canadian Network for Research on Terrorism, Security, and Society (TSAS). Her work aims to inform effective, legally responsible, and socially engaged violence-prevention policies and programs, both within and outside the context of terrorism and violent extremism.

Nicole Tishler is a Research Fellow at Carleton University's Norman Paterson School of International Affairs and a Senior Policy Adviser for the Government of Canada. Her research explores various dimensions of terrorist activity, emphasizing tactical decision-making and weapons adoption and national security policy. In 2017 her doctoral dissertation, "Fake Terrorism: Examining Terrorist Groups' Resort to Hoaxing as a Mode of Attack," won the best PhD thesis award in the field of terrorism and counterterrorism studies, from the Terrorism Research Initiative.

Edith Wu is a PhD student in the School of Criminology at Simon Fraser University. Her research interests include terrorism, violent extremism, homicide, legal studies, and network analyses.

Index

www.ingramcontent.com/pod-product-compliance
Lightning Source LLC
Chambersburg PA
CBHW030235030426
42336CB00009B/110